MW01122334

Employment for people with intellectual ...

Ralph Kober

Employment for people with intellectual disabilities

The effect of different methods of employment on job satisfaction and quality of life

VDM Verlag Dr. Müller

Impressum/Imprint (nur für Deutschland/ only for Germany)
Bibliografische Information der Deutschen Nationalbibliothek: Die Deutsche Nationalbibliothek
verzeichnet diese Publikation in der Deutschen Nationalbibliografie; detaillierte bibliografische
Daten sind im Internet über http://dnb.d-nb.de abrufbar.
 Alle in diesem Buch genannten Marken und Produktnamen unterliegen warenzeichen-, marken-
oder patentrechtlichem Schutz bzw. sind Warenzeichen oder eingetragene Warenzeichen der
jeweiligen Inhaber. Die Wiedergabe von Marken, Produktnamen, Gebrauchsnamen,
Handelsnamen, Warenbezeichnungen u.s.w. in diesem Werk berechtigt auch ohne besondere
Kennzeichnung nicht zu der Annahme, dass solche Namen im Sinne der Warenzeichen- und
Markenschutzgesetzgebung als frei zu betrachten wären und daher von jedermann benutzt
werden dürften.

Coverbild: www.purestockx.com

Verlag: VDM Verlag Dr. Müller Aktiengesellschaft & Co. KG
Dudweiler Landstr. 99, 66123 Saarbrücken, Deutschland
Telefon +49 681 9100-698, Telefax +49 681 9100-988, Email: info@vdm-verlag.de
Zugl.: Perth, The University of Western Australia, Diss., 2006

Herstellung in Deutschland:
Schaltungsdienst Lange o.H.G., Berlin
Books on Demand GmbH, Norderstedt
Reha GmbH, Saarbrücken
Amazon Distribution GmbH, Leipzig
ISBN: 978-3-639-21908-1

Imprint (only for USA, GB)
Bibliographic information published by the Deutsche Nationalbibliothek: The Deutsche
Nationalbibliothek lists this publication in the Deutsche Nationalbibliografie; detailed
bibliographic data are available in the Internet at http://dnb.d-nb.de .
Any brand names and product names mentioned in this book are subject to trademark, brand or
patent protection and are trademarks or registered trademarks of their respective holders. The use
of brand names, product names, common names, trade names, product descriptions etc. even
without a particular marking in this works is in no way to be construed to mean that such names
may be regarded as unrestricted in respect of trademark and brand protection legislation and
could thus be used by anyone.

Cover image: www.purestockx.com

Publisher:
VDM Verlag Dr. Müller Aktiengesellschaft & Co. KG
Dudweiler Landstr. 99, 66123 Saarbrücken, Germany
Phone +49 681 9100-698, Fax +49 681 9100-988, Email: info@vdm-publishing.com

Printed in the U.S.A.
Printed in the U.K. by (see last page)
ISBN: 978-3-639-21908-1

Table of Contents

Acknowledgements _____ **5**

Chapter 1 – Introduction _____ **7**

1.1 Introduction _____ 7
1.2 Performance Measurement in the Not-For-Profit Sector_____ 7
1.3 The Choice of the Disability Employment Sector_____ 9
1.4 Performance Measurement Framework_____ 13
1.5 Research Method and Results _____ 15
1.6 Conclusion _____ 16

Chapter 2 – Employment for People with Intellectual Disabilities_____ **17**

2.1 Introduction _____ 17
2.2 Selection of Outcome Measures _____ 17
2.3 Job Satisfaction _____ 19
2.4 Quality of Life _____ 22
  2.4.1 Objective (Social) Indicators _____ 22
  2.4.2 Subjective (Psychological) Indicators _____ 23
  2.4.3 Quality of Life for People with Intellectual Disabilities _____ 24
  2.4.4 Relationship between Quality of Life and Employment _____ 26
    2.4.4.1 Does Employment Make a Difference? _____ 26
    2.4.4.2 Does Type of Employment Make a Difference? _____ 27
2.5 Conclusion _____ 29

Chapter 3 – Research Method _____ **30**

3.1 Introduction _____ 30
3.2 Development of Outcome Evaluation Questionnaire _____ 30
  3.2.1 Job Satisfaction _____ 30
    3.2.1.1 Participant Observation _____ 31
    3.2.1.2 Using Questionnaires Developed for People without Disabilities_____ 32
    3.2.1.3 Modifying Questionnaires Developed for People without Disabilities ____ 32
    3.2.1.4 Developing a New Job Satisfaction Questionnaire Specific for People
      with Intellectual Disabilities_____ 35
    3.2.1.5 Selection of the Job Satisfaction Questionnaire to be used _____ 35
  3.2.2 Quality of Life _____ 36
    3.2.2.1 QOL.Q (Schalock and Keith 1993) _____ 39
    3.2.2.2 ComQoL-ID4 (Cummins 1993) _____ 40
    3.2.2.3 Selection of the Quality of Life Questionnaire to be used _____ 41

3.3 Possible Intervening Factors _____ 41
   3.3.1 Type of Occupation _____ 43
   3.3.2 Level of Disability _____ 44

3.4 Participant Selection _____ 46
   3.4.1Participant Recruitment - Agency A _____ 46
   3.4.2Participant Recruitment - Agency B _____ 49
   3.4.3Participant Recruitment - Agency C _____ 50
   3.4.4Participant Recruitment - Agency D _____ 51
   3.4.5Participant Recruitment - Agency E and Agency F _____ 51

3.5 Interview Process _____ 52

3.6 Conclusion _____ 52

Chapter 4 – Psychometric Properties of Research Instruments _____ **53**

4.1 Introduction _____ 53

4.2 Psychometric Assessment Techniques _____ 53
   4.2.1 Factor Analysis _____ 53
   4.2.2 Reliability Analysis _____ 54

4.3 Functional Assessment Inventory _____ 55
   4.3.1 FAI Factor Structure _____ 56
      4.3.1.1 Seven-Factor FAI Structure _____ 60
         4.3.1.1.1 Further Refinement of the Seven-Factor FAI Solution ___ 62
      4.3.1.2 Six-Factor FAI Structure _____ 66
         4.3.1.2.1 Further Refinement of the Six-Factor FAI Solution _____ 69
      4.3.1.3 Five-Factor FAI Structure _____ 74
         4.3.1.2.1 Further Refinement of the Five-Factor FAI Solution _____ 74
   4.3.2 Comparison of FAI Factor Structures _____ 79
   4.3.3 Factor Stability of the FAI _____ 81
   4.3.4 Summary of FAI _____ 83

4.4 Job Satisfaction _____ 83
   4.4.1 Questionnaire Refinement _____ 84
   4.4.2 Internal Reliability of the Derived JSQ Scores _____ 86
   4.4.3 Factor Stability of the Derived JSQ _____ 88
   4.4.4 Comparison of JSQ to the Barlow and Kirby (1991) Questionnaire __ 90
   4.4.5 Summary of JSQ _____ 92

4.5 Quality of Life Questionnaire _____ 92
   4.5.1 Refinement of the QOL.Q _____ 95
   4.5.2 Reliability Analysis of the QOL.Q _____ 100
   4.5.3 Rescaling of the Refined QOL.Q _____ 103
   4.5.4 Summary of QOL.Q _____ 104

4.6 Conclusion _____ 104

Chapter 5 – Demographics and Sub-Sample Selection _____ **106**

5.1 Introduction _____ 106

5.2 Data _____ 106

5.3 Normality of the Data _____ 109

5.4 Non Response Bias _____ 109

5.5 Demographics _____ 109

5.6 Demographics by Method of Employment _____ 112

5.7 Controlling for Differences between Open Employment and Supported

   Employment _____ 113
   5.7.1 Occupation Type _____ 118
   5.7.2 Living Environment _____ 118
   5.7.3 Occupation Type and Living Environment _____ 118
   5.7.4 Functional Work Ability _____ 118
   5.7.5 Matched Pairs Analysis of Open Employment versus Supported
   Employment _____ 119
   5.7.6 Non-Controllable Differences _____ 120

5.8 Demographics of Participants in Unskilled Labouring Positions _____ 121

5.9 Demographics of Participants Living with their Family _____ 122

5.10 Demographics of Participants in Unskilled Labouring Positions Living with

   their Family _____ 124

5.11 Demographics of Matched Pairs Sub-Sample _____ 125

5.12 Correlations among Demographic Variables_____ 127

5.13 Conclusion _____ 128

Chapter 6 – Results and Discussion _____ **129**

6.1 Introduction _____ 129

6.2 Job Satisfaction _____ 129
   6.2.1 Job Satisfaction Results for Participants with High Functional Work
   Ability _____ 130
   6.2.2 Job Satisfaction Results for Participants with Low Functional Work
   Ability _____ 131
   *6.2.3 Discussion of Job Satisfaction Results*_____ 132
   6.2.4 Summary of Job Satisfaction Results _____ 135

6.3 Quality of Life _____ 135
   6.3.1 Quality of Life Results for Participants with High Functional Work
   Ability _____ 141
   6.3.2 Quality of Life Results for Participants with Low Functional Work
   Ability _____ 143
   6.3.3 Discussion of Quality of Life Results _____ 146
   6.3.4 Summary of Quality of Life Results _____ 152

6.4 Conclusion _____ 153

Chapter 7 – Conclusion _____ **154**

7.1 Background _____ 154

7.2 Aim and Importance_____ 154

7.3 Method _____ 155
   7.3.1 Research Instruments _____ 155

7.3.2 Statistical Analyses _____ 155

7.4 Results _____ 155

7.5 Conclusions _____ 156

7.6 Limitations and Further Research _____ 157

Bibliography _____ **159**

Appendix 1: Questionnaire _____ **171**

Appendix 2: Correlates of Job Satisfaction and Quality of Life _____ **177**

A2.1 Introduction _____ 177

A2.2 Correlates of Job Satisfaction _____ 177
    A2.2.1 Correlates of Job Satisfaction for Participants with High Functional Work Ability _____ 179
    A2.2.2 Correlates of Job Satisfaction for Participants with High Functional Work Ability _____ 183
    A2.2.3 Discussion of Job Satisfaction Results _____ 185

A2.3 Correlates of Quality of Life _____ 186
    A2.3.1 Correlates of Quality of Life for Participants with High Functional Work Ability _____ 193
    A2.3.2 Correlates of Quality of Life for Participants with Low Functional Work Ability _____ 196
    A2.3.3 Discussion of Quality of Life Results _____ 199

A2.4 Conclusion _____ 200

Acknowledgements

I would like to thank Professor Ian Eggleton, who has been a constant source of guidance and support throughout the course of this research. I thank you for all the knowledge that you have imparted on me in relation to what is required to do research.

I wish to thank my wife, Alicia, for your undying love and support. Your love and unending support has kept me going through those challenging and demanding times. Thank you to my parents, for your continual love, encouragement, and supporting me through my formative years.

I am also extremely grateful to: the disability employment agencies that allowed me to interview their customers; the staff from those agencies, who were always helpful; and especially to the people who were willing to be interviewed, without whom, it goes without saying, this research would not have been possible. I hope that in some small way this research will make a difference.

Chapter 1 - Introduction

1.1 Introduction

Measurement of performance in the not-for-profit sector is an area of research that has received increasing attention over recent years. It is extremely important in terms of measuring efficiency and effectiveness of organisations in achieving their goals. Performance indicators assist management in strategic decision making and fulfilling their accountability obligations for the best use of limited resources to funders, purchasers, consumers, and other stakeholder groups. This thesis seeks to further research into performance measurement in the not-for-profit sector by evaluating the effectiveness of different methods of employment for people with intellectual disabilities.

The remainder of this chapter is organised as follows. In the next section I provide a brief review of the literature on performance measurement in the not-for-profit sector. I then discuss the reasons for investigating the disability employment sector and specifically whether the different methods of employment result in different outcomes[1] to consumers. The fourth section presents and explains the performance measurement framework that will be used in this research followed by a brief, discussion of the research method and major findings of this research, including potential stakeholders who may have an interest in these results.

1.2 Performance Measurement in the Not-For-Profit Sector

While extensive literature exists on performance evaluation and the development of appropriate performance indicators in the for-profit sector (a recent example being the balanced scorecard; for example, Kaplan and Norton 1992, 1993, 1996, 2001), until recently there has been little research on performance measurement in the not-for-profit sector. While there are readily observable performance measures in the for-profit sector (for example, profit, return on equity, return on assets, sales turnover, *etc.*), in the not-for-profit sector the goals of the agency are often less quantifiable than in the for-profit sector and, as such performance measurement is more problematic. Managers in the not-for-profit sector have neither the luxury of a *bottom line* nor market forces (via the stockmarket) to assist in the measurement of their performance. Instead they must pursue much wider objectives than maximisation of profit.

During the past two decades, governments around the world have faced increased pressure to reform their public sectors. Most governments[2] have either undergone reform or are undergoing reforms, such as privatisation, reduction in size, commercialisation, and deregulation (Martin 1993; Nolan 2001). These reforms, which have been referred to as either *managerialism* (Broadbent and Guthrie 1992) or *new public management* (Hood 1991, 1995; Guthrie *et al.* 2003), have significantly increased the focus on performance measurement in the public sector (McCulloh and Ball 1992; Guthrie 1998; Newberry 2003, Modell 2005). This greater emphasis on performance measurement is in line with the major aims of the public sector reform process, which include: (1) to improve the performance of the public sector, (2) to increase the accountability of the public sector, and (3) to promote efficiency and effectiveness in the allocation and use of government resources (McCulloch and Ball 1992; Ball 1994; McGregor 1999; Hoque and Moll 2001).

---

[1] The difference between outcomes and outputs will be discussed in greater detail later in this chapter, in Section 1.4 (Performance Measurement Framework). However, it is important to note at this point that outcomes differ from outputs in that, outputs reflect the direct effects of programmes on the recipients of services, whereas outcomes reflect the more indirect and often long-term effects of programmes on specific recipients of services (Modell 2005).

[2] For example, Australia (Hoque and Moll 2001), Canada (Rayner 1995), China (Tsao and Worthley 1996), Denmark (Jensen 1998), Hong Kong (Awty 2002), Japan (Elliot 1996), Netherlands (Bac 2002), New Zealand (Ball 1994), Singapore (Awty 2001), South Korea (Kim 1996), Thailand (Bowarnwathana 1996), UK (Ellwood 2002), and USA (Martin 1993).

Modell (2004) notes that the initial development of performance measures in the public sector during the 1980s and 1990s was characterised by growing concerns with accountability and fiscal probity. In response to growing economic constraints and accusations of public sector inefficiency the importance placed on accounting grew (Hopwood 1984; Lapsley 1996), resulting in an emphasis on measuring performance in financial terms (Carter 1991; Hood 1995; Carter and Greer 1996). This initial emphasis on purely financial measures of performance led to calls for a broadening of the measures of performance to better reflect aspects of greater relevance to public sector organisations (Kloot 1997; Ballentine et al. 1998; Kloot and Martin 2000). It was argued that performance of government agencies could not simply be assessed in terms of financial measures (Barton 1999) and that it was imperative public sector performance measures take into consideration the sector's multiple stakeholders (Chow et al. 1998; Jones 1999a, 1999b). However, to satisfy a diverse range of stakeholders requires the development of a much wider range of performance indicators, making the problem of quantification even more acute (Fitzgerald 1988). In this respect performance measurement methods such as the balanced scorecard (Kaplan and Norton 1992), which emphasise non-financial measures as well as financial measures, have been touted as a possible solution.

However, research that has investigated public sector organisations that do report multiple indicators of performance note that these organisations often have an excessive proliferation of performance indicators, that these performance indicators tend to change over time, and that often the wrong things have been measured (Midwinter 1994; Atkinson et al. 1997; Carlin 2004; Modell 2004). Modell (2005) notes that the development of these performance measures are rarely driven by formally stated objectives, strategies, or targets. This over-proliferation of non-financial performance indicators may be attributable to the fact that the practices of some public sector organisations may be considered too broad and unfocused to be narrowly defined. This has led Chow et al. (1998, p. 278) to note that many public sector organisations need to "sharpen their focus when identifying the long-term issues of mission, objectives, and strategy". Such a focus would then allow for more appropriate and narrowly defined performance measures to be developed. However, it must be realised in relation to public sector agencies the specification of goals and objectives is an inherently political process, often involving negotiation and bargaining between conflicting interests (Stewart and Walsh 1994).

An alternative explanation of the lack of appropriately defined outcome indicators observed in some public sector organisations is offered by Smith (1995). He notes that over proliferation of performance indicators and inappropriate performance measures relative to the organisation's goals could be due to: (1) the difficulties in attributing the specific effects of services offered by one agency, when customers are receiving services from more than one agency, or when services are produced conjointly by more than one agency; (2) the different environments faced by different agencies, which may include differences in the type, extent and intensity of needs presented by consumers (in relation to disability employment agencies an example of the differences in consumers could relate to the differing levels of customers' intellectual disabilities); (3) the extended duration of time that may pass before outcomes can be felt or become measurable; and (4) the influence of random factors outside the agency's sphere of control that impact on the outcomes experienced by the recipients of services.

Even if an agency does clearly define its mission and the outcomes it is striving to achieve, the issue of whether it is economically feasible to measure the outcomes then needs to be considered. Modell (2005) notes that the compilation of outcome measures is often time consuming, results in significant administrative costs, and may also be associated with measurement problems.

The problems identified above with the definition and measurement of non-financial indicators in the public sector, together with the emphasis that governments have placed on cost-cutting and the lack of political commitment to developing truly reflective performance indicators, have resulted in continued primary emphasis being placed on financial performance indicators and internally focused measures of inputs, with scant attention being placed on outcomes (Modell 2005). Further, the recipients of services by public sector agencies are often not able to exert sufficient power to ensure that their interests are reflected in the outcome measures (Brignall and Modell 2000; Modell 2005).

In addition to the greater emphasis on performance measurement associated with *new public management*, has been the separation of the roles of funding, purchasing, and providing public sector services (Mason and Morgan 1995; Enthoven 1988; Boston *et al.* 1996; Kaul 1997; Ormsby 1998; Eggleton *et al.* 1999; Worthington and Dollery 2002). Under the funder-purchaser-provider model, government takes responsibility for achieving desired social and economic outcomes through the purchase of services from service provides who can come from both within and outside the public sector (Eggleton *et al.* 1999). Funders are responsible for obtaining and allocating funds to purchasers who then assess the needs of their constituents, on which they set priorities, develop specifications and contract directly with providers for the delivery of the required services (Mason and Morgan 1995). Providers are then required to deliver services against specific contracts or service arrangements and are held accountable to purchasers for the quantity and quality of services provided (Mason and Morgan 1995). Kaul (1997) notes that this clear delineation between purchaser and provider allows areas free from bureaucratic constraint to be created, in which a more business like environment can be maintained. It is argued the separation of the purchasing and provision of services will lead to greater competition between service providers, and therefore help governments in their pursuit of increased efficiency and effectiveness (Kaul 1997; Ormsby 1998). Consumers should also benefit from having a greater range of services from which to choose. Parmenter (1999) notes in relation to disability services that the split between the purchaser and provider has been encouraged by policy promulgations that have occurred across both Commonwealth and State levels of Australian Governments.

1.3 The Choice of the Disability Employment Sector
This thesis attempts to further research into performance measurement in the not-for-profit sector by evaluating the effectiveness of different methods of employment for people with intellectual disabilities. There are hundreds of disability employment agencies across Australia which either support people with intellectual disabilities in supported employment or place them into open employment. In line with the separation of purchaser and provider detailed above, each of these agencies contracts directly with the Australian Commonwealth Government for the services they must provide to people with intellectual disabilities in order to receive funding. The two major categories of employment for people with intellectual disability offered by disability employment agencies in Australia are referred to as open employment and supported employment. Open employment is where people with intellectual disabilities work alongside people without disabilities in integrated, meaningful employment in a community setting, supported by their employment agency. The alternative terms of "competitive employment" or "supported employment" are often used in other countries. However, in Australia the term "supported employment" refers to the situation where people with an intellectual disability work alongside other people with a disability in a segregated, specially tailored setting. Typically, in this setting, the only people without disabilities with whom people with intellectual disabilities would interact in the workplace would be their supervisors. In most other countries this type of employment is referred to as "sheltered employment".

To qualify for the services of either an open employment or supported employment agency a person must be considered to have some form of disability. The definition of disability (which includes intellectual disability) is, for the purposes of determining eligibility for disability employment services, based on the definition in the Disability Services Act (1986) and assessed by Centrelink.

There are several reasons for the selection of the disability employment sector as the setting in which to conduct this research. First, as Schalock and Lilley (1986) note, the overriding issues of today are economic and the major issue for agencies that assist people with intellectual disabilities is to demonstrate their effectiveness and efficiency. That is, agencies must demonstrate measurability of outcomes, reportability, and accountability. To this end there has been scant research on these issues for disability employment agencies. It is, however, interesting to note that consistent with the literature reviewed above on performance measures used in the public sector (Carter 1991; Carter and Greer 1996; Hood 1995;) the primary focus of government interest in the results achieved by agencies in this sector has related to financial performance. This can be evidenced by the "Report on the Survey of Service Costs" (1994), which was commissioned by the then Department of Human Services and Health of the Australian Commonwealth Government to conduct a survey of costs associated with service provision. The report concentrates primarily on the costs associated with placing people with intellectual disabilities into employment and notes the average annual cost per customer in employment varies across agencies from a low of $1,100 to a high of $42,770. However, the report places little emphasis on potential differences in service quality or customer outcomes across agencies. Moreover, although the financial measure of the average wages of customers is noted, no mention is made of any non-financial customer-referenced outcomes, such as job satisfaction or quality of life. This lack of attention to non-financial performance measures has since continued, and culminated with the introduction by the Australian Commonwealth Government on 1 July 2005 of a case based funding model for disability employment services that is based on input and output measures.[3]

Interestingly, the primary focus of research into open employment versus supported employment has also concentrated on financial measures of performance, investigating whether the financial benefits (for example, increased tax revenues, decreased service expenditure, decreased government pensions) of open employment exceed the associated costs (for example, employment agency funding, subsidies paid to employers) (for example, Hill and Wehman 1983; Hill *et al.* 1987; Conley *et al.* 1989; Tines *et al.* 1990; Noble *et al.* 1991; McCaughrin *et al.* 1993; Rusch *et al.* 1993, Tuckerman *et al.* 1999, Shearn *et al.* 2000). The above calls made in relation to the need for non-financial measures to assess public sector performance (Kloot 1997; Ballentine *et al.* 1998; Kloot and Martin 2000) have been echoed in disability sector in general by Parmenter (1990), and specifically in relation to the disability employment sector by Inge *et al.* (1988), who contends that although open employment has been shown to result in positive financial outcomes, it is equally important to determine whether open employment has a positive effect on the lives of individuals.

Another reason for interest in the disability employment sector, and assessing whether open employment and supported employment deliver different customer outcomes, relates to the issue of the economics of limited resources and how those limited resources can best be allocated to achieve maximum desired outcomes. This issue of how to allocate limited resources has been tackled in various different ways. As Schalock and Keith (1986) describe, in Arizona, programmes are reimbursed for customer-referenced employment outcomes. The State of Illinois reimburses programmes based on measurable customer-referenced outcomes, such as skill acquisition or customer movement. In the State of Washington the level of funding is based on projected employment related outcomes. In Australia, in line with the implementation of the funder-purchaser-provider model, discussed above in Section 1.2 (Performance Measurement in the Not-For-Profit Sector), the Australian Commonwealth Government has moved all disability employment agencies off the traditional *grant-in-aid* or *input-based* models of funding to *case based funding,* in which agencies are reimbursed, based on the mix of the level of intellectual

---

[3] It should be noted that both open and supported employment agencies were required to have achieved independent quality assurance under the appropriate ISO classification by December 2004, as well as being required to gain Disability Support Certification. Both of these quality assurance instruments require that agencies meet all of the Disability Service Standards listed in the Disability Services Act (1986). However, these quality assurance procedures are based on processes and not outcomes *per se.*

disabilities and hence needs of their customers, and the outcomes they deliver in terms of job starts and job tenure. Although, it is acknowledged that these are outcome measures, they do not capture the more subjective customer-referenced outcome measures. It is argued in Chapter 2 that although disability employment agencies are concerned with placing people with intellectual disabilities, they also have a much broader focus and, as such, it is important that their performance is also assessed, based on customer-referenced outcome measures.

A third reason for the interest in the disability employment sector is that coupled with the public sector reforms of the past two decades, which were briefly discussed in Section 1.2 (Performance Measurement in the Not-For-Profit Sector), Schalock (1999, 2004) notes that the quality revolution of the 1980s and the reform movement of the 1990s has caused a significant change in how the public views the purposes, characteristics, responsibilities, and desired outcomes of education, health care, and social service programmes. There has been a change in focus from inputs to outcomes (Schalock 2004), clients have been redefined as either consumers or customers, citizens have become more empowered (Kaul 1997; Schalock 1999), and the expectation is now that agencies are guided by goals related to person-referenced outcomes (Schalock 2004). As such, it seems appropriate, given there has been no previous comprehensive analysis of the effectiveness of the different methods of employment (open employment and supported employment) based on customer-referenced outcome measures, that one should be conducted.

Schalock and Bonham (2003) and Schalock (2004) note that programmes that assist people with intellectual disabilities also face the challenge of using person and organisation outcomes for continuous programme improvement. This challenge provides the fourth reason for assessing the performance of the different methods of employment (open employment versus supported employment) based on customer-referenced outcome measures. By assessing the customer outcomes of job satisfaction and quality of life arising from the different methods of employment, agencies will be provided with data on their customers' outcomes that they can use to improve services to their customers. It should be noted that the instruments selected to measure both job satisfaction and quality of life, which are detailed in Chapter 3, not only provide an aggregate overall score, but also separate scores for the four factors that comprising each construct. Such disaggregated information on both job satisfaction and quality of life should assist in the usefulness of the findings of this research to be of practical use to disability employment agencies to improve the levels of service they provide to their customers.

A fifth reason for the importance of this research lies in the fact that the *Disability Services Act* (Australian Commonwealth Government 1986) incorporates seven principles against which services to people with disabilities are to be assessed. As Parmenter (1999) notes, the first objective stating that services should have as their focus the achievement of positive outcomes for people with disabilities has not been appropriately tested. Therefore, a comprehensive analysis of the outcomes achieved by the different forms of employment (open employment and supported employment) appears warranted.

A sixth reason relates to the fact that some recipients of services by public sector agencies are often not able to exert considerable enough power to ensure that their interests are reflected in the outcome measures (Brignall and Modell 2000; Modell 2005). This lack of institutional power in affecting the selected outcome measures is apparent in the disability employment sector, given the power exerted over agencies by the Australian Commonwealth Government in terms of their funding method and the fact that they cap the number of customers each disability employment agency can have on its register. Given that in most regions of Australia there are more potential customers than agencies to serve these customers, this capping of customer numbers greatly reduces customers' powers in influencing agencies' performance measures.[4] An example of this can be seen in the Australian city of Wollongong, where there are over 10,000 people registered on the

---

[4] For a more detailed discussion on institutional theory see Modell (2003).

disability support pension, yet the Australian Commonwealth Government until recently capped the number of beneficiaries to disability employment services in this region to just over 200.[5]

A seventh reason for the importance of this research is the value that people with intellectual disabilities place on employment. Research has shown that Western societies place a very high social value on employment (Pascoe and Lee 1980; Schneider and Ferritor 1982). Schneider and Ferritor (1982) argue that it is through employment that individuals in a Western industrialised society demonstrate their self-worth. Furthermore, they note that people with intellectual disabilities not only realise the high importance that Western society places on employment, but place even greater importance on employment than do people without intellectual disabilities. Wilkinson (1975) explains this greater importance that people with intellectual disabilities place on employment by the fact that employment gives the person a sense of identity, that people with intellectual disabilities believe they are what they do. Furthermore, Wolfensberger (1983) argues that by attaining socially valued roles, such as employment, traditionally devalued people, such as those with intellectual disabilities, can re-establish themselves as valuable members of society. He argues that this occurs because by attaining socially valued roles, the individual will be better treated by society in general, including the lifting of restrictions that may have been placed on them. Therefore, the greater importance that people with intellectual disabilities place on employment compared with people without disabilities is not surprising.

Given this importance that people with intellectual disabilities place on employment it would seem appropriate to conduct an assessment of the outcomes that the different methods of employment (open employment and supported employment) deliver to people with intellectual disabilities. While numerous studies have investigated the outcomes achieved by different methods of accommodation services for people with intellectual disabilities (for example, Hemming *et al.* 1981; Heal and Chadsey-Rusch 1985; Schalock and Lilley 1986; Schalock and Genung 1993; Conroy 1996), there has been scant research investigating whether supported or open employment for people with intellectual disabilities results in different outcomes.

An eighth reason for the importance of this research is that considerable moral debate has occurred over the future of supported employment. Opponents have typically levelled value laden arguments against supported employment in terms of the manner in which it operates and its philosophical underpinnings (for example, Bellamy et al 1986; Rusch *et al.* 1987; Schuster 1990). Typically these arguments relate to the fact that supported employment, rather than adhering to the principles of normalisation and deinstitutionalisation (Wolfensberger 1972; Nirje 1976), places individuals in institutions, so as to shelter them from the normal conditions of life (Rosen *et al.* 1993). Gill (2005) provides an example of the level of emotiveness employed by authors arguing against supported employment. He notes that supported employment exists:

"on the basis and replication of a structure that incarcerates disabled people [sic] within vocational-like setting.... The workshop is no longer a place of societal liberation that affords the individual the opportunity to learn vocational skills, but rather it has become an institution that creates its own army of workers that will forever be subjected to a life in the workshop because of their disability status." (Gill 2005, p. 613)

The problem with the extremely emotive arguments presented by authors arguing against supported employment is that they do not provide any evidence of whether supported employment is in fact delivering inferior customer-referenced outcomes relative to open employment. Therefore, an understanding of customer-referenced outcomes that both open employment and supported employment deliver would help to inform debate about the most appropriate form of employment for people with intellectual disabilities, or if the most suitable form of employment is dependent on level of intellectual disability and/or other factors. This reason for this research is all the more

---

[5] The Australian Government has now introduced uncapped capacity into the disability employment sector as part of its welfare-to work agenda.

pertinent in Australia, given the Australian Commonwealth Government now recognises supported employment as a legitimate option for people with intellectual disabilities (Parmenter 2001). This acceptance of supported employment as a legitimate vocational option for people with intellectual disabilities is contrary to the Australian Commonwealth Government's prior commitment to reducing the relative size of the supported employment sector (Parmenter 2001).

Therefore, the importance of this research is that it is the first research to conduct a comprehensive review of the customer-referenced outcomes being achieved by customers of both open employment and supported employment services. Outcomes are assessed using psychometrically validated job satisfaction and quality of life questionnaires on a comparatively large and representative sample of people with intellectual disabilities. The framework for assessing performance is discussed in the next section.

1.4 Performance Measurement Framework

The framework on which performance is determined in this thesis is the Eggleton (1991) performance measurement framework. This framework, which is partially depicted in Figure 1.1, can be viewed as a cascading hierarchy, in that, first, the mission statement (which identifies the social function or need for which the or organisation or agency has been created to fulfil) guides the formulation of the agency's goals (which should explicitly state what outcomes the agency plans to achieve for its customers). Next, the goals guide the formulation of the agency's operationalised objectives (which identify more specifically the particular outputs or the agency plans to deliver in pursuing its outcome focused goals). Once the operationalised objectives have been set, they determine the costs and inputs (which are the resources both human and physical) required to undertake the processes that deliver the outputs and outcomes specified in their opeartionalised objectives and goals respectively.

An important aspect of the framework is the distinction it makes between outputs and outcomes. Outputs are the goods and services produced by the organisation or agency through the conversion process applied to its inputs (Eggleton 1991). In relation to a disability employment agency the main outputs are the hours of job search and job support provided to job seekers and placed workers, respectively. In contrast, the outcomes are the consequences of these aforementioned outputs on the job seeker or previously placed worker (Eggleton, 1991). For the job seeker these might include the acquisition of interviewing skills, greater confidence and a job. For the worker, outcomes may include continuing employment, take home pay, higher self esteem, job satisfaction and increased quality of life. Modell (2005) notes that outcomes may be more indirect or accrue over long time periods. Outcomes may also accrue to stakeholders other than job seekers and workers. Family members and carers, for example, may have more time for respite; employers may gain a more diverse workforce and associated benefits in the form of higher productivity levels, lower absenteeism rates, *etc*. Broader societal outcomes may also be identified, such as greater levels of participation of people with intellectual disabilities in the workforce, changes in citizens' attitudes towards people with disabilities, removal of impediments so as to enhance access to public buildings, modifications to pavements to improve mobility, and greater inclusion of people with disabilities in other socially valued roles.

In relation to disability employment services the outcome measures selected in this thesis are consumers' job satisfaction and quality of life. The detailed reasons behind the selection of these two variables are more fully explained in Chapter 2. However, it should be noted that these two measures were selected as they are both customer-referenced outcome measures and they differ from the traditional financial measures mentioned in Section 1.3 (The Choice of the Disability Employment Sector) that have assessed the financial benefits versus cost of open employment relative to supported employment. Calls for customer-referenced outcomes in the disability services

Figure 1.1:   Partial replication of the Eggleton (1991) Basic Performance Measurement
Framework

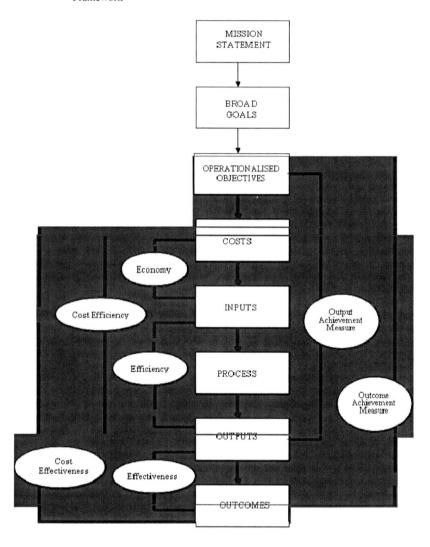

sector in general have been made by several researchers. Cummins and Baxter (1994) argue that the measurement of objective (output) variables alone would not reflect the value of a service to recipients, and that the only way such value can be appropriately reflected is through the use of subjective customer-focused outcome measures. Similarly, Wehmen *et al.* (1987), in relation to employment programs, noted the need for non-monetary, consumer-focused outcome evaluations, which they stated were far more important to consumers than monetary outcomes. They argued that to ignore such non-monetary, consumer-focused measures would be an injustice to the consumers of disability employment agencies. DeStefano (1990) specifically notes that an assessment of quality of life is an essential part of any comprehensive outcome evaluation. As stated by Landesman (1986, p. 142):

> "To judge the effectiveness of any ... [programme], we must establish evaluative standards. Despite the tremendous concern with accountability, we have failed to develop clear procedures for measuring the "success" of a given programme *at an individual level*, that is, sensitive to a person's own perceptions of quality of life...."

As noted by Modell (2005, p. 3), given that "the ultimate objectives of public sector operations are typically related to the enhancement of the usefulness of services to beneficiaries and citizens rather than the maximisation of service provision (outputs) or efficiency aspects, adequate measures of outcomes are pivotal for ascertaining the effectiveness of public sector organizations." As such the selection of customer-referenced measures, such as job satisfaction and quality of life, as outcome measures will enable an assessment of the effectiveness of the different methods of employment (open employment and supported employment) for people with intellectual disabilities. Furthermore, the selection of these two outcome measures will provide information to disability service providers that will, consistent with the *quality revolution* (Schalock 1996), enable them to manage their programmes to maximise the quality of outcomes received by their clients.

The Eggleton (1991) framework pivots around the *three e's* of *economy, efficiency,* and *effectiveness,* and explicitly links these performance measures to the main stages of the framework of converting inputs to outputs and then the subsequent outcomes of the agency's processes. From the framework it can be seen that *economy* is the cost per unit of input (or units of input per dollar), *efficiency* is the output per unit of input (or inputs per unit of outputs), and *effectiveness* is the process success rate in terms of outputs being converted to successful outcomes. Whether the agency's goals (and hence mission) are accomplished is measured in terms of objectives and goal achievement indicators.

Relating the Eggleton (1991) framework to the outcomes measures selected in this thesis, effectiveness is therefore viewed in terms of the effect that the different methods of employment (open employment and supported employment, which are different service delivery processes for generating outputs) have on the job satisfaction and quality of life (the outcome measures) of the participating individuals.

1.5 Research Method and Results
To determine the effectiveness of the two different methods of employment for people with intellectual disabilities, 117 people with intellectual disabilities who are employed in either open or supported employment are interviewed. These people are drawn from the registers of six disability employment agencies that worked within the metropolitan area of one of Australia's capital cities. As stated previously, the outcome measures used are job satisfaction and quality of life. The Barlow and Kirby (1991) job satisfaction questionnaire and Schalock and Keith (1993) quality of life questionnaire are selected to ascertain customers' levels of attainment on these scales. Both instruments are then tested to ensure they are psychometrically valid and necessary refinements are made to both instruments to enhance their internal reliability. Given the previous extensive use of the Schalock and Keith (1993) quality of life questionnaire, results are also presented for the original version of the questionnaire without the aforementioned refinements.

As the data collected for this thesis are non-normally distributed, non-parametric tests are conducted throughout this thesis. Furthermore, not only are statistical analyses conducted on the entire sample, but so as to control for underlying demographic differences between participants in open employment and participants in supported employment, participants are partitioned into various sub-samples. These sub-samples control for differences between the two populations in terms of: (1) the type of occupation performed (only participants in unskilled labouring positions are statistically analysed); (2) living environment (only participants living with their family are statistically analysed); (3) both type of occupation and living environment (only participants were in unskilled labouring positions and living with their family are statistically analysed); and (4) type of occupation, living environment, functional work ability, work hours, and gender (by conducting a matched-pairs analysis). The effect of functional work ability on the results of the statistical analyses is then controlled by splitting the sample, based on functional work ability and re-running the statistical analyses.

The results of this thesis indicate that after controlling for demographic differences between participants in open employment and those in supported employment, there is no difference in terms of job satisfaction based on method of employment (open employment versus supported employment). In relation to quality of life, it appears that for participants with high functional work ability, open employment results in a higher quality of life. While, for people with low functional work ability, there appear to be no difference in quality of life or its four factors arising from method of employment (open employment versus supported employment).

These findings, as to which outcomes and when they differed between participants in open employment and supported employment, should be of interest to: (1) people with intellectual disabilities and their families who currently use or are thinking of engaging the services of a disability employment agency; (2) all members of agencies who offer employment programmes and services for people with intellectual disabilities; (3) employers and business organisations who employ or are considering employing people with intellectual disabilities; (4) the Australian Commonwealth Government, especially the two departments responsible for funding disability employment agencies (the Department of Employment and Workplace Relations, who fund open employment agencies, and the Department of Family and Community Services, who fund supported employment agencies); (5) the community at large; and (6) researchers and others interested in enhancing outcomes (and their measurement) for people with intellectual disabilities through employment.

1.6 Conclusion
This chapter commenced with an introduction as to the importance of performance measurement in the not-for-profit sector and the effect that recent world-wide public sector reforms have had on performance measurement in this sector. The importance of investigating the outcomes of customers in the disability employment sector was then presented and formed the basis for the justification of the importance of the research conducted as part of this thesis. The framework for assessing performance was then presented along with a brief introduction as to why the customer-referenced outcome measures of job satisfaction and quality of life are selected. Finally, the research method employed in this thesis was introduced and a brief summary of the results presented.

The remainder of this thesis is organised as follows. The next chapter contains a discussion of the selection of outcomes measures and then reviews the literature in relation to whether prior research has found any differences in the outcomes achieved by participants in the different forms of employment (open employment versus supported employment). Chapter 3 describes the research method employed in this thesis, describing the instruments used to measure job satisfaction and quality of life, and participant recruitment. Chapter 4 describes the refinement of the job satisfaction, quality of life, and functional work ability instruments used in this thesis, and investigates the psychometric properties of each instrument. Chapter 5 provides information on the demographic details of the participants involved in this research and then describes how various sub-samples were formed to control for demographic differences apparent between participants in open employment and supported employment. The results of this thesis are then presented in Chapter 6, along with discussion of the results. Finally, Chapter 7 summarises the work conducted in this thesis, presents some conclusions, acknowledges the limitations of this research, and mentions areas for further research.

Chapter 2 – Employment for People with Intellectual Disabilities

2.1 Introduction

In the last chapter the difficulties of assessing the performance of not-for-profit service providers were discussed. To make any meaningful comparison of the relative effectiveness of disability employment agencies, adequate performance measures need to be developed. As mentioned in the last chapter these performance measures need to adequately reflect the outcomes that agencies are trying to achieve. This chapter describes the outcome measures that were selected to gauge the performance of agencies that provide supported employment and/or place in open employment people with intellectual disabilities. First, I justify the selection of job satisfaction and quality of life as my outcome measures. This is followed by a literature review which first presents research concerning the job satisfaction of people with intellectual disabilities and second synthesises research on the effect of employment on the quality of life of people with intellectual disabilities.

2.2 Selection of Outcome Measures

Prior to measuring the outcomes being achieved by agencies that either placed into employment or employed people with intellectual disabilities, it was essential to ascertain outcomes the agencies were striving to achieve. As stated previously, outcome measures should be logically connected to an agency's goals and objectives. While, the mission of these agencies is to gain employment for people with intellectual disabilities, a question that needs to be considered is: whether this is an end in itself? Alternatively stated, what is it that employment delivers to people with intellectual disabilities that other alternatives do not?

The answer to this question allows disability employment agencies to frame the goals and objectives they are trying to achieve by placing people with intellectual disabilities into employment. This then facilitates a comparison of the outcomes achieved by the different methods of employment for people with intellectual disabilities, thus providing agencies an assessment of their performance. As evident from the basic performance measurement framework presented in Section 1.4 (Performance Measurement Framework), without an understanding of an agency's goals it is impossible to measure their performance accurately, as performance should be measured in terms of the desired outcomes.

The answer to the question, as to what is it that the disability employment agencies believe that employment delivers to people with intellectual disabilities that alternatives such as day programmes do not, also allows for a meaningful comparison of employment methods versus alternatives to employment, to determine whether employment is indeed the best manner in which to achieve the desired outcomes.

Through discussions with managers from the two disability agencies initially involved in this research[6] it was determined that part of what each agency was trying to do was to:

- give people with intellectual disabilities an increased feeling of self-worth; and
- help people with intellectual disabilities to realise their potential for physical, social, emotional, spiritual and intellectual development.

Though the manner in which the two agencies were trying to achieve these goals differed (open employment versus supported employment), their goals were very similar. A review of the psychology literature suggested that these outcomes were closely connected to the concept of quality of life. According to Donegan and Potts (1988) quality of life is a global concept that encompasses all aspects of life; social, physical, emotional and spiritual.

---

[6] At the commencement of this research only two disability employment agencies were involved.

Furthermore, Baker and Itagliata (1982) identified five reasons why an agency supported in the provision of services to people with intellectual disabilities should focus on quality of life, rather than other outcome measures. They termed the first reason *comfort rather than cure*, since intellectual disability is not a curable condition and quality of life defines the individual's condition in positive terms, not in terms of symptoms or absence of symptoms (Murrell and Norris 1983). Their second reason was that *complex programmes require complex outcome measures*. A complex set of interventions are involved in the provision of different types of employment. The outcomes of these programmes are complicated and difficult to measure; as such a multi-dimensional variable such as quality of life serves to offer the hope of assessing the synergistic interaction of a number of smaller, less powerful outcome variables. The third reason was the desirability of *keeping the customer happy*. If the method of employment does not in some way improve consumer outcomes such as self-worth, job satisfaction, or quality of life, etc. it is hard to justify the placement. *Re-emergence of the holistic perspective* was their fourth reason. Quality of life offers a way to look at the whole life situation of a person as opposed to narrowly focusing on one aspect. Such an approach is consistent with the move made by the World Health Organisation in the late 1970s, when they adopted the definition of health as a "state of complete physical, mental and social well-being" (Baker and Intagliata 1982, p. 70), as opposed to the earlier narrow definition of health as being an absence of disease. The final reason that Baker and Intagliata (1982) identified, is that *quality of life is good politics*. It is part of our current Western cultural philosophy that a person should be able to enjoy their life, and hence it is politically sound for governments to attempt to increase people with intellectual disabilities enjoyment of life. Additionally, having a low quality of life does not stigmatize the individual as having any sort of deficit; rather it suggests that the individual is not well suited to their current environment (Murrell and Norris 1983). Moreover, McVilly and Rawlinson (1998) and Schalock (1999) noted that both society as a whole and individual consumers prefer the measurement of agencies' achievements to be person-referenced. These five reasons have resulted in the use of quality of life measures to assess the effectiveness of service provision for people with intellectual disabilities (see Schalock and Lilley 1986; Eggleton *et al.* 1999; Stancliffe and Keane 1999). However, having such a broad goal as increasing the quality of life of people with intellectual disabilities can be problematic for agencies in terms of trying to develop outcome measures that accurately capture such a broad concept.

As the two agencies were specifically involved in the provision of employment or placement of people with intellectual disabilities into employment they emphasised that a measure of customer satisfaction specifically relating to the employment aspect of the agencies services would also be useful. The agencies expressed the view that as quality of life was such a broad concept it was also likely to be affected by factors external to the employment environment and as such outside the control of agencies. Consequently, an additional, more specific and controllable outcome measure, such as job satisfaction was considered appropriate. It was felt that a job satisfaction measure would provide information to agencies concerning aspects of their service that required attention.

It could be argued, given that quality of life is such a broad and all-encompassing concept, the level of satisfaction a person experiences at work and the work environment itself could have an impact on the person's quality of life, particularly given the large number of hours spent at work each week and the social contacts made through the work environment. This positive correlation between satisfaction with work and overall quality of life has been observed in several studies investigating the relationship for people without disabilities (for example, Judge and Watanabe 1993; Efraty *et al.* 2000; Cimete *et al.* 2003; Kim and Cho 2003). It seems likely that this association between employment and quality of life applies equally, if not to a greater extent, to people with intellectual disabilities, given the importance people with intellectual disabilities place on employment (Schneider and Ferritor 1982).

A literature review of the outcome measure of job satisfaction and the effect of employment on job satisfaction will be discussed next, followed by a similar review on quality of life. Job satisfaction is discussed first, given the obvious association between an outcome measure of job satisfaction and agencies that were established to find either employment for people with intellectual disabilities or to employ people with intellectual disabilities.

2.3 Job Satisfaction

There is a dearth of research on the job satisfaction of people with intellectual disabilities. Locke (1976) estimated that by 1972 over 3,000 academic articles or dissertations had already been written on job satisfaction for people without disabilities. Doubtless, there have been many more written since, yet even today only a handful of articles have been concerned with the job satisfaction of people with intellectual disabilities.

Reasons for this lack of research have been contemplated by several authors, who have offered different explanations. Nisbet and York (1989) noted that traditionally a high rate of unemployment for people with intellectual disabilities has existed and consequently job satisfaction has not been seen as a matter of importance. This high rate of unemployment was in part due to the fact that until recently there were very few vocational programmes for people with intellectual disabilities (Nisbet and York 1989). Consequently, people with intellectual disabilities who are employed are often regarded as lucky to have a job (McAfee 1986) and, as such, job satisfaction is unlikely to be of great concern. Further, in terms of finding employment for people with intellectual disabilities, Seltzer (1984) noted that the person often has little control over where they were placed, such decisions often being made by counsellors. As McAfee (1986) and Lam and Chan (1988) both note, given the economic imperatives faced by agencies trying to find employment for people with intellectual disabilities, counsellors themselves often regarded the issue of job satisfaction to be of secondary or tertiary concern. Given such an environment, where it is hard to find employment for people with intellectual disabilities and society views the person as being lucky to have employment, even though they may have no say where they are placed, it is not surprising that research into the job satisfaction of people with intellectual disabilities has received little attention.

Even if a person wishes to assess the job satisfaction of people with intellectual disabilities, there are as yet no generally accepted instruments to measure this construct for this population. McAfee (1986) and Nisbet and York (1989) noted that instruments developed to measure the job satisfaction of people without disabilities are not applicable to people with intellectual disabilities. Most job satisfaction instruments developed for people without disabilities require a reasonable level of cognitive ability to complete and are self administered. Seltzer (1984) states that to asses the job satisfaction of a person with an intellectual disability requires interviewing/talking to the person. The difficulty that may be associated with doing so may be another factor why people have not wished to conduct such research.

Studies that have been concerned with assessing the job satisfaction of people with intellectual disabilities find people with intellectual disabilities have generally a high degree of job satisfaction (for example, Lam and Chan 1988; Houser and Chace 1993; Test et al. 1993; Shanly and Rose 1993). Lam and Chan (1988) interviewed 50 people with intellectual disabilities from two supported employment agencies using an adapted version of the Minnesota short-form Satisfaction Questionnaire (MSQ) (Weiss et al. 1969). They found supported employees to be satisfied generally with all aspects of work, with a mean rating in excess of four (out of a maximum of five) for overall job satisfaction. They also noted there was a statistically significant negative correlation between IQ scores and total job satisfaction, that is, people with higher IQ scores had lower levels of job satisfaction. Lam and Chan (1988) attributed this finding to the fact that people with lower levels of intellectual functioning were likely to be less discerning and, as such, happy with more things than people with higher levels of intellectual functioning. Additionally, they noted it was possible that people with higher IQ scores (lower levels of intellectual disability) may compare themselves to people without disabilities, causing them dissatisfaction with their work. This would be due to the person realising that they are not gainfully employed and are in a segregated, supported setting.

Houser and Chace (1993) investigated the job satisfaction among people with various disabilities, including intellectual disabilities, in open employment. They mailed the short form of the MSQ (Weiss *et al.* 1969) with no modifications, using the original five-point scale, to 290 people who had been placed into employment by one US state rehabilitation project. From the 30 responses they received they found high scores for each of the 20 questions of the MSQ and an overall mean score of 77.03 out of 100. As such, they concluded that people with disabilities in open employment were satisfied. A major limitation with this study is that the questionnaire was distributed to people of various disabilities, and no record was made of the disability of the person returning the questionnaire. Given the low response rate, and the fact that the MSQ is used in its original form, it is entirely possible that none of the respondents had an intellectual disability.

Test *et al.* (1993) also investigated job satisfaction in open employment, though only for people with intellectual disabilities. They interviewed 34 people from one North Carolinian agency using a 20 item questionnaire they developed based on items that Nisbet and York (1989) identified as indices/traits of job satisfaction.[7] Test *et al.* (1993) reported that 67.7 percent of people interviewed stated they were satisfied with their current job, 76.5 percent were satisfied with the money they earned, and 97.1 percent indicated they had friends at work.

Shanly and Rose (1993) interviewed 18 people with a mild intellectual disability who had been placed in a work-experience programme through a day-centre. They assessed job satisfaction using six open-ended questions that addressed areas of the work itself (3 questions), people at work (1 question), wages (1 question), and work structure and responsibility (1 question). They found that people generally expressed satisfaction with the work itself and the people with whom they work. However, responses were mixed as to the structure and responsibility of work, and generally negative in relation to the level of wages participants received. The negative comments in relation to wages were due to the fact that none of the participants received any form of remuneration for participating in the work-experience programme.

Although the above studies report that people with intellectual disabilities who are employed have a high degree of job satisfaction, due to the limitations of research methods employed, caution needs to be exercised in generalising from these results. None of the studies reports any measures of internal reliability of its questionnaire (for example, Cronbach alpha). Given that for three of the articles they either developed their own questionnaire (Test *et al.* 1993; Shanly and Rose 1993) or modified an existing questionnaire (Lam and Chan 1988) to be applicable for people with intellectual disabilities, it is extremely important that some form of psychometric evaluation be undertaken. Without such validation it is not possible to assert that these questionnaires have internal reliability, and consequently, the results of the research may be brought into question. However, using a psychometrically validated questionnaire developed for people without disabilities without any form of modification, as per House and Chace (1993), is also not valid, given that it is unlikely to be understood by people with intellectual disabilities. Other limitations of the above research relate to the issue of : (1) sample size, which was small (Lam and Chan 1988; Houser and Chace 1993; Test *et al.* 1993; Shanly and Rose 1993); (2) the limited representativeness of the sample, given that they interview only people with mild intellectual disabilities (Shanly and Rose 1993); and or (3) limited disclosure, in that the levels of intellectual disabilities for participants are not reported (Houser and Chace 1993; Test *et al.* 1993). This latter issue questions the applicability of the above results to the wider population of people with intellectual disabilities (including people with severe intellectual disabilities).

---

[7] Based on observing six people with intellectual disabilities in employment and interviews with five of the six and their parents, teachers and carers, Nisbet and York (1989) developed a set of indices they believe indicates job satisfaction when observed in a person with an intellectual disability.

Additionally, none of these studies compared the reported satisfaction levels with a reference group of individuals. Consequently, it is not possible to draw conclusions on the extent to which people with intellectual disabilities experience job satisfaction. However, two studies (Rosen et al. 1970; Jiranek and Kirby 1990) addressed this issue by investigating job satisfaction of people with intellectual disabilities compared with people without disabilities.

Rosen et al. (1970) compared the job satisfaction of previously institutionalised people with intellectual disabilities who are now living in the community and working in open employment with the job satisfaction of people without disabilities.[8] They interviewed 94 people, using the Minnesota Satisfaction Scale (Carlson et al. 1962). Rosen et al. (1970) found no significant differences in terms of job satisfaction between people with intellectual disabilities and people without a disability in either unskilled or blue-collar jobs.[9] As mentioned above, in relation to Houser and Chace (1993), the findings of Rosen et al (1970) may be questioned as it unlikely that the majority of people with intellectual disabilities would be able to meaningfully answer the questions of the MSS, which requires responses on both five-point and seven-point scales. Consequently, for their results to be meaningful they must relate to people with only a mild intellectual disability. However, Rosen et al. (1970) state that they interviewed people with a range of intellectual disabilities and, consequently, little if any weight can be placed on their results.

Jiranek and Kirby (1990) compared the job satisfaction of young adults with a mild intellectual disability who were placed into open employment or in supported employment, or were unemployed, with young adults without a disability who were either employed or unemployed. They interviewed 15 people with intellectual disabilities from one supported employment agency and 15 people with intellectual disabilities drawn from three open employment agencies. Job satisfaction for the people with intellectual disabilities was measured using a modified version of a job satisfaction scale developed by Warr et al (1979). Jiranek and Kirby (1990) found that on all but one of the 16 questions comprising the questionnaire there were no statistically significant differences between people with intellectual disabilities who were in open employment compared with people without disabilities in employment. The only difference between the two samples was that people with intellectual disabilities were statistically significantly more satisfied with their boss than their counterparts without disabilities. In this regard Jiranek and Kirby's (1991), results were similar to those of Rosen et al. (1970). However, Jiranek and Kirby's (1991) results also suggested[10] that people with intellectual disabilities in supported employment were statistically significantly less satisfied than workers without a disability in terms of their freedom to make decisions, relationship with co-workers, responsibilities they are entrusted with, attention paid to their suggestions, and the variety in their work. Further, Jiranek and Kirby (1991) found that people with intellectual disabilities in open employment reported a statistically significantly higher job satisfaction score and were statistically significantly more satisfied than those employed in a supported setting on seven of the 16 questions, these being: freedom to make decisions, relationships with co-workers, relationship with the boss, amount of responsibility, pay, attention paid to suggestions, hours of work, and variety in work.

Given the results of Jiranek and Kirby (1991), open employment might appear more suitable for people with intellectual disabilities in terms of providing a greater degree of job satisfaction.

---

[8] The job satisfaction scores for people without disabilities are those from Carlson (1962) who provided his data to the authors.

[9] All participants in Rosen et al. (1970) were employed in either unskilled or blue-collar positions.

[10] The word "suggested" is used as Jiranek and Kirby (1991) initially conducted a one-way ANOVA to test for differences among the three groups of open employment workers, supported employment workers and workers without a disability. They found significant results for eight of the 16 questions and overall job satisfaction. They then only report the post-hoc test comparing open employment workers to workers without a disability. However, given the figures they report it appears that in these instances there must also be a significant difference between supported workers and workers without a disability.

However, as found in other studies conducted on people with intellectual disabilities, which used a modified questionnaire developed for people without intellectual disabilities (for example, Lam and Chan 1988), Jiranek and Kirby (1991) did not conduct any psychometric validation of their revised instrument. Without having conducted such reliability analysis it is not possible to have confidence in their results. Also, as in Shanly and Rose (1993), Jiranek and Kirby (1991) interviewed people with only mild intellectual disabilities and consequently no assertion can be made on whether their results also apply to people with more severe levels of intellectual disabilities.

Furthermore, it is questionable whether the statistical tests conducted by Jiranek and Kirby (1991) were appropriate. They conducted one-way ANOVAs, but a central assumption of ANOVA is that data are normally distributed. However, as Siegel and Castellan (1988) noted, in satisfaction surveys data are often non-normally distributed. Given the relatively small sample size and the fact that Petrovski and Gleeson (1997), who used the same questionnaire, reported that their data were highly non-normal, it appears that the tests conducted by Jiranek and Kirby (1991) do not comply with those tests' underlying assumptions and, as such, their results must be questioned.

Overall, an initial reading of the limited studies conducted on the job satisfaction of people with intellectual disabilities may imply that people with intellectual disabilities generally exhibit a reasonable level of job satisfaction, with people in open employment more satisfied than those in supported employment. However, as detailed, the above studies all have major methodological issues that either cast doubt on the validity of their results or the generalisability of results to the greater population of people with intellectual disabilities. Consequently, it is not possible to reach any consensus on levels of job satisfaction for people with intellectual disabilities placed into either open employment or supported employment, or compared to people without disabilities.

2.4 Quality of Life
Quality of Life is a term with diverse usage, which has different meanings to different people, as is evident from the numerous ways it is defined (for example Schneider 1975; Flanagan 1978; Murrell and Norris 1983; Sirgy 1986; Liss 1994; Nordenfelt 1994). The reason for these diverse usages and definitions lies in the problem of clarifying what quality of life encompasses, and the quantifying it. According to Donegan and Potts (1988) quality of life is a global concept which encompasses all aspects of life; social, physical, emotional and spiritual. Moreover, they stated that it should take into account normative cultural standards as well as an individual's needs, desires, experiences and aspirations.

The problems associated with defining and measuring quality of life are evidenced in the different approaches taken in its measurement. The concept of measuring quality of life has its origins in the early work of Thorndike (1939). Since then many researchers have been attempting to improve on the quantification of the quality of life concept. In relation to people without disabilities, these attempts can broadly be categorised as being based either on objective (social) indicators or subjective (psychological) indicators.

2.4.1 Objective (Social) Indicators
Objective or social indicators generally refer to external, environmentally-based conditions. Among researchers in this area there exists a general consensus on the broad categories from which these variables should be drawn (Schneider 1975). These categories are: (1) income, wealth and employment; (2) the environment, especially housing; (3) health, both physical and mental; (4) education; (5) social disorganisation, which include crime and social pathologies such as alcoholism, drug addiction, etc; and (6) alienation and participation (Schneider 1975; Diener and Suh 1997).

As Diener and Suh (1997) noted, the advantages of measuring quality of life in terms of objective (social) indicators are they can be defined and quantified without reliance on individual perceptions, and they are easier to compare and contrast across nations, demographic sectors, and time. However, Diener and Suh (1997) also noted the weaknesses associated with assessing quality of life using objective (social) indicators, which are: (1) they can suffer from measurement problems (for example, how do you measure access to healthcare facilities? Should it be by waiting list size, or mean waiting time, or distance to nearest healthcare facility?); (2) the subjective selection of which variables to include and omit; (3) if variables are weighted, the subjective nature of the decision on what weighting should be given to the various variables; and (4) the difficulty in agreeing on an optimum level of *good* and *bad*.

A further issue associated with the use of objective (social) indicators to measure quality of life is that they are primarily concerned with describing the quality of the life experience of the population. However, the quality of life experienced by the individual is a more highly subjective condition than implied by descriptive social indicators research based on aggregate data (Schneider 1976). Schneider (1975; 1976) illustrated this point in his studies on the quality of life in large American cities. He found no evidence, as measured by the above mentioned social indicators, that "the objective social conditions of cities have any relationship with the level of subjective life quality of their citizens" (Schneider 1975, p. 505). This lack of relationship highlights that objective (social) indicators are insufficient to measure an individual's perceived quality of life (Campbell *et al.* 1976) and gave rise to the belief that the major determinates of quality of life are psychological rather than economic or demographic (Campbell 1976).

2.4.2 Subjective (Psychological) Indicators
The premise behind using subjective (psychological) indicators to assess a person's quality of life is based on the presumption that to understand a person's quality of life, you must understand how he/she feels about life in the context of his/her own standards (Diener and Suh 1997). Quality of life is seen to be about how people internally react to and experience life events and circumstances (Diener and Suh 1997). To gain such an understanding, the person must be asked directly, and reliance cannot be placed on external objective indicators (Schneider 1976; Diener and Suh 1997).

Under this category, two major approaches have been used in the measurement of quality of life (Baker and Intagliata 1982): (1) a global measure of well-being, happiness or satisfaction is used as a criterion, and a variety of more specific measures are studied as they relate to it; and (2) specific life domains are identified, conceptually and/or empirically, and quality of life is defined in terms of the individual's reaction to these specific life areas.

The first area of research (that is, global measures of well-being) emphasises the affective aspects of experience. The most prominent research in this area was conducted by Bradburn (1969) with the development of the 10-item Affect Balance Scale. Bradburn (1969) undertook to assess the subjective feeling states that individuals' experience in their daily lives by enumerating particular positive and negative episodes that had occurred in the individual's lives in the recent past (Campbell 1976). Bradburn (1969) finds that his ten questions form two five-item clusters; a positive affect scale and a negative affect scale, which are surprisingly unrelated to each other. Through the operationalisation of the Affect Balance Scale, Bradburn (1969) concludes that a person's overall psychological well-being (quality of life) is a function of the difference between one's positive and negative affect scale (Baker and Intagliata 1982).

The second approach to operationalising a person's quality of life is to question them about various aspects of their lives. This approach describes a person's quality of life as the discrepancy between their perceived life and their aspired-to life. This discrepancy is expressed as a measure of satisfaction-dissatisfaction, and greater satisfaction is taken as an indicator of a sense of well-being (Campbell 1976). An example of this approach can be seen in the work of Flanagan (1978), who identified fifteen components of quality of life: (1) material well-being and financial security; (2) health and personal safety; (3) relations with spouse, girlfriend, or boyfriend; (4) having and raising children; (5) relations with parents, siblings, or other relatives; (6) relations with friends; (7) activities related to helping or encouraging other people; (8) activities relating to local and national governments; (9) intellectual development; (10) personal understanding and planning; (11) occupational role (job); (12) creativity and personal expression; (13) socialising; (14) passive and observational recreational activities; and (15) active and participatory recreational activities. The individual is asked to rate in relation to importance, each of the fifteen components on a five-point scale. They are also asked to rate on the five-point scale how well their needs and wants are being met. Quality of life is then assessed in relation to the difference between the importance the person places on each component and how well the individual perceives their needs and wants as being met.

The advantages to measuring quality of life through the use of subjective (psychological) indicators are that they capture people's experiences that are important to them (Diener and Suh 1997) and they are constant in unchanging situations and sensitive to change when it takes place (Atkinson 1982). However, the weaknesses associated with the use of subjective (psychological) indicators are that they suffer from methodological shortcomings (for example, the subjective nature of the selection process of which variables to ask questions on and which not to) (Diener and Suh 1997) and they may be more dependent on personal characteristics than on external factors (Diener and Suh 1997; Cummins 2000b).

2.4.3 Quality of Life for People with Intellectual Disabilities
The origins of concern with the quality of life for individuals with intellectual disabilities, and the current trend to incorporate quality of life as an outcome goal in service provision, has its origins in the normalisation principle, as developed and detailed in Nirje (1969). The normalisation principle grew out of an endeavour to understand the conditions of the life of persons with intellectual disabilities (Nirje 1985).

O'Bryne and Tyne (1981) extend the concept of quality of life beyond objective (social) indicators relating to the physical environment, by arguing that the normalisation infers the development and support of personal behaviour, experiences and characteristics that are valued by society (Donegan and Potts 1988). The "normalisation principle rests on the understanding of how normal rhythms, sequences and patterns of life in any cultural circumstances relate to the development, maturity and life of the handicapped (sic), and on the understanding of how these patterns apply as indicators for development of proper human services" and actions (Nirje 1985, p. 67). The normalisation principle means making available to all people with disabilities, "patterns of life and conditions of everyday living which are as close as possible to or indeed the same as the regular circumstances and ways of life of society" (Nirje 1985, p. 67).

The following basic formulation can be used to summarise the normalisation principle: it means that you act right when you let the person with a disability "obtain the same or as close as possible to the same conditions of life as you would prefer if you were in his[/her] situation"[11] (Nirje 1985, p. 67). Application of the normalisation principle should make the conditions, and thus the quality, of life of people with intellectual disabilities "as normal as possible, respecting the degrees and complications of the handicap (sic), the training received and needed, and the social competence and maturity acquired and attainable" (Nirje 1985, p. 67). Accordingly, an ideal social environment should be one that enables people with disabilities to develop their independent skills, be gainfully employed and have both friends with disabilities and without disabilities (Reiter et al. 1981).

The basic philosophy of the normalisation policy has been incorporated into Australian government policy (for example, The Western Australian Disability Services Policy, "A Fair Go for Everyone: A Disability Policy for Western Australia in Plain English", 1991) and Australian Law (for

---

[11] The term *situation* in this sense encompasses both physical circumstances and also personal circumstances (for example, intellectual disability).

example, Disability Services Act, Australian Commonwealth Government 1986; Disability Services Act, Government of Western Australia 1992). Within the Western Australian Disability Services Policy it states that the purpose of the policy is to enable people "with disabilities the best opportunity to live a purposeful and meaningful life; to be independent and responsible, and to have their rights protected." (Government of Western Australia, 1991, p. 1) In order to achieve this, the Western Australian Disability Services Policy lists seven principles, which are incorporated into Schedule 1 of the "Disability Services Act 1992" (Western Australia), to form the "Principles Applicable to People with Disabilities".

The seven principles listed in the Western Australian Disability Services Policy are based on the normalisation principle developed by Nirje (1969), inferring that people with disabilities should experience as closely as possible the "normal conditions of life"[12] and that they have the same rights as everyone else. The seven principles state (Government of Western Australia, 1991, pp. 5-11):

1. That people with disabilities should be treated with respect;
2. That people with disabilities have the same rights as everyone else;
3. That people with disabilities have the right to work towards fulfilling their personal dreams;
4. That people with disabilities have the same right to services to help them lead as full a life as everyone else;
5. That people with disabilities have the right to make decisions about what happens in their lives;
6. That people with disabilities have the right to freedom of choice; and,
7. That people with disabilities have the right to complain about services if they are not happy with them.

Through implementation of these principles, it was believed that people with disabilities will "have the opportunity for a better quality of life." (Government of Western Australia 1991, p. 14).

Early attempts to measure quality of life of people with intellectual disabilities adopted a subjective (psychological) approach. For example, Rosen and Kivitz (1973) suggested use of a personal adjustment measure, defined in terms of: (1) self concept; (2) independence; (3) reality testing; (4) emotional development; (5) goal-directed behaviour; (6) interpersonal relationships; and (7) sexual development. They infer individuals' with higher personal adjustment to have a higher quality of life. Likewise Gunzberg's (1977) Progress Assessment Charts of Social Development, which are completed by support staff associated with people with intellectual disabilities, infers people with higher scores have higher quality of life. However, the validity of such inferences are questionable given that no established link between either personal adjustment or social development and quality of life was made. Attempts, such as that of Reiter *et al.* (1981), to measure people with intellectual disabilities quality of life using the above measures suffers from stigmatising a person with a low personal adjustment or social development score as somehow being deficient, and this deficiency results in the low score.

More recent attempts to conceptualise quality of life for people with intellectual disabilities views individuals' quality of life as being a result of the 'fit' (or lack of) between the individual and his/her environment. This approach has been referred to as the *goodness of fit approach* (Schalock *et al.* 1989). Murrell and Norris (1983) presented a model in which quality of life was defined as the criterion for establishing the goodness of fit between the human unit and its environment; the better the fit, the higher the quality of life of the human unit (Murrell and Norris 1983). They assume that the characteristics of a given human group interact with resources and stressors of their environment, with the level of quality of life resultant from these interactions. Consistent with Campbell (1981), Murrell and Norris (1983) they state the assessment of quality of life must be comprehensive, in order to reflect a global state of well-being. As such, no one domain can completely determine quality of life, which clearly encompasses more than just mental health.

---

[12] Normal conditions of life is used in the sense implied by Nirje (1985).

As Schalock and Lilley (1986) noted, the significance of the model Murrell and Norris (1983) developed was that it conceptualised quality of life as both an outcome from human service programmes, and the criterion for establishing the goodness of fit between a population and its environment (Schalock and Lilley 1986). Such an idea of quality of life has an additional appealing trait, in that with such a definition, having a low quality of life does not stigmatise the individual as having any sort of deficit. Instead, it reflects how well the current environment suits the individual (Murrell and Norris 1983). Consequently, quality of life is seen as an important criterion for addressing social policies (for example, Murrell and Norris 1983; Schalock and Lilley 1986).

Schalock and Lilley (1986) extend the idea of quality of life as being a goodness of fit between persons' and their environment, through the development of a Quality of Life Questionnaire, which, after revision and modification, resulted in the Schalock and Keith (1993) Quality of Life Questionnaire. The Schalock and Lilley (1986) Quality of Life Questionnaire was developed as a tool for programme evaluation, to assess both the individual with an intellectual disability, and their environment (Schalock et al. 1990). The structure and composition of various quality of life questionnaires, including the Schalock and Keith (1993) Quality of Life Questionnaire, are discussed further in Section 3.2.2 (Quality of Life).

2.4.4 Relationship between Quality of Life and Employment
There have been numerous studies using quality of life measures to investigate the outcomes achieved by different methods of accommodation services for people with an intellectual disability (for example, Hemming et al. 1981; Heal and Chadsey-Rusch 1985; Schalock and Lilley 1986; Schalock and Genung 1993; Conroy 1996). However, there has been surprisingly little research investigating whether supported or open employment for people with intellectual disabilities results in different quality of life outcomes. As such, this section first summarises the literature on whether employment affects the quality of life of people with intellectual disabilities, and then reports those papers that investigate whether differences exist in the quality of life of people with intellectual disabilities employed in supported employment compared with open employment.

2.4.4.1 Does Employment Make a Difference?
Schalock and Lilley (1986) developed a quality of life questionnaire to evaluate the successfulness, in living and work, of individuals eight to ten years after being deinstitutionalised. In relation to work, they found that those individuals who had successful work placements had a higher quality of life than those who have unsuccessful work placements. Schalock and Lilley (1986) found that living success appears to be independent of work success, but the converse does not hold. However, they also found that individuals who retained their jobs are generally higher functioning and have fewer disabilities. Thus, it is not clear whether it is the employment or the level of disability that is impacting on their result.

Fabian (1992) used the Lehman (1988) Quality of Life Interview to assess whether people with severe intellectual disabilities in open employment report higher quality of life scores compared with people with intellectual disabilities seeking employment. Fabian (1992) found that people in open employment reported statistically significantly higher scores than job seekers in two of the eight areas of the Quality of Life Interview; the two areas being *work* and *finance*. Neither of these findings are surprising. First, it could be expected that people in work would be more satisfied with their work situation than those unemployed. Second, it could be expected that those earning a wage would be more satisfied with their finances than those not earning a regular income. It is interesting to note, that employment does not lead to higher scores in the other six areas of the Quality of Life Interview. The results of Fabian (1992) suggest that employment does not impact on quality of life, thus contradicting the findings of Schalock and Lilley (1986).

2.4.4.2 Does Type of Employment Make a Difference?
Relatively few studies compare the quality of life of people participating in open employment compared with those in supported employment (Inge *et al.* 1988; Pedlar *et al.* 1990; E-QUAL and Donovan Research 2000; Sinnott-Oswald *et al.* 1991; Eggleton *et al.* 1999). Pedlar *et al.* (1990) conducted a qualitative study of 12 people placed in open employment. Based on content analysis of the interviews they concluded that open employment considerably enhanced participants' quality of life. However, exactly how this conclusion was drawn is not clear, as no established link between the content of the interviews and quality of life was made. Additionally, given that no statistical analysis was conducted, it is not possible to determine whether the enhancement in quality of life is statistically significant.

Inge *et al.* (1988) and Sinnott-Oswald *et al.* (1991) both conducted quantitative analysis and found that people participating in open employment experienced a higher quality of life than those employed in a supported environment. Inge *et al.* (1998) identified 20 people employed in supported employment and matched them to people in open employment based on gender, age, physical and sensory involvement, parental support, and functioning level. They assessed participants' quality of life using three proxy measures: first, the AAMD Adaptive Behaviour Scale (Nihira *et al.* 1974); second, a parent/guardian survey that measured participants' community participation, social vocational skills, fiscal responsibility, financial activity, and weekly work income; and finally, five physical health measures, including weight, resting pulse, blood pressure, hand strength, and body fat.

Inge *et al.* (1998) found that participants in open employment had statistically significantly higher scores for three of the five sub-scales of the adaptive behaviour scale (economic activity, language development, and numbers and time) as well as all five aspects of the parent/guardian survey. No significant differences were found in terms of the health of the two samples. Though not explicitly stated, they assumed that the higher scores for the adaptive behaviour scale and parent/guardian survey meant that participants in open employment had a higher quality of life. However, whether such a conclusion can be drawn is questionable. In the absence of theoretical underpinning, a person's assessment of the quality of life he/she experiences can neither be assumed to be related to his/her adaptive behaviour, nor necessarily others' opinions on his/her level of community participation, social vocational skills, fiscal responsibility, financial activity, and weekly work income.

Sinnott-Oswald *et al.* (1991) compared the quality of life of ten people employed in open employment with ten people employed in supported employment who were matched based on age, gender, and degree of intellectual disability. Quality of life was assessed using a questionnaire the authors developed, based on Schalock and Lilley's (1986) quality of life questionnaire. Sinnott-Oswald *et al.* (1991) found participants in open employment reported statistically significantly higher scores for ten of the 18 questions contained in their questionnaire (ability to make independent decisions, self esteem, use of public transport, frequency of use of public transport, participation in leisure/recreation activities, with whom they eat out, use of leisure time in the past year, changes in mobility during the past year, changes in job skills during the past year, changes in income during the past year). Based on these statistically significant differences Sinnott-Oswald *et al.* (1991) concluded that people with intellectual disabilities placed in open employment had a higher quality of life than those people placed in supported employment. Whether such a conclusion can be drawn is questionable, given the small sample size, the quality of life questionnaire did not undergo any form of psychometric validation, the non-significant changes in eight of the questions, and the fact that their questionnaire does not allow the calculation of a total quality of life score.

E-QUAL and Donovan Research (2000), as part of their Australian satisfaction survey of clients of disability services assessed the quality of life of people with disabilities in open employment and supported employment. They interviewed 1,449 people with various disabilities, including intellectual disabilities, and found the majority of people using either open employment or supported employment services liked their place of work (83 percent), felt safe at work (94 percent), believed the pay was fair (77 percent), were happy with their work hours (73 percent), and would like their employment to continue (77 percent). E-QUAL and Donovan Research (2000), based on the Core Indicators Project (Human Services Research Institute 1998) claim that these aspects of a person work life relate to the *life situation* quality of life domain. However, E-QUAL and Donovan Research (2000) find no statistically significant difference in percentage responses between open employment and supported employment.

Although E-QUAL and Donovan Research (2000) report that of their sample 43.4 percent of open employment clients had intellectual disabilities and that 76.1 percent of supported employment clients had intellectual disabilities, no separate employment analyses or results are presented exclusively for people with intellectual disabilities. As such, it is not possible to determine whether the above results hold for people with intellectual disabilities. Furthermore, the relationship between the questions asked and quality of life has not been proven, casting doubts upon whether E-QUAL and Donovan Research (2000) were even actually measuring quality of life.

Overcoming the above problems of small sample size (Inge *et al.* 1988; Sinnott-Oswald *et al.* 1991) and the use of quality of life questionnaires that had not been psychometrically validated or proven to be capturing the construct of quality of life (Inge *et al.* 1988; Sinnott-Oswald *et al.* 1991; E-QUAL and Donovan Research 2000), Eggleton *et al.* (1999) used the Schalock and Keith (1993) QOL.Q to investigate the impact of open employment on people with intellectual disabilities. They interviewed 25 people who were in open employment, and a matched sample of 25 people who were seeking open employment. As in Fabian (1992), Eggleton *et al.* (1999) found that people with intellectual disabilities in open employment reported statistically significantly higher quality of life scores than job seekers. Further, Eggleton *et al.* (1999) also compared a subset of their sample who were working in open employment, but had previously worked in a supported employment setting, with those people still working in a supported employment setting but seeking open employment (supported employment participants were included in their job seekers sample). Eggleton *et al.* (1999) found that those in open employment reported statistically significantly higher quality of life scores than their supported employment counterparts.

However, what is driving the result of Eggleton *et al.* (1999) is not entirely clear. Given that Eggleton *et al.* (1999) noted all participants in their research were drawn from the list of an open employment agency, this means those people who were in supported employment and now seeking open employment were probably not satisfied with their supported employment situation, otherwise they would not have been seeking open employment. Likewise, it is possible that those people who were previously in supported employment but now in open employment, were dissatisfied with their previous (supported) employment placement, otherwise they would not have moved to open employment. As such, it is not clear whether the results of Eggleton *et al.* (1999) are driven by the differences in the nature of the two methods of employment (open employment versus supported employment), or due to sample bias.

Summarising the above research, it is not clear whether open employment and supported employment produce different outcomes in terms of quality of life. Hence, part of the importance of this thesis lies in the fact that it uses an established quality of life questionnaire, which has had its psychometric properties validated, and has a comparatively large sample size to investigate the quality of life of individuals with intellectual disabilities who participate in open employment versus those placed in supported employment.

2.5 Conclusion

The review of literature undertaken in this chapter has shown there is a dearth of literature relating to the effect of different methods of employment (open employment and supported employment) on job satisfaction and quality of life. As such, this research is important in that it is the first major review of the person-referenced outcomes (job satisfaction and quality of life) achieved by the two major methods of employment for people with intellectual disabilities. As mentioned in the next chapter (Research Methods), this research will also overcome some of the limitations of prior research by controlling for demographic differences apparent between people in supported employment compared with those in open employment; thus ensuring that any results are in fact due to differences in the types of employment and not confounding variables.

Chapter 3 - Research Method

3.1 Introduction

In this chapter, the research method employed in examining the outcomes between the different methods of employment for people with intellectual disabilities is discussed. First, there is discussion of how the instruments used to measure outcomes were decided on. Each outcome measure is described, and the theoretical and practical considerations in selecting a particular outcome measure are given. Intervening factors that could affect the outcome measures are considered, and how they are controlled is also described. Next, follows a description of the process of sample selection, the interview processes, and the problems encountered.

3.2 Development of Outcome Evaluation Questionnaire

Having decided on the outcome measures of job satisfaction and quality of life, the next phase of the research was to identify whether measurement instruments existed or needed to be developed to measure those outcomes. Given the nature of the concepts of job satisfaction and quality of life it was apparent that to determine such outcomes from a person referenced perspective it would be necessary to interview people with intellectual disabilities. This necessitated that the measurement instruments should be readily comprehensible to people with intellectual disabilities. This factor was further compounded by the varying range of levels of intellectual disability across the agencies and that any measurement instrument had to be comprehensible to this cross-section of people with intellectual disabilities.

3.2.1 Job Satisfaction

Even though relatively few studies have investigated the job satisfaction of people with intellectual disabilities the manner in which the construct of job satisfaction for people with intellectual disabilities has been measured varies greatly. Consequently, each instrument that purported to measure job satisfaction was first assessed for its applicability to this research. Not only was each instrument assessed in terms of its psychometric rigour, but also in terms of its practicality. I had to be mindful that the instrument needed to be acceptable to the two agencies initially involved in this research. One agency indicated that any job satisfaction measure used would need to ask fairly specific questions about the work environment for it to gain their approval to be used in this research. The reason was a desire by this agency to have a measure in which a solution would be fairly self-evident, if the analysis of responses highlighted a problem. For example, if a question asked *do you have to stand up too much at work?* and the majority of respondents answered in the affirmative, it is fairly self-evident that the agency should investigate the possibility of restructuring the job to allow the people to sit down more often.

Given the disparate nature of measuring job satisfaction for people with intellectual disabilities, each instrument that had been used with people with intellectual disabilities was critically reviewed in terms of its applicability to this research. A review of the literature identified 12 questionnaires previously used in determining the job satisfaction of people with intellectual disabilities. Although the instruments differed, they could be placed into one of either four categories, depending on the method used to measure job satisfaction. Table 3.1 shows the 12 different questionnaires categorised by the different methods, which were: (1) by participant observation (this method was used in research undertaken by Talkington and Overbeck 1975; Nisbet and York 1989); (2) by using an established questionnaire developed for people without intellectual disabilities (Rosen *et al.* 1970; Houser and Chace 1993); (3) by modifying an established instrument developed for people without intellectual disabilities to make it applicable for people with intellectual disabilities (Gray and Weiss 1971; Seltzer and Seltzer 1978; Seltzer 1984; Lam and Chan 1988; Jiranek and Kirby 1990; Barlow and Kirby 1991; Petrovski and Gleeson 1997); and (4) developing a new questionnaire (Test *et al.* 1993; Shanly and Rose 1993). Each of these approaches will be discussed in turn.

Table 3.1: Job satisfaction questionnaires used with people with intellectual disabilities.

Scale	Author(s) of scale
Participant Observation	
Comments made in relation to job satisfaction	Talkington and Overbeck (1975)
Job Satisfaction Indices	Nisbet and York (1989)
Questionnaire developed for people without a disability	
Minnesota Satisfaction Scale (MSS)	Carlson (1962)
Short form of the Minnesota Satisfaction Questionnaire (MSQ)	Weiss (1969)
Modification of a questionnaire developed for people without a disability	
Modification of the short form of the MSQ	Gray and Weiss (1971)
Modification of the Smith *et al.* (1969) Job Description Index	Seltzer and Seltzer (1978)
Modification of the short form of the MSQa	Lam and Chan (1988)
Modification of the Warr *et al.* (1979) Job Satisfaction Scale	Jiranek and Kirby (1990)
Modification of the Seltzer and Seltzer (1978) Job Satisfaction Questionnaire	Barlow and Kirby (1991)
Developed a new questionnaire	
Job Satisfaction Questionnaire	Test *et al.* (1993)
Job Satisfaction Questionnaire	Shanly and Rose (1993)

a   Although both Gray and Weiss (1971) and Lam and Chan (1988) developed a job satisfaction questionnaire for people with intellectual disabilities based on a modification of the MSQ, the modifications they made differed substantially.

3.2.1.1 Participant Observation
Both Talkington and Overbeck (1975) and Nisbet and York (1989) used the indirect method of participant observation to assess job satisfaction. Talkington and Overbeck (1975), in their study on the relationship between job satisfaction and job performance for females with intellectual disabilities, determined job satisfaction based on the person's comments made to his/her residential supervisor.[13] If people continually made disparaging remarks about their work or workplace they were categorised as being dissatisfied with their employment. Conversely, if people made positive comments about their work or workplace they were categorised as being satisfied. Based on interviews with people with intellectual disabilities, their parents, teachers, and employers, and participant observation, Nisbet and York (1989) developed 22 indices that they claimed indicated job satisfaction when observed in people with intellectual disabilities. The list of indices included factors such as *consistently attends work, shows positive facial expressions, accepts instruction/supervision, expresses satisfaction with job verbally/non-verbally at home/school/other, responds positively toward going to work*, etc.

The approaches used by Talkington and Overbeck (1975) and Nisbet and York (1989) to assess job satisfaction merely seek to establish whether people with intellectual disabilities are satisfied with their job. They do not seek a deeper understanding of what aspects of the job with which the person is either satisfied or dissatisfied. Given that job satisfaction is a multidimensional construct, such approaches could be criticised for being too simplistic and for not capturing the different aspects of work that comprise job satisfaction. Additionally, as Seltzer (1984) noted, given that job satisfaction of the person is being determined by someone else, such studies cannot assess the subjective experience of work that is an integral part of the concept of job satisfaction. Consequently, neither approach adopted by Talkington and Overbeck (1975) and Nisbet and York (1989) to determine job satisfaction is considered appropriate for this research.

---

[13] All the females that participated in Talkington and Overbeck's (1975) study were drawn from the same group home.

3.2.1.2 Using Questionnaires Developed for People without Disabilities

Both Rosen *et al.* (1970) and Houser and Chace (1993) assessed the job satisfaction of people with intellectual disabilities, using established questionnaires developed for people without disabilities. Rosen *et al.* (1970) used the Minnesota Satisfaction Scale (MSS) (Carlson 1962), which has 80 questions; 76 required a response on a one to five-point scale (strongly agree, agree, undecided, disagree, strongly disagree), and four questions required a response on a seven-point scale, which used different adjectives from *I love it* to *I hate it*. Houser and Chace (1993) used the short-form of the Minnesota Satisfaction Questionnaire (MSQ) (Weiss *et al.* 1969), which contained 20 questions, to assess a person's job satisfaction. The MSQ required participants to respond on a five-point scale of *not satisfied* (1 point), *only slightly satisfied* (2 points), *satisfied* (3 points), *very satisfied* (4 points), and *extremely satisfied* (5 points).

Even though both the MSS and MSQ have undergone psychometric validation when used on samples of people without disabilities (for example, Gillet *et al.* 1975; Bledsoe and Brown 1977; Tan and Hawkins 2000; Hancer and George 2004), I believe the validity of responses for people with intellectual disabilities using these questionnaires is questionable. Given the level of cognitive comprehension of people with intellectual disabilities, it is unlikely that the majority of people would have been able to respond meaningfully on a five or seven-point scale. This belief was confirmed in discussions with staff from the two agencies initially involved in this research. Staff felt that possibly people with mild intellectual disabilities may be able to respond to such scales. However, people with more severe levels of intellectual disability would definitely not have possessed the necessary levels of cognitive ability to respond to five and seven point scales. Given that I wished to include people with varying levels of intellectual disability, both the MSS and MSQ were considered inappropriate questionnaires to assess the job satisfaction of people with intellectual disabilities.

3.2.1.3 Modifying Questionnaires Developed for People without Disabilities

Gray and Weiss (1971) reported on the development of a questionnaire for people with intellectual disabilities, based on the 20 question short-form of the MSQ (Weiss *et al.* 1969). They modified the questionnaire from being self-administered to being administered by an interviewer. They also changed the wording of the questions to make them understandable to people with intellectual disabilities. The five-point scale was replaced with five schematic faces that ranged from a scowl (not satisfied: 1 point) to a happy face (extremely satisfied: 5 points). The faces were a modification of the ones used previously by Kunin (1955) and Kendall *et al.* (1964).

Likewise, Lam and Chan (1988) developed a job satisfaction questionnaire for people with intellectual disabilities based on the short-form of the MSQ. As in Gray and Weiss (1971), Lam and Chan (1988) changed the questionnaire to be interviewer administered and replaced the five-point scale with five faces; though the five faces are faces they developed themselves. However, unlike Gray and Weiss (1971), Lam and Chan (1988) decided to omit eight of the 20 questions, thus reducing the questionnaire to 12 questions. The eight questions are omitted because Lam and Chan (1988) did not consider them to be relevant to people with intellectual disabilities employed in supported settings.[14, 15]

Though the MSQ has been psychometrically validated (for example, Tan and Hawkins 2000; Hancer and George 2004) on samples drawn from people without a disability, this does not mean that, with the modifications undertaken by Gray and Weiss (1971) and Lam and Chan (1988), the modified questionnaire for people with intellectual disabilities is also psychometrically sound. In

---

[14] The eight MSQ questions that Lam and Chan (1988) omit relate to authority, creativity, independence, moral values, responsibility, social service, social status, and autonomy.
[15] The samples of Gray and Weiss (1971) and Lam and Chan (1988) differ, in that Gray and Weiss's (1971) sample was drawn from people with intellectual disabilities placed in open employment, while Lam and Chan's (1988) sample was drawn from people with intellectual disabilities in supported employment.

both instances substantial modifications are made (rewording of questions, changing the instrument from self administration to interviewer administered, and in the case of Lam and Chan (1988) the omission of eight questions), all of which would impact on the psychometric properties of the questionnaire. Unfortunately, neither Gray and Weiss (1971) nor Lam and Chan (1988) reported any psychometric properties for their modified MSQs. Consequently, the reader is unsure whether reliability can be attributed to the scores these two modified questionnaires obtained. However, this alone is insufficient grounds on which to disregard use of either questionnaire. As will become evident from discussion of other modified questionnaires below and the ones developed from scratch (next section), only one questionnaire has undergone any form of psychometric validation, and then only on a very limited basis (the reporting of an overall Cronbach alpha). Consequently, it became evident that whichever instrument was selected the psychometric properties of the questionnaire would need to be validated.

A further matter that confounds the issue of internal reliability is the use of the faces scale and whether people with intellectual disabilities can appropriately differentiate between the faces. That is, do people with intellectual disabilities rank the faces in the order that the researcher intended them to interpret the faces, and what emotion do they allocate to each face? In relation to the issue of rank ordering the faces, Gray and Weiss (1971) noted that when participants were given the five faces randomly and asked to place them in rank order, only 50 percent of the sample could do so. This inability of half the sample to reflect the intended rankings of the faces scale brings the reliability of using faces into question. Lam and Chan (1988) do not report any form of validation on whether their participants interpreted their five faces as they hoped. Further, it cannot be easily determined whether the emotion that people with intellectual disabilities place on the faces are the emotions researchers intend. This point is especially pertinent given that none of the researchers justifies the faces used to represent scowling through to happy faces, based on empirical research linking emotions to facial expressions.

Given that I wished to interview people from both open and supported employment, it was felt that the Lam and Chan (1988) derivation of the MSQ, despite its omission of questions they considered irrelevant to supported employment, would be a more appropriate questionnaire than the Gray and Weiss (1971) modification. Consequently, the Gray and Weiss (1971) questionnaire was not considered a possible instrument for this research. Further it was recognised that if I used the Lam and Chan (1988) derivation of the MSQ, I would need to ask participants to rank order the five faces themselves to see whether they placed them in the correct order. This would not be an ideal situation, however as revealed in the discussion below, only one modified questionnaire did not use a faces scale.

Jiranek and Kirby (1990) measured the job satisfaction of people with intellectual disabilities based on a modification of the job satisfaction scale developed by Warr et al. (1979). Jiranek and Kirby (1990) simplified the wording of the questions to make them understandable to people with intellectual disabilities and also reduced the scale from seven points to five points. Like Lam and Chan (1988) they used a faces scale which they developed to represent their five points, ranging from very happy (represented by a smile: scored as 1 point) to very unhappy (represented by a scowl: scored as 5 points). Thus, the higher the score the more dissatisfied a person is with their job. This modified version of the Warr et al. (1979) job satisfaction questionnaire was subsequently also used by Petrovski and Gleeson (1997).

Similar to the concerns stated above, neither Jiranek and Kirby (1990) nor Petrovski and Gleeson (1997) reported any psychometric validation statistics and, as such, the reader is not sure of the reliability of scores obtained by this questionnaire. Also, as mentioned above, the use of the faces scale is a point of concern. Neither Jiranek and Kirby (1990) nor Petrovski and Gleeson (1997) attempted to ascertain whether respondents interpreted the faces scale in the rank order they intended. However, as stated above, given the fact that none of the modified or developed questionnaires had been validated, the lack of validation cannot preclude consideration of that instrument. Consequently, though I had reservations about the validity of the instrument, especially the use of the faces scale, I decided to present the modified Warr *et al.* (1979) job satisfaction questionnaire to the two agencies as a possible instrument.

Seltzer and Seltzer (1978) measured the job satisfaction of people with intellectual disabilities using a modification of the Job Description Index (JDI) (Smith *et al.* 1969). As Seltzer (1984) noted, the reasons for selecting the JDI were its wide usage in job satisfaction research, the fact the instrument had been used successfully with blue-collar workers, and that the instrument had been psychometrically validated. Seltzer and Seltzer (1978) modified the JDI from a self-administered instrument to an interviewer administered instrument, and replaced the adjectives or short phrases for the different aspect of a job with questions they believed would be understandable to people with intellectual disabilities. They also omitted any questions that related to aspects of the work environment they believed did not apply to people with intellectual disabilities or made reference to co-workers' levels of intelligence. This resulted in 61 questions which they placed into five sub-scales of type of work, supervision, co-workers, pay, and opportunities for promotion.[16] Seltzer and Seltzer (1978) retained the original JDI responses and scoring of *yes* (3), *no* (0), and *not sure* (1) (reverse scored for questions phrased in the negative).[17] Seltzer (1984), who reported in greater detail the results relating to job satisfaction from Seltzer and Seltzer (1978), reported that the Cronbach alpha for the overall questionnaire was .80, but did not report any Cronbach alphas for any of the sub-scales.

Barlow and Kirby (1991) further modified the Seltzer and Seltzer (1978) version of the JDI by changing some of the wordings to questions, adding some questions, omitting others, changing the scoring, and changing the sub-scales. Some of the Seltzer and Seltzer (1978) questions were omitted and other questions added to better reflect the working environment of the Barlow and Kirby (1991) sample. Seltzer and Seltzer's (1978) sample was drawn from people with intellectual disabilities in open employment, whereas the sample from Barlow and Kirby (1991) was from a supported work environment, and consequently certain questions (for example, ones relating to promotions) were irrelevant. Wording on some questions was also changed to make hopefully the questions more understandable to people with intellectual disabilities. The scoring system was changed to be consistent with other questions that formed part of Barlow and Kirby's (1991) overall questionnaire, and also because the authors wished to compare two samples and were concerned only with differences in scores and not absolute scores.[18] This resulted in a questionnaire that had 33 questions, scored 2 for *yes*, 1 for *not sure* and 0 for *no* (scored in reverse order for negatively phrased questions) and formed five sub-scales that they termed *physical*, *task*, *pay*, *social*, and *staff*.

The questionnaire used by Barlow and Kirby (1991) has since been modified by the authors to further increase hopefully the understandability of the questions and capture better the construct of job satisfaction.[19] These further modifications resulted in some minor wording changes to the

---

[16] Titles of the sub-scales are drawn from Smith et al. (1969) and the questions that comprise each sub-scale are the ones drawn from the respective sub-scale in Smith et al. (1969).

[17] Smith et al. (1969) stated that the reason for scoring *yes* as 3, *not sure* as 1, and *no* as 0 (scored in reverse order for negatively phrased questions) was that their pilot-testing revealed that *not sure* was not a mid-point between *yes* and *no*, but closer to a *no* response than it was a *yes* response. Therefore, it was not appropriate to score 2 (Yes), 1 (Not sure), and 0 (No). This was confirmed by their psychometric assessments of the JDI.

[18] The reasons for these changes were revealed through a personal discourse with both authors. Further, Barlow and Kirby's (1991) assessment of the job satisfaction of participants was only a minor part of their overall study, which was concerned with comparing the residential satisfaction of people with intellectual disabilities living in the community versus those living in institutions. Consequently the instrument they used to assess satisfaction had ten different sections, one of which related to job satisfaction.

[19] These further changes to the Barlow and Kirby (1991) questionnaire were revealed through a personal discourse with both authors.

Barlow and Kirby (1991) questionnaire and also the addition of two further questions, bringing the total number to 35, while still retaining the five sections. Given that the authors have yet to publish an article using this further modified questionnaire, for referencing ease, all future references to the Barlow and Kirby (1991) questionnaire will be to this further modified questionnaire.

Given that this research will interview people with intellectual disabilities in both open employment and supported employment, and the questions must be equally applicable to both samples, I believe the Barlow and Kirby (1991) derivation of the JDI to be more appropriate than the Seltzer and Seltzer (1978) derivation. However, given that the Seltzer and Seltzer (1978) derivation is shown to have good reliability and that I wished to confirm my views with the two agencies involved with this research I presented both versions to the agencies.

3.2.1.4 Developing a New Job Satisfaction Questionnaire Specific for People with Intellectual Disabilities

Both Shanly and Rose (1993) and Test et al. (1993) measured the job satisfaction of people with intellectual disabilities using questionnaires they had developed themselves. Both instruments used open-ended questions to assess job satisfaction. Shanly and Rose's (1993) questionnaire comprised six questions that covered four areas of work, the areas being: work itself (3 questions), people at work (1 question), wages (1 question), and work structure and responsibility (1 question). Depending on participants' responses, supplementary questions could be asked to clarify initial responses. Test et al. (1993) developed a 20-item questionnaire built around the 22 items that Nisbet and York (1990) believed to be indices of job satisfaction for people with intellectual disabilities. The questionnaire contained a mix of open-ended questions and forced yes/no questions. Test et al. (1993) noted that depending on a person's level of understanding, some questions had to be substantially rephrased, sometimes to the extent of changing an open-ended question to a forced yes/no response. In both papers, job satisfaction was determined by the rater's interpretation of respondents' answers.

Neither of the instruments developed by Shanly and Rose (1993) and Test et al. (1993) are considered appropriate for this research, given that the determination of job satisfaction relies on the rater's interpretation of peoples' responses. However, Test et al. (1993) noted that they had 100 percent inter-rater reliability based on a sample of 20 percent of the interviews they conducted. Additionally, neither questionnaire enables the degree of job satisfaction to be determined as, based on the rater's interpretation of the participants' responses, participants are deemed to be either satisfied or not for each question, with questions not being additive. The degree of rewording required for the Test et al. (1993) job satisfaction questionnaire is of further concern. Consequently, neither instrument is considered to be appropriate to the needs of this research.

3.2.1.5 Selection of the Job Satisfaction Questionnaire to be used

The above review of questionnaires previously used to assess the job satisfaction of people with intellectual disabilities resulted in four questionnaires (Seltzer and Seltzer 1978; Lam and Chan 1988; Jiranek and Kirby 1990; Barlow and Kirby 1991) being considered potentially useful for this thesis. Each of these questionnaires was presented and discussed with the two agencies initially involved in this research. Both agencies expressed reservations similar to those mentioned above in Section 3.2.1.2 (Using Questionnaires Developed for People without Disabilities) about the use of the two questionnaires that used faces scales (Lam and Chan 1988; Jiranek and Kirby 1990). Additionally, the agency that placed people with intellectual disabilities into supported employment noted that neither of these questionnaires contained an adequate level of specificity in relation to aspects of work.

Having omitted the Lam and Chan (1988) and Jiranek and Kirby (1990) questionnaires, the agency placing people into open employment was equally happy with use of either the Seltzer and Seltzer (1978) job satisfaction questionnaire or Barlow and Kirby's (1991) subsequent modification of this questionnaire. The other agency, which places people with intellectual disabilities into supported employment, was happy with the level of specificity of the questions of both questionnaires. That is, the supported employment agency felt that responses to individual questions would allow them to pin-point specific issues that may need addressing. However, this agency had a very strong preference for the Barlow and Kirby (1991) modification, as it felt the questions were more appropriate to people with intellectual disabilities in a supported employment environment, while still being appropriate to an open employment setting. The agency also felt that the rewording by Barlow and Kirby (1991) made the questions easier to understand and would thus increase the likelihood of obtaining meaningful responses from people with higher levels of intellectual disability. This was an important consideration, given that the agency had mentioned previously that some people it placed in supported employment had high levels of intellectual disabilities, and I wished to survey as wide a range of levels of intellectual disability as possible. As mentioned in Section 2.3 (Job Satisfaction), a limitation of prior research into the job satisfaction of people with intellectual disabilities is the fact that often people with only mild intellectual disabilities were surveyed.

Having stated that the supported employment agency had a strong preference for the Barlow and Kirby (1991) job satisfaction questionnaire, it should also be noted that given the review of all the job satisfaction questionnaires detailed above this was also the instrument that I believed to be the most appropriate instrument to measure job satisfaction. Given this, the fact that the supported employment agency had a strong preference for the Barlow and Kirby (1991) job satisfaction questionnaire, and that the open employment agency was indifferent to the choice between the Barlow and Kirby (1991) and Seltzer and Seltzer (1978) questionnaires, the Barlow and Kirby (1991) questionnaire was selected. I believe that in providing the two agencies with the four questionnaires (Seltzer and Seltzer 1978; Lam and Chan 1988; Jiranek and Kirby 1990; Barlow and Kirby 1991), and each of them reaching the same conclusion as myself regarding the best instrument, increased my confidence in concluding which questionnaire was the most appropriate. The questions that make up the questionnaire are shown in Table 3.2.

The Barlow and Kirby (1991) questionnaire also had the added benefit that while it is comprehensive (35 questions) it is not prohibitively long compared with other questionnaires (for example, the MSS used by Rosen et al. (1970) has 80 questions). This is important, given that I am also measuring quality of life, which necessitates the use of an additional questionnaire, and that I did not wish to make the interview too long and arduous for the participant. However, as noted above, in Section 3.2.1.3 (Modifying Questionnaires Developed for People without Disabilities), the Barlow and Kirby (1991) modification of the Seltzer and Seltzer (1978) job satisfaction questionnaire has not undergone any form of psychometric validation, necessitating the need for such validation to be conducted as part of this research prior to any weight being placed on the findings of this thesis. Unfortunately, it was not possible to undertake this psychometric validation prior to commencing interviews for this research due to agencies wishing me to undertake only one set of interviews, and the fact that if a person were interviewed for the psychometric validation of the questionnaire I would have precluded myself from interviewing the person again for the main part of the research. Given the limited number of disability employment agencies in the particular Australian city where this research was conducted, this would have severely limited my sample size for this research and made it impossible to conduct meaningful analysis. Consequently, the risk had to be taken to use an untested questionnaire in the main part of the research. Nevertheless, this limitation also provided the opportunity to perform appropriate psychometric testing following data collection, thereby contributing to our knowledge concerning this instrument.

3.2.2 Quality of Life
As stated in the previous chapter, it is important that the outcome measures used in this thesis are customer-referenced. As such, in identifying an appropriate instrument to assess quality of life, only those instruments that directly involved responses from people with intellectual disabilities were

considered. A review of the literature identified 13 possible questionnaires that purported to assess the quality of life of people with intellectual disabilities. The 13 questionnaires are shown in Table 3.3.

Table 3.2:   Barlow and Kirby's (1991) Job Satisfaction Questionnaire

Physical
1.1   Do you like the place where you work?
1.2   Is it a nice building to work in?
1.3   Is it a nice place to work?
1.4   Do you have to stand up/sit down too much while you work?
1.5   Is it too hot/cold, noisy there?
1.6   Do the days seem very long, like they will never end, when you are working?
1.7   Would you rather be working in a different section?

Task
2.1   Do you think your work is interesting?
2.2   Do you think your work is too easy?
2.3   Does your work make you feel that you are doing something important?
2.4   Is your work boring?
2.5   Do you have enough to do at work?
2.6   Would you rather be doing a different type of work?
2.7   Do you have to push yourself very hard?

Pay
3.1   Is your pay too little to let you make ends meet?
3.2   Do you think you should be paid more for what you do?
3.3   Do you think that you get paid less than you are worth?
3.4   Do you ever worry that the amount of your pay will change from week to week?
3.5   Does your pay let you buy special things when you want to?
3.6   Do you think that you are paid very well?

Social
4.1   Do you like the people you work with?
4.2   Is it hard to meet people at work?
4.3   Do you sometimes have lunch with the people you work with?
4.4   Do they talk to you very much?
4.5   Do you see them (socially) after work?
4.6   Would you rather be working with different people?
4.7   Would the people at work help you if you had a problem?
4.8   Do the people you work with respect (understand) you?

Staff
5.1   Does your supervisor tell you honestly what he/she thinks about your work?
5.2   Does he/she let you work by yourself enough?
5.3   Is he/she there when you need help with your work?
5.4   Does he/she praise you when you do a good job?
5.5   If you had a personal problem would he/she help you?
5.6   Do you think that he/she respects (understands) you?
5.7   Does your supervisor help you to learn new work skills?

For a review of these instruments, refer to Cummins (1997a, 2000a). Since this research investigates the effects of different methods of employment on quality of life, the following five questionnaires cannot be used as they focus on assessing satisfaction with residential and community settings: Quality of Life Questionnaire (Cragg and Harrison 1984), Lifestyle Satisfaction Scale (Heal and Chadsey-Rusch 1985), Assessment of Residents' Satisfaction and Family Perceptions Index (Bowd 1988), Residential Satisfaction Inventory (Burnett 1989), and Multifaceted Lifestyle Satisfaction Scale (Harner and Heal 1993). Furthermore, the Leisure

Satisfaction Scale (Hoover *et al.* 1992) should be omitted, given its focus on leisure activities. As neither the Quality of Life Survey (Sinnott-Oswald *et al.* 1991) nor the Quality of Life Questionnaire (Brown and Bayer 1992) resulted in quantifiable total quality of life scores, they also had to be omitted; in order to allow a comparison across methods of employment it is imperative that quality of life scores be calculable.

Table 3.3: Quality of Life scales for people with intellectual disabilities.

Scale	Author(s) of scale
Quality of Life Questionnaire	Cragg and Harrison (1984)
Lifestyle Satisfaction Scale	Heal and Chadsey-Rusch (1985)
Assessment of Residents' Satisfaction and Family Perceptions Index	Bowd (1988)
Quality of Life Interview	Lehman (1988)
Residential Satisfaction Inventory	Burnett (1989)
Refined Quality of Life Interview Schedule (refined QUOLIS)	Ouellette-Kuntz (1990)
Quality of Life Survey	Sinnott-Oswald (1991)
Quality of Life Questionnaire	Brown and Bayer (1992)
Leisure Satisfaction Scale	Hoover *et al.* (1992)
Multifaceted Lifestyle Satisfaction Scale	Harner and Heal (1993)
Comprehensive Quality of Life Scale (ComQoL-ID4)	Cummins (1993)
Quality of Life Questionnaire (QOL.Q)	Schalock and Keith (1993)
Perceived stress, Affect, Loneliness and Satisfaction (PALS)	Rosen *et al.* (1995)

Having eliminated the eight above-mentioned quality of life questionnaires, due to their inappropriateness to the objectives of this research, the remaining five are assessed for suitability. The Quality of Life Interview (Lehman 1988) is not considered appropriate given that responses are sought on a seven-point Likert scale. Given the level of disability of some customers of the employment agencies it is doubtful they would be able to respond meaningfully on a seven-point scale. The refined QUOLIS (Ouellette-Kuntz 1990) also uses a seven-point scale; however, with faces. As discussed above, in relation to selecting the job satisfaction questionnaire, serious reliability concerns are associated with the use of faces scales. As such, given the use of the faces and the fact that prior to using this questionnaire all interviewers must attend a two-day training course (typically held in Canada), this questionnaire is not considered suitable.[20] Furthermore, the implementation of the questionnaire is estimated to take two hours (Cummins 1997a), which is considered too long, given that I would also use the Barlow and Kirby (1991) job satisfaction questionnaire. As Cummins (1997a, p. 208) noted, in his review on quality of life scales for people with intellectual disabilities, "the magnitude of this instrument seems excessive."

After having also excluded the Quality of Life Interview (Lehman 1988) and the refined QUOLIS (Ouellette-Kuntz 1990), only three quality of life questionnaires remained; namely the fourth edition of ComQoL-ID4 (Cummins 1993), QOL.Q (Schalock and Keith 1993), and PALS (Rosen *et al.* 1995). As Cummins (1997a) noted, the QOL.Q (Schalock and Keith 1993) and the ComQoL-ID4 (Cummins 1993) both meet the basic requirements for useful instruments to measure quality of life. Cummins (1997a) believed that the satisfaction scale of PALS (Rosen *et al.* 1995), which was the only part of the questionnaire associated with quality of life, could not be regarded as an adequate measure of quality of life. He formed this opinion given that coverage of the satisfaction scale missed domains shown by Cummins (1997b) to be central to assessing quality of life, and that the five domains covered are differently weighted due to containing different numbers of questions (ranging from one question to three questions). Consequently, the PALS instrument (Rosen *et al.* 1995) was excluded as a possible measure of quality of life.

Having eliminated PALS (Rosen *et al.* 1995), and given Cummins' (1997a) assertion that both the QOL.Q (Schalock and Keith 1993) and ComQoL-ID4 (Cummins 1993) were adequate measures of

---

[20] As described below masters students were initially recruited to conduct the interviews and it was not financially viable to fly them to Canada to undertake a two-day training course.

quality of life, it was decided that both instruments should be presented to the two disability employment agencies and their opinions sought. Consequently, both instruments are now described in more detail.

3.2.2.1 QOL.Q (Schalock and Keith 1993)

As Cummins (1997a) noted, the QOL.Q is the most widely used quality of life instrument in the field of intellectual disability. The QOL.Q has 40 items, each relating to an aspect of a person's life. The interviewer, who asks the interviewee each of the 40 questions, administers the QOL.Q. For each item the interviewer provides the interviewee with three possible responses, and the interviewee selects the response most appropriate to their life situation. These responses are scored from 1 (low) to 3 (high), thus giving the overall quality of life score a theoretical range of 40 to 120. In addition to being able to compute an overall quality of life score, the QOL.Q is designed to allow the computation of four sub-dimensions (factors), which measure the following different aspects of quality of life: (1) personal life satisfaction, (2) individual competence and productivity at work, (3) feelings of empowerment and independence in the living environment, and (4) feelings of belonging and community integration (Schalock and Keith 1993). As each factor contains ten questions, each factor has a theoretical range of 10 to 30. Given that each sub-dimension has an equal number of items, the QOL.Q gives equal weight to each of the four sub-dimensions in calculating an individual's overall quality of life score.

The QOL.Q allows the interviewer to re-phrase items if the person with the intellectual disability does not understand the original question. Though for this research the person with an intellectual disability would be questioned directly, the QOL.Q allows for proxy respondents when the person with the intellectual disability is unable to complete an interview unassisted.

Cummins (2000a) noted there had been relatively little research carried out on the psychometric properties of quality of life instruments specific to people with intellectual disabilities, with the QOL.Q regarded as being no different to other instruments in this respect. The factor structure of the QOL.Q had been broadly confirmed by Rapley and Lobley (1995) and Caballo et al. (2005), both of whom conducted a replication of the factor structure of the QOL.Q. Rapley and Lobley (1995) found that 32 of the 40 questions loaded in concordance with the loadings of Schalock and Keith (1993), while the results of Caballo et al. (2005)[21] showed 34 questions to load on the same factors as those reported by Schalock and Keith (1993). Rapley and Lobley (1995) noted that the divergences in item loadings they found seemed to be a function of differences in human services provisions and life situations of their sample compared with Schalock and Keith's (1993) sample, rather than a fundamentally different factor structure.

As can be seen from Table 3.4 the internal reliability of the overall QOL.Q and its four factors is generally found to be acceptable (that is, in excess of .700: Hair et. al 1995). The exceptions being the *social belonging/community integration* factor, which on two occasions (Schalock and Keith 1993; Eggleton et al. 1999) report a Cronbach alpha below .700, and the *satisfaction* factor, which in Eggleton et al. (1999) has a Cronbach alpha coefficient below .700. Given that on each occasion the Cronbach alpha score is only marginally below .700, the factors and overall questionnaire are considered reliable.

Although the factor structure and internal reliability of the QOL.Q have been confirmed, Cummins (1997a) noted four areas of concern about the implementation of the QOL.Q. First, he noted that some questions were complex and ambiguous, for example, *Do you feel your job or other daily activity is worthwhile and relevant to either yourself or others?* Second, the responses read out after questions were sometimes also complex, for example, to the question, *what about opportunities for*

---

[21] Reference is made only to the Spanish participants of Caballo et al. (2005), as only this sub-sample comprised people with intellectual disabilities. Their Mexican sub-sample comprised people with physical disabilities.

dating or marriage? the three responses are *I am married or have the opportunity to date anyone I choose*, *I have limited opportunities to date or marry*, and *I have no opportunity to date or marry*. Third, the manual allowed interviewers to paraphrase questions to enhance the respondents' understanding. Cummins (1997a) noted that different interviewers were likely to paraphrase questions differently, which might result in them asking different questions than originally intended. Fourth, in addition to paraphrasing, the manual instructed interviewers that they could repeat items as often as necessary to ensure respondent understanding. The problem with this, Rapley and Antaki (1996) found, was that if the answer provided by a person with an intellectual disability was queried (for example, the interviewer may not be sure whether the interviewee understood the question) the person often changed his/her response when the question was repeated.

Table 3.4: Cronbach alpha scores for the QOL.Q

	Caballo *et al.* (2005)	Eggleton *et al.* (1999)	Rapley & Lobley (1995)	Schalock & Keith (1993)
Satisfaction	.70	.688	.70	.78
Competence/Productivity	.91	.951	.86	.90
Empowerment/Independence	.69	.827	.70	.82
Social belonging/Community integration	.62	.652	.80	.67
Questionnaire	.83	.900	.84	.90

3.2.2.2 ComQoL-ID4 (Cummins 1993)
The ComQoL-ID4 was the fourth edition of the Comprehensive Quality of Life Scale (ComQoL) developed by Professor Robert Cummins. The ComQoL had three parallel forms, one for adults without a disability (ComQoL-A), one for adolescents without a disability (ComQoL-S), and the one discussed here for people with intellectual disability (ComQoL-ID). Cummins developed these three questionnaires in parallel form to allow comparisons to be made across the three populations.

The ComQoL-ID4 had one question on importance and one question on satisfaction for each of the seven domains Cummins (1997b) showed to be central to quality of life. Importance was scored on a five-point scale of *could not be more important* (5), *very important* (4), *somewhat important* (3), *slightly important* (2), *no importance at all* (1), and satisfaction was also scored on a five-point scale, but this time with the points being *very happy* (4), *happy* (2.5), *neither happy nor sad* (1), *sad* (-2.5), *very sad* (-4). The score for each domain was calculated by multiplying the importance by satisfaction, thus giving a theoretical range of minus 20 to positive 20 for each domain, with total quality of life being the average score of the seven domains. The scores could be kept as is or rescaled to a score ranging from zero to 15, as per Cummins *et al.* (1997b). The ComQoL-ID4 also allowed the calculation of separate scores for *Importance* and *Satisfaction*.

The ComQoL-ID4 included a pre-testing procedure designed to determine the extent of Likert scale complexity the respondent can comprehend. Depending on the results of the pre-testing, the interviewer used a binary system, three-point scale, or a five-point scale. The manual contained tables to convert either the binary system or three-point scale to the five-point scales for importance and satisfaction.

I have two issues of concern with regard to the potential use of the ComQoL-ID4 in this research. First, as Cummins (1997a) noted, the ComQoL-ID4 has not been used widely outside his own research. This has prohibited any extensive psychometric validation of the questionnaire. Second, given the lack of psychometric validation by other authors, the Cronbach alpha scores reported in Cummins (1997b) are of concern, as they are all below the satisfactory level of .700. For *importance* the alpha reported is .48, for *satisfaction* .65, and for *importance x satisfaction* .68. Although, the scores for *satisfaction* and *importance x satisfaction* are just below .700, the low alpha for *importance* is of concern. As Pallant (2001) noted, it is not uncommon for questionnaires with less than ten questions to have lower Cronbach alpha scores. Even then, the minimum alpha score Pallant (2001) suggested as being acceptable is .500, which is still higher than the reported score for *satisfaction*.

3.2.2.3 Selection of the Quality of Life Questionnaire to be used

As stated above, Cummins (1997a) asserted that both the QOL.Q and ComQoL-ID4 were adequate measures of quality of life. However, as noted in the above discussion of the QOL.Q and ComQoL-ID4, neither instrument is perfect and there are issues of concern in relation to both instruments. In spite of these, I personally feel, given the ComQoL-ID4 has not been widely used, coupled with the reported low Cronbach alphas, that the QOL.Q is the more appropriate instrument.

Although I believed the QOL.Q to be the more appropriate instrument I still presented both the QOL.Q and ComQoL-ID4 to the two disability employment agencies initially involved in this research to seek their opinions. Both agencies had a strong preference for the QOL.Q. The open employment agency had previously participated in a research project that used the QOL.Q (results reported in Eggleton *et al.* (1999)) and, as such, was familiar with the instrument. This agency also thought it beneficial that I use the QOL.Q, as they could put me in touch with people who conducted interviews in the previous research project and I could then discuss with them any problems with the instrument, and thereby effectively use that research project as a pilot study for this research. The supported employment agency was aware of the QOL.Q and the amount of research conducted using this instrument, but had reservations about using a relatively untested instrument (the ComQoL-ID4).

Consequently, given the preference by myself and by both disability employment agencies for the QOL.Q, this instrument was selected for this research. As with the selection of the job satisfaction questionnaire, the above approach of providing the two questionnaires to the two disability employment agencies and the fact that both agencies independently selected the QOL.Q endorsed my personal selection of the QOL.Q. The questions that form the QOL.Q are shown in Table 3.5.

As noted above, one of the disability employment agencies had previously been involved in a research project that used the QOL.Q. On selecting the QOL.Q as the instrument to be used for this research, the agency placed me in contact with the people who conducted the interviews in the prior research project. They stated that generally they found most people understood most questions. However, there were several questions people occasionally had problems understanding. Some of the issues of understanding related to different vernacular usage between Australia and US, for example, the use of the word *civic* in question 31. In these instances the wording on the question was changed to a more understandable form for Australians. For example, question 31 is simplified to, *to how many clubs or organisations (including church or other religious activities) do you belong?*

Apart from difficulties in understanding, due to different English usage between Americans and Australians, there were also other questions some people had difficulty understanding. To maintain consistency for paraphrasing, alternate phrasings were developed by the previous interviewers for questions with which people had problems.

In the questionnaire used in this research, these alternate phrasings are also included below the originally stated question. As detailed below, in the initial phases of interviews masters of psychology students conducted them; hence, by providing these alternate phrasings, consistency of questioning was maintained. The QOL.Q used in this research, with rewordings, alternate phrasings, and full response items, is shown in Appendix 1. Appendix 1 contains the full outcome evaluation questionnaire used in this research, containing the JSQ and QOL.Q.

3.3 Possible Intervening Factors

Having selected the job satisfaction and quality of life questionnaires, demographic factors that may affect job satisfaction and quality of life then had to be determined. Based on a review of literature,

Table 3.5: Schalock and Keith's (1993) Quality of Life Questionnaire

Factor 1: Satisfaction	
1	Overall, would you say that life brings out the best in you, treats you like everybody else, or doesn't give you a chance?
2	How much fun and enjoyment do you get out of life?
3	Compared to others, are you better off, about the same, or less well off?
4	Are most of the things that happen to you rewarding, acceptable, or disappointing?
5	How satisfied are you with your current home or living arrangement?
6	Do you have more or fewer problems than other people?
7	How many times per month do you feel lonely?
9	How successful do you think you are, compared to others?
8	Do you ever feel out of place in social situations?
10	What about your family members? Do they make you feel an important part of the family, sometimes a part of the family, or like an outsider?
Factor 2: Competence/Productivity	
11	How well did your educational or training programme prepare you for what you are doing now?
12	Do you feel your job or other daily activity is worthwhile and relevant to either yourself or others?
13	How good do you feel you are at your job?
14	How do people treat you on your job?
15	How satisfied are you with the skills and experience you have gained or are gaining from your job?
16	Are you learning skills that will help you get a different or better job? What are these skills?
17	Do you feel you receive fair pay for you work?
18	Does your job provide you with enough money to buy the things you want?
19	How satisfied are you with the benefits you receive at the workplace?
20	How closely supervised are you on your job?
Factor 3: Empowerment/Independence	
21	How did you decide to do the job or other daily activities you do now?
22	Who decides how to spend your money?
23	How do you use health care facilities (doctor, dentist, etc.)?
24	How much control do you have over things you do every day, like going to bed, eating, and what you do for fun?
25	When can friends visit your home?
26	Do you have a key to your home?
27	May you have a pet if you want?
28	Do you have a guardian?
29	Are there people living with you who sometimes hurt you, pester you, scare you, or make you angry?
30	Overall, would you say that your life is free, somewhat planned for you, or that you cannot usually do what you want?
Factor 4: Social belonging/Community integration	
31	To how many civic or community clubs or organisations (including church or other religious activities) do you belong?
32	How satisfied are you with the clubs or organisations (including church or other religious activities) to which you belong?
33	Do you worry about what people expect of you?
34	How many times per week do you talk to (or associate with) your neighbours, either in the yard or in their home?
35	Do you have friends over to visit your home?
36	How often do you attend recreational activities (homes, parties, dances, concerts, plays) in your community?
37	Do you participate actively in those recreational activities?
38	What about opportunities for dating or marriage?
39	How do your neighbours treat you?
40	Overall, would you say that your life is very worthwhile, okay, or useless?

quality of life has been reported to be affected by level of disability (Schalock and Lilley 1986; Schalock *et al.* 1994), living arrangements (Seltzer 1981; Schalock and Lilley 1986; Schalock *et al.* 1994; Conroy 1996), and income level (Schalock *et al.* 1994). Details of the participant's living arrangements were ascertained during the interview with the person, and information on the wages and level of disability of participants was collected from the disability employment agencies once participants agreed to participate. This information was collected from the disability employment agencies as they had ready access to such information, and collecting this information directly from agencies was more likely to have higher levels of reliability, rather than ascertaining the information from participants during interviews. Level of disability was measured using the Functional Assessment Inventory (FAI) (Crew and Athelstan 1984), which is explained in Section 3.3.2 (Level of Disability).

Further demographic data were also collected, and reported on a participant's age, gender, current job tenure, total length of time in employment, length of time with the disability employment agency, number of previous jobs, type of job (as per Australian Standard Classification of Occupations (ASCO) classifications), and average hours worked per week. These are reported in Chapter 5 (Demographics and Sub-Sample Selection). There had been no prior literature on these demographic variables affecting either job satisfaction or quality of life; however, as such data were available it was considered pertinent for collection and analysis.

Demographic data were also requested on whether participants still received the disability support pension and hours of formal recreation activities attended. In over 90 percent of instances, agencies did not have information on what formal recreation activities their customers attended; what information was collected is not reported. In relation to whether the person received the disability support pension, the only participants who were receiving the disability support pension were those employed in supported employment and, as such, the reporting of this variable was regarded as superfluous. Due to the confidential nature of the amount of disability support pension customers received, agencies indicated they would not be willing to reveal this information, thus this information was not sought.

3.3.1 Type of Occupation
The Australian Bureau of Statistics (ABS) codes all Australian occupations based on a skills-based system of classifications. This system is referred to as the Australian Standard Classification of Occupations (ASCO). The ASCO structure has five levels. The first level, called the major occupation group, is the broadest of all classifications and contains nine groups denoted by single-digit codes. Groups are distinguished from each other based on skill levels. The second level comprises 35 sub-major groups, which are sub-divisions of the major groups, and are represented by double-digit codes (being the relevant major group code with the addition of an extra digit). Sub-major groups are separated from others in the same major group on the basis of broadly stated skills specialisations. The third level contains in total 81 minor groups, which are sub-divisions of the sub-major groups, and are represented by triple-digit codes (being the double-digit sub-major code with the addition of an extra digit). These minor groups are distinguished from other minor groups in the same sub-major group based on less broadly stated skill sets. The fourth level contains a total of 340 unit groups, which are sub-divisions of the minor groups, and are represented by quadruple-digit codes (being the minor group code with the addition of a digit). Unit groups are distinguished from one another, based on a finer degree of skill specialisation. The fifth, and final level are the 986 occupations, which are sub-divisions of the unit groups. Occupations are represented by six-digit codes (being the quadruple-digit codes of the unit group with the addition of two digits) and can be separated from other occupations in the same unit group on the basis of detailed skill specialisation.

ASCO codes for each participant were obtained in two different manners. One agency did not have on file the occupations performed by their customers. For this agency, which is involved in the provision of supported employment to its customers, I visited each of their sites and observed their customers perform their daily work functions. Through this observation of the agency's customers and in discussion with workshop staff as to the functions performed by each customer, I was able to match each customer with a quadruple-digit ASCO code. For the other agencies involved in this research they each had on file the occupation performed by their customers. Though the systems used by each of these agencies varied, the various occupation classifications used by each agency could be mapped directly to a two-digit ASCO code. This made it relatively straightforward to classify their customers.

3.3.2 Level of Disability

As the Disability Services Commission, which retains on file IQ scores for all people with intellectual disabilities in Western Australia, does not release them to non-government employees, an alternative measure of functional ability had to be obtained. Further, Schalock *et al.* (1994) showed that it was the level of adaptive and challenging behaviour that was associated with QOL. Therefore, whether IQ scores would be the most suitable demographic variable to collect in this instance is questionable, even if they had been made available to me.

Given that this research relates to the outcomes achieved by different methods of employment for people with intellectual disabilities, it was considered appropriate that the measure of functional ability be related, if possible, to functional work ability. Parmenter *et al.* (1996) conducted a review of assessment instruments to determine which would be the most appropriate to classify the support needs, and thus funding requirements, of people with intellectual disabilities, if a performance based funding system were to be implemented in the Australian disability employment sector. Of the three instruments[22] investigated the authors recommended that the FAI be further investigated as a possible classification tool, reflecting the employment support needs of people with intellectual disabilities. Further, in personal discussions with the first-mentioned author it was noted that the FAI, though not totally satisfactory in his opinion, was probably the best available measure of functional work ability for the purposes I required. As such, the FAI is selected as the measure of functional work ability to be used in this research.

The FAI is a rating instrument designed to be completed by vocational rehabilitation counsellors to measure the employment related disability of their customers. It also incorporates a rating of factors such as appearance and attitude that affect a person's employability (Heineman *et al.* 2000). The FAI is designed to be used with adults or late adolescents who have any type of disability, and has been used on post-stroke patients (Heineman *et al.* 2000), the elderly[23] (Pfeifer *et al.* 1989), and five types of disabilities – orthopaedic/amputation, chronic-physical condition, mental illness, intellectual, and learning disability (Neath *et al.* 1997).

The FAI, as shown in Table 3.6, contains 30 behaviourally anchored questions that assess the customer's vocational capabilities and deficiencies. The 30 behaviourally anchored questions ask the counsellor to assess their customer's disability on a four-point scale, ranging from 0 (no significant impairment) to 3 (severe impairment), thus giving a theoretical range of 0 (full functional work ability) to 90 (has no functional work ability). It was these 30 questions that Crew and Athelstan (1984) asserted factored into the seven factors of *adaptive behaviour, motor functioning, cognition, physical condition, communication, vocational qualification,* and *vision*.[24] Consequently, they contended that it was possible to establish separately a person's employment capacity in these seven categories.

---

[22] The three instruments that were investigated by Parmenter *et al.* (1996) were the Inventory for Client and Agency Planning, the Functional Assessment Inventory, and the Post Schools Option Programme – Individual Needs Assessment.

[23] It is acknowledged that age is not a disability; however, given the physical limitations often resultant from the aging process the FAI has also been used to assess the functional work capabilities of the elderly.

[24] Even though Crewe and Athelstan (1984) stated they believed the FAI comprised seven factors, the evidence they provided was inconclusive. Whether the FAI does have seven factors is an issue that is explored in Chapter 4.

Table 3.6:   Seven-Factor Solution as per Crew and Athelstan (1984)

Item	
Dimension 1: Cognition	
1	Learning ability
2	Ability to read and write in English
3	Memory
4	Spatial and form perception
Dimension 2:Vision	
5	Vision
Dimension 3: Communication	
6	Hearing
7	Speech
8	Language functioning
Dimension 4: Motor Functioning	
9	Upper extremity functioning
10	Hand functioning
11	Motor speed
12	Ambulation and mobility
Dimension 5: Physical condition	
13	Capacity for exertion
14	Endurance
15	Loss of time from work
16	Stability of disabling condition
Dimension 6: Vocational qualifications	
17	Work history
18	Acceptability to employers
19	Personal attractiveness
20	Skills
21	Economic disincentives
22	Access to job opportunities
23	Requirements for special working conditions
Dimension 7: Adaptive behaviour	
24	Work adjustment
25	Social support system
26	Accurate perception of capabilities and limitations
27	Effective interaction with employers and co-workers
28	Judgement
29	Congruence of behaviour with rehabilitation plans and goals
30	Initiative

The FAI was sent to the job coordinator (or equivalent position depending on agency structure) for each participant who agreed to be interviewed (participant selection is detailed below). Often this resulted in a single job coordinator completing multiple FAIs as they were responsible for several customers who participated in this study. The two agencies initially involved in this research expressed a concern that job coordinators may not wish to complete the FAI due to its length and hence likely time it would take to complete. Furthermore, given that job coordinators in both agencies expressed opinions to management concerning very high case loads, it was felt that if the FAIs were to be completed by the job coordinators, it would be during personal time and not work time. Given it was vital that I received a completed FAI for each participant, a ten dollar gift-voucher was offered per completed FAI.[25] All FAIs that were distributed were returned fully completed.

3.4 Participant Selection

The people who participated in this research were drawn from six agencies that placed people with intellectual disabilities into employment. Each agency operated within the metropolitan area of the same major Australian city. The six agencies participating in this research were contacted, based on contacts known to either myself or Professor Ian Eggleton.[26]

The research commenced with the involvement of two agencies (hereafter called Agency A and Agency B). These agencies were initially contacted as Professor Ian Eggleton knew that they would be willing to participate in this research. Once the participants from these two agencies were interviewed it was decided to increase the sample and involve more agencies. The CEO of Agency B recommended an agency where she personally knew the CEO. Another agency was contacted as Professor Eggleton knew a member of the board. Agency A, at the same time as this research was being conducted, had involved a disability consultant to do some work and had informed this person of the research I was conducting. The disability consultant subsequently contacted me and we met to discuss research on several occasions. This disability consultant was a member of the board of another disability employment agency and subsequently introduced me to the CEO of that agency. A senior member of one of the above agencies also suggested another agency which he thought would be willing to participate in the research, and consequently that agency was contacted. All these agencies agreed to participate in this research (the four agencies will hereafter be referred to as agencies C, D, E, and F). The disability consultant also recommended another agency that she thought would be interested in participating in this research. That agency, however, declined, stating it did not have the time to be involved.

The selection of participants and recruitment techniques varied across each agency. This could not be avoided, as each agency had a different manner in which it wished to conduct the participant selection and recruitment process. It was felt that given time sacrifices and effort each agency was making to be involved in this research, it would be inappropriate to exert undue pressure for consistency across agencies. However, where possible, every attempt was made for consistency across agencies. As the methods of participant selection and recruitment differed across each agency, the processes are detailed below for each agency.

3.4.1 Participant Recruitment - Agency A

This agency is a supported employment agency that at the time of conducting this research had 11 workshops, employing 438 people with intellectual disabilities operating within the metropolitan area of the city.[27] The agency suggested sampling customers from ten of these workshops, which accounted for 433 of the 438 customers. Having identified the ten workshops from which participants would be drawn I visited each workshop and was given a site tour to familiarise myself with the operations of each. During each visit customers were observed performing their normal work duties. By observing customers perform their work duties and noting what functions each performed, I was able to determine the ASCO code for each of the 433 customers from which I was to sample.

---

[25] The funds to purchase the gift vouchers were made available through a University of Western Australia Business School Research Grant.

[26] At the time of commencing this doctoral thesis, Professor Ian Eggleton was the Deputy Chairperson of the Western Australian Disability Services Commission Board and the Research and Development Director on the Board of Edge Employment Solutions.

[27] Since completing the interviews of customers from this agency, the agency has undergone a substantial re-organisation. This re-organisation was due to reductions in funding and the greater requirement for quality assurance of its employment practices. The re-organisation resulted in the closure of several workshops and the merging of others.

Given the time associated with data collection on the agency's behalf, Agency A initially indicated a willingness to send letters seeking participation to 70 of the 433 customers. Seventy customers were selected so as to give a representative sample of ASCO codes from each of the ten workshops. Given that there was a requirement to complete an FAI by the job coordinator for each of the participants involved, selection of participants was conducted, ensuring that no support co-ordinator would have to complete more than eight FAIs. In most instances it was attempted to keep this number down to six.

Having selected the 70 customers to whom a letter seeking participation would be sent, the agency felt that given the differing level of comprehension of the people it may not always be appropriate to address the letter to the customer, but rather, in some instances, the family and potentially a letter to both the individual and the family. Each of the ten workshops was then contacted to determine to whom the letter should be addressed. This resulted in 29 letters being sent solely to the customer, 18 being sent solely to the customer's family, and on 23 occasions letters were sent to both the customer and his/her family.[28] The letters to both the individual and family were signed by both the manager of employment services for Agency A and myself. As the letters were going to a different demographic (the parents versus the person with an intellectual disability) they were worded differently. Each letter, irrespective of whether it was addressed to the individual or the individual's family, was mailed to the appropriate workshop where the staff had agreed to distribute the letters to the people in question, or their families. This was so that customers' personal contact details remained confidential. All letters contained a form to be completed by respondents, indicating that they either *did* or *did not* give their consent to be interviewed, and a reply-paid envelope.

Within seven weeks of the initial mail-out 26 responses had been received indicating a willingness to be interviewed. Reminder letters were then sent to the individuals and/or families that did not respond.[29] This resulted in a further eight people agreeing to be interviewed, giving an overall sample of 34 (response rate 48.57 percent).

Given this response rate, Agency A agreed to conduct another mail-out to bolster the number of participants. The same stipulations as stated above applied to the resampling in terms of ensuring that no support worker had an excessive amount of FAIs to complete, and that the people selected provided a good representation of all occupation types and were from all workshops. Given these constraints, the agency in conjunction with myself selected a further 67 people to whom a letter was sent seeking participation in this research. Agency A decided that to make things administratively easier letters would be sent to both the individuals and their families on all occasions. Once more, the letters were mailed to the appropriate workshops, where staff had agreed to distribute the letters to the people and their families. Within seven weeks 25 people had replied, indicating a willingness to be interviewed. Again a reminder letter was sent to those people and their families that did not reply. This resulted in a further three people indicating a willingness to be interviewed, giving a sample for this second mail-out of 28 (response rate 41.79 percent) and an overall sample of 62 (response rate 45.26 percent).

A list of all individuals who agreed to participate in the research was compiled and sent to the agency so they could forward me their customers' phone numbers and I could establish contact. This list was initially compiled after seven weeks, which comprised respondents to the initial mail-out to that date. Another list of phone numbers of customers who agreed to participate was received three weeks after the follow-up mail-out. These same time-frames were also applied to the second set of customers sampled from this agency. This procedure was adopted so as to minimise the

---

[28] Prior to mailing the letters, ethics approval was obtained for this research by The University of Western Australia's Human Research Ethics Committee.

[29] Some people responded indicating they did not wish to be interviewed and these people were not sent a follow-up letter.

workload on the staff of Agency A.

As stated earlier, Agency A was one of the original two agencies that agreed to participate in this research. As I had only limited experience interacting with people with intellectual disabilities, it was thought best by Agency A and Agency B that a qualified person should conduct the interviews. However, after contacting the appropriate agencies it became clear the cost of hiring a professional was prohibitive. Agencies A and B then agreed it would be acceptable to hire psychology masters students, as it was felt their background would give them the requisite skills for conducting interviews with people with intellectual disabilities. I then organised through a staff member at The University of Western Australia's Psychology Department to give a brief presentation at the commencement of a psychology masters unit on the details of my project and how much interviewers would be paid. This resulted in nine people contacting me, stating they wanted more information. I met personally with each of the nine for approximately half an hour, during which time the full details and time-frame of the project were stated. Each person was also given a copy of Biklen and Moseley (1988), which discusses issues associated with interviewing people with intellectual disabilities. This process resulted in seven of the nine masters students agreeing to conduct the interviews.

The respondents were then randomly allocated to one of the seven interviewers, with the interviewers being given the names and phone numbers of respondents. Agency A wished for only the interviewer, and not myself, to know the street address of the individuals. Consequently, when the interviewer phoned the individual or family to organise a time, they also asked for their street address details.

The above process, though minimising the amount of work on the staff of Agency A led to some delays in contacting people to organise an interview time. This problem was compounded by the fact that some interviewers did not meet the deadline set for contacting respondents. This was due to the interviewers being masters students, and having study and other work commitments. Additionally, on a few occasions the phone numbers provided for the individuals were found to be incorrect and staff at Agency A had to make contact with the individual to obtain their correct phone numbers. Several interviewers had to be reminded on a few occasions that they had to speed up the interviewing process and at least contact all of their allocated respondents to organise an interview time. Where I discovered there were long delays in contacting people to organise interviews I personally contacted the individual or family to thank them for agreeing to be involved in the research and to assure them they would be contacted soon to organise an interview time. Although, one interviewer stated she had been conducting interviews, she had conducted only one within a period of two months and no longer wished to conduct any interviews. On discovering this, the respondents assigned to this person were immediately contacted by myself to apologise for the delay and assure them they would be contacted soon to organise an interview time. The six remaining interviewers were then asked if they could conduct extra interviews, to which three responded positively. However, two of them could only do one extra and consequently the majority of the extra interviews fell to one interviewer. This resulted in an unequal allocation of interviews to the different interviewers. However, this was unavoidable.

When contacted to organise a time for an interview, 16 people from Agency A stated they no longer wished to be interviewed, which resulted in 46 people being interviewed (62 – 16). Given the sensitive nature of this research, and not wishing to offend either the agency or the individual, no reason was sought for the individual no longer wishing to participate.

It is felt that the long delay in contacting some people contributed to the number of people declining to be interviewed. However, a senior staff member of Agency A stated that she was not surprised I had a number of people who initially said *yes* and then later changed their mind.

3.4.2 Participant Recruitment – Agency B

Agency B places people with a range of disabilities (both intellectual and physical) into open employment. At the time of conducting this research the agency had 237 customers with intellectual disability on their register. Of these, 132 customers were classified as having an intellectual disability. Agency B also agreed to allow me to send letters seeking participation to 70 customers. These 70 were selected in an attempt to match the occupation codes of the initial 70 selected from Agency A.

Agency B also stipulated that it did not wish any of its job coordinators to complete more than eight FAIs and preferably no more than six. Consequently, 70 customers were selected from the list of 132 so as to match the two-digit ASCO occupation codes with the initial 70 customers selected from Agency A, ensuring that where possible no employment co-ordinator had more than six customers selected and definitely no more than eight.

The 70 people selected were each sent a letter by the CEO of the agency, introducing the researchers and research topic. The letter ensured participants that no information would be revealed to the agency. As the letter seeking participation in this research had to be mailed to the person's home address, it was felt by the CEO that to reassure people the agency was not revealing private and confidential information to other people, it should be sent by her on agency letterhead. Each letter contained a form to be completed by the individual, indicating either that they *did* or *did not* wish to be interviewed and a reply-paid envelope.

Twenty-eight people responded to the initial mail-out, agreeing to be interviewed. After approximately four weeks the same letter was resent to anyone who did not respond to the initial mail-out. This resulted in a further three people agreeing to participate. The overall response rate for Agency B, therefore, was 44.29 percent (31 of 70). Due to other commitments the agency was facing at the time it indicated it did not wish to select additional customers as prospective interviewees.

Similar to procedures described above, a list of people agreeing to be interviewed was compiled and sent to the agency, which then provided phone numbers for each person. These phone numbers were then given to the seven interviewers when they were allocated people. Interviewers asked for the person's address when contacting the person to organise an interview time. As above, it was felt that these procedures would ensure that customers' private information was kept as confidential as possible.

When the list of respondents who agreed to participate in this research was given to Agency B, they noted that four of the respondents were unemployed at the time and consequently would not be suitable for our research purposes. These four people were then contacted and thanked for their agreement to being involved in the research; however, they were informed that only people who were currently placed in employment were being interviewed, and consequently we would not be interviewing them. This left a sample 27 customers whom I wished to interview.

Again, the procedures documented above concerning the use of Masters of Psychology students resulted in time delays in terms of contacting people. Additionally, the problems discussed above, with some interviewers taking an inordinate amount of time to contact participants and one interviewer after two months revealing she had conducted only one interview, impacted on the scheduling of interviews for participants from Agency B as well. It was felt these delays contributed to six people stating that they no longer wished to be interviewed when contacted by telephone. As with the procedures outlined for Agency A, no reason was sought as to why the individual had changed his/her mind. This resulted in 21 people initially being interviewed from Agency B.

Agency B had previously been involved in a research project investigating the quality of life of people with intellectual disabilities in open employment versus those unemployed. That research resulted in the subsequent publication of Eggleton *et al.* (1999). Once it was decided to expand the number of agencies participating in this research and after I commenced interviewing participants from other agencies (detailed below), I approached the CEO of Agency B to see whether she would be interested in assisting in a longitudinal study, where the people who were interviewed in Eggleton *et al.* (1999) were interviewed again, and changes in their quality of life and possible causes traced and documented. The CEO responded favourably to this idea and agreed that these people could be contacted again and that I could use the data for this thesis as well as a longitudinal study.

As part of Eggleton *et al.* (1999), 58 people with intellectual disabilities were interviewed from Agency B. At the time of conducting this research, 32 of those 58 were still registered with Agency B. These 32 people were sent a letter seeking their participation in the follow-up study, with a form to complete if they were willing to participate and a reply-paid envelope.[30] To expedite the process on this occasion, and to minimise the workload on the agency, the form asked participants for their phone number.

Thirteen people initially responded, stating that they were willing to be interviewed. Agency B felt it would not be worth conducting a reminder mail-out as many of the customers who were being targeted in this mail-out had limited association with the agency and, consequently, they felt the response rate would not increase. This limited exposure to the agency was due to the customers having maintained a job for a considerable period of time and consequently had little or no need for support from the agency. Agency B, however, agreed that they would call the 19 people who had not responded, asking them if they would agree to participate. These follow-up calls led to one more person agreeing to be interviewed, thus the sample for this second mail-out from Agency B was 14 (response rate 43.75 percent).

Given the problems associated with having interviewers (detailed above) and the fact that by this time I had substantial exposure to, and dealings with, people with intellectual disabilities, Agency B was now comfortable in letting me conduct interviews with their customers. This, combined with the fact that people placed their telephone numbers on the return form, meant that I could contact the respondents to organise an interview time as soon as I received their consent forms. This resulted in all 14 people being interviewed.

Overall, 35 interviews were conducted with customers from Agency B. However, of the 14 customers interviewed by myself, 2 had previously been interviewed by an interviewer during the earlier stages of this research. Consequently, the two earlier interviews conducted by the master of psychology students were omitted.[31] This meant 33 people from Agency B participated in this research.

3.4.3 Participant Recruitment – Agency C
Agency C is an employment agency that places only people with intellectual disabilities into open employment. At the time of conducting this research the agency had 74 customers with an intellectual disability on its register. Agency C agreed to allow me to send a letter to all 74

---

[30] It is acknowledged that some of these 32 people had been previously contacted seeking participation in the first stages of this study. However, as noted below, only two people who responded to this request to be interviewed had been interviewed in the initial stages of this research.

[31] As would be expected there were some differences in the responses given to interview questions to the Master of Psychology students and myself by the two customers of Agency B that were interviewed twice. These differences were expected, given the time difference between the first interviews (conducted by the Masters of Psychology students) and the interviews conducted by myself was in excess of one year. Further, one of the respondents was in a different job to that when interviewed earlier, and as, such different responses to the interview questions would be expected.

customers seeking participation in my research. The agency felt that to highlight the independence of the research it was best if the letter came from me and not the agency. Each letter also included a consent form and a reply-paid envelope.

Eleven people responded to the original mail-out within four weeks of receiving the original letter (response rate 14.86 percent). Agency C agreed that I could send a reminder letter to those people who had not responded. This resulted in a further five people responding. Consequently, 16 people from Agency C agreed to be interviewed, giving an overall response rate of 21.62 percent.

As I had experience of dealing with people with intellectual disabilities by this stage of the research, Agency C felt it was acceptable that I conduct the interviews. The consent forms for Agency C had a space where people responding filled-in their phone number, thus allowing me to contact the person to schedule an interview time as soon as I received their consent form. This expedited the process and resulted in 15 of the 16 agreeing to be interviewed when contacted. As stated above, not wishing to upset the person, their family, or the agency, no reason was sought from the one person who no longer wished to be interviewed.

3.4.4 Participant Recruitment – Agency D
Agency D operates four branches across the metropolitan area of the Australian city where this research was conducted. It places people with intellectual disabilities into either open employment or enclaves, which it operates.[32] As at the time of conducting this research the agency had 233 customers with an intellectual disability on its register. Agency D agreed to allow me to send a letter to all 233 of its customers.

Agency D suggested that I should write a letter seeking participation in this research and that this letter be signed solely by myself to highlight the independence of the research. Agency D would then include in the mail-out a signed letter from the manager of the branch with which the individual was associated, introducing the research project, commending participation, and stressing the independence of the research. The letters were sent by Agency D, so as to maintain the confidentiality of their customers' street addresses. Also enclosed in the mail-out was a consent form and reply-paid envelope. As per the procedures outlined above, the consent form asked respondents for their telephone number, allowing me to contact the respondents as soon as I received the consent form. Agency D was also comfortable with me conducting the interviews.

Twenty-six people responded to the initial mail-out, giving a response rate of 11.2 percent. Given the time and cost associated with the mail-out process Agency D did not wish to conduct a reminder mail-out. When contacted to organise an interview time, 25 of the 26 people who indicated their willingness to participate in this research agreed to be interviewed. Again no explanation was sought from the one person who did not wish to be interviewed.

3.4.5 Participant Recruitment – Agency E and Agency F
Agency E and Agency F are both employment agencies that place people with intellectual disabilities into open employment. At the time of conducting this research Agency E had 60 customers on its register and Agency F had 113 customers. Both agencies agreed to allow me to

---

[32] Enclaves are categorised as supported employment given that it is the disability employment agency that pays the customers wage and not the hiring organisation. The hiring organisation contracts with the disability employment agency for the agency to provide services (for example, cleaning of cars, clerical work) and as such the disability employment agency is the employer of the customers. In the case of clerical enclaves, although the enclave is typically located at the hiring organisation's premise in the case of participants I interviewed, the enclaves were located in rooms separate from people without disabilities (in one instance a separate building) and there is little if any interaction between enclave members and employees of the hiring organisation. Furthermore, enclaves along with workshops are both classified by the Commonwealth Government as supported employment.

send a letter to all of their customers, which included a consent form (including a request for phone number) and reply-paid envelope. So as to highlight the independence of the research, both agencies felt that the letter should only be signed by myself. However, to maintain confidentiality of their customers' private details, agencies E and F mailed the letters themselves.

The mail-out resulted in eight people from Agency E and seven from Agency F responding, stating they would be willing to participate. This gave a response rate of 16.00 percent from Agency E and 6.19 percent from Agency F. Respondents were then contacted by me to organise an interview time, with all fifteen being interviewed. Neither agency wished for a reminder mail-out to occur, as they felt that if people didn't respond they did not wish to participate, coupled with the fact that neither agency wished to inundate their customers with requests to participate in research.

3.5 Interview Process
The above participant recruitment process resulted in a total of 162 people agreeing to be interviewed. However, as noted above, when contacted not all the people indicated a willingness to be interviewed. As such, only 134 of the original 162 respondents were interviewed and responded to questions from the Barlow and Kirby (1991) job satisfaction questionnaire and the QOL.Q. The interviews were conducted by either myself or a masters of psychology student. A more detailed analysis on the exact number of interviews conducted by each is contained at the commencement of Chapter 5 (Demographics and Sub-Sample Selection). These interviews were conducted at the participant's normal place of residence outside working hours, typically in the evenings, though also often on weekends, and were on average 38 minutes in duration.

3.6 Conclusion
This chapter commenced by describing how the questionnaires used to measure the job satisfaction and quality of life of participants were selected. A description was also provided of the various demographic variables collected, including a measure of functional work ability as assessed by the FAI. Information on these variables were collected as it was considered that they could impact on the job satisfaction and quality of life experienced by participants and, as such, may need to be controlled for. Finally, the procedures undertaken to recruit participants to take part in this research were described.

In the next chapter the psychometric properties of the Barlow and Kirby (1991) job satisfaction questionnaire, the QOL.Q, and the FAI, are explored. To ensure the results of this research are robust, it is vital that the instruments are reliable, that the underlying factor structure and the scores obtained for each of these questionnaires are valid.

Chapter 4 – Psychometric Properties of Research Instruments

4.1 Introduction
In this chapter I describe the development of a job satisfaction questionnaire for people with intellectual disabilities, as well as describing my assessment of the psychometric properties of: (1) the Functional Assessment Inventory questionnaire (FAI) (Crew and Athelstan), (2) the Barlow and Kirby (1991) job satisfaction questionnaire (JSQ), and (3) the Schalock and Kieth (1993) Quality of Life Questionnaire (QOL.Q). The reliability of the scores for each of the three questionnaires was assessed by calculating the Cronbach alphas (both for the total scores as well as scores for each factor of the respective questionnaire) and by investigating the stability of the factor structure.

4.2 Psychometric Assessment Techniques
4.2.1 Factor Analysis
A principal axis factor analysis is conducted on all three instruments to determine whether they factor in the manner expected. It is acknowledged that the samples for these three factor analyses are not as large as would have been liked. Tabachnick and Fiddell (1989) stated that to conduct factor analyses it was preferable to have sample sizes of over 200. Although the sample used in this thesis is not as large, a principal axis factor analysis is still conducted. As Hair *et al.* (1995) noted, it was acceptable to conduct factor analysis with a sample of 100 or larger, and past studies have achieved meaningful results with samples of less than 200 (for example, Rapley and Lobley 1995; Kober and Eggleton 2002). Once the factors and factor loadings were obtained they are then compared with those reported for the original instruments.

Depending on the degree of correlation between pairs of factors, different rotation methods are used. For both the job JSQ and the QOL.Q varimax rotation is used as factor correlation matrices reveal that on nearly all occasions the factors are uncorrelated (correlation of below .30). Varimax rotation, which is an orthogonal rotation that assumes factors are uncorrelated, is used as it gives a clearer separation of factors (Hair *et al.* 1995). Principal axis factor analysis with an oblique rotation is also conducted in all instances. Oblique rotations do not require factor axes to be orthogonal, as dimensions are not assumed to be uncorrelated with each other (Hair *et al.* 1995). As such, oblique rotations may reflect variables more accurately as it is reasonable to expect different sets of variables measuring the same underlying construct (for example, quality of life) to be correlated. Cattell (1952) noted that in nature, factors are unlikely to be orthogonal and, as such, argues exclusively for the use oblique rotations.

Only the results of the principal axis factor analysis with varimax rotation are reported for the JSQ and QOL.Q, as the results using the oblique rotations do not vary greatly and the factor correlation matrices from the oblique rotations clearly show that on nearly all occasions the factors are uncorrelated (correlation of below .30). Tabachnick and Fidell (2001) suggested that if results of the factor analyses were similar, as they often will be if patterns of correlations in the data were fairly clear, then it was advantageous to use the varimax rotation approach due to the practical disadvantages of interpreting, describing, and reporting the results of oblique rotations.

For the FAI there are several occasions when reported correlations between factors are greater than .30 and are as high as .448. Due to this high degree of correlation, oblimin rotations are used (Hair *et al.* 1995) and reported. In all instances the results of the pattern matrix are reported,[33] as the pattern matrix is best for determining the clustering of variables (Cattell 1962), which defines the

---

[33] When an oblique rotation is conducted, two matrices are produced. The first is a structure matrix, which reports the correlations between each variable and the factor. The second is the pattern matrix, which reports the beta weights to reproduce the variable scores from factor scores. As the pattern matrix reports beta weights, the value may in some instances be in excess of 1.

simple structure (Rummel 1970).[34]

4.2.2 Reliability Analysis

Having assessed the factor structure of the three instruments, the reliability of the scores attained by each instrument is assessed using Cronbach's (1951) alpha and a factor stability analysis. Everett (1983, p. 199) emphasised that it was important "that the same factor procedures applied to different sets of respondents ... should provide factors which are stable between different sets of respondents." If this was not the case, it would bring the reliability of the scores attained by an instrument into question.

Factor stability of the three instruments is assessed using the coefficient of congruence (Harman 1967). Kober and Eggleton (2002) showed how the coefficient of congruence could be used to assess the reliability of questionnaire scores. Assessing the reliability of an instrument's scores, using the coefficient of congruence, involves dichotomising the sample across various heterogeneities and calculating a coefficient of congruence based on the congruence of factor loadings across the two respective samples. As explained by Everett and Entrekin (1980), if there are n items, where A and B represent the factor structure matrices for the two sets of respondents, then the factor congruence between the jth factor in one set and the kth factor in the other set is given by:

$$\frac{\sum_{i=1}^{n} a_{ij} b_{ik}}{\sqrt{\sum_{i=1}^{n} a_{ij}^2 \sum_{i=1}^{n} b_{ik}^2}}.$$

Factor stability for all three instruments is investigated by splitting the sample on the basis of each of:
(1) random selection (half-half);
(2) gender (female versus male);
(3) the level of functional work ability, as measured by the FAI;[35]
(4) an examination of employment, when the sample is dichotomised into participants employed in open employment versus participants employed in supported employment and job seekers;[36,37]
(5) an examination of employment, when the sample is dichotomised into participants employed in open employment versus those employed in supported employment.
It is not possible to conduct a factor stability analysis comparing employed respondents versus job seekers as not enough participants were job seekers. Coefficients of congruence are calculated based on principal axis factor analyses with varimax rotation for the JSQ and the QOL.Q. For the FAI, principal axis factor analysis with oblimin rotation is used to calculate the coefficients of congruence due to the factors not being orthogonal.

---

[34] An added advantage of using the pattern matrix for interpreting the factor results is that the pattern matrix often reports a simpler structure (fewer multi-vocal items) compared to the structure matrix.

[35] The FAI was dichotomised for each sample around the median. The median was selected as the mid-point since there are no generally accepted ranges that define participants with intellectual disabilities as having either a high functional work ability or low functional work ability.

[36] This dichotomisation results in the same dichotomisation as dichotomisation five for the job satisfaction instrument, as only participants who were employed could complete this instrument.

[37] When it was discovered prior to the interview that a respondent who agreed to be interviewed was a job seeker the respondent was contacted and thanked for agreeing to participate, but that as this research was concerned with investigating the effects of different methods of employment on people with intellectual disabilities we would not be interviewing them. However, on several occasions it was not discovered that a respondent was a job seeker until commencing the interview. In these instances the participants were asked questions only from the QOL.Q.

4.3 Functional Assessment Inventory

As stated in Section 3.3.2 (Level of Disability), the FAI, which contains 30 behaviourally anchored questions assessing participants' functional ability on a four-point scale (from 0 [no significant impairment] to 3 [severe impairment]), was completed by the job coordinators of each participant and is used to assess the level of functional ability of the participants. Job coordinators completed FAIs for 156 clients[38], for whom the demographic data are presented in Table 4.1.

Table 4.1: Demographic information for the FAI

	Number	Percentage
Gender:		
Female	54	35
Male	102	65
Employment:		
Open employment	78	50
Supported employment	65	42
Job seeker[39]	13	8
Functional ability[40]:		
Low (FAI 24 to 65)	77	49
High (FAI 1 to 23)	79	51

4.3.1 FAI Factor Structure

As stated in Chapter 3 (Research Methods), Crewe and Athelstan (1984) contended that the FAI has seven factors that measure different aspects of a person's functional ability: adaptive behaviour, motor functioning, cognition, physical condition, communication, vocational qualification, and vision. However, they fail to provide conclusive proof of this factor structure. Crewe and Athelstan (1984) revealed the results of three factor analyses conducted on samples from three different populations, which found three different factor structures. One analysis revealed the seven factors (six multi-item factors and one single-item factor) shown in Table 3.6. This is the analysis that in Crew and Athelstan's (1984, p. 48) opinion "provides the most complete and satisfactory view of the dimensions of the FAI." Although why they believe this is not revealed. The other two factor analyses reported revealed, respectively, eight factors (five multi-item factors and three single-item factors) and five factors (all multi-item factors). The results of these two factor analyses are not reported in this thesis since neither has been used in subsequent research.

In addition to the inconclusive results reported in Crewe and Athelstan (1984), Neath *et al.* (1997) found that six factors were more appropriate when analysing the factor structure of the FAI across five relatively homogeneous groups of people with disabilities (orthopaedic/amputation, chronic-physical condition, mental illness, intellectual, and learning disability). Neath *et al.* (1997) also found differing factor structures for the five different disability types. The results for the intellectual

---

[38] As stated in Section 3.5 (Interview Process) the number of participants who were interviewed as part of this thesis was 134. However, the FAI was completed for 156 of the 162 participants who initially stated they were willing to be interviewed. The FAIs not completed were due to participants withdrawing consent to be interviewed prior to the distribution of FAIs to the employment agency staff and, as such, agency staff were not requested to complete an FAI for those participants.

[39] As I am concerned in this thesis with investigating the effectiveness of different methods of employment for people with intellectual disabilities, Chapter 6 (Results and Discussion) uses the responses only from employed participants. However, as job seekers were also unintentionally interviewed, the responses from these participants are also used to validate the FAI. The reason for their use is to increase sample size.

[40] A low functional ability is defined as a FAI score of 23 or greater, with a high functional ability defined as a FAI score of less than 23. The median of 23 is selected as the mid-point since there are no generally accepted ranges for the FAI that define participants with intellectual disabilities as having either a high functional ability or low functional ability.

and learning disabilities are presented in Table 4.5. The results of only these two factor solutions are presented, as the sample for this thesis combines people that Neath *et al.* (1997) classified as having either an intellectual or learning disability, and does not include individuals with the other three disability types. To facilitate comparative analysis their results are first presented in item order (Table 4.2(a)) and then grouped according to their resulting factors (Table 4.2(b)).

As such, it is inappropriate to assume that the FAI has seven well-established factors, even though most of the subsequent research (for example, Bellini *et al.* 1998; Heinemann *et al.* 2000) has assumed as much. Consequently the factor structure of the FAI is first investigated, with the factor solution for the thesis data compared with those of Crewe and Athelstan (1984) and Neath *et al.* (1997).

Principal axis factor analysis with oblimin rotation is conducted to determine the factor structure of the FAI. The Bartlett test of sphericity is significant (χ^2 (435, n = 156) = 2,265.03, $p \le .001$), and the Kaiser-Meyer-Okin measure of sampling is greater than .6 (KMO = .876), which indicate that it is possible to conduct a factor analysis on the sample. Given the aforementioned inconclusive results as to the factor structure of the FAI, it is important to correctly identify the number of factors to be extracted for this sample.

Hair *et al.* (1995) stated there were numerous methods to determine the number of factors to be extracted. These included the eigenvalues greater than one rule, *a priori* criteria, and the scree test (Cattell 1966). The eigenvalues greater than one approach is not used in this thesis as it does not indicate how many factors will be reliable (Cliff 1988). Zwick and Velicer (1986) and Cliff (1988) both showed that the eigenvalues greater than one rule tends to over-estimate the number of factors. Cliff (1988) also highlighted that it was relatively simple to construct population matrices that would result in the rule either systematically over-estimating or under-estimating the appropriate number of factors. Gorsuch (1983), in reviewing the literature on methods for selecting the appropriate number of factors, noted that the eigenvalues greater than one rule was not a mathematical criterion, but a rule of thumb. Gorsuch (1983) reviewed several studies (Humphreys 1964; Cattell and Jaspers 1967; Browne 1968; Linn 1968; Tucker *et al.* 1969; Mote 1970) which all showed that the eigenvalues greater than one rule is not accurate in selecting the appropriate number of factors.[41]

To determine the number of factors using the scree test, the researcher determines where the plot of eigenvalues (scree plot) flattens out. The number of factors selected being the number immediately prior to the flattening out of the plot (Cattell and Jaspers 1967). Gorsuch (1983), in his review of literature on determining the appropriate number of factors, showed that in the majority of cases the scree test provided the correct number of factors.[42] On occasions, typically when less than optimal conditions existed,[43] the scree test does over-estimate or under-estimate the number of factors. However, it is still usually accurate within one or two factors (Tabachnick and Fidell 2001) and preferable to the eigenvalues greater than one rule. For a more detailed review on the different methods of selecting the number of factors and the problems associated with the eigenvalues greater than one rule refer to Cliff (1988) and Gorsuch (1983).

Unfortunately the scree plot fails to reveal clearly the appropriate number of factors to extract, with the point at which the Scree plot curve flattened either revealing five or eight factors,[44] depending on interpretation. *A priori* criteria would suggest either six (Neath *et al.* 1997) or seven (Crew and

---

[41] These studies either generated matrices from a known number of factors or from an examination of the distributions of residual matrices.

[42] *Ibid.*

[43] Optimal conditions are when the "sample size is large, communality values are high, and each factor has several variables with high loadings."(Tabachnick and Fidell 2001, p. 621).

[44] Eight factors are also the number suggested by the eigenvalues greater than one rule.

Athelstan 1984) factors.

Given that it is not clear how many factors should be extracted, principal axis factor analysis with oblimin rotation is conducted specifying in turn five, six, seven and eight factors. As stated previously, oblimin rotation is used as there is a high degree of correlation among factors, as evidenced by the factor correlation matrices. This high degree of correlation among factors was also observed by Neath *et al.* (1997). The extracted factors are then examined to see if the sets of related items make theoretical sense. The factors extracted for the five, six, and seven factor iterations make theoretical sense. However, the factors extracted for the eight-factor iteration result in sets of items that do not make theoretical sense. Accordingly, this factor solution is not investigated further. The five, six, and seven factor extractions result in factors as shown in Tables 4.3 to 4.5 respectively. Factor headings are selected to match the items in each factor.

Table 4.2(a): FAI Six-Factor Solutions for Intellectual and Learning Disability Samples as per Neath *et al.* (1997) ordered by item number

Item		Intellectual disability factors	Learning disability factors
1	Learning ability	Cognition	Cognition
2	Ability to read and write in English	Cognition	Cognition
3	Memory	Cognition	Cognition
4	Spatial and form perception	Cognition	Cognition
5	Vision	Communication	Physical capacity
6	Hearing	Communication	Communication
7	Speech	Communication	Communication
8	Language functioning	Communication	Communication
9	Upper extremity functioning	Physical capacity	Physical capacity
10	Hand functioning	Physical capacity	Physical capacity
11	Motor speed	Physical capacity	Physical capacity
12	Ambulation and mobility	Physical capacity	Physical capacity
13	Capacity for exertion	Physical capacity	Physical capacity
14	Endurance	Physical capacity	Physical capacity
15	Loss of time from work	Physical capacity	Physical capacity
16	Stability of disabling condition	Physical capacity	Physical capacity
17	Work history	Motor functioning/work history	Motor functioning/work history
18	Acceptability to employers	Motor functioning/work history	Communication
19	Personal attractiveness	Motor functioning/work history	Communication
20	Skills	Cognition	Vocational qualifications
21	Economic disincentives	Adaptive behaviour	Vocational qualifications
22	Access to job opportunities	Vocational qualifications	Vocational qualifications
23	Requirements for special working conditions	Vocational qualifications	Vocational qualifications
24	Work adjustment	Adaptive behaviour	Adaptive behaviour
25	Social support system	Adaptive behaviour	Adaptive behaviour
26	Accurate perception of capabilities and limitations	Adaptive behaviour	Adaptive behaviour
27	Effective interaction with employers and co-workers	Adaptive behaviour	Adaptive behaviour
28	Judgement	Adaptive behaviour	Adaptive behaviour
29	Congruence of behaviour with rehabilitation plans and goals	Adaptive behaviour	Adaptive behaviour
30	Initiative	Cognition	Adaptive behaviour

Table 4.2(b):   FAI Six-Factor Solutions for Intellectual and Learning Disability Samples as per Neath *et al.* (1997) ordered by resultant factors

Intellectual disability		Learning disability	
Item		Item	
Factor 1: Adaptive behaviour		*Factor 1: Adaptive behaviour*	
21	Economic disincentives		
24	Work adjustment	24	Work adjustment
25	Social support system	25	Social support system
26	Accurate perception of capabilities and limitations	26	Accurate perception of capabilities and limitations
27	Effective interaction with employers and co-workers	27	Effective interaction with employers and co-workers
28	Judgement	28	Judgement
29	Congruence of behaviour with rehabilitation plans and goals	29	Congruence of behaviour with rehabilitation plans and goals
		30	Initiative
Factor 2: Cognition		*Factor 2: Cognition*	
1	Learning ability	1	Learning ability
2	Ability to read and write in English	2	Ability to read and write in English
3	Memory	3	Memory
4	Spatial and form perception	4	Spatial and form perception
20	Skills		
30	Initiative		
Factor 3: Physical capacity		*Factor 3: Physical capacity*	
		5	Vision
9	Upper extremity functioning	9	Upper extremity functioning
10	Hand functioning	10	Hand functioning
11	Motor speed	11	Motor speed
12	Ambulation and mobility	12	Ambulation and mobility
13	Capacity for exertion	13	Capacity for exertion
14	Endurance	14	Endurance
15	Loss of time from work	15	Loss of time from work
16	Stability of disabling condition	16	Stability of disabling condition
Factor 4: Motor functioning/work history		*Factor 4: Motor functioning/work history*	
17	Work history	17	Work history
18	Acceptability to employers		
19	Personal attractiveness		
Factor 5: Communication		*Factor 5: Communication*	
5	Vision		
6	Hearing	6	Hearing
7	Speech	7	Speech
8	Language functioning	8	Language functioning
		18	Acceptability to employers
		19	Personal attractiveness
Factor 6: Vocational qualifications		*Factor 6: Vocational qualifications*	
		20	Skills
		21	Economic disincentives
22	Access to job opportunities	22	Access to job opportunities
23	Requirements for special working conditions	23	Requirements for special working conditions

Looking at factors of the three different factor solutions, the various factors generally make sense. In discussing factors of the various factor solutions, I shall first comment on the seven-factor solution, since the number of factors is consistent with that espoused in the original instruction manual by Crewe and Athelstan (1984). I then discuss the six-factor solution compared with the two six-factor solutions derived by Neath *et al.* (1997)[45] and, finally, discuss the five-factor solution in general and whether it makes theoretical sense. In discussing each factor solution I shall begin by discussing the factor solutions from the above tables (Table 4.3 to Table 4.5) and compare them with the factor solutions derived in prior studies. This approach is taken since both Crewe and Athelstan (1984) and Neath *et al.* (1997) retained all 30 items without applying cut-off values, below which items are omitted.

Table 4.3: Factor loadings for the five-factor extraction of the FAI

Item		Factor loadings
Factor 1: Cognition and skill development		
20	Skills	.397
1	Learning ability	.378
6	Hearing	-.276
15	Loss of time from work	-.267
Factor 2: Sensory ability		
5	Vision	.737
4	Spatial and form perception	.649
3	Memory	.260
Factor 3: Communication		
8	Language functioning	.789
7	Speech	.763
2	Ability to read and write English	.457
19	Personal attractiveness	.300
Factor 4: Physical condition and vocational opportunities		
10	Hand functioning	.739
13	Capacity for exertion	.732
9	Upper extremity functioning	.687
11	Motor speed	.624
16	Stability of disabling condition	.438
22	Access to job opportunities	.419
14	Endurance	.395
21	Economic disincentives	.393
18	Acceptability to employers	.376
17	Work history	.349
12	Ambulation and mobility	.324
Factor 5: Vocational suitability and adaptive behaviour		
28	Judgement	.832
29	Congruence of behaviour with rehabilitation plans and goals	.696
27	Effective interaction with employers and co-workers	.672
30	Initiative	.636
26	Accurate perception of capabilities and limitations	.614
24	Work adjustment	.613
23	Requirements for special working conditions	.408
25	Social support system	.406

Given there has been little psychometric assessment of the FAI and the appropriateness of using it to assess the functional work ability of people with intellectual disabilities, I conducted further factor analyses, omitting items with factor loadings below .32. This cut-off score was selected

---

[45] One six-factor solution for each of the Neath *et al.* (1997) disability groupings of *intellectual disability* and *learning disability*.

based on the rule-of-thumb suggested by Tabachnick and Fidell (2001). Tabachnick and Fidell (2001) noted that even though different benchmarks existed, suggested by different authors, the choice of the cut- off loading was largely a matter of researcher preference.[46]

Table 4.4: FAI Factor loadings for the six-factor extraction of the FAI

Item		Factor loadings
Factor 1: Cognition and vocational qualifications		
20	Skills	.513
12	Ambulation and mobility	.457
1	Learning ability	.435
11	Motor speed	.372
3	Memory	.270
Factor 2: Sensory ability		
5	Vision	.712
4	Spatial and form perception	.685
6	Hearing	.274
Factor 3: Communication		
7	Speech	.802
8	Language functioning	.792
2	Ability to read and write English	.452
18	Acceptability to employers	.332
19	Personal attractiveness	.286
Factor 4: Upper functional ability		
9	Upper extremity functioning	.930
10	Hand functioning	.716
Factor 5: Vocational opportunities		
16	Stability of disabling condition	-.559
13	Capacity for exertion	-.471
22	Access to job opportunities	-.403
21	Economic disincentives	-.396
17	Work history	-.345
23	Requirements for special working conditions	-.336
14	Endurance	-.319
Factor 6: Vocational suitability and adaptive behaviour		
28	Judgement	.805
29	Congruence of behaviour with rehabilitation plans and goals	.760
27	Effective interaction with employers and co-workers	.623
26	Accurate perception of capabilities and limitations	.572
30	Initiative	.563
24	Work adjustment	.531
25	Social support system	.407
15	Loss of time from work	.254

4.3.1.1 Seven-Factor FAI Structure
Table 4.6 shows a comparison of the seven-factor solution that I derive (Table 4.5) and the original Crewe and Athelstan (1984) seven-factor solution (Table 3.6). Comparison of the two seven-factor solutions shows some noticeable differences in the factor structure. First, however, beginning with

---

[46] A review of the factor analyses presented later in the chapter reveals that even though .32 was selected as the factor loading cut-off, most factor loadings for the refined questionnaires are in excess of .40 (an alternative benchmark often used). This was due to the results of the other psychometric tests employed in determining the questions that form part of a factor (for example, omitting items if this resulted in an increase in the Cronbach alpha of the factor).

the similarities, the seven items (24, 25, 26, 27, 28, 29, 30) comprising the *adaptive behaviour* factor are the same across the two solutions. Additionally, the factor I label *vocational suitability* is very similar to Crewe and Athelstan's (1984) *vocational qualifications*. Two differences are that the factor I term *vocational suitability* has the inclusion of one extra item (16, stability of disabling condition) and excludes item 20 (skills). It is easy to see how the stability of disabling condition could load with *vocational suitability*, thus this factor makes theoretical sense. Item 20 (skills) I find to load on the factor I term *cognition and physical development*.

Table 4.5: Factor loadings for the seven-factor extraction of the FAI

Item		Factor loadings
Factor 1: Cognition and physical development		
12	Ambulation and mobility	.530
20	Skills	.489
11	Motor speed	.448
1	Learning ability	.432
13	Capacity for exertion	.417
14	Endurance	.407
3	Memory	.402
Factor 2: Sensory ability		
5	Vision	.754
4	Spatial and form perception	.592
6	Hearing	.271
Factor 3: Communication		
8	Language functioning	.813
7	Speech	.779
2	Ability to read and write English	.373
Factor 4: Upper functional ability		
9	Upper extremity functioning	.982
10	Hand functioning	.696
Factor 5: Loss of time from work		
15	Loss of time from work	.590
Factor 6: Vocational suitability		
23	Requirements for special working conditions	-.605
16	Stability of disabling condition	-.490
22	Access to job opportunities	-.471
18	Acceptability to employers	-.449
19	Personal attractiveness	-.334
17	Work history	-.308
21	Economic disincentives	-.288
Factor 7: Adaptive behaviour		
28	Judgement	.774
29	Congruence of behaviour with rehabilitation plans and goals	.737
27	Effective interaction with employers and co-workers	.564
26	Accurate perception of capabilities and limitations	.538
24	Work adjustment	.534
30	Initiative	.512
25	Social support system	.353

The factor I term *cognition and physical development* differs markedly from any factors identified by Crewe and Athelstan (1984) and actually comprises items from four of Crewe and Athelstan's (1984) seven factors: items 1 (learning ability) and 3 (memory) from their factor *cognition*; items

11 (motor speed) and 12 (ambulation and mobility) from their factor *motor functioning*; items 13 (capacity for exertion) and 14 (endurance) from their factor *physical condition*; and item 20 (skills) from their factor *vocational qualifications*.

Items 4 (spatial and form perception), 5 (vision), and 6 (hearing), although coming from three different factors in the Crew and Athelstan (1984) solution, I find to load together on a single factor I term *sensory ability*. The fact that these three items would load together, given their strong relationship to an individual's sensory ability, makes theoretical sense. So also does my finding that items 2 (ability to read and write English), 7 (speech), and 8 (language functioning) load together on a single factor that I term *communication*, in line with the original Crew and Athelstan (1984) *communication* factor. The *communication* factor I find in my iteration is similar to the original Crew and Athelstan (1984) *communication* factor in that it contains two of the same items (7 and 8), with the omission of item 6 (hearing) and the addition of item 2 (ability to read and write English). It can easily be seen how an individual's ability to read and write English would affect their ability to communicate and, as such, item 2 loading on this factor makes theoretical sense.

I also find items 9 (upper extremity functioning) and 10 (hand functioning) load together on a factor I term *upper functional ability*. Items 9 and 10 are both from the same original Crew and Athelstan (1984) factor, *motor functioning*. However, Crew and Athelstan's (1984) *motor functioning* factor also comprised two other items, which related to motor speed and ambulation and mobility (items 11 and 12, respectively).[47] Given the exclusion of these two items, I re-label this factor *upper functional ability*. I find item 15 (loss of time from work) forms a factor by itself. Crew and Athelstan (1984) had this item in their *physical condition* factor. However, its association with an individual's physical condition could be seen as tenuous, given that there are many other causes other than a physical condition that could lead to a person failing to turn up for work. Consequently, given the individualistic nature of this item, its forming a singlet is not seen as a problem.

In summary, compared to Crew and Athelstan's (1984) seven factors (1, *Cognition*; 2, *Vision*; 3, *Communication*; 4, *Motor functioning*; 5, *Physical condition*; 6, *Vocational qualifications*; and 7, *Adaptive behaviour*) my analysis results in seven somewhat different factors (1, *Cognition and physical development*; 2, *Sensory ability*; 3, *Communication*; 4, *Upper functional ability*; 5, *Loss of time from work*; 6, *Vocational suitability*; and 7, *Adaptive behaviour*).

4.3.1.1.1 Further Refinement of the Seven-Factor FAI Solution
As can be seen in Table 4.5 three items have factor loadings below .32: item 6 (hearing) from the *sensory ability* factor, item 17 (work history) from *vocational suitability*, and item 21 (economic disincentives) from *vocational suitability*. Each of these items is omitted and the factor analysis with oblimin rotation is repeated. Items with multiple loadings are not omitted, but are retained in the factor in which they have the highest loading.[48] This necessitated omitting items 14 (endurance) from the *cognition and physical development* factor and item 17 (work history) from *vocational suitability* as they report factor loadings below .32. The omission of these two items produces the following factor structure (Table 4.7), with all items reporting loadings above .32.

Having arrived at the above factor solution, the internal reliability of the scores for the above factors of the FAI is now explored by computing the Cronbach's alpha score for each factor

---

[47] I found these two items (11 and 12) to load on the factor I termed *cognition and physical development*.
[48] This approach is taken for the items that had multiple loadings above .32, as one loading was always substantially greater than the other. Once refined, FAI solutions are derived for the seven-factor solution, six-factor solution, and five-factor solutions; multiple weightings that existed (which are minimal) are always retained in the factor in which they loaded the highest. This is because this is the factor it made theoretical sense in which to place the item (Hair *et al.* 1995), plus an analysis of the Cronbach alpha scores when the item is placed in the alternate factor always reveals a reduced Cronbach alpha score for that factor as well as the factor to which the item has the highest loading.

(reported in Table 4.8) and then determining the alpha for each factor if any one of the items is deleted (reported in Table 4.9 (a), (b), (c), (d), (e), and (f)). As evident in Table 4.8, the Cronbach alpha score for the overall questionnaire was excellent at .917 and the Cronbach alpha scores for five of the six factors, where it is possible to calculate a Cronbach alpha score, are in excess of .70 (Hair *et al.* 1995; Nunnally 1978). The Cronbach alpha score of .562 for the *sensory ability* factor appears to be of concern. However, as Pallant (2001) noted, it is common for scales with less than ten items, as is the case for each factor, to report low Cronbach alpha scores.[49] This highlights the good internal reliability of the scores for the other five factors, given that they all have less than ten items, yet report Cronbach alpha scores in excess of .70. It may also suggest that the reported Cronbach alpha score for the *Sensory ability* factor is not as problematic as it may initially appear to be; especially given it has only two items.

Table 4.6: Comparison of Crew and Athelstan (1984) seven-factor FAI solution to PhD seven-factor solution

Item		Crew and Athelstan (1984) factor	PhD thesis factor
1	Learning ability	Cognition	Cog & physical develop
2	Ability to read and write English	Cognition	Communication
3	Memory	Cognition	Cog & physical develop
4	Spatial and form perception	Cognition	Sensory ability
5	Vision	Vision	Sensory ability
6	Hearing	Communication	Sensory ability
7	Speech	Communication	Communication
8	Language functioning	Communication	Communication
9	Upper extremity functioning	Motor functioning	Upper functional ability
10	Hand functioning	Motor functioning	Upper functional ability
11	Motor speed	Motor functioning	Cog & physical develop
12	Ambulation and mobility	Motor functioning	Cog & physical develop
13	Capacity for exertion	Physical condition	Cog & physical develop
14	Endurance	Physical condition	Cog & physical develop
15	Loss of time from work	Physical condition	Loss of time from work
16	Stability of disabling condition	Physical condition	Vocational suitability
17	Work history	Vocational qualifications	Vocational suitability
18	Acceptability to employers	Vocational qualifications	Vocational suitability
19	Personal attractiveness	Vocational qualifications	Vocational suitability
20	Skills	Vocational qualifications	Cog & physical develop
21	Economic disincentives	Vocational qualifications	Vocational suitability
22	Access to job opportunities	Vocational qualifications	Vocational suitability
23	Requirements for special working conditions	Vocational qualifications	Vocational suitability
24	Work adjustment	Adaptive behaviour	Adaptive behaviour
25	Social support system	Adaptive behaviour	Adaptive behaviour
26	Accurate perception of capabilities and limitations	Adaptive behaviour	Adaptive behaviour
27	Effective interaction with employers and co-workers	Adaptive behaviour	Adaptive behaviour
28	Judgement	Adaptive behaviour	Adaptive behaviour
29	Congruence of behaviour with rehabilitation plans and goals	Adaptive behaviour	Adaptive behaviour
30	Initiative	Adaptive behaviour	Adaptive behaviour

Abbreviations: Cog & physical develop – Cognition and physical development

Referring to Table 4.9 (a) - (f), it can be seen that with exception of the *cognition and physical development* and *adaptive behaviour* factors the omission of any single item would not improve the Cronbach alpha scores for the factors. The deletion of item 3 (memory) from the *cognition and*

---

[49] Pallant (2001) provides the example of .5.

63

physical development factor (Table 4.9(a)) improves the Cronbach alpha score for that factor from .848 to .851, and the deletion of item 25 (social support system) from the *adaptive behaviour* factor (Table 4.9(f)) improves the Cronbach alpha score for that factor from .834 to .842. Accordingly, these two items are omitted and principal axis factor analysis with oblimin rotation is conducted on the remaining items. This, however, results in items 18 (acceptability to employers) and 19 (personal attractiveness), both of the *vocational suitability* factor, reporting factor loadings below .32. Accordingly, these items are omitted.

Table 4.7: Revised factor loadings for the seven-factor extraction of the FAI

Item		Factor loadings
Factor 1: Cognition and physical development		
20	Skills	.650
1	Learning ability	.539
11	Motor speed	.460
12	Ambulation and mobility	.442
13	Capacity for exertion	.351
3	Memory	.346
Factor 2: Sensory ability		
4	Spatial and form perception	.756
5	Vision	.640
Factor 3: Communication		
7	Speech	.905
8	Language functioning	.706
Factor 4: Upper functional ability		
9	Upper extremity functioning	1.003[50]
10	Hand functioning	.664
Factor 5: Loss of time from work		
15	Loss of time from work	.513
Factor 6: Vocational suitability		
23	Requirements for special working conditions	-.545
16	Stability of disabling condition	-.519
22	Access to job opportunities	-.406
18	Acceptability to employers	-.394
19	Personal attractiveness	-.369
Factor 7: Adaptive behaviour		
28	Judgement	.741
29	Congruence of behaviour with rehabilitation plans and goals	.722
27	Effective interaction with employers and co-workers	.601
24	Work adjustment	.546
26	Accurate perception of capabilities and limitations	.518
30	Initiative	.461
25	Social support system	.325

Principal axis factor analysis with oblimin rotation is then conducted on the remaining items. The Bartlett test of sphericity is significant (χ^2 (210, n = 156) = 1537.383, $p \leq .001$) and the Kaiser-Meyer-Okin measure of sampling is greater than .6 (KMO = .868), indicating it is possible to

---

[50] As the pattern matrix is reported for oblique rotations factor loadings of greater than 1 may occur in some instances. This is due to the fact that the pattern matrix reports beta weights.

conduct a factor analysis on the sample. The results of this factor analysis are presented in Table 4.10 below. Note that the heading of factor one has been changed slightly from *cognition and physical condition* to *cognition and skill development* to reflect better the items now comprising that factor.

Table 4.8: Cronbach alpha scores for the refined seven-factor FAI

	Cronbach alpha
Factor:	
1: Cognition and physical development	.848
2: Sensory ability	.562
3: Communication	.779
4: Upper functional ability	.789
5: Loss of time from work	---[a]
6: Vocational suitability	.814
7: Adaptive behaviour	.834
Overall questionnaire	.917

a   It is not possible to calculate a Cronbach alpha score for a one item factor.

Table 4.9(a):   Analysis of scale reliability and unidimensionality of the *cognition and physical development* factor (1) of the refined FAI

Item	Mean	Std deviation	Corrected item-total correlation	Alpha if item deleted
20	1.38	.853	.704	.810
1	1.48	.926	.618	.826
11	.92	.974	.745	.799
12	.36	.753	.600	.830
13	.89	1.000	.660	.818
3	.85	.881	.475	.851

Alpha for *cognition and physical development* factor = .848

Table 4.9(b):   Analysis of scale reliability and unidimensionality of the *sensory ability* factor (2) of the refined FAI

Item	Mean	Std deviation	Corrected item-total correlation	Alpha if item deleted
4	.54	.757	.436	---[a]
5	.15	.470	.436	---

Alpha for *sensory ability* factor = .562
a   It is not possible to calculate a Cronbach alpha score for a one item scale.

Table 4.9(c):   Analysis of scale reliability and unidimensionality of the *communication* factor (3) of the refined FAI

Item	Mean	Std deviation	Corrected item-total correlation	Alpha if item deleted
7	.52	.723	.639	---[a]
8	.96	.769	.639	---

Alpha for *communication* factor = .779
a   It is not possible to calculate a Cronbach alpha score for a one item scale.

Table 4.9(d):   Analysis of scale reliability and unidimensionality of the *upper functional ability* factor (4) of the refined FAI

Item	Mean	Std deviation	Corrected item-total correlation	Alpha if item deleted
9	.17	.442	.662	---[a]
10	.22	.528	.662	---

Alpha for *upper functional ability* factor = .789
a   It is not possible to calculate a Cronbach alpha score for a one item scale.

Table 4.9(e):   Analysis of scale reliability and unidimensionality of the *vocational suitability* factor
(6) of the refined FAI

Item	Mean	Std deviation	Corrected item-total correlation	Alpha if item deleted
23	1.28	.961	.701	.747
16	.51	.807	.522	.801
22	.74	.943	.590	.782
18	1.20	1.031	.676	.755
19	.84	.919	.536	.798

Alpha for *vocational suitability* factor = .814

Table 4.9(f):   Analysis of scale reliability and unidimensionality of the *adaptive behaviour* factor
(7) of the refined FAI

Item	Mean	Std deviation	Corrected item-total correlation	Alpha if item deleted
28	1.23	.810	.751	.783
29	.83	.805	.671	.797
27	.73	.837	.589	.811
24	1.14	.905	.604	.809
26	1.07	.820	.530	.820
30	.90	.670	.596	.811
25	.35	.651	.350	.842

Alpha for *adaptive behaviour* factor = .834

Having arrived at the above factor solution (Table 4.10), the internal reliability of scores for the
above factors of the FAI are assessed by investigating the Cronbach alpha score for each factor
(reported in Table 4.11) and then determining the alpha for each factor if any items are deleted
(reported in Table 4.12 (a), (b), (c), (d), (e), and (f)). As can be seen referring to Table 4.11, the
Cronbach alpha score for the overall questionnaire is still excellent at .903, and the Cronbach alpha
scores for five of the six factors, where it is possible to calculate a Cronbach alpha score, are again
in excess of .70 (Hair *et al.* 1995; Nunnally 1978). The Cronbach alpha score for the *sensory ability*
factor is still .562 (as this factor still contains the same two items as the previous iteration). As
mentioned above, Pallant (2001) noted that for scales with only a few items, such a score may not
be of great concern. Although, comparing Table 4.8, (initial refinement) to Table 4.11, reveals that
there has been a decrease in the Cronbach alpha scores for the overall questionnaire (.917 to .903),
cognition and skill development (.848 to .819), and *vocational suitability* (.814 to .796), the final
refinement (Table 4.11) is still considered the psychometrically superior version of the FAI, given
(as discussed below) it has a superior level of scale unidimensionality, while still having excellent
Cronbach alpha scores.

Tables 4.12 (a) – (f) show the reliability of scores for each factor and also the unidimensionality of
each factor. As evident from these tables, on no occasions would omission of an item result in an
increase of the Cronbach alpha score for that factor. As such, it can be concluded that all items for
each factor contribute to the measurement of each factor. The corrected item to scale total
correlations for each factor exceeds .30, which indicates an acceptable level of scale
unidimensionality (de Vaus 1995).

Consequently, the factor structure presented in Table 4.10 is accepted as the final seven-factor
solution to be compared with the five-factor and six-factor solutions.

4.3.1.2 Six-Factor FAI Structure
Having compared my seven-factor iteration with that of Crew and Athelstan (1984) and further
refining the seven-factor solution, I now compare my six-factor solution (Table 4.4) with the two

six-factor solutions[51] found by Neath *et al.* (1997) (Table 4.2). To facilitate this comparison, both six-factor solutions that Neath *et al.* (1997) derive and the six-factor solution that I obtain (Table 4.4) are shown in Table 4.13.

Table 4.10:   Factor loadings for the refined seven-factor extraction of the FAI

Item		Factor loadings
Factor 1: Cognition and skill development		
20	Skills	.546
12	Ambulation and mobility	.505
1	Learning ability	.501
11	Motor speed	.469
Factor 2: Sensory ability		
5	Vision	.743
4	Spatial and form perception	.573
Factor 3: Communication		
7	Speech	-.832
8	Language functioning	-.813
Factor 4: Upper functional ability		
9	Upper extremity functioning	.981
10	Hand functioning	.657
Factor 5: Loss of time from work		
15	Loss of time from work	.474
Factor 6: Vocational suitability		
16	Stability of disabling condition	-.749
23	Requirements for special working conditions	-.455
22	Access to job opportunities	-.439
13	Capacity for exertion	-.379
Factor 7: Adaptive behaviour		
29	Congruence of behaviour with rehabilitation plans and goals	.777
28	Judgement	.750
24	Work adjustment	.621
27	Effective interaction with employers and co-workers	.603
26	Accurate perception of capabilities and limitations	.568
30	Initiative	.482

Table 4.11:   Cronbach alpha scores for the final refined seven-factor FAI

	Cronbach alpha
Factor:	
1: Cognition and skill development	.819
2: Sensory ability	.562
3: Communication	.779
4: Upper functional ability	.789
5: Loss of time from work	---[a]
6: Vocational suitability	.796
7: Adaptive behaviour	.842
Overall questionnaire	.903

a   It is not possible to calculate a Cronbach alpha score for a one item factor.

---

[51] Neath *et al.* (1997) conducts separate factor analyses for participants with intellectual disabilities and participants with learning disabilities.

Table 4.12(a): Analysis of scale reliability and unidimensionality of the *cognition and skill development factor* (1) of the refined FAI

Item	Mean	Std deviation	Corrected item-total correlation	Alpha if item deleted
20	1.38	.853	.701	.744
12	.36	.753	.582	.799
1	1.48	.926	.627	.779
11	.92	.974	.668	.761

Alpha for *cognition and skill development* factor = .819

Table 4.12(b): Analysis of scale reliability and unidimensionality of the *sensory ability* factor (2) of the refined FAI

Item	Mean	Std deviation	Corrected item-total correlation	Alpha if item deleted
4	.54	.757	.436	--- [a]
5	.15	.470	.436	---

Alpha for *sensory ability* factor = .562
a   It is not possible to calculate a Cronbach alpha score for a one item scale.

Table 4.12(c): Analysis of scale reliability and unidimensionality of the *communication* factor (3) of the refined FAI

Item	Mean	Std deviation	Corrected item-total correlation	Alpha if item deleted
7	.52	.723	.639	--- [a]
8	.96	.769	.639	---

Alpha for *communication* factor = .779
a   It is not possible to calculate a Cronbach alpha score for a one item scale.

Table 4.12(d): Analysis of scale reliability and unidimensionality of the *upper functional ability* factor (4) of the refined FAI

Item	Mean	Std deviation	Corrected item-total correlation	Alpha if item deleted
9	.17	.442	.662	--- [a]
10	.22	.528	.662	---

Alpha for *upper functional ability* factor = .789
a   It is not possible to calculate a Cronbach alpha score for a one item scale.

Table 4.12(e): Analysis of scale reliability and unidimensionality of the *vocational suitability* factor (6) of the refined FAI

Item	Mean	Std deviation	Corrected item-total correlation	Alpha if item deleted
16	.51	.807	.560	.769
23	1.28	.961	.601	.748
22	.74	.943	.655	.720
13	.89	1.000	.620	.739

Alpha for *vocational suitability* factor = .796

When comparing the two six-factor solutions of Neath *et al.* (1997) with the one I derive, a substantial number of differences are evident. First, however, looking at the one similarity, the *adaptive behaviour* items from the original Crew and Athelstan (1984) factor solution (Table 3.6) (items 24, 25, 26, 27, 28, 29, and 30) are similar to those in the *adaptive behaviour* factors in the two Neath *et al.* (1997) factor solutions. All of the items from the Crew and Athelstan (1984) *adaptive behaviour* factor formed part of the factor that I term *vocational suitability and adaptive behaviour*. In addition to these seven items, I find this factor also includes items 15 (loss of time from work), 17 (work history), and 19 (personal attractiveness), thus predicating the need to incorporate vocational suitability in the name for the factor. These three items are distributed across the two factors of *physical capacity* (item 15) and *motor functioning/work history* (items 17 and 19) in the Neath *et al.* (1997) intellectual disability factor solution. For the learning disability factor solution, Neath *et al.* (1997) reported items 15, 17, and 19 as being distributed across three different factors; with item 15 (loss of time from work) loading on the *physical capacity* factor, item 17 (work history) loading on the *motor functioning/work history* factor, and item 19 (personal attractiveness) loading on the *communication* factor.

Table 4.12(f): Analysis of scale reliability and unidimensionality of the *adaptive behaviour* factor (7) of the refined FAI

Item	Mean	Std deviation	Corrected item-total correlation	Alpha if item deleted
29	.83	.805	.658	.809
28	1.23	.810	.767	.787
24	1.14	.905	.616	.819
27	.73	.837	.588	.823
26	1.07	.820	.523	.836
30	.90	.670	.596	.823

Alpha for *adaptive behaviour* factor = .842

As for the other five factors of my six-factor extraction, there are surprisingly few similarities when compared with the two six-factor extractions of Neath *et al.* (1997) (both listed in Table 4.7), with most items loading on different factors. This is disconcerting given the high degree of agreement that Neath *et al.* (1997) found between their two six-factor solutions (21 of the 30 factors loading on the same items)[52]. The substantial differences between my six-factor solution and the two derived by Neath *et al.* (1997) suggest the possibility that the factors in a six-factor extraction of the FAI are not well defined. This possibility is tested later in this chapter when the results of factor stability analyses are reported.

Examining whether the factors I derive in my six-factor solution make theoretical sense, it can be seen that on the whole, the groupings seem intuitive. The two factors that initially appear slightly questionable are the ones I term *cognition and vocational qualifications* and *vocational suitability and adaptive behaviour*. The items comprising the *cognition and vocational qualifications* factor seem slightly disparate; however, it is easy to see how the cognition items that form part of this factor (item 1 (learning ability) and item 3 (memory)) could impact on the employment suitability of an individual in a similar manner to their qualifications. Likewise, for the factor *vocational suitability and adaptive behaviour*, it is reasonable to expect that adaptive behaviour (items 24 – 30) would impact on the vocational suitability of an individual. While I acknowledge there might be some degree of questionability on the items that loaded on the two factors discussed above, this by itself is not enough to cast doubt on the suitability of a six factor solution for the FAI.

4.3.1.2.1 Further Refinement of the Six-Factor Solution
As evident from Table 4.14, there are six items with factor loadings below .32: item 3 (memory) from the *cognition and vocational qualifications* factor; item 6 (hearing) from the *sensory ability* factor; item 18 (acceptability to employers) and item 19 (personal attractiveness) both from the *communications* factor; item 14 (endurance) from the *vocational opportunities* factor; and item 15 (loss of time from work) from the *vocational suitability and adaptive behaviour* factor. Each of these items is omitted and the factor analysis with oblimin rotation is repeated. This necessitates omitting item 14 (endurance) from *cognition and physical development*, as the item reports a factor loading below .32. The further omission of this item results in the following factor structure (Table 4.14), with all items reporting factor loadings above .32.

---

[52] Neath *et al.* (1997) did not conduct any statistical analysis comparing their different factor analyses.

Table 4.13: Comparison of the two six-factor FAI solutions of Neath *et al.* (1997) to PhD six-factor solution

Item		Neath *et al.* (1997) intellectual disability factor	Neath *et al.* (1997) learning disability factor	PhD thesis factor
1	Learning ability	Cognition	Cognition	Cog & vocational qualifications
2	Ability to read and write English	Cognition	Cognition	Communication
3	Memory	Cognition	Cognition	Cog & vocational qualifications
4	Spatial and form perception	Cognition	Cognition	Sensory ability
5	Vision	Communication	Physical capacity	Sensory ability
6	Hearing	Communication	Communication	Sensory ability
7	Speech	Communication	Communication	Communication
8	Language functioning	Communication	Communication	Communication
9	Upper extremity functioning	Physical capacity	Physical capacity	Upper funct ability
10	Hand functioning	Physical capacity	Physical capacity	Upper funct ability
11	Motor speed	Physical capacity	Physical capacity	Cog & vocational qualifications
12	Ambulation and mobility	Physical capacity	Physical capacity	Cog & vocational qualifications
13	Capacity for exertion	Physical capacity	Physical capacity	Cog & vocational qualifications
14	Endurance	Physical capacity	Physical capacity	Cog & vocational qualifications
15	Loss of time from work	Physical capacity	Physical capacity	Voc suitability & adap behaviour
16	Stability of disabling condition	Physical capacity	Physical capacity	Vocational opportunities
17	Work history	Motor functioning/ work history	Motor functioning/ work history	Voc suitability & adap behaviour
18	Acceptability to employers	Motor functioning/ work history	Communication	Cog & vocational qualifications
19	Personal attractiveness	Motor functioning/ work history	Communication	Voc suitability & adap behaviour
20	Skills	Cognition	Vocational qualifications	Cog & vocational qualifications
21	Economic disincentives	Adaptive behaviour	Vocational qualifications	Vocational opportunities
22	Access to job opportunities	Vocational qualifications	Vocational qualifications	Cog & vocational qualifications
23	Requirements for special working conditions	Vocational qualifications	Vocational qualifications	Cog & vocational qualifications
24	Work adjustment	Adaptive behaviour	Adaptive behaviour	Voc suitability & adap behaviour
25	Social support system	Adaptive behaviour	Adaptive behaviour	Voc suitability & adap behaviour
26	Accurate perception of capabilities and limitations	Adaptive behaviour	Adaptive behaviour	Voc suitability & adap behaviour
27	Effective interaction with employers and co-workers	Adaptive behaviour	Adaptive behaviour	Voc suitability & adap behaviour
28	Judgement	Adaptive behaviour	Adaptive behaviour	Voc suitability & adap behaviour
29	Congruence of behaviour with rehabilitation plans and goals	Adaptive behaviour	Adaptive behaviour	Voc suitability & adap behaviour
30	Initiative	Cognition	Adaptive behaviour	Voc suitability & adap behaviour

Abbreviations: Cog & vocational qualifications – Cognition and vocational qualifications
Voc suit & adap behaviour – Vocational suitability and adaptive behaviour
Upper funct ability – Upper functional ability

Table 4.14: FAI Factor loadings for the six-factor extraction of the FAI

Item		Factor loadings
Factor 1: Cognition and vocational qualifications		
20	Skills	.661
1	Learning ability	.593
12	Ambulation and mobility	.516
11	Motor speed	.479
Factor 2: Sensory ability		
5	Vision	.755
4	Spatial and form perception	.543
Factor 3: Communication		
8	Language functioning	-.779
7	Speech	-.778
2	Ability to read and write in English	-.396
Factor 4: Upper functional ability		
9	Upper extremity functioning	.865
10	Hand functioning	.685
Factor 5: Vocational opportunities		
16	Stability of disabling condition	.670
22	Access to job opportunities	.447
13	Capacity for exertion	.387
23	Requirements for special working conditions	.385
21	Economic disincentives	.344
Factor 6: Vocational suitability and adaptive behaviour		
29	Congruence of behaviour with rehabilitation plans and goals	.853
28	Judgement	.732
27	Effective interaction with employers and co-workers	.609
26	Accurate perception of capabilities and limitations	.554
24	Work adjustment	.503
30	Initiative	.467
25	Social support system	.413

Table 4.15: Cronbach alpha scores for the six-factor refined FAI

	Cronbach alpha
Factor:	
1: Cognition and vocational qualifications	.819
2: Sensory ability	.562
3: Communication	.715
4: Upper functional ability	.789
5: Vocational opportunities	.755
6: Vocational suitability and adaptive behaviour	.834
Overall questionnaire	.905

Having arrived at the above six-factor solution for the FAI, the internal reliability of the scores for the factors is explored by investigating the Cronbach's alpha score for each factor (reported in Table 4.15) and then determining the alpha for each factor as each item is deleted in turn (reported in Table 4.16 (a), (b), (c), (d), (e), and (f), respectively). The Cronbach alpha score for the overall questionnaire is excellent at .905 and, as in the analysis of the seven factor solution, all Cronbach alpha scores for the factors are in excess of .70, with the exception of the *sensory ability* factor (.562). As stated above, the score for this factor may not be of great concern, given it has only two items.

Looking at the Cronbach alpha scores reported in Table 4.16 (a) – (f), it is apparent that three of the six factors the Cronbach alpha scores can be increased with the deletion of an item. For the *communication* factor, if item 2 (ability to read and write English) is omitted, the Cronbach alpha score increases from .715 to .779 (Table 4.16(c)). For the *vocational opportunities* factor, the deletion of item 21 (economic disincentives) increases the Cronbach alpha score from .755 to .796 (Table 4.16(e)) and if item 25 (social support system) is omitted from the *vocational suitability and adaptive behaviour* factor the Cronbach alpha score increases from .834 to .842 (Table 4.16(f)).

Table 4.16(a): Analysis of scale reliability and unidimensionality of the *cognition and vocational qualifications* factor (1) of the refined FAI

Item	Mean	Std deviation	Corrected item-total correlation	Alpha if item deleted
20	1.38	.853	.701	.744
1	1.48	.926	.627	.779
12	.36	.753	.582	.799
11	.92	.974	.668	.761

Alpha for *cognition and vocational qualifications* factor = .819

Table 4.16(b): Analysis of scale reliability and unidimensionality of the *sensory ability* factor (2) of the refined FAI

Item	Mean	Std deviation	Corrected item-total correlation	Alpha if item deleted
5	.15	.470	.436	---[a]
4	.54	.757	.436	---

Alpha for *sensory ability* factor = .562
a   It is not possible to calculate a Cronbach alpha score for a one item scale.

Table 4.16(c): Analysis of scale reliability and unidimensionality of the *communication* factor (3) of the refined FAI

Item	Mean	Std deviation	Corrected item-total correlation	Alpha if item deleted
8	.96	.769	..676	.444
7	.52	.723	.533	.630
2	.2.07	.843	.417	.779

Alpha for *communication* factor = .715

Table 4.16(d): Analysis of scale reliability and unidimensionality of the *upper functional ability* factor (4) of the refined FAI

Item	Mean	Std deviation	Corrected item-total correlation	Alpha if item deleted
9	.17	.442	.662	---[a]
10	.22	.528	.662	---

Alpha for *upper functional ability* factor = .789
a   It is not possible to calculate a Cronbach alpha score for a one item scale.

Table 4.16(e): Analysis of scale reliability and unidimensionality of the *vocational opportunities* factor (5) of the refined FAI

Item	Mean	Std deviation	Corrected item-total correlation	Alpha if item deleted
16	.51	.807	.560	.701
22	.74	.943	.617	.675
13	.89	1.000	.629	.669
23	1.28	.961	.578	.690
21	.98	.791	.240	.796

Alpha for *vocational opportunities* factor = .755

Table 4.16(f): Analysis of scale reliability and unidimensionality of the *vocational suitability and adaptive behaviour* factor (6) of the refined FAI

Item	Mean	Std deviation	Corrected item-total correlation	Alpha if item deleted
29	.83	.805	.671	.797
28	1.23	.810	.751	.783
27	.73	.837	.589	.811
26	1.07	.820	.530	.820
24	1.14	.905	.604	.809
30	.90	.670	.596	.811
25	.35	.651	.350	.842

Alpha for *vocational suitability and adaptive behaviour* factor = .834

Given that the omission of items 2, 21, and 25 improves the Cronbach alpha scores for their respective factors, these items are omitted and a principal axis factor analysis with oblimin rotation is then conducted on the remaining items. The Bartlett test of sphericity is significant (χ^2 (190, n = 156) = 1506.150, $p \leq .001$) and the Kaiser-Meyer- Okin measure of sampling is greater than .6 (KMO = .872), indicating that it is possible to conduct a factor analysis on the sample. The results of this factor analysis are reported in Table 4.17.

Table 4.17: FAI factor loadings for the refined six-factor extraction of the FAI

Item		Factor loadings
Factor 1: Cognition and skill development		
20	Skills	.558
1	Learning ability	.535
12	Ambulation and mobility	.440
11	Motor speed	.373
Factor 2: Sensory ability		
5	Vision	.720
4	Spatial and form perception	.604
Factor 3: Communication		
7	Speech	.829
8	Language functioning	.806
Factor 4: Upper functional ability		
9	Upper extremity functioning	.877
10	Hand functioning	.718
Factor 5: Vocational suitability		
16	Stability of disabling condition	-.703
22	Access to job opportunities	-.509
23	Requirements for special working conditions	-.425
13	Capacity for exertion	-.417
Factor 6: Adaptive behaviour		
29	Congruence of behaviour with rehabilitation plans and goals	-.836
28	Judgement	-.772
27	Effective interaction with employers and co-workers	-.647
24	Work adjustment	-.570
26	Accurate perception of capabilities and limitations	-.560
30	Initiative	-.516

As can be seen from Table 4.17, the factors are exactly the same as factors in the refined seven-factor solution (Table 4.10), with the exclusion of the *loss of time from work* factor, which was a single item factor. Consequently, the factor headings for the six-factor solution are renamed to be consistent with the titles of the seven-factor solution and to reflect better the content of items remaining in each factor. The Cronbach alpha scores for each of the factors and the questionnaire overall are reported in Table 4.18. These scores are the same as those reported in Table 4.11, with the exception of the questionnaire overall, which is slightly higher, .907 compared to .903 for the seven-factor solution.

Table 4.18:   Cronbach alpha scores for the refined six-factor FAI

	Cronbach alpha
Factor:	
1: Cognition and skill development	.819
2: Sensory ability	.562
3: Communication	.779
4: Upper functional ability	.789
5: Vocational suitability	.796
6: Adaptive behaviour	.842
Overall questionnaire	.907

Given that the items comprising each of the six factors are consonant with the multiple item factors of the seven-factor solution, there is no need to report the details of the scale analysis and unidimensionality as they are the same as those reported in Table 4.12 (a) - (f). As reported for the seven-factor FAI solution in Table 4.12 (a) – (f), on no occasion would omission of an item increase the Cronbach alpha score for a factor, indicating that each item contributes to the factor, and the corrected item to scale total correlations for each factor exceeds .30, indicating an acceptable level of scale unidimensionality (de Vaus 1995).

4.3.1.3 Five-Factor FAI Structure
An examination of the derived five-factor solution (Table 4.3) reveals that most factors make theoretical sense. The first three factors (*cognition and skill development*, *sensory ability*, and *communication*) appear logical in terms of the items that load on them. As with the concerns raised above regarding to the six-factor solution, there may be a degree of questionability concerning items that load on the factors I termed *physical condition and vocational opportunities* and *vocational suitability and adaptive behaviour*. The issues in relation to the *vocational suitability* and *adaptive behaviour* factor are identical to those raised above in the discussion of the six-factor solution and, as such, are not repeated here. In relation to the factor *physical condition and vocational opportunities* it is easy to see how both an individual's physical condition and vocational opportunities directly affect his/her employment opportunities. However, one might question whether they should load together, given that they are rather disparate conceptual constructs. As stated above in relation to the six-factor solution, these issues by themselves are not enough to dismiss the appropriateness of the five-factor solution for the FAI.

4.3.1.3.1 Further Refinement of the Five-Factor Solution
As can be seen from Table 4.3, four items have factor loadings below .32: item 6 (hearing) and item 15 (loss of time from work), both from the *cognition and skill development* factor; item 3 (memory) from the *sensory ability* factor; and item 19 (personal attractiveness) from the *communication* factor. Each of these items are omitted and another factor analysis with oblimin rotation is conducted. This results in the need to omit items 12 (ambulation and mobility), 14 (endurance), 17 (work history), and 21 (economic disincentives), all from the *physical condition and vocational opportunities* factor, as they report factor loadings below .32. The further omission of these items results in the factor structure reported in Table 4.19, with all items reporting factor loadings above .32.

Having arrived at the above five-factor solution for the FAI, the internal reliability of the factor scores is assessed in terms of the Cronbach's alpha score for each factor (reported in Table 4.20).

74

The Cronbach alpha score for the overall questionnaire is excellent at .910 and, as in the above analysis of the six-factor and seven-factor solutions, all Cronbach alpha scores for the factors are in excess of .70, with the exception of the *sensory ability* factor (.677). The score for *sensory ability* is higher than that reported for the six-factor and seven-factor solutions due to the inclusion of two additional items; item 16 (stability of disabling condition) and item 18 (acceptability to employers). The inclusion of these two items in this factor does not make much theoretical sense. However, given the other factors appear to make theoretical sense, further scale analysis is conducted in terms of the Cronbach alpha scores for each factor if each of the items is omitted in turn, the results of which are reported in Table 4.21 (a) – (e).

Table 4.19: Factor loadings for the five-factor extraction of the FAI

Item		Factor loadings
Factor 1: Cognition and skill development		
20	Skills	.635
1	Learning ability	.434
23	Requirements for special working conditions	.427
22	Access to job opportunities	.418
Factor 2: Sensory ability		
5	Vision	.584
16	Stability of disabling condition	.574
4	Spatial and form perception	.458
18	Acceptability to employers	.347
Factor 3: Communication		
8	Language functioning	-.845
7	Speech	-.755
2	Ability to read and write English	-.355
Factor 4: Physical condition and vocational opportunities		
9	Upper extremity functioning	.874
10	Hand functioning	.757
13	Capacity for exertion	.440
11	Motor speed	.415
Factor 5: Vocational suitability and adaptive behaviour		
29	Congruence of behaviour with rehabilitation plans and goals	.828
28	Judgement	.779
27	Effective interaction with employers and co-workers	.636
26	Accurate perception of capabilities and limitations	.565
30	Initiative	.518
24	Work adjustment	.493
25	Social support system	.385

Table 4.20: Cronbach alpha scores for the five-factor FAI

	Cronbach alpha
Factor:	
1: Cognition and skill development	.808
2: Sensory ability	.677
3: Communication	.715
4: Physical condition and vocational opportunities	.792
5: Vocational suitability and adaptive behaviour	.834
Overall questionnaire	.910

Table 4.21(a): Analysis of scale reliability and unidimensionality of the *cognition and skill development factor* (1) of the FAI

Item	Mean	Std deviation	Corrected item-total correlation	Alpha if item deleted
20	1.38	.853	.679	.736
1	1.48	.926	.605	.769
23	1.28	.961	.662	.741
22	.74	.943	.560	.791

Alpha for *cognition and skill development* factor = .808

Table 4.21(b): Analysis of scale reliability and unidimensionality of the *sensory ability* factor (2) of the FAI

Item	Mean	Std deviation	Corrected item-total correlation	Alpha if item deleted
5	.15	.470	.384	.671
16	.51	.807	.449	.617
4	.54	.757	.564	.543
18	1.20	1.031	.523	.585

Alpha for *sensory ability* factor = .677

Table 4.21(c): Analysis of scale reliability and unidimensionality of the *communication* factor (3) of the FAI

Item	Mean	Std deviation	Corrected item-total correlation	Alpha if item deleted
8	.96	.769	..676	.444
7	.52	.723	.533	.630
2	.2.07	.843	.417	.779

Alpha for *communication* factor = .715

Table 4.21(d): Analysis of scale reliability and unidimensionality of the *upper functional ability* factor (4) of the FAI

Item	Mean	Std deviation	Corrected item-total correlation	Alpha if item deleted
9	.17	.442	.603	.778
10	.22	.528	.612	.760
13	.89	1.000	.704	.701
11	.92	.974	.716	.687

Alpha for *upper functional ability* factor = .792

Table 4.21(e): Analysis of scale reliability and unidimensionality of the *vocational suitability and adaptive behaviour* factor (5) of the FAI

Item	Mean	Std deviation	Corrected item-total correlation	Alpha if item deleted
29	.83	.805	.671	.797
28	1.23	.810	.751	.783
27	.73	.837	.589	.811
26	1.07	.820	.530	.820
30	.90	.670	.596	.811
24	1.14	.905	.604	.809
25	.35	.651	.350	.842

Alpha for *vocational suitability and adaptive behaviour* factor = .834

As evident from Table 4.21 (a) – (e), the deletion of item 2 (ability to read and write English) from the *communication* factor (Table 4.21 (c)) and item 25 (*social support system*) from the *vocational suitability and adaptive behaviour* factor (Table 4.21(e)) improves the reported Cronbach alpha score for each factor. Consequently, these two items are omitted and a principal axis factor analysis with oblimin rotation is conducted on the remaining items.

The resultant factor solution (not reported) has factor loadings in excess of .32 for all items. However, analysis of the Cronbach alpha scores reveals that the further omission of item 5 (vision) improves the Cronbach alpha score items. A further principal axis factor analysis is conducted with the omission of item 5. This results in item 4 (spatial and form perceptions) reporting a factor loading below .32 (results not reported). Consequently, item 4 is deleted and a principal axis factor analysis with oblimin rotation is conducted once more. The Bartlett test of sphericity for this factor analysis is significant (χ^2 (153, n = 156) = 1400.687, $p \le .001$) and the Kaiser-Meyer-Okin measure of sampling is greater than .6 (KMO = .880), which indicates that it is possible to conduct a factor analysis on the sample. The results of this factor analysis are reported in Table 4.22.

Looking at the above factor structure, the items comprising the five factors are similar to the six-factor and seven-factor solutions and substantially different from the original five-factor solution prior to the omission of any items (Table 4.3). Consequently, factor headings are renamed to reflect better the items comprising each factor.

Having arrived at the above refined five-factor solution for the FAI, the internal reliability of the scores for each factor is investigated by looking at the Cronbach alpha score for each factor (reported in Table 4.23). As can be seen from Table 4.23 the Cronbach alpha score for the overall questionnaire is excellent at .906. The Cronbach alpha scores for each of the five factors are in excess of .700, indicating a high degree of reliability for the scores of each factor.

Table 4.22:   Factor loadings for the refined five-factor extraction of the FAI

Item		Factor loadings
Factor 1: Cognition and skill development		
20	Skills	-.690
1	Learning ability	-.658
Factor 2: Communication		
8	Language functioning	.836
7	Speech	.772
Factor 3: Upper functional ability		
9	Upper extremity functioning	.832
10	Hand functioning	.711
Factor 4: Vocational suitability		
16	Stability of disabling condition	.698
22	Access to job opportunities	.597
23	Requirements for special working conditions	.551
13	Capacity for exertion	.465
18	Acceptability to employers	.433
11	Motor speed	.340
Factor 5: Adaptive behaviour		
29	Congruence of behaviour with rehabilitation plans and goals	-.850
28	Judgement	-.756
27	Effective interaction with employers and co-workers	-.635
26	Accurate perception of capabilities and limitations	-.557
24	Work adjustment	-.504
30	Initiative	-.471

Table 4.23:   Cronbach alpha scores for the refined five-factor FAI

	Cronbach alpha
Factor:	
1: Cognition and skill development	.787
2: Communication	.779
3: Upper functional ability	.789
4: Vocational suitability	.868
5: Adaptive behaviour	.842
Overall questionnaire	.906

To assess the contribution of each item to the overall factor, the Cronbach alpha score for each factor with the omission of that item is calculated and reported in Table 4.24 (a) – (e). As can be seen from Table 4.24 (a) – (e), on no occasions does deletion of an item improve the Cronbach alpha score of any of the factors. This indicates that each item is contributing to the overall factor. Unidimensionality is also assessed by looking at the corrected item-total correlation. Again, referring to Table 4.24 (a) – (e), on all occasions the corrected item to scale total correlations are in excess of .30, indicating an acceptable level of unidimensionality (de Vaus 1995).

Table 4.24(a): Analysis of scale reliability and unidimensionality of the *cognition and skill development* factor (1) of the refined FAI

Item	Mean	Std deviation	Corrected item-total correlation	Alpha if item deleted
20	1.38	.853	.651	--- [a]
1	1.48	.926	.651	---

Alpha for *cognition and skill development factor* = .787
[a]   It is not possible to calculate a Cronbach alpha score for a one item scale.

Table 4.24(b): Analysis of scale reliability and unidimensionality of the *communication* factor (2) of the refined FAI

Item	Mean	Std deviation	Corrected item-total correlation	Alpha if item deleted
8	.96	.769	.639	--- [a]
7	.52	.723	.639	---

Alpha for *communication* factor = .779
[a]   It is not possible to calculate a Cronbach alpha score for a one item scale.

Table 4.24(c): Analysis of scale reliability and unidimensionality of the *upper functional ability* factor (3) of the refined FAI

Item	Mean	Std deviation	Corrected item-total correlation	Alpha if item deleted
9	.17	.442	.662	--- [a]
10	.22	.528	.662	---

Alpha for *upper functional ability* factor = .789
[a]   It is not possible to calculate a Cronbach alpha score for a one item scale.

Table 4.24(d): Analysis of scale reliability and unidimensionality of the *vocational suitability* factor (4) of the refined FAI

Item	Mean	Std deviation	Corrected item-total correlation	Alpha if item deleted
16	.51	.807	.542	.865
22	.74	.943	.672	.844
23	1.28	.961	.676	.843
13	.89	1.000	.708	.837
18	1.20	1.031	.670	.845
11	.92	.974	.722	.835

Alpha for *vocational suitability* factor = .868

Table 4.24(e): Analysis of scale reliability and unidimensionality of the *adaptive behaviour* factor (5) of the refined FAI

Item	Mean	Std deviation	Corrected item-total correlation	Alpha if item deleted
29	.83	.805	.658	.809
28	1.23	.810	.767	.787
27	.73	.837	.588	.823
26	1.07	.820	.523	.836
24	1.14	.905	.616	.819
30	.90	.670	.596	.823

Alpha for *adaptive behaviour* factor = .842

Table 4.25: Comparison of the three different derived factor structures of the FAI

Item		7-factor solution	6-factor solution	5-factor solution
1	Learning ability	Cog & skill	Cog & skill	Cog & skill
2	Ability to read and write English	---	---	---
3	Memory	---	---	---
4	Spatial and form perception	Sensory ab	Sensory ab	---
5	Vision	Sensory ab	Sensory ab	---
6	Hearing	---	---	---
7	Speech	Comm	Comm	Comm
8	Language functioning	Comm	Comm	Comm
9	Upper extremity functioning	Up fun ab	Up fun ab	Up fun ab
10	Hand functioning	Up fun ab	Up fun ab	Up fun ab
11	Motor speed	Cog & skill	Cog & skill	Voc suit
12	Ambulation and mobility	Cog & skill	Cog & skill	---
13	Capacity for exertion	Voc suit	Voc suit	Voc suit
14	Endurance	---	---	---
15	Loss of time from work	Loss	---	---
16	Stability of disabling condition	Voc suit	Voc suit	Voc suit
17	Work history	---	---	---
18	Acceptability to employers	---	---	Voc suit
19	Personal attractiveness	---	---	---
20	Skills	Cog & skill	Cog & skill	Cog & skill
21	Economic disincentives	---	---	---
22	Access to job opportunities	Voc suit	Voc suit	Voc suit
23	Requirements for special working conditions	Voc suit	Voc suit	Voc suit
24	Work adjustment	Adap behav	Adap behav	Adap behav
25	Social support system	---	---	---
26	Accurate perception of capabilities and limitations	Adap behav	Adap behav	Adap behav
27	Effective interaction with employers and co-workers	Adap behav	Adap behav	Adap behav
28	Judgement	Adap behav	Adap behav	Adap behav
29	Congruence of behaviour with rehabilitation plans and goals	Adap behav	Adap behav	Adap behav
30	Initiative	Adap behav	Adap behav	Adap behav

Abbreviations: Adap behave - Adaptive behaviour; Cog & skill - Cognition and skill development; Comm – Communication; Loss - Loss of time from work; Sensory ab - Sensory ability; Up fun ab - Upper functional ability; Voc suit - Vocational suitability; --- - item omitted

4.3.2 Comparison of FAI Factor Structures

Table 4.25 shows a comparison of the three different refined factor solutions; there is a high degree of stability in that factors appear to load consonantly across the three different solutions. First, comparing the factors that make up the three different factor solutions, the difference between the seven-factor and six factor solution is the omission of the *loss of time from work* factor from the six-factor solution. Apart from the omission of this factor, containing a single item, all items load on the same factors in the six-factor solution compared to the seven factor solution. Comparing the six-factor solution with the five factor solution reported in Table 4.25, the factors that comprise the five-factor solution are the same as the six-factor solution except for the omission of the *sensory ability* factor. The sensory ability factor (a factor in both the seven-factor and six-factor solutions) contains item 4 (spatial and form perception) and item 5 (vision), both of which are omitted in the five factor solution. This factor is also the only factor that reports a Cronbach alpha score below .70 (.562).

As stated above, the six-factor and seven-factor solutions are the same, except for the omission of the single item factor *loss of time from work*, from the six-factor solution. Similar to the six-factor solution, the five-factor solution also omits the *loss of time from work* factor, but different to both the six-factor and seven-factor solutions the five-factor solution omits the *sensory ability* factor and the two items that form this factor. Looking horizontally across the three different factor solutions reported in Table 4.25, three factors are identical in that they contain exactly the same items across the three factor solutions; these factors being *communication* (items 7 and 8), *upper functional ability* (items 9 and 10), and *adaptive behaviour* (items 24, 26, 27, 28, 29, and 30).

It is interesting to note that these three factors are similar to the original ones developed by Crew and Athelstan (1984) (Table 3.6). Crew and Athelstan's (1984) *communication* factor contains in addition to items 7 and 8, item 6 (hearing), which was omitted from all the five-factor, six-factor, and seven-factor solutions. Likewise, Crew and Athelstan's (1984) *adaptive behaviour* factor contains an extra item to that reported in Table 4.25, (items 24, 26, 27, 28, 29, and 30) which is omitted from the five-factor, six-factor, and seven-factor solutions I derive; the additional item being 25 (social support system). Crew and Athelstan (1984) have a factor they refer to as *motor functioning*, which contains four items (9, 10, 11, and 12). Item 9 (upper extremity functioning) and item 10 (hand functioning) form part of the factor I term *upper functional* ability, which is consistent across the five-factor, six-factor, and seven-factor solutions. Item 11 (motor speed) and 12 (ambulation and mobility) form part of the factor I term *cognition and skill development* in my six-factor and seven-factor solutions. For the five-factor solution, item 11 forms part of the *vocational suitability* factor and item 12 is omitted.

Looking at the other two factors common to the three solutions, *vocational suitability* contains the same four items (13, 16, 22, and 23) across the three solutions, with the only difference in the composition of this factor being the inclusion of two extra items in the five-factor solution; item 12 (ambulation and mobility) from the *cognition and skill development* factor in the six-factor and seven-factor solutions, and item 18 (acceptability to employers), which is omitted from the six-factor and seven-factor solutions. The other factor common to the three solutions, *cognition and skill development*, for the five-factor solution contains only two of the four items that load on this factor; in the six-factor and seven-factor solutions, these two items are 1 (learning ability) and 20 (skills). The two items that do not load on this factor in the five-factor solution are item 11 (motor speed), which loads on the *vocational suitability* factor in the five-factor solution, and item 12 (ambulation and mobility), which is omitted in the five-factor solution.

Initially, one possible explanation for the different factor solutions across the three studies (Crewe and Athelstan 1984; Neath *et al.* 1997; this thesis) could be due to the fact that the FAI is not stable across different types of disability. That is, the FAI may factor differently for different disability types, for example, physical disabilities compared with intellectual disabilities. However, this possibility is not supported by the results of Crewe and Athelstan (1984). Crewe and Athelstan (1984), although they did not report the results, stated they conducted separate factor analyses for physical and behavioural[53] disabilities, which resulted in similar solutions. The results of Neath *et al.* (1997) contrast the results of Crewe and Athelstan (1984), in that Neath *et al.* (1997) found a

---

[53] Crew and Althelstan's (1984) behavioural disability group included participants with intellectual disabilities.

different factor structure for each of their five different disability groups. Neath *et al.* (1997) found that the factor structures of the intellectual and learning disability groups[54] differed markedly from the other three disability groups (orthopaedic/amputation, chronic-physical condition, and mental illness).

4.3.3 Factor Stability of the FAI

As the five-factor, six-factor, and seven-factor extractions I derive make theoretical sense and have acceptable Cronbach alpha scores, a factor stability analysis is conducted to examine further the reliability of scores for each factor. As mentioned in Section 4.2.2 (Reliability Analysis), to conduct a factor stability analysis the sample is split (1) randomly (half-half), (2) by gender (male-female), (3) by level of functional work ability (as measured by the FAI[55]), (4) by employment when the sample is dichotomised into participants employed in open employment versus participants employed in supported employment and job seekers, and (5) by employment when the sample is dichotomised into participants employed in open employment versus those employed in supported employment.

First, I shall discuss the seven-factor extraction, as this is the most commonly used factor structure of the FAI. Then I shall discuss the six-factor and five-factor extractions. For the sub-population sample sizes, refer to Table 4.1, which contains the demographic information for the FAI sample.

Table 4.26: Factor stability test: Coefficients of congruence for refined seven-factor FAI[a]

	Functional Assessment Inventory Factors						
	Cognition and skill development	Sensory Ability	Communication	Upper functional ability	Loss of time from work	Vocational suitability	Adaptive behaviour
Random split halves	.983	.904	.999	.994	---[b]	.999	.979
Gender	---	.999	.974	.921	1.000	.958	.966
Functional ability	.999	.978	.988	.980	---	.973	.980
Employment (open v. supported and job seekers	.992	.999	.974	.999	1.000	---	.934
Employment (open v. supported)	.999	.997	.975	.995	1.000	---	.943

a   For factors to be considered congruent the coefficient of congruence should be equal to or greater than .940.
b   The dashed lines indicate that a coefficient of congruence cannot be calculated in these instances, as no items from the relevant factor load on the same factor when the sample is dichotomised. That is, the items variously load on other factors.

Results for the seven-factor stability analysis are presented in Table 4.26. In order to conclude that factors are congruent, the coefficient of congruence should be equal to or greater than .940 (Harman 1967). As can be seen by reference to Table 4.26, it is not possible to calculate a coefficient of congruence on five occasions due to items comprising these factors not loading on similar factors across the sub-samples. Therefore the scores obtained from these factors may not represent the same underlying construct. The five occasions when it is not possible to calculate a coefficient of congruence relate to the following factors: *loss of time from work* and *vocational suitability*, both on two occasions, and *cognition and skill development* on one occasion. This inability to calculate

---

[54] As mentioned previously, Neath *et al.* (1997) found 21 of the 30 FAI items loaded on the same factors for the intellectual disability and learning disability groups.
[55] The FAI is dichotomised around the median. The median is selected as the mid-point since there are no generally accepted ranges that define participants with intellectual disabilities as having either high functional work ability or low functional work ability.

coefficients of congruence, due to no items from these factors loading on the similar factors, brings the reliability of scores for these factors of the FAI into question. These results are possibly due to having a too small sample size given that the entire sample pertaining to the FAI analysis is only 156. When this sample is dichotomised it results in factor analyses having to be conducted on samples of less than 100, which is generally considered too small a sample on which to conduct reliable factor analyses.[56] However, when Kober and Eggleton (2002) dichotomised their sample relating to the Schalock and Keith (1993) Quality of Life Questionnaire to conduct a factor stability analysis, it results in samples as small as 55, yet they still managed to find stable factors.

In those instances when it is possible to calculate a coefficient of congruence they are in excess of .940 on all but three occasions. These three occasions are for the *sensory ability* factor when the sample is split randomly, for the *upper functional ability* factor when the sample is split based on gender, and for the *adaptive behaviour* factor when the sample is split by employment (open employment compared to supported employment and job seekers).

The factor stability for the six-factor analysis is more comforting than that of the seven-factor analysis. As can be seen from Table 4.27, it is not possible to calculate a coefficient of congruence (for the *cognition and skill development* factor when the sample is split by gender) on only one occasion, and on only three occasions are the coefficients of congruence below .940: once for the *sensory ability* factor when the sample is randomly split (as was also the case for the seven-factor FAI); once for the *vocational suitability* factor when the sample is separated by functional ability; and once for the *adaptive behaviour* factor when the sample is split by gender.

Table 4.27: Factor stability test: Coefficients of congruence for refined six-factor FAI[a]

	Functional Assessment Inventory Factors					
	Cognition and skill development	Sensory ability	Communi-cation	Upper Functional ability	Vocational opportunities	Adaptive behaviour
Random split halves	.969	.890	.999	.976	.999	.976
Gender	---[b]	.976	.981	.973	.999	.923
Functional ability	.982	.999	.978	.992	.870	.988
Employment (open v. supported and job seekers	.995	.998	.965	.981	.998	.999
Employment (open v. supported)	.973	.996	.999	.988	.999	.999

a   For factors to be considered congruent the coefficient of congruence should be equal to or greater than .940.
b   The dashed lines indicate that a coefficient of congruence cannot be calculated in these instances, as no items from the relevant factor load on the same factor when the sample is dichotomised. That is, the items variously load on other factors.

The factor stability for the five-factor iteration is reported in Table 4.28. For four of the five splits it is not possible to calculate a coefficient of congruence for the *cognition and skill development* factor, indicating that the scores obtained for this factor may not reflect the same underlying construct. However, the other factors appear to be stable, with only one of the calculable coefficients of congruence being below .940: that being the coefficient of congruence for the *vocational suitability* factor when the sample is split by functional ability.

That both the five-factor and seven-factor FAI solutions have several occasions when it is not

---

[56] The sample sizes for each of the dichotomisations can be seen in Table 4.1, which lists the demographic details for the FAI sample.

possible to calculate a coefficient of congruence suggests that these are not well specified solutions. This occurs, even the case for five-factor solution, even though it is the only solution with all factors reporting Cronbach alpha scores in excess of .70. The lack of factor stability for both the five-factor and seven-factor solutions means that these solutions cannot be used.

Table 4.28: Factor stability test: Coefficients of congruence for five-factor FAI[a]

| | Functional Assessment Inventory Factors | | | | |
	Cognition and skill development	Communication	Upper functional ability	Vocational suitability	Adaptive behaviour
Random split halves	---[b]	.994	.995	.995	.972
Gender	---	.977	.981	.955	.977
Functional ability	.999	.992	.971	.933	.968
Employment (open v. supported and job seekers	---	.952	.998	.987	.974
Employment (open v. supported)	---	.984	.998	.999	.973

a   For factors to be considered congruent the coefficient of congruence should be equal to or greater than .940.
b   The dashed lines indicate that a coefficient of congruence cannot be calculated in these instances, as no items from the relevant factor load on the same factor when the sample is dichotomised. That is, the items variously load on other factors.

4.3.4 Summary of FAI
The six-factor solution is the one used hereafter in this research, given that it has the best factor stability, a high overall Cronbach alpha, and acceptable Cronbach alpha scores for all factors.[57] That I find the six-factor solution to be the best specified solution is consistent with the findings of Neath *et al.* (1997), and brings into doubt the assertions of Crew and Athelstan (1984) that the seven-factor solution is well specified. However, it should also be noted that the six-factor solution I derive is substantially different to the one that Crew and Athelstan (1984) derived.
In summary, the six-factor FAI (shown in Table 4.17) used hereafter in this thesis contains the following six factors, with the stated number of questions and theoretical ranges also noted:
1. *Cognition and skill development*, four questions, with a theoretical range of 0 to 12;
2. *Sensory ability*, two questions with a theoretical range of 0 to 6;
3. *Communication*, two questions with a theoretical range of 0 to 6;
4. *Upper functional ability*, two questions with a theoretical range of 0 to 6;
5. *Vocational suitability*, four questions with a theoretical range of 0 to 12; and
6. *Adaptive behaviour*, six questions with a theoretical range of 0 to 18.

4.4 Job Satisfaction
As mentioned in Chapter 3 (Research Method), job satisfaction is determined using a revised version of the Smith *et al.* (1969) Job Description Index (JDI). Responses to *yes*, *no*, and *not sure* questions are sought during interviews with people with intellectual disabilities. Responses are then scored in the standard JDI fashion of 3 for *yes*, 1 for *not sure*, and 0 for *no* (scored in reverse order for negatively phrased questions).[58] Of the 134 participants interviewed 118 were employed and, as

---

[57] The reason why the Cronbach alpha score of .562 for the *sensory ability* may not be of such great concern as would initially appear (given it is below .70) has previously been discussed in Section 4.3.1.1.1 (Further Refinement of the Seven-Factor FAI Solution).
[58] Smith *et al.* (1969) stated that the reason for scoring 3 (yes), 1 (not sure), and 0 (no) (scored in reverse order for negatively phrased questions) was that their pilot-testing revealed that *not sure* was not a mid-point between *yes* and *no*, but closer to a *no* response than to a *yes* response. Therefore, it was not appropriate to score 2 (yes), 1 (not sure), and 0 (no). This is confirmed by their psychometric assessments of the JDI.
To confirm the appropriateness of the scoring technique that Smith *et al.* (1969) espoused, I conduct my own analysis of scoring in the *more traditional* 2 (yes), 1 (not sure), 0 (no) (scored in reverse order for negatively phrased questions) format. However, as per Smith *et al.* (1969), I find that my JSQ factors better (the factors

such, only these 118 participants completed the JSQ. Table 4.29 shows the demographics of participants who completed the JSQ.

While the Smith *et al.* (1969) questionnaire, developed for people without a disability, has undergone extensive psychometric analysis (for example Roznowski 1989; Wu and Watkins 1994; Kinicki *et al.* 2002), neither the initial modified version for people with intellectual disability by Seltzer and Seltzer (1978), nor the subsequent modification by Barlow and Kirby (1991) have undergone extensive validation. Seltzer (1984), who reported a subset of the analysis from Seltzer and Seltzer (1984), reported that the Cronbach alpha for their modified JDI was .80. However, she does not report Cronbach alpha's for the five sub-scales. Barlow and Kirby (1991) do not report any internal reliability statistics for their version of the modified JDI. As stated in Chapter 3 (Research Method), some of the modifications to transform the original questionnaire, which was developed for people without intellectual disabilities, to one suitable for people with intellectual disabilities, are substantial. Consequently, factor analysis is initially conducted not as a confirmatory technique, but to determine the number of factors, and the questions within each of these factors.

Table 4.29: Demographic information for the JSQ

	Number	Percentage
Gender:		
Female	45	38.14
Male	73	61.86
Employment:		
Open employment	65	55.08
Supported employment	53	44.92
Functional ability[59]:		
Low (FAI 24 to 65)	60	50.85
High (FAI 1 to 23)	58	49.15

4.4.1 Questionnaire Refinement

The Bartlett test of sphericity was significant (χ^2 (595, n = 118) = 1,309.287, $p \leq .001$) and the Kaiser-Meyer-Okin measure of sampling was greater than .6 (KMO = .661), which indicated that a factor analysis could be conducted on the sample.

Given that the Barlow and Kirby (1991) derivation of the Smith *et al.* (1969) questionnaire has five sections[60] the sample might be expected to form five factors. However, when relating questions that formed the Barlow and Kirby (1991) derivation of the JDI back to Smith *et al.* (1969) they relate to only four of the five sections. Barlow and Kirby (1991) do not to include any questions relating to the *promotions* section in their questionnaire. Therefore, the job satisfaction questions might be expected to form four factors. Though, the addition by Barlow and Kirby (1991) of their own

---

make more theoretical sense), reports higher Cronbach alpha scores, and has a higher degree of factor stability when scored 3 for *yes*, 1 for *not sure*, and 0 for *no* (scored in reverse order for negatively phrased questions).

[59] As noted before, the FAI is scored on 30 behaviourally anchored questions assessing a person's functional ability on a four point scale from 0 (no significant impairment) to 3 (severe impairment). Consequently, the higher the FAI, the lower a person's functional work ability. A low functional ability was defined as a FAI score of 24 or greater, with a high functional ability defined as a FAI score of less than 24. The median of 24 was selected as the mid-point since there were no generally accepted ranges for the FAI that defined participants with intellectual disabilities as having either a high functional ability or low functional ability.

[60] The word *sections* is used in this instance, as opposed to factor, as Barlow and Kirby (1991) do not conduct factor analysis to justify the questions that form each section.

questions may have added factors.

The scree plot is inconclusive and appears to reveal that either three or seven factors may be appropriate.[61] However, as Tabachnick and Fidell (2001) noted, the scree plot is not exact when the sample is not as large as statistically desirable. In these instances the scree plot may only be accurate to within one or two factors. Also, given it was thought that due to the number of sections in the Seltzer and Seltzer (1978) and Barlow and Kirby (1991) questionnaires there may be either four or five factors, principal axis factor analysis with varimax rotation is conducted specifying three, four, five, six, and seven factors. As noted in Section 4.2.1 (Factor Analysis), factor correlation matrices using oblique rotations revealed on nearly all occasions the JSQ factors have a correlation of below .30; that is, they are not statistically significantly correlated. Consequently, Tabachnick and Fidell (2001) suggested that only the results of the factor solution with varimax rotation be reported due to the disadvantages of interpreting, describing and reporting oblique rotation results.[62]

The factor solutions are then assessed to determine which is the most appropriate. An initial review of the factor solutions reveals that the six and seven factor solutions can be discarded as both result in items clustering into factors that do not make theoretical sense. Additionally, both factor solutions result in one very large factor with more than half of the questions. There are also numerous questions with multiple loadings and all but the primary factor in both solutions comprise items with low factor loadings. The highest factor loading in either the six or seven factor solution outside the primary factor is .521. Also, if questions with a factor loading of below .32 are excluded (Tabachnick and Fidell 2001), both factor solutions result in singlets. All of the above limitations indicated that neither the six-factor or seven-factor solutions are well specified.

The three-factor solution, while better specified than the six-factor and seven-factor solutions, still has the problem of factors that do not make theoretical sense. The three-factor solution has a large primary factor with 17 questions having a factor loading greater than .32, with a variety of questions covering a range of topics, such as work conditions, pay, and work task. The second factor also contains questions from a variety of areas, such as work conditions, social aspects of work, and supervision. However, the third factor of the three-factor solution does make theoretical sense, containing only questions relating to the social aspects of work-life.

A review of the four-factor solution reveals the solution to be well specified with factors that make theoretical sense. The 35 items factor into four broad groupings that make theoretical sense once items with low factor loading are excluded. These four groups are termed *work and staff*, *task*, *pay*, and *social*.

The five-factor solution, while making more theoretical sense than the three-factor, six-factor and seven-factor solutions, still has instances of factors with questions that focus on different aspects of job satisfaction loading on the same factor. This is especially apparent with questions focusing on physical conditions, supervisory conditions, and task, loading on the first two factors, but not on factors that would make theoretical sense. Interestingly, all the questions relating to pay load on a single factor. The questions relating to the social aspect of work load exclusively on the last two factors, though it is not readily apparent as to which aspects of the work social-life these two factors capture. As such, the five-factor solution is also discarded, since the factor loadings do not make theoretical sense.[63]

---

[61] The point of flattening out (inflection point) could be interpreted as either three or seven.

[62] As noted in Section 4.2.1 (Factor Analysis) the results using oblique rotation do not vary greatly.

[63] As per the four-factor solution (the derivation of which I describe in the following paragraphs) the five-factor solution is examined and all questions with a loading of below .32 are removed. A new principal axis factor analysis with varimax rotation specifying five factors is then conducted and again all questions with a loading of below .32 are removed. This is repeated until an iteration containing only questions with factor

Given the above discussion, the only factor solution that makes theoretical sense is the four-factor solution. Comparisons are not made with the Barlow and Kirby (1991) questionnaire at this stage, given that their questionnaire did not undergo any psychometric evaluation and no justifications were provided for the questions that formed each section. However, for purposes of comparison, similarities and differences between my final JSQ and their questionnaire are noted later. It is not possible to compare factors of my JSQ with the Seltzer and Seltzer (1978) questionnaire, given the number of new questions added by Barlow and Kirby (1991). As such, I shall now describe the derivation of the final JSQ and the selection of the final set of questions that form this four-factor questionnaire.

Table 3.2 lists the questions comprising the job satisfaction questionnaire used in this thesis. As just described above the factor solution was examined to see whether it made broad theoretical sense. Having established that the four-factor solution makes theoretical sense, questions with factor loadings below .32 are omitted (Tabachnick and Fidell 2001). Items with multiple loadings are not omitted at this stage.[64] This results in the omission of the following six questions:

1.2   Is it a nice building to work in?
2.5   Do you have enough to do at work?
4.3   Do you sometimes have lunch with the people you work with?
4.5   Do you see them [work people] (socially) after work?
5.2   Does he/she [supervisor] let you work by yourself enough?
5.5   If you had a personal problem would he/she [supervisor] help you?

A principal axis factor analysis specifying four factors with varimax rotation is then conducted again to assess how the questions now factor with the omission of above listed questions. This new factor solution, shown in Table 4.30, still makes theoretical sense and questions on all factors have loadings greater than .32.

Given that responses are scored 3 (yes), 1 (not sure), and 0 (no) (scored in reverse order for negatively phrased questions), the above solution results in a theoretical scale range for the JSQ of $0 - 87$. Each of the factors has the following theoretical range: *work and staff*, $0 - 27$; *task*, $0 - 24$; *pay*, $0 - 18$; and *social*, $0 - 18$.

4.4.2 Internal Reliability of the Derived JSQ Scores

Having arrived at a factor solution for the JSQ, the internal reliability of the four factors are assessed using Cronbach alpha coefficients, which are reported in Table 4.31. As evident from Table 4.31, the factors *work and staff*, *task*, and *pay* all have a satisfactory degree of internally reliability, with alphas above .70 (Hair *et al.* 1995; Nunnally 1978). Although the reliability of the overall job satisfaction instrument is very good, with a Cronbach alpha coefficient of .840, the slightly low Cronbach alpha for the *social* factor (.624) is of potential concern. However, as Pallant (2001) noted, it is common for scales with less than ten items, as is the case for each factor, to report low Cronbach alpha scores.[65] This highlights the good level of internal reliability for the *work and staff*, *task*, and *pay* factors, given that all factors have less than ten questions, yet report

---

loadings above .32 is obtained. This factor solution is then examined to see if it makes theoretical sense. Similar to the initial five-factor solution, it has questions focusing on different aspects of job satisfaction loading on the same factor, that is, it does not make theoretical sense.

[64] This approach is taken since, for the items that do have multiple loadings above .32, one loading is substantially greater than the other. Once the refined JSQ solution is derived, only one multiple weighting remains. The question is retained in the factor which with the highest loading due to theoretical support (Hair *et al.* 1995), plus an analysis of the Cronbach alpha scores when the item is placed in the alternate factor always reveals a reduced Cronbach alpha score for that factor, as well as the factor to which the item has the highest loading.

[65] Pallant (2001) gave an example of .5.

Cronbach alphas in excess of .70. It may also suggest that the reported Cronbach alpha score for the *social* factor should not be cause for great concern.

The good internal reliability of the factors of the JSQ can be confirmed by looking at the effect on the Cronbach alphas if any of the items are deleted in turn, which are reported in Tables 4.32 (a), (b), (c), and (d). In no instances would the omission of any question cause a significant increase in the Cronbach alphas of any of the four factors,[66] indicating that each question contributes to the measurement of the respective factors. The corrected item-total correlations on all occasions exceed .30, which indicates acceptable scale unidimensionality (de Vaus 1995).

Table 4.30: Factor loadings of the JSQ used

Question number	Question	Factor loadings
Factor 1: Work and Staff		
1.1	Do you like the place where you work?	.758
5.4	Does he/she [supervisor] praise you when you do a good job?	.570
5.7	Does your supervisor help you to learn new work skills?	.481
5.6	Do you think that he/she [supervisor] respects (understands) you?	.478
5.1	Does your supervisor tell you honestly what he/she thinks about your work?	.475
2.1	Do you think your work is interesting?	.451
5.3	Is he/she [supervisor] there when you need help with your work?	.444
1.3	Is it a nice place to work?	.412
2.3	Does your work make you feel that you are doing something important?	.357
Factor 2: Task		
1.6	Do the days seem very long, like they will never end, when you are working?	.696
2.4	Is your work boring?	.599
2.6	Would you rather be doing a different type of work?	.498
1.5	Is it too hot/cold, noisy there [where you work]?	.452
1.7	Would you rather be working in a different section?	.437
1.4	Do you have to stand up/sit down too much while you work?	.377
2.7	Do you have to push yourself very hard?	.355
2.2	Do you think your work is too easy?	.352
Factor 3: Pay		
3.5	Does your pay let you buy special things when you want to?	.562
3.6	Do you think that you are paid very well?	.557
3.1	Is your pay too little to let you make ends meet?	.524
3.2	Do you think you should be paid more for what you do?	.480
3.4	Do you ever worry that the amount of your pay will change from week to week?	.475
3.3	Do you think that you get paid less than you are worth?	.445
Factor 4: Social		
4.2	Is it hard to meet people at work?	.572
4.8	Do the people you work with respect (understand) you?	.478
4.1	Do you like the people you work with?	.469
4.6	Would you rather be working with different people?	.427
4.7	Would the people at work help you if you had a problem?	.441
4.4	Do they talk to you very much?	.355

---

[66] On only one occasion would the omission of a question cause an increase of the Cronbach alpha and on that occasion it only results in an improvement of .002 (question 2.3 of the *work and staff* factor). This question is not omitted first, because the resultant increase in the Cronbach alpha is only marginal, and second, the question reports a corrected item-total correlation in excess of .3, indicating that the question is measuring the same underlying concept as the rest of the questions comprising the factor.

4.4.3 Factor Stability of the Derived JSQ

An analysis is now conducted to determine the stability of the four-factor solution. The factor stability analysis of the JSQ is assessed by splitting the sample on the basis of random selection, gender, level of functional work ability (as measured by the FAI[67]), and by employment type (open employment versus supported employment).[68]

Table 4.31: Cronbach alpha scores for the JSQ

	Cronbach alpha
Factor:	
Work and staff	.747
Task	.744
Pay	.705
Social	.624
Overall questionnaire	.840

The coefficients of congruence for the four factors are shown in Table 4.33. As can be seen from Table 4.33, when it was possible to calculate a coefficient of congruence it was above .940 on all except one occasion. This occasion was for the *social* factor when dichotomised by employment type (open versus supported). Two dichotomies for the *social* factor result in an inability to calculate a coefficient of congruence due to items from this factor not loading on similar factors. Given that only one of the four dichotomies of this factor result in an acceptable coefficient of congruence (in excess of .940), it is apparent that the *social* factor is not well specified. On one occasion a coefficient of congruence could not be calculated for the *task* factor, due to questions loading on different factors. However, in all other cases the coefficient of congruence exceeds .940. Both the *work and staff* and *pay* factors appear to be well specified with all dichotomies resulting in coefficients of congruence in excess of .940.

The above suggests that the *work and staff* and *pay* factor scores definitely measure consistent constructs. Although a coefficient of congruence cannot be calculated on one occasion for the *task* factor, given that this factor reports good levels of congruence (in excess of .940) for the three other dichotomies further investigation is warranted on this factor's stability. The three factors of *work and staff*, *task*, and *pay* also produce scores that are reliable, as evidenced by their acceptable Cronbach alpha scores (in excess of .700).

Table 4.32(a): Analysis of scale reliability and unidimensionality of the *work and staff* factor of the JSQ

Question	Mean	Std deviation	Corrected item-total correlation	Alpha if item deleted
1.1	2.788	.749	.640	.695
1.3	2.890	.536	.342	.739
2.1	2.619	.951	.422	.725
2.3	2.398	1.133	.319	.749
5.1	2.729	.792	.438	.723
5.3	2.712	.838	.433	.723
5.4	2.737	.831	.502	.713
5.6	2.695	.822.	.401	.728
5.7	2.348	1.194	.452	.724

Alpha for *work and staff* factor = .747

---

[67] The FAI is dichotomised around the median. The median is selected as the mid-point since there are no generally accepted ranges that define participants with intellectual disabilities as having either high functional work ability or low functional work ability.

[68] Refer to Section 4.2.2 (Reliability Analysis) for a more detailed explanation on the technique of factor stability analysis.

Table 4.32(b): Analysis of scale reliability and unidimensionality of the *task* factor of the JSQ

Item	Mean	Std deviation	Corrected item-total correlation	Alpha if item deleted
1.4	2.017	1.408	.330	.739
1.5	1.890	1.431	.409	.724
1.6	2.051	1.352	.502	.706
1.7	1.907	1.377	.476	.711
2.2	1.949	1.407	.327	.739
2.4	2.297	1.249	.588	.692
2.6	1.805	1.404	.550	.696
2.7	2.017	1.371	.354	.734

Alpha for *task* factor = .744

Table 4.32(c): Analysis of scale reliability and unidimensionality of the *pay* factor of the JSQ

Item	Mean	Std deviation	Corrected item-total correlation	Alpha if item deleted
3.1	1.627	1.466	.493	.646
3.2	1.153	1.424	.511	.640
3.3	1.398	1.433	.401	.677
3.4	2.229	1.284	.421	.670
3.5	2.610	.996	.377	.684
3.6	2.102	1.349	.422	.680

Alpha for *pay* factor = .705

Table 4.32(d): Analysis of scale reliability and unidimensionality of the *social* factor of the JSQ

Item	Mean	Std deviation	Corrected item-total correlation	Alpha if item deleted
4.1	2.915	.464	.450	.585
4.2	2.280	1.212	.380	.575
4.4	2.670	.943	.328	.590
4.6	2.195	1.249	.370	.582
4.7	2.602	.907	.338	.586
4.8	2.695	.790	.421	.561

Alpha for *social* factor = .624

Table 4.33: Factor stability test: Coefficients of congruence for four-factor job satisfaction solution[a]

	Job Satisfaction Factors			
	Work & staff	Task	Pay	Social
Random split halves	.983	.964	.951	---[b]
Gender	.996	.940	.992	---
Functional ability	.977	---	.975	.991
Employment (open v. supported)	.977	.998	.969	.302

a   For factors to be considered congruent the coefficient of congruence should be equal to or greater than .940.

b   The dashed lines indicate that a coefficient of congruence cannot be calculated in these instances, as no items from the relevant factor load on the same factor when the sample is dichotomised. That is, the items variously load on other factors.

The *social* factor is definitely not congruent and caution should be exercised in placing too much emphasis on this factor's scores. It is also the only factor that does not report an acceptable Cronbach alpha coefficient (α = .624).[69] However, the very good Cronbach alpha score for the overall instrument (.840) indicates the reliability of scores of the overall instrument. As noted in discussion in the preceding section on factor stability of the FAI, the lack of stability apparent for

---

[69] As noted previously the cause for the one factor having a Cronbach alpha of below .700 may be due to having less than 10 questions (Pallant 2001).

the *social* factor and the one instance where a coefficient of congruence cannot be calculated for the *task* factor could be due to a too small sample size, given the entire sample pertaining to the job satisfaction analysis was 118. When this sample is dichotomised it resulted in factor analyses being conducted on samples that were generally considered too small to conduct reliable factor analyses.[70]

However, given concern over the factor stability of the *social* factor and its slightly low Cronbach alpha score, the total JSQ score is reported, both including and excluding this factor. Questions comprising the *social* factor have been retained in calculating the total JSQ score given that the questions in this factor contribute to the overall JSQ, as evidenced by the fact that the Cronbach alpha score for the overall questionnaire does not increase by the omission of these questions. However, to further validate the results I also consider it appropriate to calculate the total JSQ score, omitting the questions that comprise the *social* factor.

To confirm that omitting the factor score does not affect the factor structure of the other three factors, further principal axis factor analysis with varimax rotation is conducted on the remaining 23 questions (excluding the six questions relating to the *social* factor). Although the results are not reported, the remaining 23 questions factor into the three appropriate factors of *work and staff*, *task*, and *pay*. The Cronbach alpha for the JSQ, excluding the *social* factor, is also good at .819. As such, confidence can be placed on the results for the total JSQ score, excluding the *social* factor.

4.4.4 Comparison of JSQ to the Barlow and Kirby (1991) Questionnaire
Table 4.34 shows a comparison of the four-factor solution for the JSQ used in this thesis with the Barlow and Kirby (1991) questionnaire from which it has been developed. Looking initially at the similarities between the two questionnaires, the *pay* factor of the JSQ comprises of the same six questions as the Barlow and Kirby (1991) *pay* section. The six questions that form the *social* factor of the JSQ all come from the *social* factor of the Barlow and Kirby (1991) questionnaire. However, the JSQ *social* factor does not include questions 4.3 (do you sometimes have lunch with the people you work with?) and 4.5 (do you see them [people you work with] (socially) after work?). Both questions are omitted from the JSQ due to having factor loadings below .32.

The JSQ *task* factor comprises of questions from the *physical* and *task* sections of the Barlow and Kirby (1991) questionnaire. Questions 2.2 (do you think your work is too easy?), 2.4 (Is your work boring?), 2.6 (would you rather be doing a different type of work?), and 2.7 (do you have to push yourself very hard?) are common to both questionnaires' *task* domain. The other four questions that form the JSQ *task* factor come from the *physical* section of the Barlow and Kirby (1991) questionnaire; these are 1.4 (do you have to stand up/sit down too much while you work?), 1.5 (is it too hot/cold, noisy there [work]?), 1.6 (do the days seem very long, like they will never end, when you are working?), and 1.7 (would you rather be working in a different section?). It is not hard to see how responses to each of these questions could relate to the task that a participant is performing and, as such, their loading on this factor is considered to make sense.

Five of the nine questions that form the JSQ *work and staff* factor come from the *staff* section of the Barlow and Kirby (1991) questionnaire; the five questions are 5.1 (does your supervisor tell you honestly what he/she thinks about your work?), 5.3 (is he/she [your supervisor] there when you need help with your work?), 5.4 (does he/she [your supervisor] praise you when you do a good job?), 5,6 (do you think that he/she [your supervisor] respects (understands) you?), and 5.7 (does your supervisor help you to learn new work skills?). Two of the remaining four questions come from the *physical* section of the Barlow and Kirby (1991) questionnaire; being questions 1.1 (do you like the place where you work?) and 1.3 (is it a nice place to work?). The other two questions

---

[70] The sample sizes that resulted from the various dichotomies are: gender - 45 females and 73 males; employment - 68 participants in open employment and 50 participants in supported employment; and functional ability - 60 participants with low functional ability and 58 participants with high functional ability.

come from Jiranek and Kirby's (1990) *task* section; 2.1 (do you think your work is interesting?) and 2.3 (does your work make you feel that you are doing something important?). Although the questions that form the *work and staff* factor of the JSQ come from three different sections of the Barlow and Kirby (1991) questionnaire, the loading of each question on this factor is seen to make theoretical sense, given that their association with the underlying work and staff (supervisor) is readily apparent.

Table 4.34: Comparison of Barlow and Kirby (1991) five-section questionnaire to four-factor JSQ

Item		Barlow & Kirby (1991) section	JSQ factor
1.1	Do you like the place where you work?	Physical	Work & staff
1.2	Is it a nice building to work in?	Physical	---
1.3	Is it a nice place to work?	Physical	Work & staff
1.4	Do you have to stand up/sit down too much while you work?	Physical	Task
1.5	Is it too hot/cold, noisy there?	Physical	Task
1.6	Do the days seem very long, like they will never end, when you are working?	Physical	Task
1.7	Would you rather be working in a different section?	Physical	Task
2.1	Do you think your work is interesting?	Task	Work & staff
2.2	Do you think your work is too easy?	Task	Task
2.3	Does your work make you feel that you are doing something important?	Task	Work & staff
2.4	Is your work boring?	Task	Task
2.5	Do you have enough to do at work?	Task	---
2.6	Would you rather be doing a different type of work?	Task	Task
2.7	Do you have to push yourself very hard?	Task	Task
3.1	Is your pay too little to let you make ends meet?	Pay	Pay
3.2	Do you think you should be paid more for what you do?	Pay	Pay
3.3	Do you think that you get paid less than you are worth?	Pay	Pay
3.4	Do you ever worry that the amount of your pay will change from week to week?	Pay	Pay
3.5	Does your pay let you buy special things when you want to?	Pay	Pay
3.6	Do you think that you are paid very well?	Pay	Pay
4.1	Do you like the people you work with?	Social	Social
4.2	Is it hard to meet people at work?	Social	Social
4.3	Do you sometimes have lunch with the people you work with?	Social	---
4.4	Do they talk to you very much?	Social	Social
4.5	Do you see them (socially) after work?	Social	---
4.6	Would you rather be working with different people?	Social	Social
4.7	Would the people at work help you if you had a problem?	Social	Social
4.8	Do the people you work with respect (understand) you?	Social	Social
5.1	Does your supervisor tell you honestly what he/she thinks about your work?	Staff	Work & staff
5.2	Does he/she let you work by yourself enough?	Staff	---
5.3	Is he/she there when you need help with your work?	Staff	Work & staff
5.4	Does he/she praise you when you do a good job?	Staff	Work & staff
5.5	If you had a personal problem would he/she help you?	Staff	---
5.6	Do you think that he/she respects (understands) you?	Staff	Work & staff
5.7	Does your supervisor help you to learn new work skills?	Staff	Work & staff

It can be seen from the above discussion that the *pay* and *social* factors of the JSQ are similar to the respective sections of the Barlow and Kirby (1991) questionnaire; however, the questions forming the other two factors of the JSQ, *work and staff* and *task* are different from all of the Barlow and Kirby (1991) sections. Given that Barlow and Kirby (1991) neither conduct factor analysis on their questions, nor provide any theoretical justifications for their groupings, the differences between the JSQ and their questionnaire are not unexpected.

4.4.5 Summary of JSQ

The JSQ (shown in Table 4.30) developed and used in this thesis contains the following four factors, with the stated number of questions and theoretical ranges noted also:

1. *Work and staff,* nine questions, with a theoretical range of 0 to 27;
2. *Task*, eight questions with a theoretical range of 0 to 24;
3. *Pay*, six questions with a theoretical range of 0 to 18; and
4. *Social*, six questions with a theoretical range of 0 to 18.

To increase the meaningfulness of the reported numbers for each of the four factors, they are converted into a percentage figure. For example, instead of reporting a figure of 22 for the *work and staff* factor the figure reported is 81.48 percent (22/27).

Total job satisfaction for a participant is the average of the four factors and not the summation of the scores for each question. Each factor is equally weighted, as I have no theoretical justification to assume that any of the factors contribute to a greater or lesser extent than any other to total job satisfaction. Given the poor reliability of the *social* factor scores, total job satisfaction is also calculated excluding this factor. The total is calculated by averaging the scores for the remaining three factors.

4.5 Quality of Life Questionnaire

As stated in Chapter 3 (Research Method), the questionnaire I use in this thesis to measure a person's quality of life is the Schalock and Keith (1993) QOL.Q. The questionnaire is administered by an interviewer asking the interviewee 40 questions. For each question, the interviewee selects one of three possible responses provided by the interviewer. The responses are then scored from 1 (low) to 3 (high), giving the QOL.Q a theoretical range of 40 to 120. Of the 134 participants interviewed there are 130 useable responses[71] to the QOL.Q, which are used in this section to determine the psychometric properties of the QOL.Q. Table 4.34 shows the demographic details of the 130 participants.

As Cummins (2000a) noted, relatively little psychometric research has been conducted on any of the quality of life instruments developed for people with intellectual disabilities. In relation to the QOL.Q, the exceptions are Eggleton *et al.* (1999) and Kober and Eggleton (2002), who undertook a factor analysis and reported the internal reliability of the questionnaire and each of its factors; Rapley *et al.* (1998), who investigated the correlation between the QOL.Q scores between two proxy respondents and between proxy respondents and clients; Rapley and Lobley (1995), who conducted a replication of Schalock and Keith's (1993) factor analysis; and Kober and Eggleton (2002), who investigated the factor stability of the QOL.Q.

The Bartlett test of sphericity is significant (χ^2 (780, n= 130) = 1,617.43, $p \leq .001$) and the Kaiser-Meyer-Okin measure of sampling is greater than .6 (KMO = .666), which indicate that it is possible to conduct a factor analysis on the sample. The scree test suggests that four factors are appropriate. Consequently, a principal axis factor analysis with varimax rotation specifying four factors is conducted. As noted in Section 4.2.1 (Factor Analysis) factor correlation matrices using oblique rotations reveal that on nearly all occasions the QOL.Q factors are uncorrelated (correlation of below .30). Consequently, following the suggestion of Tabachnick and Fidell (2001), the results using varimax rotation are reported, due to the greater ease of interpreting, describing and reporting them.[72]

---

[71] The four interviews that are not used are due to interviewees acquiescing.
[72] As noted in Section 4.2.1 (Factor Analysis) the results using oblique rotation do not vary greatly.

Table 4.34: Demographic information for the QOL.Q

	Number	Percentage
Gender:		
Female	49	38
Male	81	62
Employment:		
Open employment	68	52
Supported employment	53	41
Job seeker[73]	9	7
Functional ability:[74]		
Low (FAI 24 to 65)	63	49
High (FAI 1 to 23)	67	51

The resultant factor structure, shown in Table 4.35, is similar to the Schalock and Keith (1993) factor structure with only five of the 40 questions (3, 12, 29, 33, and 39) failing to load on the original Schalock and Keith (1993) QOL.Q factors. Interestingly, four of these five questions (12, 29, 33, and 39) now load on the first factor, which Shalock and Keith (1993) called *satisfaction*; namely question 12 (do you feel your job or other daily activity is worthwhile and relevant to either yourself or others?), which is from the Schalock and Keith (1993) *satisfaction* factor; question 29 (are there people living with you who sometimes hurt you, pester you, scare you, or make you angry?), which is from the Schalock and Keith (1993) *empowerment/independence* factor; and questions 33 (do you worry about what people expect of you?) and 39 (how do your neighbours treat you?), both of which are from the Schalock and Keith (1993) factor *social belonging/community integration*. Due to the loading of these four questions on this factor, the factor is relabelled *life satisfaction and domestic contentment* in Table 4.22, consonant with the title given to the factor by Rapley and Lobley (1995) and subsequently used by Kober and Eggleton (2002). With the addition of these four questions the new heading of *life satisfaction and domestic contentment* is believed to reflect more accurately the content of the questions. The addition of these four items to the factor makes theoretical sense as it is apparent how the items being questioned could affect a person's life satisfaction and domestic contentment.

The loading of question 3 (compared with others, are you better off, about the same, or less well off?), which is from the Schalock and Keith (1993) *satisfaction* factor, on the *empowerment/independence* factor is unexpected, as how well-off a person feels is generally not thought of relating to feelings of empowerment and independence. However, it is possible to see how a person's feelings of how well-off they are compared to others would affect their overall feelings of empowerment and independence. Given that question 3 loads onto this factor, it would appear that it is feelings of empowerment/independence on which participants are reflecting in answering this question. It is possible that individuals who felt better off than others also felt a greater overall level of empowerment/independence, with the converse also being true. Thus the loading of question 3 on the *empowerment/independence* factor is considered to make theoretical sense.

---

[73] As noted in Section 4.3 (Functional Assessment Inventory), since in this thesis I am concerned with investigating the effectiveness of different methods of employment for people with intellectual disabilities, Chapter 6 (Results and Discussion) uses the responses only from employed participants. However, as job seekers were also unintentionally interviewed the responses from these participants are also used in validating the QOL.Q. The reason for their use is to increase sample size.

[74] A low functional ability is defined as a FAI score of 24 or greater, with a high functional ability defined as a FAI score of less than 23. The median of 23 is selected as the mid-point since there are no generally accepted ranges for the FAI that define participants with intellectual disabilities as having either a high functional ability or low functional ability.

Table 4.35: Factor loadings for the QOL.Q

Factor 1:	Life satisfaction and domestic contentment[a]	Loading
4	Are most of the things that happen to you rewarding, acceptable, or disappointing?	.485
9	How successful do you think you are, compared to others?	.458
12	Do you feel your job or other daily activity is worthwhile and relevant to either yourself or others?	.449
2	How much fun and enjoyment do you get out of life?	.444
8	Do you ever feel out of place in social situations?	.443
5	How satisfied are you with your current home or living arrangement?	.436
39	How do your neighbours treat you?	.368
29	Are there people living with you who sometimes hurt you, pester you, scare you, or make you angry?	.329
1	Overall, would you say that life brings out the best in you, treats you like everybody else, or doesn't give you a chance?	.317
10[b]	What about your family members? Do they make you feel an important part of the family, sometimes a part of the family, or like an outsider?	.315
7	How many times per month do you feel lonely?	.298
33	Do you worry about what people expect of you?	-.188
6	Do you have more or fewer problems than other people?	.150
Factor 2:	Competence/Productivity	
19	How satisfied are you with the benefits you receive at the workplace?	.809
13	How good do you feel you are at your job?	.763
18	Does your job provide you with enough money to buy the things you want?	.695
15	How satisfied are you with the skills and experience you have gained or are gaining from your job?	.670
14	How do people treat you on your job?	.655
17	Do you feel you receive fair pay for you work?	.519
20	How closely supervised are you on your job?	.443
16	Are you learning skills that will help you get a different or better job? What are these skills?	.423
11[b]	How well did your educational or training programme prepare you for what you are doing now?	.148
Factor 3:	Empowerment/Independence	
23	How do you use health care facilities (doctor, dentist, etc.)?	.723
28	Do you have a guardian?	.661
22	Who decides how to spend your money?	.575
24	How much control do you have over things you do every day, like going to bed, eating, and what you do for fun?	.574
30	Overall, would you say that your life is free, somewhat planned for you, or that you cannot usually do what you want?	.501
25	When can friends visit your home?	.488
3	Compared with others, are you better off, about the same, or less well off?	.305
26	Do you have a key to your home?	.268
21	How did you decide to do the job or other daily activities you do now?	.178
27[b]	May you have a pet if you want?	.101
Factor 4:	Social belonging/Community integration	
32	How satisfied are you with the clubs or organisations (including church or other religious activities) to which you belong?	.717
37	Do you participate actively in those recreational activities?	.708
36	How often do you attend recreational activities (homes, parties, dances, concerts, plays) in your community?	.631
31	How many civic or community clubs or organisations (including church or other religious activities) do you belong to?	.584
38	What about opportunities for dating or marriage?	.369
34[b]	How many times per week do you talk to (or associate with) your neighbours, either in the yard or in their home?	.235
40[b]	Overall, would you say that your life is very worthwhile, okay, or useless?	.119
35	Do you have friends over to visit your home?	.116

a   Rapley and Lobley's (1995) factor heading.
b   This item loads weakly on two factors. It is placed in this factor due to theoretical support (Hair et al. 1995).

In comparing the above factor analysis with those of Rapley and Lobley (1995) and Kober and Eggleton (2002), it is interesting to note that in both Rapley and Lobley (1995) and Kober and Eggleton (2002) question 29 (are there people living with you who sometimes hurt you, pester you, scare you, or make you angry?), from Schalock and Keith's (1993) *empowerment/independence* factor, loads on the *life satisfaction and domestic contentment* factor. Questions 33 (do you worry about what people expect of you?) and 39 (how do your neighbours treat you?) also load onto the *life satisfaction and domestic contentment* factor in Kober and Eggleton (2002), but not in Rapley and Lobley (1995), who found these two questions loaded consistent with Schalock and Keith (1993) on the *social belonging/community integration* factor.

The other divergences in loadings compared with the original Schalock and Keith (1993) QOL.Q (questions 3 and 12) differ from those reported in Rapley and Lobley (1995) and Kober and Eggleton (2002). In this thesis, question 12 (do you feel your job or other daily activity is worthwhile and relevant to either yourself or others?) loads on the *life satisfaction and domestic contentment* factor. However, Kober and Eggleton (2002) found this question to load consistent with Schalock and Keith (1993) on the *competence/productivity* factor, while Rapley and Lobley (1995) found question 12 to load on their *empowerment/independence* factor. Question 3 (compared to others, are you better off, about the same, or less well off?) from the Schalock and Keith (1993) *satisfaction* factor, which loads on the *empowerment/independence* factor for this thesis, was found by Rapley and Lobley (1995) and Kober and Eggleton (2002) to be consistent with its original loading, in that it loaded on their *life satisfaction and domestic contentment* factor.

In spite of the above difference in the factor loadings between this thesis, Rapley and Lobley (1995) and Kober and Eggleton (2002), the fact that the loading of 35 of the 40 items (87.50 percent) is consistent with the original factor structure of Schalock and Keith (1993) is seen as supporting their instrument. The consistency of question loading in this thesis is slightly less than that reported in Kober and Eggleton (2002) (37 of the 40 items; 92.50 percent), but greater than that reported by Rapley and Lobley (1995) (32 of the 40 items; 80.00 percent). Taken in totality, the results from this thesis as well as Rapley and Lobley (1995) and Kober and Eggleton (2002) suggest that the QOL.Q has a reasonably robust factor structure.

However, the internal reliability of the four factors gives rise to some degree of concern. In Table 4.36, although the Cronbach alpha coefficient for the overall QOL.Q is acceptable at .731[75], it is only acceptable for one of the four factors (Competence/Productivity). For the other three factors the Cronbach alpha coefficient is less than .700, indicating a lack of internal reliability for those factors. This is true irrespective of whether the items comprising each factor were selected in accordance with the original QOL.Q (Schalock and Keith 1993) (Table 3.5) column one, under the heading *original QOL.Q factors*) or as per the above factor analysis (reported in Table 4.36, column two, under the heading *thesis QOL.Q factors*).

4.5.1 Refinement of the QOL.Q
Given this lack of internal reliability, and that a number of the factor loadings reported in Table 4.35 are below .32 (Tabachnick and Fiddell 2001), the factor analysis is repeated omitting any items with a factor loading below .32.[76] This results in the omission of the 13 questions listed in Table 4.37. Omitting the 13 questions listed in Table 4.37 results in a Bartlett test of sphericity that is significant (χ^2 (351, n = 130) = 1,133.552, $p \leq$ .001) and the Kaiser-Meyer-Okin measure of sampling is greater than .6 (KMO = .711), indicating that it is possible to conduct a factor analysis on the sample. The scree test suggests once more that four factors are appropriate. A principal axis factor analysis with varimax rotation is then conducted to determine how the remaining 27 questions factor. The new factor solution, shown in Table 4.38, makes theoretical sense, and all items have factor loadings greater than .32.

---

[75] Acceptable is defined as having a Cronbach alpha greater than .700 (Hair *et al.* 1995).
[76] All items that have multiple loadings have factor loadings below .32 and consequently are omitted.

Table 4.36: Cronbach alpha scores for the QOL.Q

	Original QOL.Q factors	Thesis QOL.Q factors
Satisfaction	.625	.573
Competence/ Productivity	.816	.815
Empowerment/ Independence	.666	.685
Social belonging/ Community integration	.589	.653
Questionnaire	.731	.731

Table 4.37: Items omitted from the QOL.Q

Factor 1: Life satisfaction and domestic contentment

1   Overall, would you say that life brings out the best in you, treats you like everybody else, or doesn't give you a chance?

6   Do you have more or fewer problems than other people?

7   How many times per month do you feel lonely?

10   What about your family members? Do they make you feel an important part of the family, sometimes a part of the family, or like an outsider?

33   Do you worry about what people expect of you?

Factor 2: Competence/Productivity

11   How well did your educational or training programme prepare you for what you are doing now?

Factor 3: Empowerment/Independence

3   Compared with others, are you better off, about the same, or less well off?

21   How did you decide to do the job or other daily activities you do now?

26   Do you have a key to your home?

27   May you have a pet if you want?

Factor 4: Social belonging/Community integration

34   How many times per week do you talk to (or associate with) your neighbours, either in the yard or in their home?

35   Do you have friends over to visit your home?

40   Overall, would you say that your life is very worthwhile, okay, or useless?

The internal reliability of the above factors is then investigated using Cronbach's alpha. In Table 4.39, three of the four factors (*competence/productivity*, *empowerment/independence*, and *social belonging/community integration*) now have acceptable Cronbach alphas above .700, when previously only one factor (*competence/productivity*) had an acceptable Cronbach alpha. The *life satisfaction and domestic contentment* factor still reports a Cronbach alpha less than .700. However at .642 it has improved substantially from the previous value (Table 4.36, column two) of .573, indicating an increase in the reliability of this factor. As previously mentioned, it is common for scales with less than ten items, as this factor now has, to report lower Cronbach alpha scores (Pallant 2001) and as such the Cronbach alpha for this factor is considered satisfactory. The Cronbach alpha for the overall questionnaire also rose slightly from .731 (Table 4.36, column two) to .738.

The internal reliability of the four factors of the QOL.Q are further investigated by determining the alphas if each of the questions in turn are deleted; the results of which are reported in Tables 4.40 (a), (b), (c), and (d). It can be seen from Tables 4.40 (a), (b), and (c) that on no occasion does the omission of a question result in a substantial increase of the Cronbach alpha scores of any of these factors.[77] On all but one occasion (question 29 which formed part of the *life satisfaction and domestic contentment* factor) the corrected total-item correlations are in excess of .300, as is required to show unidimensionality of the questions (de Vaus 1995). This question is not omitted since doing so

---

[77] On only one occasion does the omission of a question result in the increase of the Cronbach alpha for that factor and that was question 20 of *competence/productivity*, which would result in an increase of .004 (from .833 to .837). This question is not omitted as this is not a substantial increase in the Cronbach alpha score and also because the question reports a corrected item-total correlation in excess of .3 indicating that the question is measuring the same underlying concept as the rest of the factor.

would result in a decrease in the Cronbach alpha score for the *life satisfaction and domestic contentment* factor, that is, the internal reliability of the scores for this factor would decrease.

Table 4.38: Factor loadings for the QOL.Q with 13 questions omitted

Factor 1:	Life satisfaction and domestic contentment	Factor loading
4	Are most of the things that happen to you rewarding, acceptable, or disappointing?	.517
2	How much fun and enjoyment do you get out of life?	.453
12	Do you feel your job or other daily activity is worthwhile and relevant to either yourself or others?	.451
39	How do your neighbours treat you?	.429
9	How successful do you think you are, compared to others?	.418
5	How satisfied are you with your current home or living arrangement?	.368
29	Are there people living with you who sometimes hurt you, pester you, scare you, or make you angry?	.359
8	Do you ever feel out of place in social situations?	.358
Factor 2:	Competence/Productivity	
19	How satisfied are you with the benefits you receive at the workplace?	.806
13	How good do you feel you are at your job?	.772
18	Does your job provide you with enough money to buy the things you want?	.700
14	How do people treat you on your job?	.674
15	How satisfied are you with the skills and experience you have gained or are gaining from your job?	.673
17	Do you feel you receive fair pay for you work?	.523
20	How closely supervised are you on your job?	.439
16	Are you learning skills that will help you get a different or better job? What are these skills?	.418
Factor 3:	Empowerment/Independence	
23	How do you use health care facilities (doctor, dentist, *etc.*)?	.716
28	Do you have a guardian?	.652
22	Who decides how to spend your money?	.624
24	How much control do you have over things you do every day, like going to bed, eating, and what you do for fun?	.582
30	Overall, would you say that your life is free, somewhat planned for you, or that you cannot usually do what you want?	.499
25	When can friends visit your home?	.496
Factor 4:	Social belonging/Community integration	
32	How satisfied are you with the clubs or organisations (including church or other religious activities) to which you belong?	.712
37	Do you participate actively in those recreational activities?	.688
36	How often do you attend recreational activities (homes, parties, dances, concerts, plays) in your community?	.643
31	How many civic or community clubs or organisations (including church or other religious activities) do you belong to?	.615
38	What about opportunities for dating or marriage?	.361

Table 4.39: Cronbach alpha scores for the refined QOL.Q

	Cronbach alpha
Factor:	
Life satisfaction and domestic contentment	.642
Competence/Productivity	.833
Empowerment/Independence	.757
Social belonging/Community integration	.724
Overall questionnaire	.738

Table 4.40(a): Analysis of scale reliability and unidimensionality of the *life satisfaction and domestic contentment* factor of the QOL.Q

Question	Mean	Std deviation	Corrected item-total correlation	Alpha if item deleted
2	2.562	.597	.339	.610
4	2.285	.613	.421	.586
5	2.692	.555	.318	.615
8	2.585	.632	.335	.611
9	1.992	.591	.372	.601
12	2.631	.695	.307	.621
29	2.792	.444	.285	.624
39	2.350	.586	.315	.616

Alpha for *life satisfaction and domestic contentment* factor = .642

Table 4.40(b): Analysis of scale reliability and unidimensionality of the *competence/productivity* factor of the QOL.Q

Item	Mean	Std deviation	Corrected item-total correlation	Alpha if item deleted
13	2.646	.633	.725	.795
14	2.608	.688	.619	.807
15	2.515	.662	.664	.802
16	2.062	.805	.394	.838
17	2.285	.847	.447	.832
18	2.523	.718	.609	.807
19	2.508	.673	.753	.790
20	2.300	.774	.391	.837

Alpha for *competence/productivity* factor = .833

Table 4.40(c): Analysis of scale reliability and unidimensionality of the *empowerment/independence* factor of the QOL.Q

Item	Mean	Std deviation	Corrected item-total correlation	Alpha if item deleted
22	2.554	.660	.520	.717
23	2.054	.926	.570	.707
24	2.615	.589	.489	.727
25	2.569	.681	.426	.741
28	2.046	.756	.564	.704
30	2.462	.599	.456	.734

Alpha for *empowerment/independence* factor = .757

Table 4.40(d): Analysis of scale reliability and unidimensionality of the *social belonging/community integration* factor of the QOL.Q

Item	Mean	Std deviation	Corrected item-total correlation	Alpha if item deleted
31	1.985	.854	.502	.670
32	2.512	.678	.611	.635
36	2.331	.782	.519	.662
37	2.523	.707	.561	.650
38	2.192	.873	.285	.761

Alpha for *social belonging/community integration* factor = .724

The results presented in Table 4.40 (d), show that if question 38 (what about opportunities for dating or marriage?) is omitted from the *social belonging/community integration* factor it would result in an increase of the Cronbach alpha for the factor from .724 to .761. Given the size of this increase and the fact that this question also has a corrected item-total correlation below .300, question 38 was omitted from this factor and consequently the QOL.Q.

Table 4.41:   Factor loadings for the QOL.Q with 14 questions omitted

		Factor loading
Factor 1:	Life satisfaction and domestic contentment	
4	Are most of the things that happen to you rewarding, acceptable, or disappointing?	.514
2	How much fun and enjoyment do you get out of life?	.459
12	Do you feel your job or other daily activity is worthwhile and relevant to either yourself or others?	.456
39	How do your neighbours treat you?	.429
9	How successful do you think you are, compared to others?	.421
5	How satisfied are you with your current home or living arrangement?	.359
8	Do you ever feel out of place in social situations?	.357
29	Are there people living with you who sometimes hurt you, pester you, scare you, or make you angry?	.354
Factor 2:	Competence/Productivity	
19	How satisfied are you with the benefits you receive at the workplace?	.808
13	How good do you feel you are at your job?	.774
18	Does your job provide you with enough money to buy the things you want?	.701
14	How do people treat you on your job?	.673
15	How satisfied are you with the skills and experience you have gained or are gaining from your job?	.671
17	Do you feel you receive fair pay for you work?	.522
20	How closely supervised are you on your job?	.436
16	Are you learning skills that will help you get a different or better job? What are these skills?	.420
Factor 3:	Empowerment/Independence	
23	How do you use health care facilities (doctor, dentist, etc.)?	.717
28	Do you have a guardian?	.638
22	Who decides how to spend your money?	.618
24	How much control do you have over things you do every day, like going to bed, eating, and what you do for fun?	.584
30	Overall, would you say that your life is free, somewhat planned for you, or that you cannot usually do what you want?	.509
25	When can friends visit your home?	.503
Factor 4:	Social belonging/Community integration	
32	How satisfied are you with the clubs or organisations (including church or other religious activities) to which you belong?	.706
37	Do you participate actively in those recreational activities?	.692
31	How many civic or community clubs or organisations (including church or other religious activities) do you belong to?	.631
36	How often do you attend recreational activities (homes, parties, dances, concerts, plays) in your community?	.631

Omitting question 38 results in the need to re-conduct the factor analysis to ensure that the QOL.Q still factors consistently. The Bartlett test of sphericity is significant (χ^2 (325, n = 130) = 1,084.642, $p \leq .001$) and the Kaiser-Meyer-Okin measure of sampling is greater than .6 (KMO = .732), indicating it is possible to conduct a factor analysis on the sample. The scree test again suggests four factors are appropriate. Consequently, a principal axis factor analysis with varimax rotation specifying four factors is conducted on the remaining 26 questions. The new factor solution, which is shown in Table 4.41, factors as expected, and all items have factor loadings in excess of .32.

The factor loadings for the eight questions of the *life satisfaction and domestic contentment* factor shown in Table 4.41 are quite low, with the highest reported loading being .514 for question 4. The low factor loadings might indicate that more than one factors is present in this factor and that forcing four factors for the overall questionnaire has resulted in this grouping of questions into one factor. However, when analysed in isolation, the Scree plot for these eight questions showed clearly there was only one factor for all eight questions. Additionally, forcing the eight questions into two or three factors does not yield meaningful results, with most questions yielding lower factor loadings than when they load on just one factor. Consequently, it appears these eight questions do belong to one factor.

4.5.2 Reliability Analysis of the QOL.Q

Table 4.42 summarises the final Cronbach alpha scores obtained, using the 26 questions and four factors shown in Table 4.41 (see column two, titled *refined QOL.Q factors*) as well as the Cronbach alphas per the original 40 questions and four factors of the Schalock and Keith (1993) QOL.Q (Table 4.41, column one, titled *original QOL.Q factors*). Table 4.42 also presents Cronbach alpha coefficients reported in previous studies that investigate the internal reliability of the QOL.Q. In general, the factors report Cronbach alpha coefficients that are acceptable. The exceptions being the *social belonging/community integration* factor, which on three prior occasions (Schalock and Keith 1993; Eggleton *et al.* 1999; Kober and Eggleton 2002) reports a Cronbach alpha below .700 and the *satisfaction* factor which in two prior studies (Eggleton *et al.* 1999; Kober and Eggleton 2002) also reports a Cronbach alpha coefficient below .700.

Table 4.42: Cronbach alpha scores for the QOL.Q (ranks of Cronbach alphas reported in brackets)

	Thesis data		Comparative studies' data			
	Original QOL.Q factors	Refined QOL.Q factors	Kober & Eggleton (2002)	Eggleton *et al.* (1999)	Rapley & Lobley (1995)	Schalock & Keith (1993)
Satisfaction	.625 (3)	.642 (4)	.47 (4)	.688 (3)	.70 (= 3)	.78 (3)
Competence/ Productivity	.816 (1)	.833 (1)	.91 (1)	.951 (1)	.86 (1)	.90 (1)
Empowerment/ Independence	.666 (2)	.757 (2)	.75 (2)	.827 (2)	.70 (= 3)	.82 (2)
Social belonging/ Community integration	.589 (4)	.744 (3)	.68 (3)	.652 (4)	.80 (2)	.67 (4)
Questionnaire	.731	.738	.81	.900	.84	.90

Ranks of the Cronbach alphas are also reported in Table 4.42. The rank is determined by comparing the relative standing of the Cronbach alpha score for each of the four QOL.Q factors in turn, relative to the same QOL.Q factors for each study. Visual inspection of these ranks shows that the *competence/productivity* factor consistently ranks number one, that is, on all occasions it has the highest Cronbach alpha of the four QOL.Q factors. *Empowerment/Independence* for all but one study reports the second highest Cronbach alpha, that is, ranked number two, while the *satisfaction* and *social belonging/community integration* factors consistently rank third or fourth. Kendall's tau-b[78] correlation coefficients were calculated to measure the correlation of ranks among the different studies. The results in Table 4.43 reveal that only when there is one hundred percent correlation that the Kendall's tau-b correlation coefficient provides a significant result at the five percent level. This is due to having only a relatively small sample size in terms of ranks (only four here).

Kendall's W[79] is also calculated to measure the overall concordance of rankings of the Cronbach alphas across the different studies and found to be statistically significant ($W = .713, p \le .010$)[80].

---

[78] Kendall's tau-b is calculated in preference to the Pearson correlation coefficient as the data set is small. With large data sets, Kendall's tau-b and Pearson's coefficients give similar values with similar significance probabilities. However, with smaller data sets Kendall's tau-b is preferable, especially when there are tied observations (Kinnear and Gray 2000), as there are in this instance.

[79] Kendall's W expresses the degree of association between sets of rankings (Siegel and Castellan 1988).

[80] Significance is assessed by comparing the calculated Kendall's W to the critical values table for Kendall's W provided in Siegel and Castellan (1988), who only provide the critical values for the one percent and five percent levels of significance.

This result indicates a consistency in the findings of the different studies in terms of the rank ordering of the internal reliability of the different factors of the QOL.Q, with the *competence/productivity* factor scores having the highest internal reliability, followed by the *empowerment/independence* scores. However, the average rank for the Cronbach alpha scores for the *satisfaction* and *social belonging/community integration* factors were tied.[81]

Given that the QOL.Q, in its original form (that is, prior to the refinement I describe above) has been extensively used (for example, Schalock *et al.* 1994; Rapley and Hopgood 1997; Eggleton *et al.* 1999; McIntyre *et al.* 2004) I decided to investigate not only the factor stability of the refined QOL.Q but also to conduct a factor stability analysis of the original 40-question QOL.Q. Conducting both factor stability analyses also allows further comparison of the internal reliability of the two forms of the QOL.Q. Both factor stability analyses are conducted by splitting the sample (1) randomly (half-half), (2) by gender, (3) by level of functional work ability (as measured by FAI[82]), (4) by employment (participants employed in open employment versus participants employed in supported employment and job seekers), and (5) by employment (participants employed in open employment versus those employed in supported employment).

Table 4.43: Kendall's tau-b correlation coefficients of Cronbach alpha ranks of the QOL.Q as reported in Table 4.26 (two-tailed significance figures reported in brackets).

	Thesis data		Comparative studies' data			
	Original QOL.Q factors	Refined QOL.Q factors	Kober & Eggleton (2002)	Eggleton *et al.* (1999)	Rapley & Lobley (1995)	Schalock & Keith (1993)
Original QOL.Q factors		.667 (.174)	.667 (.174)	1.000[*] (.042)	.183 (.718)	1.000[*] (.042)
Refined QOL factors			1.000[*] (.042)	.667 (.174)	.548 (.279)	.667 (.174)
Kober & Eggleton (2002)				.667 (.174)	.548 (.279)	.667 (.174)
Eggleton *et al.* (1999)					.183 (.718)	1.000[*] (.042)
Rapley & Lobley (1995)						.183 (.718)

* Correlation is significant at the 5 percent level (2-tailed).

The results of the factor stability analyses for the original QOL.Q are presented in Table 4.44. For the subpopulation sample sizes refer to Table 4.34, which contains the demographic data relating to the QOL.Q.

Table 4.44 shows that on five occasions the reported coefficients of congruence are below the acceptable level of .940. On two occasions this relates to the *competence/productivity* factor (when the sample is split by employment – open versus supported and job seekers; open versus supported), and on one occasion to each of the factors of *satisfaction* (when the sample is split by employment – open versus supported), *empowerment* (when the sample is split by employment - open versus supported and job seekers), and *social* (when the sample is split by employment – open versus supported). On all other occasions the dichotomies result in coefficients of congruence that are acceptable (in excess of .940). Note that when the sample is dichotomised randomly by gender and by functional ability, on all occasions coefficients of congruence result that are in excess of .940. The only dichotomies relating to coefficients of congruence below .940 are those by employment,

[81] Average ranks are calculated for each factor as part of the calculations for the Kendall *W*.
[82] The FAI is dichotomised around the median. The median is selected as the mid-point since there are no generally accepted ranges that define participants with intellectual disabilities as having either a high functional work ability or low functional work ability.

either *open versus supported and job seekers* or *open versus supported*. Results for the *open versus supported* dichotomy, which accounts for three of the five instances when the coefficient of congruence is below .940, may be due to the fact that this dichotomy has the lowest sample size (68 participants in open employment and 53 participants in supported employment).

These results are in contrast to Kober and Eggleton (2002) who concluded that, using the same dichotomisations as in Table 4.44, three of the four factors were highly stable. Kober and Eggleton's (2002) analysis revealed scores in excess of .940 on all occasions for the three factors of *competence/productivity*, *empowerment/independence*, and *social belonging/community integration*. The only factor found not to be stable was *satisfaction*, which on no occasions reported a coefficient of congruence above .940.

Table 4.44:   Factor stability test: Coefficients of congruence for the original QOL.Q[a]

	Quality of life questionnaire factors			
	Satisfaction	Competence/ Productivity	Empowerment/ Independence	Social belonging/ Community integration
Random split halves	.964	.984	.980	.992
Gender	.950	.983	.988	.968
Functional ability	.974	.989	.949	.954
Employment (open v. supported & job seekers)	.979	.905	.939	.999
Employment (open v. supported)	.709	.794	.945	.934

a   For factors to be considered congruent the coefficient of congruence should be equal to or greater than .940.

Kober and Eggleton (2002) concluded that scores obtained for the factors of *competence/productivity*, *empowerment/independence*, and *social belonging/community integration* were reliable since all three factors were highly stable and had acceptable Cronbach alpha coefficients. However, they expressed concern over the internal reliability of the *satisfaction* factor given that it was not stable and below the acceptable Cronbach alpha coefficient (.700). Kober and Eggleton (2002) stated that it was therefore difficult to attribute reliability to the scores obtained for this factor. However, as Cummins (2000a) noted, there is a lack of psychometric assessment of quality of life questionnaires used to measure the quality of life for people with intellectual disabilities. This means that although Kober and Eggleton (2002) raised concern about one of the QOL.Q factors, it is impossible to state whether the QOL.Q is inferior to other measures of the quality of life of people with intellectual disabilities since other instruments have not undergone rigorous psychometric assessments.

The psychometric validation results obtained in this thesis in relation to the QOL.Q (that is, Cronbach alphas and the factor stability analysis), using the four original Schalock and Keith (1993) factors, interpreted on their own might raise concern about the stability of the factors and the internal reliability of the factor scores. However, it is suspected that these results are in part due to the sample size of only 130 participants. Kober and Eggleton (2002) had a sample of 172 participants, of whom 116 are also included in the analysis reported in this thesis. The Kober and Eggleton (2002) sample was drawn from 56 participants who were interviewed as part of Eggleton *et al.* (1999) (all drawn from agency B) and the 116 participants who had been interviewed as at that time from my PhD sample. Given there is a large overlap in terms of the sample between Kober and Eggleton (2002) and this PhD and the fact that Kober and Eggleton (2002) had a larger sample size, I believe more weight should be placed on the results of Kober and Eggleton (2002) than those obtained in this section of the PhD. This is especially so, considering that in conducting the current factor stability analysis some of the factor analyses are conducted on samples as low as 51 (the number of females in the gender dichotomisation).[83]

Even though Kober and Eggleton (2002) conclude that the QOL.Q had three stable factors and produced reliable scores for these three factors as well as for the instrument overall, as stated previously, due to concerns over the Cronbach alpha coefficients reported for the original QOL.Q (presented in Table 4.36), a refined version of the QOL.Q is obtained here using factor analysis (presented in Table 4.41). Table 4.45 reports the results of the factor stability analysis conducted on this refined QOL.Q. On all occasions the coefficients of congruence for the *competence/productivity*, *empowerment/independence*, and *social belonging/community integration* factors are in excess of .940, indicating that these three factors are stable. For three of the five dichotomies (Random split halves, gender, and functional ability) the coefficient of congruence for the *satisfaction* factor is in excess of .940. On the two other instances, when the sample is dichotomised by employment (open versus supported and job seekers; open versus supported) a coefficient of congruence cannot be calculated as no items from this factor load on similar factors.

Table 4.45: Factor stability test: Coefficients of congruence for the refined QOL.Q[a]

| | Quality of life questionnaire factors | | | |
	Satisfaction	Competence/ Productivity	Empowerment/ Independence	Social belonging/ Community integration
Random split halves	.991	.998	.971	.997
Gender	.977	.987	.985	.971
Functional ability	.945	.990	.950	.955
Employment (open v. supported & job seekers)	---[b]	.986	.959	.942
Employment (open v. supported)	---	.979	.964	.985

a   For factors to be considered congruent the coefficient of congruence should be equal to or greater than .940.
b   The dashed lines indicate that a coefficient of congruence cannot be calculated in these instances, as no items from the relevant factor load on the same factor when the sample is dichotomised. That is, the items variously load on other factors.

These results presented for the refined QOL.Q developed in this thesis are not only better than those for the original QOL.Q, but are consistent with those reported in Kober and Eggleton (2002), in that the three factors of *competence/productivity*, *empowerment/independence*, and *social belonging/community integration* are found to be stable and to report acceptable Cronbach alpha scores.[84] Given that, as in Kober and Eggleton (2002), the *satisfaction* factor is found not to be stable and has a below satisfactory Cronbach alpha score (.642), caution should be taken in interpreting the scores obtained for this factor.

4.5.3 Rescaling of the Refined QOL.Q
The scores of each of the four factors of the refined QOL.Q, as well as the overall QOL.Q, are rescaled. This rescaling is undertaken for several reasons. First, given the wide usage of the original QOL.Q it is though appropriate to rescale the refined QOL.Q to facilitate comparisons with prior studies. Second, given that each factor of the original Schalock and Keith (1993) QOL.Q has ten questions, each with a one to three response range, in summing all 40 questions each factor is effectively given equal weighting. However, as a result of the above refinement process the refined QOL.Q comprises four factors with an unequal number of questions in each factor; *life satisfaction and domestic contentment* and *competence/productivity* both have eight questions,

---

[83] Another low sample results when the sample is split based on type of employment (open employment versus supported employment), which results in a sample of 54 for supported employment. The other dichotomisations, though not resulting in such low samples still result in factor analysis being conducted on samples in the 60s.
[84] The similarities in results between Kober and Eggleton (2002) and this thesis are expected given the sample overlap. Of the 130 participants used to validate the QOL.Q in this thesis, 116 also form part of Kober and Eggleton's (2002) sample of 172 participants.

empowerment/independence has six questions, and *social belonging/community integration* has four questions. As a consequence, if the questions are summed to obtain the total refined QOL.Q score, each factor would no longer be weighted equally. Given that I have no theoretical foundation to assume that each factor contributes differently to overall quality of life, and to maintain consistency with the original QOL.Q it is considered appropriate to rescale each factor to an equal weighting.

To rescale the scores for the *satisfaction, competence/productivity, empowerment/independence*, and *social belonging/community integration* factors of the refined QOL.Q, they are multiplied by 1.25 (10/8), 1.25 (10/8), (10/6), and 2.5 (10/4), respectively. This results in each factor having a theoretical range of 10 – 30. Total quality of life is then calculated by summing the four factor scores, giving a theoretical range of 40 – 120, as per the original QOL.Q.

4.5.4 Summary of QOL.Q
As detailed above, I refine the QOL.Q based on the data collected for this thesis. The refined QOL.Q reports higher Cronbach alpha coefficients for each factor and the overall questionnaire and has better factor stability than the original QOL.Q. I believe it is possible to attribute reliability to the overall refined QOL.Q score as well as the scores of the three factors of *competence/productivity, empowerment/independence*, and *social belonging/community integration*. However, a degree of caution needs to be exercised when interpreting results for the *satisfaction* factor.

Given the results of Kober and Eggleton (2002), I believe that the original 40-question QOL.Q shown in Table 3.5, can also be used in this research with the scores obtained for the overall QOL.Q as well as the three factors of *competence/productivity, empowerment/independence*, and *social belonging/community integration* being considered reliable. As per Kober and Eggleton (2002), a degree of caution should be exercised when interpreting the *satisfaction* score. The reporting of the outcome results, as per the original QOL.Q and the factors specified by Schalock and Keith (1993), also allows for comparisons to be made with prior research. However, emphasis will be given to the refined QOL.Q as it reports higher Cronbach alpha coefficients and has better factor stability the scores. The reporting of the original QOL.Q scores is conducted on a confirmatory basis.

In summary, the refined QOL.Q (Table 4.41) used in this thesis contains the following four factors, with the stated number of questions and rescaled theoretical ranges noted also:
1. *Life satisfaction and domestic contentment*, eight questions, rescaled theoretical range 10 – 30;
2. *Competence/Productivity*, eight questions, rescaled theoretical range 10 – 30;
3. *Empowerment/Independence*, six questions, rescaled theoretical range 10 – 30; and
4. *Social belonging/Community integration*, four questions, rescaled theoretical range 10 – 30.

4.6 Conclusion
In this chapter I assessed firstly the psychometric properties of the FAI. Given the inconclusive results of prior research (Crew and Athelsatn 1984; Neath *et al.* 1997) on the factor structure of the FAI for people with intellectual disabilities, I initially investigated the FAI's factor structure. I investigated five, six and seven factor structures for the FAI which revealed, consistent with Neath *et al.* (1997), that the six-factor solution is the best defined solution for the FAI. However, there are surprisingly few similarities between my factor structure and that of Neath *et al.* (1997).

Next, I developed a job satisfaction questionnaire based on an instrument initially developed for people without a disability by Smith *et al.* (1969) and subsequently modified to be used with people with intellectual disabilities by Seltzer and Seltzer (1978) and then Barlow and Kirby (1991). The resultant questionnaire has 29 questions which factor into the following four constructs: *work and staff* (9 questions), *task* (8 questions), *pay* (6 questions), and *social* (6 questions). The reliability analysis revealed that the questionnaire has three reliable factors – the factors being *work and staff*, *task* and *pay*. As the *social* factor is not stable and has a Cronbach alpha score below .700 little weight can be placed on the scores associated with this factor.

Finally, the psychometric properties of the Schalock and Keith (1993) QOL.Q were assessed. The QOL.Q factored slightly differently to that reported in Schalock and Keith (1993); five questions load on to different factors from those Schalock and Keith (1993) reported. Given there were several questions with factor loadings below .32 and the Cronbach alphas of three factors were below .700, the QOL.Q was refined by first, omitting questions with factor loadings below .32, and second, questions that when omitted increased the Cronbach alpha scores of the factors. This resulted in a 26-question refined QOL.Q with four factors that reported acceptable Cronbach alpha scores; the four factors were, *life satisfaction and domestic contentment* (8 questions), *competence/productivity* (8 questions), *empowerment/independence* (6 factors), and *social belonging/community integration* (4 questions). Factor stability analysis revealed that this refined QOL.Q has three stable factors, with only the *life satisfaction and domestic contentment* factor not being stable. These results, in relation to the stability of factors, are consistent with those reported in Kober and Eggleton (2002).

Kober and Eggleton (2002) found that the QOL.Q in its original 40-question form was an instrument that had three stable factors with, on the whole, acceptable Cronbach alpha scores. Consequently, the outcome results are presented in the next chapter based on both my refined QOL.Q and the original 40-question QOL.Q. Reporting both results not only facilitates comparisons for the purposes of this study, but also allows increased comparability with other studies that have used the QOL.Q in its original form.

The poor factor stability results for some factors mentioned above bring into question the reliability of the scores for those particular dimensions and suggest that when using the scores for these dimensions caution should be exercised. As discussed throughout the chapter, part of the reason for these poor results may be driven by small sub-sample sizes. However, the above psychometric assessments should not preclude the use of the three instruments analysed and refined here (FAI, JSQ, and QOL.Q), as alternative instruments have not undergone such extensive assessments and, as such, it is impossible to ascertain how they compare. However, it is reassuring that the overall Cronbach alpha scores are acceptable for each questionnaire, suggesting that the overall score for each instrument can be used with confidence.

Chapter 5 – Demographics and Sub-Sample Selection

5.1 Introduction
In this chapter I first analyse and discuss the properties of the job satisfaction and quality of life data. A description is then given of the demographics of the entire sample followed by a breakdown by method of employment (open employment versus supported employment). Given there are statistically significant demographic differences between participants in open employment and supported employment it is important that these differences are controlled to allow for a meaningful analysis of the different outcomes for the two methods of employment. This is possible through the formation of sub-samples described next. Finally, the demographic data of each sub-sample are then discussed.

5.2 Data
As detailed in Section 3.4 (Participant Selection), letters seeking participation in this research were sent to 707[85] people with an intellectual disability. The letters were sent to clients drawn from the registers of six disability employment agencies who operated within metropolitan area of a major Australian city. Of the 707 letters sent, a total 162 people agreed to be interviewed; 142 from initial mail-outs and 20 after either a follow-up mail-out or reminder calls.[86,87] This gave an overall response rate of 22.91 percent.

The response rates differ by agency from a low of 6.19 percent to a high of 45.26 percent. The different response rates in terms of the number of people agreeing to be interviewed for each agency are reported in the third column of Table 5.1. One possible explanation for the different response rates may be due to the difference in terms of people's association with an agency. The highest response rate is for Agency A, which exclusively operates workshops and thus people identify with the agency, as each day they work in one of Agency A's workshops. However, for the agencies that place people into open employment, there is no such connection, in that the clients work for an independent organisation and only liaise, typically with one person, from the disability employment agency, being their job coordinator. In some instances if the person is performing well in his/her job, he/she may not have any contact with his/her employment co-ordinator for extended periods of time, occasionally in excess of a year.

However, the explanation in the above paragraph does not explain the great variation in the response rates that is apparent across agencies B to F, all of whom place people into open employment.[88] Agency B, as stated in section 3.4.2 (Participant Recruitment – Agency B), initially sent the letter from the CEO seeking participation, and this may have led to a higher response rate as people may be more likely to respond to a request from someone or an agency they are familiar with, rather than a letter from an unknown university post-graduate student. However, Agency D, along with the letter seeking participation which I signed, also enclosed a supporting letter from a manager commending participation. Yet Agency D's response rate is far lower than Agency B's. Additionally, 32 of the people selected from Agency B for the mail-out had participated in a prior study and therefore this might account for the high response rate for this agency, as these people

---

[85] Summing the number of letters sent to the clients of each agency would total 709, however, as stated in Section 3.4.2 (Participant Recruitment – Agency B), two people were interviewed twice and consequently although 709 letters were sent, they went to 707 people. The numbers reported in this chapter exclude these two people and consequently, the numbers reported for the number of people who initially agreed to be interviewed and those actually interviewed will be two less than the total that would be achieved if the numbers for each agency reported in Section 3.4 (Participant Selection) are summed.

[86] Three of the agencies allowed a follow-up mail-out to those people who did not respond to the original mail-out, while three agencies did not wish for a follow-up mail-out to be undertaken.

[87] The breakdown of the 20 is: 19 as a result of follow-up mail-outs and one as a result of a reminder call.

[88] As stated in Section 3.4.4 (Participant Recruitment – Agency D), Agency D not only places people into open employment but also has some enclaves that are considered supported employment.

have previously shown themselves to be willing to participate in research projects. However, if the separate response rates for Agency B between the two sub-samples (the initial mail-out versus the second mail-out of people who had previously participated in a prior study) are compared, there is not great disparity. Of the 32 specifically targeted people (second mail-out of people who had previously participated in a prior study), 14 agreed to participate, giving a response rate of 43.75 percent, compared with 29 of the other 68 people not specifically targeted (the initial mail-out), which yields a response rate of 42.65 percent (29 of 68).

Table 5.1: Number of participants by agency

Agency	Letters distributed	Respondents agreeing to participate (response rate)	Number interviewed (response rate)	Number used in analysis (response rate)
A	137	62 (45.26%)	46 (33.58%)	43 (31.39%)
B	100	43 (43.00%)	33 (33.00%)	30 (30.00%)
C	74	16 (21.62%)	15 (20.27%)	11 (14.86%)
D	233	26 (11.16%)	25 (10.73%)	25 (10.73%)
E	60	8 (16.00%)	8 (16.00%)	3 (6.00%)
F	113	7 (6.19%)	7 (6.19%)	5 (4.39%)
Total	707	162 (22.91%)	134 (18.95%)	117 (16.55%)

Agencies A, B, and C also allowed a follow-up letter to be sent to people who had not responded to the initial mail-out, which may partially explain why these three agencies have higher response rates. However, it is unlikely this alone would explain all the variation. No other explanations can be provided to explain the dispersion of response rates among the different agencies.

Of the 162 people, when contacted to organise an interview time, 24 stated they no longer wished to be interviewed. The majority of these 24 came from Agency A and as described in Section 3.4.1 (Participant Recruitment – Agency A), the delays in obtaining persons' contact details and then contacting them no doubt contributed to the large number of people who no longer wished to be interviewed. In accordance with ethical guidelines and not wishing to upset the individual, their family, or the employment agency, no reason was sought as to why the people no longer wished to be interviewed. It was also discovered that four of the respondents from Agency B were unemployed and consequently they were not interviewed. This resulted in 134 people being interviewed. The breakdown of the exact number of people interviewed by agency is reported in the fourth column of Table 5.1.

The fifth column of Table 5.1, reports the number of interviews by agency used in this analysis. Data from 17 interviews are not used in the final analysis due to one of the following reasons discovered during the interviews: nine people were unemployed; four people acquiesced;[89,90] two people had found their current employment without the assistance of their employment agency; one person worked fewer than eight hours per week;[91] and one person left an agency soon after the interview and in accordance with that agency's confidentiality guidelines the agency subsequently

---

[89] This acquiescence rate on initial inspection might appear low. However, it should be noted that the participants of this study are not representative of the general population of people with an intellectual disability. The reasons for this are: 1) Agency A sent out participation letters only to clients whom they considered to have adequate understanding and comprehension skills; 2) there is likely to be a selection bias in the participants who agreed to be interviewed, in that they (and/or their family/carer) would believe that they possessed adequate comprehension skills to participate; and 3) it could be expected for those people placed into open employment that their understanding and comprehension skills would be relatively high. Note that the four people who acquiesced came from supported employment.

[90] To ensure the validity of responses, if a person acquiesced in one part of the questionnaire the entire interview is not used.

[91] Eight hours is selected as the minimum number of hours a person must work per week due to this being the number of hours used by the Australian Commonwealth Government to define a successful outcome in terms of employment for people with intellectual disability.

did not provide other required information on the person. This resulted in a final sample size of 117 people.

The initial stages of this research involved Agency A and B, both of which requested the interviewing of their clients be conducted by a suitably qualified person. This resulted in the recruitment of seven masters of psychology students to conduct the interviews.[92] Once a decision was made to expand the scope of this research beyond these two agencies the remaining interviews were conducted by me. I undertook to conduct the interviews myself due to the unreliability of the masters students in scheduling interviews and the fact that the four new agencies felt comfortable with me conducting interviews due to the experience I had gained during the course of conducting my research to that point in time. At the time the scope of the research was expanded, Agency B also agreed to allow me to conduct further interviews. Of the 117 interviews used in this research, 59 were conducted by the masters students and 58 by myself. A breakdown of the number of interviews conducted by each masters students and myself is shown in Table 5.2.

Table 5.2: Number of interviews by interviewer

| Interviewer | Number of interviews conducted | | | |
	Agency A	Agency B	Agencies C - F	Total
MPS 1	7	1	0	8
MPS 2	6	3	0	9
MPS 3	7	2	0	9
MPS 4	6	2	0	8
MPS 5	12	6	0	18
MPS 6	1	0	0	1
MPS 7	4	2	0	6
Myself	0	14	44	58
Total	43	30	44	117

Abbreviations: MPS – master of psychology student

To test whether the interviewer has an effect on the scores for participants, Mann Whitney U Tests are conducted comparing the responses for the masters of psychology students with those obtained by me.[93] Given that, as a proportion of participants, I interviewed more participants from open employment, to control for any effect that the method of employment (open employment versus supported employment) might have on the results, the analysis on interviewer differences is conducted separately for both open employment and supported employment. The results for participants from open employment revealed no statistically significant differences between participants interviewed by either the masters of psychology students or myself for job satisfaction or quality of life or any of their respective factors. The results for participants from supported employment revealed statistically significant differences depending on the interviewer for two of the four factors of job satisfaction (*work* and *staff and task*) as well as *total job satisfaction* as well as for the *social belonging/community integration* factor of both the refined QOL.Q and the original QOL.Q. On each of these occasions the participants interviewed by me reported the higher scores. However, the reason for these differences could be a result of differences in the form of supported employment undertaken by the different participants and not necessarily the interviewer. All the participants interviewed by the masters of psychology students worked in workshops, whereas all the participants I interviewed worked in enclaves (for example, car cleaning crews, clerical enclave located at an organisation's premises[94]). Furthermore, I do not believe that the differences found

---

[92] A full discussion of the use of the seven masters students to conduct interviews is contained in Section 3.4.1 (Participant Recruitment – Agency A).

[93] It is not possible to analyse differences between the masters of psychology students given the number of interviews conducted by each student.

[94] Enclaves are categorised as supported employment given that it is the disability employment agency that pays the clients wage and not the hiring organisation. The hiring organisation contracts with the disability employment agency for the agency to provide services (for example, cleaning of cars, clerical work) and as

between interviewers for participants from supported employment bring into doubt the results of the research as the results from participants in open employment showed no differences among open employment participants based on interviewer. This should to some extent indicate that there are no biases based on interviewer.

5.3 Normality of the Data

Participant scores for total quality of life and its four factors, of both the refined and original QOL.Q, the four factor-scores and total score of the JSQ, and both the refined and original FAI total scores are tested for normality. The Kolmogrov-Smirnov test, with Lilliefors significance correction,[95] reveals that all of the variables have statistically significant scores ($p \leq .05$). Given that it is only when the significance score is greater than .05 that normality can be assumed, the null hypothesis that the sample is normally distributed is rejected and, consequently, all tests conducted are non-parametric.

5.4 Non Response Bias

To test for non-response bias, the participants who responded to the initial mail-out are compared with those who responded after follow-up mail-outs or phone calls. Mann-Whitney U tests are conducted to compare total scores, and sub-totals, for the QOL.Q (refined and original), JSQ, and the FAI (refined and original). The results of the Mann-Whitney U tests suggest that the samples come from populations having the same distribution. That is, on no occasions could the null hypothesis that both samples are drawn from the same sample population be rejected at the five percent significance level. Consequently, the results presented in this thesis should not be affected by non response bias.

5.5 Demographics

Table 5.3, which reports the demographic information of the 117 participants in this research, shows that 61.54 percent are male. This predominance of males accessing disability employment services is consistent with both state and federal figures. For example, Anderson *et al.* (2000) notes that 64 percent of clients who access open employment services in Australia are male. The most recent Australian Government Disability Services Census conducted in 2002 (released 2004)[96] shows that for Western Australia 64.56 percent of clients who access open and supported employment services are male.[97] As can be seen in Table 5.3, the average age of the participants in my sample is 30 years. This average age is also consistent with data from Anderson *et al.* (2000) and the Australian Government Disability Services Census (2004), which shows the majority of clients accessing employment services are in their twenties and thirties.

In terms of accommodation, the majority of people (68 people; 58.12 percent) live with their family, 31 people (26.50 percent) live independently, and 18 (15.38 percent) live in group housing.

---

such the disability employment agency is the employer of the clients. In the case of clerical enclaves, although the enclave is typically located at the hiring organisation's premise in the case of participants I interviewed the enclaves were located in rooms separate from people without disabilities (in one instance a separate building) and there is little if any interaction between enclave members and employees of the hiring organisation. Furthermore, enclaves along with workshops are both classified by the Commonwealth Government as supported employment.

It is not possible to conduct meaningful analysis categorising enclave workers as a separate category of method of employment given the small sample size for this population. The results of all analyses reported in Chapters 6 (Results: Outcome Evaluation) and 7 (Results: Correlates of Job Satisfaction and Quality of Life) were repeated excluding enclave workers from the supported employment section, and the results remained qualitatively similar.

[95] The Lilliefors significance correction is conducted when the means and variances of the population are not known and have to be estimated from the sample.

[96] The Australian Commonwealth Government conducts a Disability Services Census every five years.

[97] The data reported in both the AIHW report (Anderson *et al.* 2000) and the Australian Government Disability Services Census (2004) in relation to gender is for all disability types.

Unfortunately, Comparisons in relation to living arrangements with the Australian Government Disability Services Census (2004) are not possible as the census did not distinguish between people living with their family or living independently. However, Anderson *et al.* (2000) reported that for clients placed in open employment across Australia 66.18 percent of clients lived with their family, 20.75 percent lived independently, and 13.07 percent live in group housing. It can be seen by comparing the figures of Anderson *et al.* (2000) with those for open employment reported in Table 5.5, it appears that the open employment sample for this thesis has a slightly greater proportion of people living independently and a lesser proportion living in group housing than would be the norm.

Table 5.3: Participant demographics (n=117)

		n (%)		n (%)	Total
Gender:	Female	45 (38.46%)	Male	72 (61.54%)	117
Living:	Independently	31 (26.50%)	With family	68 (58.12%)	
	Group home	18 (15.38%)			117
Employment:	Open	64 (54.70%)	Supported	53 (45.30%)	117

	Median	Mean	Interquartile range	Standard deviation	Maximum	Minimum
Age:	28.82	30.88	13.42	9.24	61.07	17.87
Current job tenure (yrs):	4.10	5.27	6.64	5.29	25.12	0.02
Years in employment:	5.84	7.68	7.27	6.49	34.99	0.65
Hours worked per week:	32.50	26.78	20.50	10.72	48.00	8.00
Weekly wage:	$72.00	$153.09	$238.25	$149.43	$502.00	$3.30
Hourly wage:	$4.10	$5.70	$8.66	$4.57	$15.00	$0.17
Refined FAI score:	14.00	16.77	13.50	9.99	46.00	0.00
Original FAI score:	24.00	25.61	21.00	13.87	65.00	1.00

In terms of employment, 64 people (54.70 percent) are drawn from open employment, while 53 people (45.30 percent) work in a supported employment setting. Compared with the Australian Government Disability Services Census (2004) my sample is over-represented by people in open employment. The Australian Government Disability Services Census (2004) reveals that Australian people with intellectual disabilities are predominantly placed in supported employment settings. The Australian Government Disability Services Census (2004) reports that 66.29 percent of people with intellectual disabilities who are employed are employed in supported employment, while 31.12 percent are employed in open employment, and 2.59 percent are employed in *other settings*.[98]

In terms of job tenure, the median (mean) length of employment in a participant's current job is 4.10 (5.27) years, with a median (mean) of 5.84 (7.68) years of total employment. Though, as can be seen from Table 6.3, both job tenure and total years of employment vary greatly; job tenure from one week (.02 years) to in excess of 25 years (25.12 years), and total years of employment from 34 weeks (0.65 years) to effectively 35 years (34.99).[99]

The mean (median) hours worked per week is 32.50 (26.78) hours, with a median (mean) hourly wage of $4.10 ($5.70), resulting in a median (mean) weekly wage of $72.00 ($153.09).[100] As with

---

[98] The term *other settings* is not defined in the Australian Government Disability Services Census (2004).

[99] No figures in terms of length of employment are reported in the Australian Government Disability Services Census (2004).

[100] Multiplying the figures given in Table 5.3 for mean hours worked per week by the mean hourly wage results in a slightly different figure for the mean weekly wage to that presented in Table 5.3. This slight difference is due to the rounding of the figures presented in Table 5.3 for mean hourly wage and mean hours worked.

job tenure, these figures also vary greatly. Hours worked vary from eight hours to well above the standard 37.5 hour working week (48 hours), while hourly wages vary from 17 cents per hour through to $15 per hour. Due to these two factors the weekly wages vary from $3.30 to $502. The figures in relation to hours worked appear to be consistent with the Australian Government Disability Services Census (2004), which reveals that 45.59 percent of people with a disability[101] work 30 hours or more a week. However, the census also reports that 52.6 percent of people with intellectual disabilities earn less than $60 per week. It is likely that the higher weekly wage for my sample is due to the fact that my sample is made up of a substantially larger proportion of people from open employment (54.70 percent) (who earn higher wages) compared with the national average (31.12 percent). Even though the participants for this research have a higher average weekly wage (compared with the national average for people with intellectual disabilities), this average wage is still substantially below the national mean wage at the time of $610 per week (ABS, 1998, Cat No 6306.0).

Apart from the fact that the sample for this thesis has a higher representation of people placed in open employment than the national average, the sample of participants appears to be fairly representative of clients accessing disability employment services across Australia. This higher proportion of participants from open employment is not an issue here, as I am comparing whether differences exist in the outcomes achieved by the two methods of employment.

Table 5.4: Breakdown of occupation types by ASCO major groupings

ASCO Number	Occupation Grouping	Number	Percent
LABOURING POSITIONS			
9	LABOURERS AND RELATED WORKERS		
91	Cleaners	11	9.40%
92	Factory labourers	39	33.33%
99	Other labourers and related workers	24	20.51%
		74	63.25%
7	INTERMEDIATE PRODUCTION AND TRANSPORT WORKERS		
72	Intermediate machine operators	17	14.53%
79	Other intermediate production and transport workers	3	2.56%
		20	17.09%
4	TRADESPERSON AND RELATED WORKERS		
41	Mechanical and fabrication engineering tradespersons	1	0.85%
NON-LABOURING POSITIONS			
8	ELEMENTARY CLERICAL, SALES AND SERVICE WORKERS		
81	Elementary clerks	11	9.40%
82	Elementary sales workers	3	2.56%
83	Elementary service workers	6	5.13%
		20	17.09%
6	INTERMEDIATE CLERICAL, SALES AND SERVICE WORKERS		
61	Intermediate clerical workers	1	0.85%
63	Intermediate service workers	1	0.85%
		2	1.70%
TOTAL		117	100.00%

[101] This figure is for all disabilities. No figures are reported based on type of disability in relation to work hours.

Table 5.4 lists the types of occupations in which participants are involved by Australian Standard Classification of Occupation (ASCO) groupings.[102] As can be seen from Table 5.4 the majority of people are employed in physical labouring positions – ASCO major groupings four, seven, and nine. These three groupings account for 95 of the 117 participants (81.20 percent).[103]

5.6 Demographics by Method of Employment

To provide an appreciation of the participants by method of employment Table 5.5 lists separately the demographics for both open employment and supported employment participants. Additionally, as this research is concerned with examining the effect that different methods of employment (open employment versus supported employment) have on the job satisfaction and quality of life of people with intellectual disabilities, tests are conducted to examine if any differences exist in the demographics between the two populations. The Chi-square test for independence reveals there is no statistically significant difference in terms of gender distribution between open employment and supported employment ($\chi^2 = 0.002$, $p \leq .965$). However, there is a statistically significant difference in terms of living patterns between the two populations ($= 20.749$, $p \leq .001$), with a greater proportion of participants who are placed in open employment living either independently or with their family. Those participants placed in supported employment are more likely to be living in a group home compared with those participants placed in open employment.

Mann-Whitney U tests are conducted to determine whether any demographic differences exist between the two populations (open employment and supported employment) in terms of age, job tenure, total years of employment, hours worked, and hourly and weekly wages. As shown in Table 5.5, many statistically significant differences exist between participants in open employment and supported employment. On average, participants in supported employment are older ($Z = -4.720$, $p \leq .001$), have been employed in their current jobs longer ($Z = -3.604$, $p \leq .001$), have worked more years in total ($Z = -5.672$, $p \leq .001$), and earn less per week and per hour ($Z = -7.906$, $p \leq .001$; $Z = -9.005$, $p \leq .001$, respectively). As such it is important to control for these differences between open employment and supported employment. This is discussed further in the next section, Section 5.7 (Controlling for Differences between Open Employment and Supported Employment) where reasons why these differences in demographic variables occur are also discussed.

Table 5.6 lists the occupation types in which participants are involved, by method of employment (supported employment versus open employment). The great majority of participants in both open and supported employment are employed in physical labouring positions (*labourers and related workers, intermediate production and transport workers*, and t*radespersons and related workers*), accounting for 95 of the 117 participants (81.20 percent). Though the relative percent of employees in labouring positions is greater for supported employment compared with open employment (51 of 53 employees [96.23 percent] versus 43 of 64 employees [67.19 percent]).

A Chi-square test reveals in terms of participant occupation that statistically significant differences exist between open employment and supported employment ($\chi^2 = 22.637$, p $\leq .001$).[104] Some

---

[102] ASCO groupings are based on a standard classification of occupations issued by the Australian Bureau of Statistics and were explained in Section 3.3.1 (Type of Occupation).

[103] It is not possible to make comparisons with national figures to determine whether the occupations in which participants in this research are placed are representative of the Australian population of people with intellectual disabilities, as the Australian Government Disability Services Census (2004) does not report statistics on types of occupation. Anderson *et al.* (2000) provides a breakdown of occupation types in accordance with ASCO groupings. However, this breakdown is for all disability types (including physical, hearing, visual, *etc.*). Given that placement into different occupations can vary greatly depending on the type of disability, no meaningful comparison can be made.

[104] The Chi-square test was conducted comparing ASCO single-digit occupation groupings, that is, *labourers and related workers* (9); *intermediate production and transport workers* (7); *and elementary clerical, sales and service workers* (8). The occupation groupings *tradespersons and related workers* (4) and *intermediate*

noticeable differences apparent from Table 5.6 are that only participants in open employment were in the *tradespersons and related workers* and *intermediate clerical, sales and service workers* groupings. The occupation grouping of *elementary clerical, sales and service workers* comprises predominantly participants from open employment, while participants from supported employment form the majority of employees in the *intermediate production and transport workers* occupation group.

Table 5.5: Differences in demographics between open employment and supported employment

	Supported employment	Open employment	Pearson Chi-Square	Significance
Gender: Female	21 (39.62%)	24 (37.50%)	0.002[a,d]	.965
Male	32 (60.38%)	40 (62.50%)		
	53 (100.00%)	64 (100.00%)		
Living: Independently	11 (20.75%)	20 (31.25%)	20.749[b]	.000
With family	25 (47.17%)	43 (67.19%)		
Group home	17 (32.08%)	1 (1.56%)		
	53 (100.00%)	64 (100.00%)		
Work: Labouring position	51(96.23%)	44 (68.75%)	12.891[c,d]	.000
Non-labouring position	2 (3.77%)	20 (31.25%)		
	53 (100.00%)	64 (100.00%)		

	Supported Employment	Open Employment	Mann-Whitney Z	Significance
Median (mean) age:	34.46	25.94	-4.520	.000
	(35.31)	(27.21)		
Median (mean) current job tenure in years:	6.71	1.81	-5.492	.000
	(8.04)	(2.99)		
Median (mean) years in employment:	8.14	5.31	-3.444	.001
	(10.09)	(5.68)		
Median (mean) hours worked per week:	32.50	23.00	-0.527	.598
	(27.66)	(26.05)		
Median (mean) weekly wage:	$33.00	$252.70	-7.865	.000
	($37.64)	($248.70)		
Median (mean) hourly wage:	$1.33	$9.73	-9.000	.000
	($1.53)	($9.15)		
Median (mean) refined FAI score:	18.00	12.00	-3.872	.000
	(20.72)	(13.50)		
Median (mean) original FAI score:	28.00	18.50	-3.928	.000
	(31.25)	(20.94)		

a   Zero cells have expected count less than five. The minimum expected count is 20.38.
b   Zero cells have expected count less than five. The minimum expected count is 8.15.
c   Zero cells have expected count less than five. The minimum expected count is 10.05.
d   The reported Chi-square coefficient is corrected for continuity using the Yates' correction, which compensates for the overestimation of the Chi-square value when used with a two-by-two table (Pallant 2001).

5.7 Controlling for Differences between Open Employment and Supported Employment

To ensure that results of this research are valid, the demographic differences between the open employment clients and supported employment clients need to be controlled. This will ensure that

---

clerical, sales and service workers (6) are not included given that each occupation type only includes one and two participants, respectively. If these two groups are included then 40 percent of cells have an expected count of less than five, which violates the requirements of a meaningful analysis. For information completeness it should be noted that with the inclusion of *tradespersons and related workers* and *intermediate clerical, sales and service workers* the results of the Chi-square test are still significant (χ^2= 25.276, $p \leq .001$).

113

any results achieved are due to differences in the method of employment and not due to some other difference between the two populations.

Table 5.6: Breakdown of occupations: open employment versus supported employment

No.	ASCO Occupation grouping	Supported Employment n	Supported Employment %	Open Employment n	Open Employment %	Total n	Total %
LABOURING POSITIONS							
9	LABOURERS AND RELATED WORKERS						
91	Cleaners	8	15.09%	3	4.69%	11	9.40%
92	Factory labourers	19	35.85%	20	31.25%	39	33.33%
99	Other	7	13.21%	17	26.56%	24	20.51%
		34	64.15%	40	62.50%	74	63.24%
7	INTERMEDIATE PRODCUTION AND TRANSPORT WORKERS						
72	Machine operators	17	32.08%	0	0.00%	17	14.53%
79	Other	0	0.00%	3	4.69%	3	2.56%
		17	32.08%	3	4.69%	20	17.09%
4	TRADESPERSON AND RELATED WORKERS						
41	Mechanical tradespersons	0	0.00%	1	1.56%	1	0.85%
NON-LABOURING POSITIONS							
8	ELEMENTARY CLERICAL, SALES AND SERVICE WORKERS						
81	Elementary clerks	2	3.77%	9	14.06%	11	9.40%
83	Elementary sales workers	0	0.00%	3	4.69%	3	2.56%
83	Elementary service workers	0	0.00%	6	9.38%	6	5.13%
		2	3.77%	18	28.13%	20	17.09%
6	INTERMEDIATE CLERICAL, SALES AND SERVICE WORKERS						
61	Intermediate clerical workers	0	0.00%	1	1.56%	1	0.85%
63	Intermediate service workers	0	0.00%	1	1.56%	1	0.85%
		0	0.00%	2	3.12%	2	1.71%
TOTAL		53	100.00%	64	100.00%	117	100.00%

First Spearman Rank Order Correlation Tests[105] are conducted to gain an understanding of which of the collected demographic variables are correlated with the outcome measures of job satisfaction and quality of life. An understanding of these relationships is important in determining which demographic variables will need to be controlled, so as to allow a meaningful comparison of whether open employment or supported employment have different effects on the outcomes achieved by people with intellectual disabilities.

Table 5.7 shows the Spearman rhos between the collected demographic variables and the four factors of the JSQ, the total JSQ score, as well as total score excluding the *social* factor. The results in Table 5.7 reveal that there is a statistically significant positive correlation between the *work and staff* factor of the JSQ, and both the refined FAI score ($r_s = .217$, $p \leq .019$) and the original FAI score ($r_s = .216$, $p \leq .020$). This relationship suggests that the lower the functional work ability (higher the refined and original FAI scores) the more satisfied participants are with the work they perform, and the staff at the workplace. As such, it appears important, in relation to this factor of

---

[105] Spearman rank order correlation coefficients are calculated as opposed to Pearson correlation coefficients given the non-normal distribution of the data.

the JSQ, that level of functional work ability is controlled when doing statistical analysis to examine whether a statistically significant difference exists between the job satisfaction of participants in open employment and supported employment.

Table 5.7: Spearman rank order correlation coefficients between job satisfaction and demographic variables

	Weekly wage	Hourly wage	Refined FAI Score	Original FAI Score	Age	Current job tenure (years)	Total years of employment
Work and staff	-.126	-.067	.217*	.216*	.007	.017	-.030
	(.175)^a	(.473)	(.019)	(.020)	(.944)	(.853)	(.745)
Task	-.054	.060	.160	.158	-.091	-.145	-.085
	(.566)	(.522)	(.084)	(.088)	(.331)	(.120)	(.361)
Pay	.100	.104	-.020	-.035	-.080	-.054	-.070
	(.285)	(.267)	(.828)	(.710)	(.390)	(.561)	(.451)
Social	.117	.145	.080	.058	-.117	-.009	-.010
	(.209)	(.119)	(.389)	(.531)	(.208)	(.924)	(.911)
Total job satisfaction	.016	.083	.153	.138	-.139	-.086	-.104
	(.861)	(.373)	(.099)	(.137)	(.135)	(.357)	(.262)
Total job satisfaction (exc. social)	.009	.068	.147	.134	-.131	-.093	-.111
	(.924)	(.468)	(.133)	(.149)	(.159)	(.318)	(.233)

a   Figures in parentheses represent significance levels.
*   Significant at the 5 percent level.
Note: *Method of employment* and *living environment* were not included in the above correlation analysis as both are categorical variables.

Spearman Rank Order Correlation tests are conducted to determine whether any of the collected demographic variables are correlated with total quality of life, as well as its four factors, as measured by both the refined and original QOL.Q. Table 5.8 reveals that *empowerment/independence* is statistically significantly positively correlated with participants' weekly wage ($r_s = .508$, $p \leq .001$) and hourly wage ($r_s = .497$, $p \leq .001$) and statistically significantly negatively correlated with functional work ability, measured by either the refined FAI ($r_s = -.447$, $p \leq .001$) or original FAI ($r_s = -.432$, $p \leq .001$). Table 5.4 also reveals that *social belonging/community integration* is statistically significantly positively correlated with the refined FAI score ($r_s = .207$, $p \leq .025$),[106] and statistically significantly negatively correlated with both age ($r_s = -.260$, $p \leq .005$) and total years of employment ($r_s = -.249$, $p \leq .007$). *Quality of life* is found to be statistically significantly positively correlated with hourly wage ($r_s = .274$, $p \leq .003$). These results indicate that when conducting statistical analysis investigating whether there are statistically significant differences in the outcomes achieved by participants in open employment and supported employment, it is important to control for the effects weekly wages (correlated to *empowerment/independence*), hourly wages (correlated to *empowerment/independence* and *quality of life*), functional work ability measured by either refined FAI or original FAI (correlated to *empowerment/independence* and *social belonging/community integration*), age of participants (correlated to *social belonging/community integration*), and total years of employment (correlated to *social belonging/community integration*).

Spearman Rank Order Correlation tests are conducted for the original QOL.Q and its four factors

---

[106] The Spearman rho between *social belonging/community integration* and original FAI for Table 5.3 just fails to meet the five percent significance level ($r_s = .181$, $p \leq .051$). Given the results in Table A2.4 of Appendix 2, which shows that both the refined FAI and original FAI are statistically significantly positively correlated with *social belonging/community integration* for participants in unskilled labouring positions (Panel B, Table A2.4), participants living with their family (Panel C, Table A2.4), and for participants living with their family and in unskilled position (Panel D, Table A2.4), it is safe to conclude that functional work ability is negatively correlated with the *social belonging/community integration* factor of the QOL.Q.

(Table 5.9). In many respects the results are similar to those shown in Table 5.8, for the refined QOL.Q. Similar to Table 5.8, Table 5.9 shows *empowerment/independence* to be statistically significantly positively correlated with weekly wages ($r_s = .527$, $p \leq .001$) and hourly wages ($r_s = .504$, $p \leq .001$), and statistically significantly negatively correlated with refined FAI score ($r_s = -.468$, $p \leq .001$) and original FAI score ($r_s = -.460$, $p \leq .001$). However, different to the result in for the refined QOL.Q (Table 5.8), Table 5.9 reveals a statistically significant negative correlation between *empowerment/independence* and current job tenure ($r_s = -.194$, $p \leq .036$).

Table 5.8: Spearman rank order correlation coefficients between refined QOL.Q and demographic variables

	Weekly wage	Hourly wage	Refined FAI Score	Original FAI Score	Age	Current job tenure (years)	Total years of employment
Satisfaction	-.055	-.040	.151	.123	-.007	.025	-.060
	(.553)[a]	(.667)	(.103)	(.188)	(.938)	(.786)	(.519)
Competence/	.008	.005	.083	.099	.027	.019	-.116
Productivity	(.928)	(.961)	(.376)	(.288)	(.521)	(.836)	(.215)
Empowerment/	.508**	.497**	-.447**	-.432**	.086	-.165	.026
Independence	(.000)	(.000)	(.000)	(.000)	(.356)	(.075)	(.779)
Social	-.073	.099	.207*	.181	-.260**	-.098	-.249**
belonging[b]	(.433)	(.291)	(.025)	(.051)	(.005)	(.291)	(.007)
QOL	.166	.274**	-.028	-.037	-.108	-.111	-.175
	(.074)	(.003)	(.767)	(.691)	(.246)	(.233)	(.060)

a	Figures in parentheses represent significance levels.
b	Social belonging/Community integration.
*	Significant at the 5 percent level.
**	Significant at the 1 percent level.
Note:	*Method of employment* and *living environment* were not included in the above correlation analysis as both are categorical variables.

Table 5.9: Spearman rank order correlation coefficients between original QOL.Q and demographic variables

	Weekly wage	Hourly wage	Refined FAI Score	Original FAI Score	Age	Current job tenure (years)	Total years of employment
Satisfaction	.035	.009	.090	.047	-.003	.081	-.056
	(.709)[a]	(.921)	(.332)	(.614)	(.970)	(.388)	(.549)
Competence/	-.026	-.060	.108	.115	.060	.040	-.087
Productivity	(.777)	(.521)	(.248)	(.216)	(.521)	(.666)	(.354)
Empowerment/	.527**	.504**	-.468**	-.460**	-.033	-.194*	-.060
Independence	(.000)	(.000)	(.000)	(.000)	(.726)	(.036)	(.522)
Social	.014	.157	.075	.049	-.307**	-.117	-.260**
belonging[b]	(.885)	(.091)	(.424)	(.600)	(.001)	(.207)	(.005)
QOL	.216*	.252**	-.080	-.097	-.130	-.085	-.183*
	(.020)	(.006)	(.388)	(.296)	(.164)	(.361)	(.048)

a	Figures in parentheses represent significance levels.
b	Social belonging/Community integration.
*	Significant at the 5 percent level.
**	Significant at the 1 percent level.
Note:	*Method of employment* and *living environment* were not included in the above correlation analysis as both are categorical variables.

The results in Table 5.9, for *social belonging/community integration* are also similar to the results for the refined QOL.Q shown in Table 5.8, in that *social belonging/community integration* is found to be statistically significantly negatively correlated with age ($r_s = -.307$, $p \leq .001$) and total years of employment ($r_s = -.260$, $p \leq .005$). However, different to the results shown in Table 5.8, there is no statistically significant correlation between *social belonging/community integration* and the refined

FAI score.

The results for quality of life also vary between Table 5.8 (refined QOL.Q) and Table 5.9 (original QOL.Q). Similar to Table 5.8, the results in Table 5.9 reveal a statistically significant positive correlation between quality of life and hourly wages (r_s = .252, $p \leq$ .006). However, unlike the results in Table 5.8, Table 5.9 also reveals a statistically significant positive correlation between quality of life and weekly wages (r_s = .216, $p \leq$ .020), and a statistically significant negative correlation between *quality of life* and total years of employment (r_s = -.183, $p \leq$ .048).

Although there are some differences in correlations between the collected demographic variables and quality of life and its four factors depending on which instrument is used (refined QOL.Q or original QOL.Q), results relating to the original QOL.Q (Table 5.9) largely confirm the need to control the same demographic variables in subsequent statistical analysis. That is, both Table 5.8 and Table 5.9 show that it is important to control for the effects of weekly wages, hourly wages, functional work ability measured by either refined FAI or original FAI, age of participant, and total years of employment. Table 5.9, would also suggest that it is important to control for the effects of current job tenure.

Given that data are non-normally distributed, to determine if ANOVAs or ANCOVAs can be used to control for the statistically significant differences highlighted in Table 5.5, and the correlates identified above in Tables 5.7, 5.8, and 5.9, an attempt is undertaken to normalise the data. Histograms of job satisfaction and its four factors as well as quality of life (measured by both the refined and original versions of the QOL.Q) and its four factors are examined. Based on the distributions, the appropriate data transformations recommended by Tabachnick and Fidell (2001) are conducted for each measure (for example, the *work and staff* factor scores of the JSQ are inversed and squared, *job satisfaction* scores are logged). However, when the transformed data are tested for normality, using the Kolmogrov-Smirnov test, on no occasion are the transformed data normally distributed. As Hair *et al.* (1998) noted, for data transformation to have a noticeable effect on the normality of the data, the ratio of the mean to standard deviation should be less than four. For only two of the outcome measures (the factor *task* and the factor *pay*, both from the JSQ) is this ratio less than four, though the conversion still does not result in the data becoming normally distributed. On all other occasions this ratio is well in excess of four; on one occasion it is as high as 12. Consequently, ANOVAs and ANCOVAs are not conducted.

Regression analyses are conducted for each of the different outcome measures (job satisfaction and its four factors, and both the refined and original QOL.Q scores, and the four factors for each), controlling for functional work ability, living environment, and length of employment. These regression analyses are not reported as plots of the residuals reveal hetroscedasticity to be a problem. Hair *et al.* (1998) noted that hetroscedasticity of the residuals often occurred when the dependent variables were not normally distributed, as in this instance. Hair *et al.* (1998) recommended that to overcome the problem of hetroscedasticity of the residuals, the dependent variables should be transformed from a non-normal distribution to a normal distribution. However, as mentioned above, such transformations are not possible with this data and, as such, it is not possible to conduct meaningful regression analyses.

Even if transformations of the data had resulted in the outcome measures being normally distributed, caution would need to be exercised in drawing inferences from the results. Hair *et al.* (1998) noted that when data were transformed so as to alter the underlying distribution, the results of any analysis on the transformed data related to transformed data and not the pre-transformed data. Hair *et al.* (1998) suggested caution in drawing inferences based on the results of analyses conducted on transformed data. Consequently, had it been possible to transform the distribution of the outcome variables to a normal distribution, it is still not clear that the results of the ANOVAs

117

ANCOVAs and regression analyses would necessarily have translated to the underlying non-normally distributed data.

To overcome the problem of not being able to conduct ANOVAs, ANCOVAs, and regression analyses, sub-samples are selected that control for some of the demographic differences between open and supported employment highlighted in Table 5.5 and the correlates identified in Tables 5.7, 5.8, and 5.9.

5.7.1 Occupation Type

As is apparent from Table 5.6 the vast majority of participants placed into supported employment, are placed into labouring positions (96.23 percent), compared with only 68.75 percent of clients in open employment. To control for any potential effect that the nature of the job may have on the results, all analyses are repeated for a sub-sample, comprising only those participants employed in unskilled labouring positions (n = 94). The unskilled labouring occupations comprise the two groupings *labourers and related workers* and *intermediate production and transport workers* (see Table 5.4). The labouring grouping *tradesperson and related workers* is not included since this type of occupation differs from the other two labouring categories and is considered *skilled*. To be classified in the occupation grouping *tradesperson and related workers*, a person must have completed at least either a trade certificate or an apprenticeship.

5.7.2 Living Environment

A substantial body of literature highlights that people accommodated in institutional settings report lower quality of life scores compared with non-institutionalised individuals (for example, Hemming *et al.*, 1981; Heal and Chadsey-Rusch, 1985; Schalock and Lilley, 1986; Schalock and Genung, 1993). As in Table 5.5 the participants who work in open employment differ statistically significantly in terms of their living arrangements compared with participants in supported employment. To control for the effect that living environment may have on the results, all analyses are repeated for only those individuals living with their family (n = 68). Due to small sample sizes in the other two categories (living independently and living in a group home) it is not possible to conduct separate analyses for these sub-samples.

5.7.3 Occupation Type and Living Environment

To control both demographic variables of occupation type and living environment, analyses are repeated on the sub-sample of participants who work in unskilled labouring positions and live with their family (n = 54). As mentioned below, in an attempt to gain a greater understanding of the results, the entire sample is dichotomised, based on functional work ability (high versus low). However, when such analyses are conducted, it is not possible to conduct further analysis on the sub-sample of participants who work in unskilled labouring positions and who live at home due to the sub-sample being too small.

5.7.4 Functional Work Ability

It is reasonable to expect that the functional work ability of a person with an intellectual disability will to some extent dictate whether they were placed in open or supported employment. Table 5.5 reveals that participants placed in open employment have statistically significantly higher functional work ability (as measured by the both the refined FAI and original FAI) compared with participants placed in supported employment. This statistically significant difference in functional work ability is also apparent in the above mentioned three sub-samples: (1) participants in unskilled labouring positions, (2) participants who live with their families, (3) participants in unskilled labouring positions who live with their families.[107] Functional work ability is primarily measured by

---

[107] These statistically significant differences will be reported later when each of the three sub-samples are discussed in more detail.

the refined FAI.[108] The refined FAI consists of 20 behaviourally anchored rating items, ranging from zero (no significant impairment) to three (severe impairment), which assess a person's work capabilities and deficiencies, thus giving a theoretical range of zero to 60; the *higher* the score, the *lower* the person's functional work ability. Given that the original FAI, containing 30 questions (range zero to 90) has been widely used as a measure of functional work ability (although not for people with intellectual disabilities), the scores of the original FAI are also reported in all instances. This should facilitate comparisons with other studies.

Consequently, to control for differences in the functional work ability of the two populations (open employment and supported employment) and to gain further insight into the initial results, Mann-Whitney U Tests are conducted separately for participants with high and low functional work abilities. Low functional work ability is defined as a refined FAI score of equal to or greater than 17, with a high functional work ability defined as a refined FAI score of 12 or less. These cut-off scores were selected as they represent approximately the top and bottom 40 percent of the sample, respectively. The mid-point is not selected, given that the FAI was completed by different support workers. As such, potential rater-differences could decrease the power of the statistical tests if the sample were dichotomised around the median. This is because the rater-differences might affect in which half of the dichotomised sample a participant is categorised.[109]

5.7.5 Matched Pairs Analysis of Open Employment versus Supported Employment
A matched pair analysis is also conducted to control for differences between participants placed in open employment and those placed in supported employment. The matching is conducted as follows:
1. Given that there are fewer people in supported employment (53) compared with open employment (64), I commenced with the list of supported employment participants and proceeded to match each one with open employment participants.
2. Matching is based on gender, type of occupation (unskilled labouring position or non-labouring position), functional work ability (refined FAI), and hours worked per week. As it is not always possible to match exactly, based on the refined FAI, and given that rater differences may result in participants being rated differently had they been rated by someone else, plus or minus three points is considered an acceptable match in relation to the refined FAI.[110] In relation to work hours, participants are deemed to be matched if their work hours were within five hours of the other participant.[111]
3. For each supported employment participant I searched all the open employment participants to identify all possible matches. All potential matches are listed next to each supported employment participant. Open employment participants who matched a supported employment participant are listed as a match, irrespective of the number of times they have been previously listed as a match. This stage of the matching process results in 23 supported employment participants being matched with open employment participants. It is not possible to match 30 supported employment participants and as such they are omitted. Of the 23 supported employment participants with matches, 12 matched to only one open employment participant, six matched to two participants in open employment, and five matched to multiple open employment participants (ranging between four and ten participants).

---

[108] The refinement of the original FAI (Crewe and Athelstan 1984) to arrive at the refined FAI was detailed in Section 4.3 (Functional Assessment Inventory).

[109] Different cut-off scores were used and the results remain qualitatively the same.

[110] The matching process was also attempted with a more stringent matching criterion for the FAI, but this resulted in a substantial reduction in the number of matches, which would not have allowed for meaningful statistical analysis to be conducted. Matching was also attempted with a more lax criterion for the FAI, but this resulted in the matching not effectively controlling for differences in the functional work ability between the two populations (open employment versus supported employment).

[111] Five hours is selected, as any reduction in the number of hours substantially reduces the sample size and, consequently, meaningful statistical analysis is not possible.

4. The supported employment participants with single matches are examined first and four of the 12 are dropped as they match against the same open employment participant as another single match. In deciding which single matches to keep, the ones that most closely match in terms of refined FAI and work hours are retained.
5. The remaining 11 supported employment participants who have multiple matches are then investigated. As on a number of occasions the same open employment participants had been matched to several supported employment participants I commenced the process of selecting the best match for these 11 supported employment participants by looking firstly at those participants with only two potential matches, then those with four potential matches,[112] and so on. This process is carried out to ensure as many matches as possible. Unfortunately, two more supported employment participants have to be dropped due to multiple matchings with the same open employment participants. As stated above, in deciding which open employment participant to match with the supported employment participant, the ones that most closely matched are retained. On two occasions there are no differences based on the refined FAI and work hours. The best match is then based on ASCO occupation type.
6. The above process results in 17 matched pairs being selected.

5.7.6 Non-Controllable Differences
Controlling for differences in either the hourly or weekly wage between participants in open employment and those in supported employment is not possible, as there is a requirement for open employment to pay at least the minimum wage, whereas no such requirement exists for people working in a supported environment. The consequence, as highlighted in the figures at the bottom of Table 5.5, is that it is not uncommon for people in supported employment to be paid as little as 20 cents per hour. Thus, the differences in wages are inherent in the different methods of employment (open employment versus supported employment).

Age and length of employment are also not controlled as the higher age and length of employment by participants in supported employment reflected differences in the two methods of employment. The higher average age of people in supported employment is due to this form of employment having a longer history. Supported employment agencies have operated in Perth, Australia since 1951, with Agency A being the first (Agency A's web page). Whereas, the first open employment agency was not established in Western Australia until 1984, being Agency B (Agency B's web page). Even with the establishment of the first open employment agency in Western Australia in the mid 1980s, this method of employment for people with intellectual disabilities was not readily accepted as being a suitable alternative until the 1990s.[113] Given the relative newness of open employment agencies it is not surprising that the average age of their clients is younger.

This relative newness of open employment agencies and the younger average age of clients partially explain why the average length of employment for people in supported employment is higher compared with participants in open employment. However, another factor is due to the underlying different nature of the two methods of employment. Supported employment is a relatively stable form of placement. Once a client is placed in a supported environment (for example, a workshop), most stay in that placement for a long period of time. If a person changes jobs, it is typically to another job within the same supported setting. This contrasts rather dramatically with open employment, where a placement may fail due to a variety of reasons. As noted by Schalock and Lilley (1986) the major reasons why people with intellectual disabilities lose open employment are due to slow work, inappropriate behaviour, low motivation, lack of physical stamina, and poor personal appearance. Once a placement has failed, open employment agencies recommence searching for another placement for their client. As such, the client may spend periods of time out

---

[112] No supported employment person matches with three open employment participants.
[113] This statement is made based on discussions with staff from both open and supported employment agencies and can be evidenced by the fact that the majority of open employment agencies operating in this Australian city did not commence operations until the 1990s.

of employment and hence the average length of a job is less than in supported employment. It is also acknowledged that open employment might offer a greater range of job opportunities, allowing for job changes for people in jobs which they do not find fulfilling, or for some people to progress their careers by accepting higher level jobs. These two factors would further reduce the average length of a job in open employment relative to supported employment.

Demographic information for each of the above control sub-samples (participants in unskilled labouring positions, participants living with their family, participants in unskilled labouring positions living with their family, and the matched pairs sub-sample) is presented in the following sections. For each sub-sample an analysis is also conducted to examine whether participants in open employment and supported employment differed demographically at a statistically significant level (that is, $p \leq .05$).

5.8 Demographics of Participants in Unskilled Labouring Positions
Table 5.10 has demographic data for those participants who are employed in unskilled labouring positions. Comparing the demographic data in Table 5.10 with the entire sample (Table 5.3) this sub-sample appears slightly different. Participants in unskilled labouring positions are slightly older (median (mean) age 29.70 (31.60) compared with 28.82 (30.88)), have been in employment and their current jobs longer (6.15 (8.12) and 4.51 (5.89) years compared with 5.84 (7.68) and 4.10 (5.27) years), earn less per week and hour ($51.50 ($135.11) per week and $2.42 ($4.81) per hour compared with $72.00 ($153.09) per week and $ $4.10 ($5.70) per hour), a greater percentage live in group homes (19.15 percent compared with 15.38 percent), and less live independently (23.40 percent compared with 26.50 percent). The reason for these differences is due to a greater representation of supported employment participants in this sub-sample than the entire sample; 54.26 percent compared with 45.30 percent. As is apparent from Table 5.6, non-labouring positions are predominantly occupied by participants in open employment, and the exclusion of participants in such positions results in this sub-sample having a greater proportion of participants from supported employment.

Table 5.10: Demographics of participants working in unskilled labouring positions (n=94)

		n (%)		n (%)	Total
Gender:	Female	38 (36.8%)	Male	56 (63.2%)	94
Living:	Independently	22 (23.40%)	With family	54 (57.45%)	94
	Group home	18 (19.15%)			
Employment:	Open	43 (45.74%)	Supported	51 (54.26%)	94

	Median	Mean	Interquartile range	Standard deviation	Maximum	Minimum
Age:	29.70	31.60	13.74	9.44	61.07	17.87
Current job tenure (yrs):	4.51	5.89	6.40	5.57	25.12	0.02
Years in employment:	6.15	8.12	6.26	6.54	34.99	0.65
Hours worked per week:	32.50	27.58	20.00	10.91	48.00	8.00
Weekly wage:	$51.50	$135.11	$229.24	$147.85	$495.00	$3.00
Hourly wage:	$2.42	$4.81	$7.69	$4.32	$13.27	$0.17
Refined FAI score:	14	17.34	14	10.33	46	0
Original FAI score:	23.50	26.39	21.25	14.20	65	1

Table 5.11 shows separately the demographics by method of employment (open employment and supported employment) for this sub-sample. Similarly for Table 5.5, which shows a breakdown for the entire sample, significant differences exist between the two groups of participants. As found in the entire sample there is a statistically significant difference in terms of living patterns (· = 14.834, $\underline{p} \leq .001$), with a greater percentage of participants from open employment living independently or with their family. Also as found in the entire population, participants in supported employment are older (Z = -4.705, $p \leq .001$), have been employed in their current jobs longer (Z = -

121

5.096, $p \le .001$), worked more years in total ($Z = -3.427$, $p \le .001$), and earn less per week and per hour ($Z = -6.443$, $p \le .001$; $Z = -7.993$, $p \le .001$, respectively). There is also a statistically significant difference in terms of functional work ability (as measured by the FAI – both the refined and original versions) between participants in open employment compared with supported employment ($Z = -3.362$, $p \le .001$; $Z = -3.394$, $p \le .001$, respectively); participants in open employment have a higher functional work ability. Consequently, though this sub-sample of only participants in unskilled labouring positions controls for differences in the types of occupations that participants were placed in across open employment and supported employment, and gender ($\chi^2 = 0.000$, $p \le 1.000$), it does not control for demographic differences in terms of living arrangements, or levels of functional work ability.

Table 5.11: Differences in demographics between open employment and supported employment for participants working in unskilled labouring positions (n=94)

	Supported employment	Open employment	Pearson Chi-Square	Significance
Gender: Female	21 (41.18%)	17 (39.53%)	$0.000^{a,c}$	1.000
Male	30 (58.82%)	26 (60.47%)		
	51 (100.00%)	43 (100.00%)		
Living: Independently	11 (21.57%)	11 (25.58%)	14.834^{b}	.001
With family	23 (45.10%)	31 (72.09%)		
Group home	17 (33.33%)	1(2.33%)		
	51 (100.00%)	43 (100.00%)		

	Supported Employment	Open Employment	Mann-Whitney Z	Significance
Median (mean) age:	34.55	26.17	-4.705	.000
	(35.84)	(26.57)		
Median (mean) current job tenure in years:	7.03	1.85	-5.096	.000
	(8.30)	(3.03)		
Median (mean) years in employment:	8.15	5.39	-3.427	.001
	(10.39)	(5.44)		
Median (mean) hours worked per week:	32.50	37.50	-1.245	.213
	(28.00)	(27.08)		
Median (mean) weekly wage:	33.00	$269.00	-6.443	.000
	($37.15)	($251.29)		
Median (mean) hourly wage:	1.33	$9.00	-7.993	.000
	($1.50)	($8.73)		
Median (mean) refined FAI score:	18.00	12.00	-3.362	.001
	(20.43)	(20.51)		
Median (mean) original FAI score:	28.00	18.00	-3.394	.001
	(30.82)	(21.14)		

a   Zero cells have expected count less than five. The minimum expected count is 17.38.
b   Zero cells have an expected count less than five. The minimum expected count is 8.23.
c   The reported Chi-square coefficient is corrected for continuity using the Yates' correction, which compensates for the overestimation of the Chi-square value when used with a two-by-two table (Pallant 2001).

5.9 Demographics of Participants Living with their Family
When comparing Table 5.12 with Table 5.3, this sub-sample of only participants who live with their family differs from the entire sample in that it is younger (median (mean) age of 24.82 (26.92) years compared with 28.82 (30.88) years), the participants have been in their current jobs for fewer years (1.97 (3.96) years compared with 4.10 (5.27) years), they have worked fewer years in total (4.77 (5.16) years compared with 5.84 (7.68) years), but they are earning a higher weekly wage ($83.50 ($163.71) compared with $72.00 ($153.09)). These differences are a consequence of this sub-sample of participants who live with their family having a higher percentage of participants from open employment than the entire sample; 63.24 percent compared with 54.70 percent.

Table 5.12: Demographics of participants living with their family (n=68)

		n (%)		n (%)	Total
Gender:	Female	25 (36.76%)	Male	43 (63.24%)	68
Employment:	Open	43 (63.24%)	Supported	25 (36.76%)	68
Work:	Non-labouring	14 (20.59%)	Labouring	54 (79.41%)	68

	Median	Mean	Interquartile range	Standard deviation	Maximum	Minimum
Age:	24.82	26.92	8.88	7.63	58.81	17.87
Current job tenure (yrs):	1.97	3.96	4.91	3.92	16.48	0.02
Years in employment:	4.77	5.16	5.31	3.89	16.48	0.65
Hours worked per week:	32.50	26.90	23.75	11.59	40.00	8.00
Weekly wage:	$83.50	$163.71	$301.94	$154.05	$502.00	$14.00
Hourly wage:	$5.67	$5.74	$7.61	$4.11	$13.39	$0.51
Refined FAI score:	14.00	16.37	11.00	9.41	46.00	0.00
Original FAI score:	24.00	25.00	19.75	13.04	65.00	1.00

Table 5.13: Differences in demographics between open employment and supported employment for participants living with their family (n=68)

	Supported employment	Open employment	Pearson Chi-Square[a]	Significance
Gender: Female	9 (36.00%)	16 (37.21%)	0.000[b]	1.000
Male	16 (64.00%)	27 (62.79%)		
	25 (100.00%)	43 (100.00%)		
Work: Labouring position	23 (92.00%)	31 (72.09%)	2.255[c]	.133
Non-labouring position	2 (8.00%)	12 (27.91%)		
	25 (100.00%)	43 (100.00%)		

	Supported Employment	Open Employment	Mann-Whitney Z	Significance
Median (mean) age:	29.75 (31.56)	24.17 (24.23)	-3.142	.002
Median (mean) current job tenure in years:	5.00 (6.01)	1.52 (2.76)	-3.504	.000
Median (mean) years in employment:	5.40 (6.63)	4.26 (4.31)	-1.991	.047
Median (mean) hours worked per week:	32.50 (27.46)	30.00 (26.58)	-1.119	.263
Median (mean) weekly wage:	$30.00 ($38.35)	$236.00 ($236.60)	-5.343	.000
Median (mean) hourly wage:	$1.35 ($1.62)	$8.95 ($8.14)	-6.501	.000
Median (mean) refined FAI score:	18.00 (20.60)	12.00 (13.91)	-3.031	.002
Median (mean) original FAI score:	28.00 (31.08)	19.00 (21.47)	-2.991	.003

a   All reported Chi-square coefficients are corrected for continuity using the Yates' correction, which compensates for the overestimation of the Chi-square value when used with a two-by-two table (Pallant 2001).
b   Zero cells have expected count less than five. The minimum expected count is 20.38.
c   One cell has an expected count less than five. The minimum expected count is 4.85.

As revealed in Table 5.13, even though this sub-sample controls for the living environment by sampling only participants who live with their family, there are still statistically significant differences between participants in open employment and supported employment in terms of average age (Z = -3.142, $p \leq .002$), average years in current job (Z = -3.504, $p \leq .001$), average years in employment (Z = -1.991, $p \leq .047$), average weekly wage (Z = -5.343, $p \leq .001$), average hourly wage (Z = -6.501, $p \leq .001$), and functional work ability as measured by the FAI (refined and original) (Z = -3.031, $p \leq .002$; Z = -2.991, $p \leq .003$, respectively). Interestingly, there is no statistically significant difference in terms of participant occupation types (labouring versus non-labouring) for open employment compared with supported employment (χ^2= 2.255, $p \leq .133$) and gender (χ^2= 0.000, $p \leq 1.000$). Thus, this sub-sample of only participants living with their family controls not only for differences in living environments but also for differences in occupation types and gender differences between participants in open employment and those in supported employment. However, this sub-population does not control for the higher functional work ability of participants in open employment compared with participants in supported employment.

5.10 Demographics of Participants in Unskilled Labouring Positions Living with their Family

As is evident from Table 5.14, this sub-sample of participants who work in unskilled labouring positions and live at home differs demographically from the entire sample (Table 5.3), in that participants have a lower median (mean) age at 26.47 (27.82) years compared with 28.82 (30.88) years), have on average been employed in their current job for fewer years (2.55 (4.32) years compared with 4.10 (5.27) years), have worked on average fewer total years (5.20 (5.61) years compared with 5.84 (7.68) years), and on average earn less per week and per hour ($55.00 ($148.95) per week and $3.69 ($5.23) per hour compared with $72.00 ($153.09) per week and $4.10 ($5.70) per hour). The differences in terms of age and length of employment can be attributed to the fact that people living at home are likely to be younger than those not living at home and consequently have not had as many employment experiences. The difference in terms of wage level can be attributed to a combination of the fact that labouring positions might receive less pay than non-labouring positions and that younger people tend to earn less than older people.

Table 5.14: Demographics of participants working in unskilled labouring positions and living with their family (n=54)

		n (%)		n (%)	Total
Gender:	Female	21 (38.89%)	Male	33 (61.11%)	54
Employment:	Open	31 (57.41%)	Supported	23 (42.59%)	54

	Median	Mean	Interquartile range	Standard deviation	Maximum	Minimum
Age:	26.47	27.82	10.36	8.23	58.81	17.87
Current job tenure (yrs):	2.55	4.32	5.30	4.10	16.48	0.02
Years in employment:	5.20	5.61	6.34	4.03	16.48	0.65
Hours worked per week:	32.50	27.19	24.25	11.99	40.00	8.00
Weekly wage:	$55.00	$148.95	$288.86	$149.60	$495.00	$14.00
Hourly wage:	$3.69	$5.23	$7.57	$4.11	$13.03	$0.51
Refined FAI score:	14.00	16.50	11.00	9.66	46.00	0.00
Original FAI score:	23.50	25.11	20.00	13.20	65.00	1.00

Though this sub-sample controls for differences between participants in open employment and supported employment in terms of living environment and types of occupations, Table 5.15 reveals there are still statistically significant differences in terms of average age (Z = -3.236, $p \leq .001$), current job tenure (Z = -3.560, $p \leq .001$), average weekly wage (Z = -4.375, $p \leq .001$), average hourly wage (Z = -5.914, $p \leq .001$), and functional work ability as measured by the FAI (both refined and original) (Z = -2.663, $p \leq .008$; Z = -2.608, $p \leq .009$, respectively). Consequently, as per the previous sub-sample (participants living with their family), this sub-sample of participants working in unskilled labouring positions and living with their family controls for differences between open employment and supported employment in terms of living environment, type of occupations, and gender ($\chi^2 = 0.000$, $p \leq 1.000$), but does not control for differences in the level of functional work ability of participants.

Table 5.15: Differences in demographics between open employment and supported employment for participants working in unskilled labouring positions and living with their family (n=54)

	Supported employment	Open employment	Pearson Chi-Square	Significance
Gender: Female	9 (39.13%)	12 (38.71%)	0.000[a,b]	1.000
Male	14 (60.87%)	19 (61.29%)		
	23 (100.00%)	31 (100.00%)		

	Supported Employment	Open Employment	Mann-Whitney Z	Significance
Median (mean) age:	29.76	24.46	-3.236	.001
	(32.41)	(24.41)		
Median (mean) current job tenure in years:	5.39	1.81	-3.560	.000
	(6.41)	(2.77)		
Median (mean) years in employment:	5.95	5.15	-1.880	.060
	(7.00)	(4.58)		
Median (mean) hours worked per week:	32.50	38.00	-1.109	.268
	(28.20)	(26.45)		
Median (mean) weekly wage:	$30.00	$269.00	-4.375	.000
	($37.33)	($231.77)		
Median (mean) hourly wage:	$1.35	$8.75	-5.914	.000
	($1.59)	($7.95)		
Median (mean) refined FAI score:	18.00	12.00	-2.663	.008
	(19.96)	(13.94)		
Median (mean) original FAI score:	27.00	18.00	-2.608	.009
	(30.13)	(21.39)		

a   Zero cells have expected count less than five. The minimum expected count is 8.94.
b   The reported Chi-square coefficient is corrected for continuity using the Yates' correction, which compensates for the overestimation of the Chi-square value when used with a two-by-two table (Pallant 2001).

Table 5.16: Demographics of matched pairs sub-sample (n=34)

		n (%)		n (%)	Total
Gender:	Female	12 (35.29%)	Male	22 (64.71%)	34
Living:	Independently	11 (32.35%)	With family	20 (58.82%)	
	Group home	3 (8.83%)			34
Employment:	Supported	17 (50.00%)	Open	17 (50.00%)	34
Work:	Non-labouring	32 (94.12%)	Labouring	2 (5.88%)	34

	Median	Mean	Interquartile range	Standard deviation	Maximum	Minimum
Age:	27.86	30.98	14.61	10.28	61.07	17.87
Current job tenure:	2.83	5.28	6.67	5.61	25.12	.15
Years in employment:	6.71	8.96	8.00	8.06	34.99	0.65
Hours worked per week:	31.25	27.26	22.50	11.23	40.00	8.00
Weekly wage:	$66.00	$148.34	$242.57	$151.65	$494.00	$13.50
Hourly wage:	$3.13	$5.20	$7.51	$4.37	$14.54	$0.68
Refined FAI score:	13.50	15.35	7.25	6.56	29	4
Original FAI score:	23.00	24.24	12.25	9.28	41	9

5.11 Demographics of Matched Pairs Sub-sample

As none of the above sub-samples effectively controls for the statistically significantly higher functional work ability of participants in open employment compared with supported employment, matching of participants is conducted. Participants are matched, based on gender, occupation type (labouring or non-labouring), functional work ability (based on the refined FAI)[114], and work hours, to control hopefully for all possible differences in the collected demographic variables between open and supported employment participants.

Table 5.16 shows the demographic information of participants in the matched pairs sub-sample. As can be seen comparing Table 5.16 with Table 5.3, this sub-sample is similar in terms of age, years of employment, hours worked per week, average wage (weekly and hourly) and functional work ability (measured by either the refined or original FAI). However, this matched pairs sub-sample has a higher proportion of supported employment participants (50.00 percent compared with 45.30 percent) due to the matching process. Interestingly, this sub-sample differs considerably in terms of living environments to the entire sample (Table 5.3); with a greater proportion of people living independently (32.35 percent compared with 26.50 percent) and considerably less in group homes (8.33 percent compared with 15.38 percent).

Table 5.17: Differences in demographics between matched pairs sub-sample (n=34)

		Supported employment	Open employment	Pearson Chi-Square	Significance
Gender:	Female	6 (35.29%)	6 (35.29%)		
	Male	11 (64.71%)	11 (64.71%)		
		17 (100.00%)	17 (100.00%)		
Living:	Independently	6 (35.29%)	5 (29.41%)	3.891[a]	.143
	With family	8 (47.06%)	12 (70.59%)		
	Group home	3 (17.65%)	0 (0.00%)		
		17 (100.00%)	17 (100.00%)		
Work:	Labouring position	16(94.12%)	16 (94.12%)		
	Non-labouring position	1 (5.88%)	1 (5.88%)		
		17 (100.00%)	17 (100.00%)		

	Supported Employment	Open Employment	Wilcoxon Z	Significance
Median (mean) age:	33.77	26.17	-2.154	.031
	(35.73)	(26.23)		
Median (mean) current job tenure in years:	6.01	1.82	-2.769	.006
	(8.03)	(2.52)		
Median (mean) years in employment:	10.29	5.57	-2.107	.035
	(12.38)	(5.54)		
Median (mean) hours worked per week:	32.50	30.00	-0.144	.886
	(27.38)	(27.15)		
Median (mean) weekly wage:	$51.50	$275.00	-3.479	.001
	($46.43)	($250.25)		
Median (mean) hourly wage:	$1.47	$8.95	-3.479	.001
	($1.86)	($8.54)		
Median (mean) refined FAI score:	14.00	13.00	-0.321	.748
	(15.41)	(15.29)		
Median (mean) original FAI score:	23.00	22.00	-0.493	.622
	(24.18)	(24.29)		

a   Two cells have expected count less than five. The minimum expected count is 1.50.

Given that the matching process is not exact, with some leeway given in terms of a match being specified for hours worked per week (hours could vary by five) and functional work ability (the refined FAI score could vary by three), Wilcoxon Signed Ranks Tests are conducted to ensure that the matched pairs sub-sample controls for these variables and also to see whether any statistically

---

[114] Matching was also conducted based on the original FAI and results are qualitatively similar.

significant differences exist between the open employment and supported employment populations. Table 5.17 shows that there are no statistically significant differences between participants in open employment and those in supported employment in terms of hours worked per week ($Z = -0.144$, $p \leq .886$) or functional work ability as measured by the refined FAI ($Z = -0.321$, $p \leq .748$) and original FAI ($Z = -0.493$, $p \leq .622$). Table 5.18 also reveals that the participants in open employment and supported employment for this sub-sample still differ statistically significantly in terms of average age ($Z = -2.154$, $p \leq .031$), current job tenure ($Z = -2.769$, $p \leq .006$), average total years in employment ($Z = -2.107$, $p \leq .035$), average weekly wage ($Z = -3.479$, $p \leq .001$), and average hourly wage ($Z = -3.479$, $p \leq .001$). However, as previously stated, these differences are inherently related to the different methods of employment and, as such, no attempt to control for these variables is made. Consequently, as in the two previous sub-samples, this matched pairs sub-sample effectively controls for differences between open employment and supported employment in terms of type of occupations (labouring versus non-labouring) and living environment. Whereas the two previous sub-samples do not effectively control for differences in functional work ability, this matched pairs sub-sample does.

Table 5.18:   Spearman rank order correlation coefficients between demographic variables

	Hourly wage	Refined FAI Score	Original FAI Score	Age	Current job tenure (years)	Total years of employment
Weekly wage	.867**	-.558**	-.573**	-.165	-.240**	-.024
	(.000)	(.000)	(.000)	(.075)	(.009)	(.800)
Hourly wage		-.435**	-.435**	-.302**	-.410**	-.200*
		(.000)	(.000)	(.002)	(.000)	(.031)
Refined FAI			.983**	.009	.134	-.027
			(.000)	(.922)	(.149)	(.769)
Original FAI				.021	.139	-.041
				(.823)	(.135)	(.658)
Age					.465**	.683**
					(.000)	(.000)
Current job tenure (years)						.718**
						(.000)

*   Significant at the 5 percent level.
**   Significant at the 1 percent level.
Note: *Method of employment* and *living environment* were not included in the above correlation analysis as both are categorical variables.

5.12 Correlations among Demographic Variables

Demographic differences between open employment and supported employment for the entire sample are highlighted in Table 5.5 and the various sub-samples in Tables 5.11, 5.13, 5.15, and 5.17. Given that Table 5.5 shows statistically significant differences exist between open employment and supported employment for all except one of the collected demographic variables (hours worked), it is not surprising that Table 5.18, which presents the Spearman rhos[115] between the various demographic variables, shows statistically significant correlations between most of the demographic variables. The statistically significant negative correlations between the measures of functional work ability (refined and original FAI scores) and wages (both weekly and hourly) are expected as this indicates that people with higher (lower) functional work ability (refined and original FAI scores) earn more (both hourly and weekly). It is highly likely the reason for statistically significant negative correlations between hourly wages and current job tenure ($r_s = -.410$, $p \leq .001$) and total years of employment ($r_s = -.200$, $p \leq .031$) is due to the fact that supported employment options have been available to people with intellectual disabilities for longer than open employment opportunities and, as such, people in supported employment have been in their current jobs longer and have been employed for more years in total. This is confirmed by results in Tables

---

[115] The Spearman Rank Order Correlation Test is used as opposed to the Pearson Correlation Test, given that the collected demographic variables are non-normally distributed.

5.5, 5.11, 5.13, 5.15, and 5.17, showing that participants in open employment have been in their current jobs statistically significantly fewer years, and have been employed statistically significantly fewer years in total compared with their counterparts in supported employment. As such, negative correlations between these demographic variables would be expected. The above explanation is also the most probable cause for the statistically significant negative correlation between weekly wages and current job tenure ($r_s = -.240$, $p \leq .009$). Though why there is no statistically significant correlation between weekly wages and total years of employment is not readily evident. The earlier establishment of supported employment services also explains the statistically significant positive correlations between age and current job tenure ($r_s = .465$, $p \leq .001$) and total years of employment ($r_s = .683$, $p \leq .001$).

5.13 Conclusion
This chapter described first the demographic data for the entire sample and then discussed the formation of different sub-samples of participants to control for demographic differences that exist between participants employed in open employment and participants employed in supported employment. The different sub samples formed are:
1) participants employed in unskilled labouring positions, to control for differences that exist in occupation types between open employment and supported employment;
2) participants living with their family, to control for differences in the living environment of participants in open employment compared with participants in supported employment;
3) participants in unskilled labouring positions who live with their family, to control for differences in both occupation types and living arrangements between open employment participants and supported employment participants; and
4) a matched pairs analysis, where participants are matched based on gender, occupation type (unskilled labouring versus non-labouring), functional work ability (based on refined FAI score), and hours worked per week.

The demographic data for each of the above sub-samples were presented and analysed to explore what, if any, demographic differences still existed between open employment and supported employment participants.

In the next chapter the scores for job satisfaction and quality of life outcome measures are presented. Differences in the scores between open employment and supported employment participants for the entire sample, as well as each of the above sub-samples, are analysed and discussed.

Chapter 6 – Results and Discussion

6.1 Introduction

In this chapter I discuss the different outcomes achieved by the different methods of employment. Initially the different methods of employment (open employment versus supported employment) are compared with see whether they result in statistically significantly different scores for job satisfaction and its four factors. These differences are then further investigated, controlling for several important underlying differences in the two populations. Likewise, the scores for quality of life and its four factors are then assessed to see whether any statistically significant differences exist between open employment and supported employment. As with job satisfaction, sub-samples are then used to control for the underlying differences in the demographics of the two populations and results are compared.

6.2 Job Satisfaction

To assess whether a statistically significant difference exists in the job satisfaction of participants placed in supported employment compared with participants placed in open employment, Mann-Whitney U Tests are conducted (except for the matched-pairs sub-sample when Wilcoxon Signed Ranks Tests are conducted) for each of the four factors of the JSQ, the total JSQ score, as well as the total score excluding the *social* factor.[116] As the data are non-normally distributed, medians are reported. However, given the prevalence of reporting means, and to aid future researchers who may wish to compare their results with those reported in this thesis, means are also shown.

The results in Table 6.1 reveal that across the entire sample (Panel A) participants placed in open employment report statistically significantly higher *social* scores compared with those placed in supported employment ($Z = -2.111$, $p \leq .035$). However, none of the other factors or total *job satisfaction* is statistically significantly different, depending on the method of employment (open employment versus supported employment).

As mentioned in Section 5.7 (Controlling for Differences between Open Employment and Supported Employment), such an analysis as reported in the above paragraph does not control for any of the demographic differences between the two populations. To control for any potential effect that the type of occupation may have on the results, the analysis is initially repeated for the sub-sample, comprising only those participants employed in unskilled labouring positions. The analysis reveals that for participants in unskilled labouring positions (Panel B, Table 6.1) there is no statistically significant difference in *job satisfaction* based on method of employment (open employment versus supported employment), and only one of the four factors differs statistically significantly between the two methods of employment; the *social* factor ($Z = -2.942$, $p \leq .003$), which is higher for participants in open employment

When the living environment is controlled, by repeating the analysis for only those participants who live with their family (Panel C, Table 6.1), no significant results are found for *job satisfaction* nor for any of the four factors. When the analysis is repeated for the sub-sample of participants who work in unskilled labouring positions and live with their family (Panel D, Table 6.1), no statistically significant differences are found for *job satisfaction* or its four factors based on method of employment (open employment versus supported employment).

For the matched-pairs sub-sample (Panel E, Table 6.1), a statistically significant difference is found in terms of the *social* factor ($Z = -2.127$, $p \leq .033$), with participants in open employment reporting higher scores relative to participants in supported employment. However, total job satisfaction and

---

[116] As mentioned in Section 4.4.2 (Internal Reliability of the Derived JSQ Scores) and Section 4.4.3 (Factor Stability of the Derived JSQ) the *social* factor of the JSQ did not produce reliable scores and consequently the total JSQ score is calculated both with and without this factor.

the three other factors are again found not to differ statistically significantly based on method of employment (supported employment versus open employment).

Table 6.1: Differences in the median (mean) of JSQ scores

	Work & Staff	Task	Pay	Social	Total	Total (x social)
Panel A: All occupations (n=117)						
Open employment	92.59%	75.00%	66.67%	100.00%	81.71%	77.78%
(n=64)	(85.88%)	(68.82%)	(65.36%)	(88.11%)	(77.04%)	(73.35%)
Supported employment	100.00%	66.67%	55.56%	83.33%	72.92%	68.06%
(n=53)	(91.82%)	(63.44%)	(56.08%)	(81.66%)	(73.25%)	(70.45%)
Z	-1.186	-1.135	-1.872	-2.111*	-1.588	-1.421
Significance (p)	.236	.257	.061	.035	.112	.155
Panel B: Unskilled labouring occupations (n=94)						
Open employment	92.59%	75.00%	66.67%	100.00%	81.83%	77.78%
(n=43)	(86.74%)	(68.90%)	(64.86%)	(92.51%)	(78.25%)	(73.50%)
Supported employment	100.00%	62.50%	55.56%	83.33%	72.22%	66.98%
(n=51)	(91.50%)	(62.25%)	(56.54%)	(81.70%)	(73.00%)	(70.10%)
Z	-0.939	-1.233	-1.559	-2.942**	-1.818	-1.404
Significance (p)	.348	.218	.119	.003	.069	.160
Panel C: Living with family (n=68)						
Open employment	92.59%	75.00%	66.67%	88.89%	81.83%	80.86%
(n=43)	(87.60%)	(69.96%)	(67.05%)	(88.89%)	(78.38%)	(74.87%)
Supported employment	100.00%	75.00%	61.11%	83.33%	81.37%	78.86%
(n=25)	(92.30%)	(67.17%)	(62.22%)	(82.89%)	(76.14%)	(73.90%)
Z	-0.970	-0.436	-0.803	-1.496	-0.916	-0.712
Significance (p)	.332	.663	.442	.135	.360	.476
Panel D: Unskilled labouring occupations and living with family (n=54)						
Open employment	88.89%	75.00%	66.67%	100.00%	81.48%	77.78%
(n=31)	(86.98%)	(69.22%)	(66.49%)	(91.40%)	(78.52%)	(74.23%)
Supported employment	92.59%	66.67%	66.67%	83.33%	81.37%	78.86%
(n=23)	(91.63%)	(64.86%)	(63.77%)	(83.09%)	(75.84%)	(73.42%)
Z	-1.051	-0.563	-0.514	-1.885	-0.805	-0.507
Significance (p)	.293	.573	.607	.059	.421	.612
Panel E: Matched-pairs sub-sample (n=34)						
Open employment	100.00%	87.50	66.67%	100.00%	89.47%	85.96
(n=17)	(93.03%)	(80.15%)	(68.30%)	(93.79%)	(83.82%)	(80.49%)
Supported employment	92.59%	75.00	50.00%	83.33%	74.54%	73.15%
(n=17)	(91.07%)	(67.16%)	(50.98%)	(85.29%)	(73.62%)	(69.73%)
Z	-0.461	-1.372	-1.761	-2.127*	-1.728	-1.810
Significance (p)	.645	.170	.078	.033	.084	0.070

*   Significant at the 5 percent level.
**   Significant at the 1 percent level.

6.2.1 Job Satisfaction Results for Participants with High Functional Work Ability

To investigate whether there are any differences in the results for participants with different levels of functional work ability, Mann-Whitney U Tests are conducted separately for participants with high and low functional work abilities. Table 6.2 reports the results for participants classified as having high functional work ability (low refined FAI). The results in Panel A of Table 6.2 reveal that when considering all participants with high functional work ability (refined FAI ≤ 12), there is a statistically significant difference in terms of the social aspect of work between open employment and supported employment; with participants in open employment reporting higher scores on the *social* factor of the JSQ ($Z = -2.588$, $p \leq .010$) than participants in supported employment. Neither

130

total *job satisfaction* nor the three other factors of the JSQ are found to differ statistically significantly between open employment and supported employment.

Table 6.2: Differences in median (mean) of JSQ scores for participants with high functional work ability (refined FAI ≤ 12)

	Work & Staff	Task	Pay	Social	Total	Total (x social)
Panel A: All occupations (n=46)						
Open employment	85.19%	64.58%	66.67%	100.00%	77.43%	69.91%
(n=34)	(79.52%)	(62.13%)	(61.76%)	(85.62%)	(72.26%)	(67.81%)
Supported employment	90.74%	52.08%	55.56%	72.22%	65.45%	62.96%
(n=12)	(87.65%)	(52.43%)	(53.24%)	(69.44%)	(65.69%)	(64.44%)
Z	-0.741	-1.030	-0.769	-2.588**	-1.226	-0.801
Significance (p)	.458	.303	.442	.010	.220	.423
Panel B: Unskilled labouring occupations (n=36)						
Open employment	85.19%	66.67%	66.67%	100.00%	77.43%	69.91%
(n=24)	(81.02%)	(62.50%)	(60.88%)	(90.97%)	(73.84%)	(68.13%)
Supported employment	90.74%	52.08%	55.56%	72.22%	65.45%	62.96%
(n=12)	(87.65%)	(52.43%)	(53.24%)	(69.44%)	(65.69%)	(64.44%)
Z	-0.769	-1.028	-0.608	-3.153**	-1.376	-0.839
Significance (p)	.456	.311	.562	.002	.177	.416
Panel C: Living with family (n=27)						
Open employment	88.89%	75.00%	66.67%	88.89%	81.48%	75.77%
(n=23)	(82.45%)	(66.30%)	(63.77%)	(87.20%)	(74.93%)	(70.84%)
Supported employment	92.59%	31.25%	72.22%	69.44	64.47%	63.73%
(n=4)	(90.74%)	(36.46%)	(66.67%)	(72.22%)	(66.52%)	(64.42%)
Z	-0.592	-1.784	-0.242	-1.669	-1.229	-0.888
Significance (p)	.576	.082	.818	.111	.243	.409

*   Significant at the 5 percent level.
**   Significant at the 1 percent level.

When controlling for occupation type, by analysing only participants with high functional work ability in unskilled labouring positions (Panel B, Table 6.2) the scores for the social factor are still found to be statistically significantly higher for participants in open employment compared with supported employment (Z = -3.153, $p ≤ .002$). As in Panel A, the three other factors and total *job satisfaction* do not differ statistically significantly, based on method of employment (open employment versus supported employment).

Panel C of Table 6.2 shows the results for those participants with high functional work ability who live with their family. As can be seen from this panel, once the living environment is controlled for, no statistically significant differences exist between open employment and supported employment participants based on total job satisfaction or any of its four factors.

The results in Table 6.2, for participants with high functional work ability, are similar to those presented in Table 6.1, for the entire sample. In both instances participants placed in open employment have statistically significantly higher *social* scores when demographic differences are not controlled (Panel A, Tables 6.1 and 6.2) and when the type of occupation is controlled (Panel B, Tables 6.1 and 6.2). However, when analysing only the responses of participants living with their families (Panel C, Tables 6.1 and 6.2), this statistically significant difference disappears.

6.2.2 Job Satisfaction Results for Participants with Low Functional Work Ability
Table 6.3 presents the results for participants with low functional work ability (high refined FAI). Panel A of Table 6.3 reveals that across all participants with a low functional work ability (refined

FAI $\geq$ 12), the only statistically significant difference between open employment and supported employment relates to *pay* (Z = -2.181, $p \leq .029$); with participants in open employment reporting higher scores than participants in supported employment. Neither *job satisfaction* nor the three other factors are found to differ statistically significantly between participants in open employment and supported employment.

When occupation type is controlled for by only investigating participants with low functional work ability who work in unskilled labouring positions (Panel B, Table 6.3), the results are qualitatively similar to those reported in Panel A. That is, participants in open employment report statistically significantly higher scores for *pay* compared with participants in supported employment (Z = -2.171, $p \leq .031$), with no statistically significant difference in the three other factors of the JSQ or *job satisfaction*.

Panel C of Table 6.3 shows the results for participants with low functional work ability living with their family. The results in this panel reveal that when living and work environments[117] are controlled for, no statistically significant differences exist between open employment and supported employment in terms of *job satisfaction* and its four factors.

Table 6.3: Differences in the median (mean) of JSQ scores for participants with low functional work ability (refined FAI $\geq$ 17)

	Work & Staff	Task	Pay	Social	Total	Total (x social)
Panel A: All occupations (n=47)						
Open employment	92.59%	87.50%	77.78%	88.89%	88.77%	85.03%
(n=18)	(90.12%)	(76.39%)	(74.69%)	(88.58%)	(82.45%)	(80.40%)
Supported employment	100.00%	75.00%	55.56%	83.33%	75.23%	68.06%
(n=29)	(93.49%)	(68.39%)	(59.00%)	(85.63%)	(76.63%)	(73.63%)
Z	-1.132	-1.171	-2.181*	-0.069	-1.324	-1.587
Significance (*p*)	.258	.242	.029	.945	.185	.113
Panel B: Unskilled labouring occupations (n=37)						
Open employment	92.59	87.50%	80.56%	100.00%	90.10%	86.81%
(n=10)	(89.63%)	(74.17%)	(78.89%)	(95.00%)	(84.42%)	(80.90%)
Supported employment	100.00%	75.00%	61.11%	100.00%	75.23%	68.06%
(n=27)	(93.00%)	(66.51%)	(60.08%)	(86.01%)	(76.40%)	(73.20%)
Z	-1.009	-0.964	-2.171*	-1.256	-1.522	-1.283
Significance (*p*)	.371	.353	.031	.257	.130	.203
Panel C: Living with family (n=27)						
Open employment	92.59%	77.08%	83.33%	88.89%	88.77%	85.03%
(n=12)	(91.67%)	(70.49%)	(77.31%)	(88.89%)	(82.09%)	(79.82%)
Supported employment	100.00%	87.50%	55.56%	83.33%	82.99%	82.41
(n=15)	(94.07%)	(75.56%)	(59.26%)	(83.33%)	(78.06%)	(76.30%)
Z	-1.130	-0.074	-1.871	-0.805	-1.122	-0.830
Significance (*p*)	.323	.943	.067	.456	.277	.427

*   Significant at the 5 percent level.
**   Significant at the 1 percent level.

6.2.3 Discussion of Job Satisfaction Results

The significant results for the *social* factor of the JSQ (Panels A, B, and E of Table 6.1, and Panels A and B of Table 6.2) are interesting in that they counter the findings of previous research, which

---

[117] As mentioned in Section 5.9 (Demographics of Participants Living with their Family), although I did not specifically attempt to control for differences in the types of occupations in this sub-sample, the Chi-square test revealed that there were no significant differences between participants in open employment and those in supported employment.

finds that workers with intellectual disabilities in open employment are interacting socially at only a superficial level in their workplaces (for example, Test *et al.* 1993; Petrovski and Gleeson 1997) or that workers with intellectual disabilities in open employment may have a reduced number of social supports available in the workforce compared with those in a supported employment setting (Jiranek and Kirby 1990). However, the significant results for the *social* factor must also be viewed in light of the poor psychometric properties of this factor that were revealed in Section 4.4.2 (Internal Reliability of the Derived JSQ Scores) and Section 4.4.3 (Factor Stability of the Derived JSQ). As this factor is not stable and does not report a satisfactory Cronbach alpha score, it is not possible to rely on the scores attained for this factor and, consequently, the statistically significant differences between open employment and supported employment for this factor must be viewed with caution. As such no weight can be placed on the statistically significant results for the *social* factor, and, consequently, no explanations are offered as to possible causes for the differences in results. However, it should also be noted that neither Test *et al.* (1993) nor Petrovski and Gleeson (1997) used psychometrically validated questionnaires.

The results in Table 6.3 for participants with low functional work ability (high refined FAI) are interesting in that they are different from those presented in Table 6.1, for the entire sample, and Table 6.2, for participants with high functional work ability (low refined FAI). Unique to the results presented in Table 6.3, participants with low functional work ability in open employment report a statistically significantly higher satisfaction with *pay* compared with participants in supported employment. This significant difference is apparent when demographic differences are not controlled (Panel A, Table 6.3) and when the type of occupation is controlled by analysing only participants in unskilled labouring positions (Panel B, Table 6.3). The result is no longer apparent when both the living and working environments are controlled for, by looking at only those participants who live with their family (Panel C, Table 6.3). However, the fact that this result is no longer apparent in Panel C of Table 6.3 may not be due to controlling for the living environment, but due to the problem of small sample size, given that this sub-sample has only 29 participants. When the sub-sample is separated, based on method of employment, there are only 12 participants in open employment and 15 in supported employment. As evident from Panel C of Table 6.3, the result for the pay factor is just above the five percent significance level ($Z = -1.871$, $p \leq .067$). Given the small size of the sub-sample, this result is not seen as necessarily being inconsistent with the results reported in Panels A and B of Table 6.3.

Given large differences in both weekly and hourly wages between open employment and supported employment, the fact that participants should report different levels of satisfaction with their pay is not in itself a surprising finding. What is surprising is that this finding is apparent only for participants with low functional work ability. One possible explanation is that those participants with low functional work ability in supported employment earn less than their counterparts with higher functional work ability and are therefore less satisfied with their pay. Consequently, when an analysis is conducted comparing these lower-paid workers with substantially higher paid participants in open employment, a statistically significant difference should result. However, if this is the case a Mann-Whitney U Test comparing the satisfaction with pay between high functional work ability and low functional work ability supported participants should reveal a difference. However, when such a test is performed, no statistically significant result is found ($Z = -0.476$, $p \leq .641$).

An alternate explanation could be that participants in open employment with low functional work ability are more satisfied with their pay than their counterparts with high functional work ability. One possible explanation to justify such a statement is that participants with low functional work ability may not expect to earn as much as they do, given their higher level of disability. Support for this argument comes from Lam and Chan (1988) who note that people with high functional work ability are more likely to reference their life situation relative to people without disabilities. Whereas for those people with low levels of functional work ability their frame of reference is more likely to be other people with low levels of functional work ability. As such, the expectations of these two groups may be highly divergent, with participants with high functional work ability expecting the same levels of pay as people without a disability, whereas participants with low levels of functional work ability may not be expecting such levels of pay given that the majority of people with low levels of functional work ability are employed (if at all) in a supported setting, receiving non-competitive wages. Consequently, participants with low functional work ability are more satisfied with the pay they receive. If this is the case then a difference in the levels of satisfaction with pay could be expected between low functional work ability and high functional work ability participants in open employment. However, a Mann-Whitney U Test finds no such difference ($Z = -1.313$, $p \leq .189$). Given there is no such difference and that there appears to be no difference in satisfaction with pay for high versus low functional work ability participants in supported employment, no explanation can be provided for the finding that only participants with low functional work ability in open employment report a statistically significantly higher *pay* score than participants in supported employment.

Taken in totality, the results in Table 6.1, Table 6.2, and Table 6.3 indicate that whether a person with an intellectual disability is placed into open employment or supported employment has no effect on their overall job satisfaction or the three of the four factors of job satisfaction that have reliable scores (*work and staff, task, pay*). This lack of statistical significance in job satisfaction between open employment and supported employment is in contrast to the findings of Jiranek and Kirby (1991), whose results suggest that people with intellectual disabilities in open employment have a higher degree of job satisfaction than those in supported employment. However, as noted in Section 2.3 (Job Satisfaction), Jiranek and Kirby (1991) did not use a psychometrically validated questionnaire and it is highly questionable as to whether they performed the correct statistical tests given the likely statistical distribution of their responses.

This lack of a statistically significant difference in job satisfaction between open employment and supported employment could be due to one or more of four reasons. First, it may indicate that participants in my sample are appropriately matched to either open employment or supported employment and consequently participants in both forms of employment are equally satisfied. Given that only one agency involved in this research (Agency D) placed people with intellectual disabilities into both open and supported employment, the selection of the appropriate form of employment for the person with the intellectual disabilities would have to be made by his or her parent or guardian; once an agency had been selected, that largely determines the type of employment the person with the intellectual disability would be placed into. Whether such this decision is made by parents or guardians, or them in conjunction with an agency, is worthy of future research, but is beyond the scope of this research.

Second, the lack of statistical significance in job satisfaction between open employment and supported employment may indicate that participants' job satisfaction is not dependent on whether the work is performed as either an open employment placement or a supported employment placement. That is, it is the intrinsic attributes of the job itself and the functions performed as part of that job that dictate the level of job satisfaction and not whether the placement is an open employment placement or a supported employment placement.

Third, as mentioned in Section 2.3 (Job Satisfaction), the studies that have investigated the job satisfaction of people with intellectual disabilities have typically reported high levels of job satisfaction. The results in Table 6.1, Table 6.2, and Table 6.3 are similar, with satisfaction on most factors, except for pay, being high. It might be that given the historically high rate of unemployment for people with intellectual disabilities and the lack of vocational places, that participants feel fortunate to have a job. Houser and Chace (1993) note that this feeling of fortunateness may result in people with intellectual disabilities overrating their job satisfaction. Consequently, it could be that participants both in open and supported employment experience equally these feelings of fortunateness, thus negating any statistically significant results in overall job satisfaction and the three factors that report reliable scores.

Fourth, as Moseley (1988) notes, any measure of satisfaction implicitly involves a comparison with something else. He further states that people who have only experienced supported employment may see this form of employment as satisfactory as that is the only form of employment that they have experienced. This can be supported by contrasting the findings of Lam and Chan (1988), who find participants in supported employment to generally report high levels of job satisfaction, with those of Seltzer (1984), who finds that individuals who return to supported employment after having experienced open employment are statistically significantly less satisfied with tasks performed and co-workers compared with individuals who remain in supported employment without having experienced open employment. Given that only five participants from the supported employment population had previously held another job (either in open or supported employment), this lack of a reference point for people in supported employment is a likely reason for the lack of statistically significant difference between the two forms of employment.

6.2.4 Summary of Job Satisfaction Results
The results for job satisfaction indicate that participants with a high level of functional work ability report statistically significantly higher *social* scores in open employment compared with supported employment, which counters the findings of previous studies that find people with intellectual disabilities interact on only a superficial level in open employment. However, as noted, it is not possible to rely on the scores of the *social* factor and, as such, the validity of this result can not be confirmed. Consequently, no weight is placed on this result.

In relation to total job satisfaction and the three factors that report reliable scores (*work and staff, task, pay*), no statistically significant difference is found between participants in open employment compared with supported employment. As Moseley (1988) noted it is highly likely that this result is due to participants in supported employment having no frame of reference by which to judge their level of job satisfaction and, as such, generally report high levels of satisfaction. Alternatively, it could be that participants in both open and supported employment feel fortunate to have a job (Houser and Chace 1993) and thus equally overrate their level of job satisfaction, thus negating any statistically significant differences between the two forms of employment. Another possible explanation is that it could indicate that participants have selected the form of employment that best suits them, or that it is the job itself that determines job satisfaction and not whether it is performed in either an open employment setting or a supported employment setting.

6.3 Quality of Life
The results presented and discussed below are for both the scores of the refined QOL.Q and its four factors and for the original QOL.Q (Schalock and Keith 1993) and its four factors. Even though the psychometric properties of the QOL.Q were enhanced through the refinements presented in Section 4.5.1 (Refinement of the QOL), the results of the original QOL.Q are also presented, given the extensive past usage of this instrument. By presenting the original QOL.Q results I am allowing comparisons to be made with past studies that have used the QOL.Q in its original form. As the data are non-normally distributed, each table is initially presented with the median data for open employment and supported employment (that is, Tables 6.4(a), 6.5(a), 6.6(a), 6.7(a), 6.8(a), and 6.9(a)). However, given the prevalence of reporting means, and to aid future researchers who may wish to compare their results with those reported in this thesis, each table is also replicated reporting the means (that is, Tables 6.4(b), 6.5(b), 6.6(b), 6.7(b), 6.8(b), and 6.9(b)).

In addition to the presentation of the raw scores, results are also presented in terms of percentage of scale maximum. The presentation of scale maximum scores facilitates future comparisons across different research studies that might use different quality of life questionnaires and, consequently, different scales. It should be noted, however, that this transformation does not control for differences in scores across studies arising from use of different questions and scale labels. Percentage of scale maximum involves the conversion of a scale into a standard form that ranges from zero to 100 percent (Cummins 2000b). As the QOL.Q has a theoretical range of 40 to 120, the QOL.Q score is converted to a percentage of scale maximum score using the following formula:

$$[(QOL.Q \text{ score} - 40) \div 80] \times 100.$$

To convert the four sub-domain QOL.Q scores, which have a theoretical range of 10 to 30, to a percentage of scale maximum score the following formula is used:

$$[(QOL.Q \text{ sub-domain score} - 10) \div 20] \times 100.$$

Table 6.4(a): Differences in medians of refined QOL.Q scores

	Satisfaction	Competence/ Productivity	Empowerment/ Independence	Social belonging/ Community integration	QOL
Panel A: All occupations (n=117)					
Open employment	25.00	26.25	26.67	25.00	100.83
(n=64)	75.00%[a]	81.25%	83.33%	75.00%	76.04%
Supported	25.00	26.25	21.67	25.00	96.67
employment (n=53)	75.00%	81.25%	58.33%	75.00%	70.83%
Z	-0.674	-0.215	-4.165**	-1.498	-2.665*
Significance (p)	.500	.830	.000	.134	.008
Panel B: Unskilled labouring occupations (n=94)					
Open employment	25.00	26.25	26.67	25.00	100.83
(n=43)	75.00%	81.25%	83.33%	75.00%	76.04%
Supported	25.00	26.25	21.67	25.00	96.67
employment (n=51)	75.00%	81.25%	58.33%	75.00%	70.83%
Z	-0.180	-0.046	-3.829**	-1.274	-2.471**
Significance (p)	.857	.963	.000	.203	.013
Panel C: Living with family (n=68)					
Open employment	25.00	26.25	25.00	25.00	99.58
(n=43)	75.00%	81.25%	75.00%	75.00%	74.48%
Supported	26.25	26.25	21.67	25.00	97.92
employment (n=25)	81.25%	81.25%	58.33%	75.00%	72.40%
Z	-1.696	-0.950	-3.459**	-0.200	-0.827
Significance (p)	.090	.342	.001	.841	.408
Panel D: Unskilled labouring occupations and living with family (n=54)					
Open employment	25.00	26.25	26.67	25.00	98.75
(n=31)	75.00%	81.25%	83.33%	75.00%	73.44%
Supported	26.25	26.25	21.67	25.00	97.92
employment (n=23)	81.25%	81.25%	58.33%	75.00%	72.40%
Z	-1.406	-1.554	-3.504**	-0.311	-0.963
Significance (p)	.160	.120	.000	.756	.336
Panel E: Matched-pairs sub-sample (n=34)					
Open employment	26.25	26.25	26.67	25.00	102.50
(n=17)	81.25%	81.25%	83.33%	75.00%	78.13%
Supported	25.00	23.75	21.67	20.00	92.08
employment (n=17)	75.00%	68.75%	58.33%	50.00%	65.10%
Z	-1.547	-1.491	-1.663	-1.785	-2.794**
Significance (p)	.122	.136	.096	.074	.005

a   All percentages reported in this table are percentage of scale maximum.
*   Significant at the 5 percent level.
**   Significant at the 1 percent level.

Table 6.4(b):   Differences in means of refined QOL.Q scores

	Satisfaction	Competence/ Productivity	Empowerment/ Independence	Social belonging/ Community integration	QOL
Panel A: All occupations (n=117)					
Open employment	24.78	25.41	25.36	24.47	100.02
(n=64)	73.88%[a]	77.05%	76.82%	72.36%	75.03%
Supported	25.19	25.35	21.64	22.55	94.73
employment (n=53)	75.94%	76.77%	58.18%	62.73%	68.41%
Z	-0.674	-0.215	-4.165**	-1.498	-2.665*
Significance (p)	.500	.830	.000	.134	.008
Panel B: Unskilled labouring occupations (n=94)					
Open employment	25.19	25.23	25.50	24.27	100.20
(n=43)	75.95%	76.16%	77.52%	71.37%	75.25%
Supported	25.17	25.39	21.67	22.30	94.53
employment (n=51)	75.86%	76.96%	58.33%	61.52%	68.17%
Z	-0.180	-0.046	-3.829**	-1.274	-2.471**
Significance (p)	.857	.963	.000	.203	.013
Panel C: Living with family (n=68)					
Open employment	24.43	25.35	24.34	24.33	98.45
(n=43)	72.17%	76.74%	71.71%	71.66%	73.07%
Supported	25.65	26.20	20.80	23.80	96.45
employment (n=25)	78.25%	81.00%	54.00%	69.00%	70.56%
Z	-1.696	-0.950	-3.459**	-0.200	-0.827
Significance (p)	.090	.342	.001	.841	.408
Panel D: Unskilled labouring occupations and living with family (n=54)					
Open employment	24.70	24.84	24.89	24.40	98.82
(n=31)	73.49%	74.19%	74.46%	71.98%	73.53%
Supported	25.65	26.36	20.80	23.37	96.18
employment (n=23)	78.26%	81.79%	53.99%	66.85%	70.22%
Z	-1.406	-1.554	-3.504**	-0.311	-0.963
Significance (p)	.160	.120	.000	.756	.336
Panel E: Matched-pairs sub-sample (n=34)					
Open employment	26.40	25.81	25.98	23.24	101.42
(n=17)	81.99%	79.04%	79.90%	66.18%	76.78%
Supported	24.71	24.04	23.04	20.88	92.67
employment (n=17)	73.53%	70.22%	65.20%	54.41%	65.84%
Z	-1.547	-1.491	-1.663	-1.785	-2.794**
Significance (p)	.122	.136	.096	.074	.005

a   All percentages reported in this table are percentage of scale maximum.
*   Significant at the 5 percent level.
**   Significant at the 1 percent level.

To assess whether a statistically significant difference exists in the quality of life of participants in supported employment compared with participants in open employment, Mann-Whitney U Tests are conducted (except for the matched-pairs sub-sample when Wilcoxon Signed Ranks Tests are conducted). As can be seen from the results reported in Panel A of Tables 6.4(a) and (b), participants employed in open employment report statistically significantly higher *quality of life* scores compared with those employed in supported employment ($Z = -2.665$, $p \leq .008$). The results in Panel A of Tables 6.4(a) and (b) also reveal that participants in open employment have statistically significantly higher scores for *empowerment/independence* ($Z = -4.165$, $p \leq .001$); but no statistically significant differences for the other factors.

As stated in Section 6.2 (Job Satisfaction), Panel A results do not control for any of the demographic differences apparent between participants in open employment and those in supported employment. Consequently, to control for the effect that the nature of the job may have on the results, Panel B presents the results for only those participants who are employed in unskilled labouring positions. As can be seen from Panel B of Tables 6.4(a) and (b), the above results also hold when the analysis is conduced on only those participants employed in unskilled labouring positions. That is, *quality of life* ($Z = -2.471$, $p \leq .013$) and *empowerment/independence* ($Z = -3.829$, $\underline{p} \leq .001$) are statistically significantly higher for participants in open employment compared with supported employment, with none of the other factors differing statistically significantly.

When the living environment is controlled by conducting analyses only on participants who live with their family (Panel C, Tables 6.4(a) and (b)) *quality of life* is no longer statistically significantly different between open employment and supported employment. The only statistically significant difference is for *empowerment/independence* ($Z = -3.459$, $p \leq .001$), with participants in open employment reporting higher scores.

Likewise, quality of life is not statistically significantly different between open employment and supported employment participants for the sub-sample of participants who work in unskilled labouring positions and live with their family (Panel D, Tables 6.4(a) and (b)). For only one of the four factors, *empowerment/independence,* is open employment statistically significantly higher than supported employment ($Z = -3.504$, $p \leq .001$).

The matched-pairs sub-sample, reported in Panel E of Tables 6.4(a) and (b), which is matched based on gender, type of occupation (unskilled labouring versus non-labouring), work hours, and functional work ability (refined FAI), and has no significant differences in terms of participants' living environments,[118] reveals a statistically significant difference in terms of *quality of life* ($Z = -2.794$, $p \leq .005$). Interestingly, Panel E of Tables 6.4(a) and (b) also shows that although participants in open employment have statistically significantly higher scores for *quality of life* there are no statistically significant differences in any of the four factors that combine to form *quality of life*, although *empowerment/independence* and *social belonging/community integration* approach significance ($p \leq .10$).

Two possible explanation as to why *quality of life* becomes statistically significant again in the matched-pairs sub-sample (Panel E, Table 6.4), is first, due to the slightly higher functional work ability (lower refined FAI) of this sub-sample compared with the previous sub-samples (Panels B – D, Table 6.4), and second, that people who live independently and in group homes again form part of the sub-sample. As discussed below, it appears that the results in relation to significant differences in terms of *quality of life* and its four factors are driven by the participants with high functional work ability and as discussed in Section 6.3.3 (Discussion of Quality of Life Results) it appears that living with family has a moderating effect on the effects of employment on quality of life. The only explanation that can be thought of as to why *empowerment/independence* is no longer statistically significantly different for the matched-pairs sub-sample, when it is so for all the other sub-samples, is due to the small sample size ($n = 34$). Even though the result for *empowerment/independence* for the matched-pairs sub-sample is not significant, it approaches significance ($p \leq .096$) and, given the small sample size, is supportive of the findings in Panels A, B, C, and D of Table 6.4.

---

[118] Although Panels C and D of Tables 6.4(a) and (b) attempt to control for living environment by only analysing the responses of participants who live with their family, it is acknowledged that the results in these panels only pertain to people who live with their family. As noted in Section 5.11 (Demographics of Matched-pairs Sub-Sample), the matched-pairs sub-sample contains participants from all three living environment (living independently, living with family, and living in a group home) and there is not statistically significant differences between the living environments of participants' in open employment and those in supported employment.

Table 6.5(a):   Differences in medians of original QOL.Q scores

	Satisfaction	Competence/ Productivity	Empowerment/ Independence	Social belonging/ Community integration	QOL
Panel A: All occupations (n=117)					
Open employment	25.00	26.00	26.00	23.00	100.00
(n=64)	75.00%[a]	80.00%	80.00%	65.00%	75.00%
Supported	25.00	26.00	22.00	21.00	95.00
employment (n=53)	75.00%	80.00%	60.00%	55.00%	68.75%
Z	-0.353	-0.637	-4.432**	-2.118*	-2.328*
Significance (p)	.724	.524	.000	.034	.020
Panel B: Unskilled labouring occupations (n=94)					
Open employment	25.00	26.00	26.00	23.00	100.00
(n=43)	75.00%	80.00%	80.00%	65.00%	75.00%
Supported	25.00	26.00	22.00	21.00	95.00
employment (n=51)	75.00%	80.00%	60.00%	55.00%	68.75%
Z	-0.149	-0.531	-4.020**	-2.302*	-2.479*
Significance (p)	.882	.595	.000	.021	.013
Panel C: Living with family (n=68)					
Open employment	24.00	26.00	25.00	23.00	97.00
(n=43)	70.00%	80.00%	75.00%	65.00%	71.25%
Supported	25.00	27.00	22.00	22.00	96.00
employment (n=25)	75.00%	85.00%	60.00%	60.00%	70.00%
Z	-1.905	-1.261	-3.676**	-0.927	-0.746
Significance (p)	.057	.207	.000	.354	.456
Panel D: Unskilled labouring occupations and living with family (n=54)					
Open employment	24.00	26.00	25.00	23.00	97.00
(n=31)	70.00%	80.00%	75.00%	65.00%	71.25%
Supported	26.00	27.00	22.00	22.00	96.00
employment (n=23)	80.00%	85.00%	60.00%	60.00%	70.00%
Z	-1.516	-1.689	-3.693**	-1.644	-1.061
Significance (p)	.129	.091	.000	.100	.288
Panel E: Matched-pairs sub-sample (n=34)					
Open employment	26.00	27.00	26.00	24.00	101.00
(n=17)	80.00%	85.00%	80.00%	70.00%	76.25%
Supported	24.00	24.00	23.00	20.00	92.00
employment (n=17)	70.00%	70.00%	65.00%	50.00%	65.00%
Z	-0.726	-0.940	-3.622**	-3.028**	-2.772**
Significance (p)	.468	.347	.000	.002	.006

a   All percentages reported in this table are percentage of scale maximum.
*   Significant at the 5 percent level.
**   Significant at the 1 percent level.

Tables 6.5(a) and (b) presents the results of the original QOL.Q. The results of the original QOL.Q are largely consistent with those of the refined QOL.Q presented in Tables 6.4(a) and (b), with a few notable differences. As found in Tables 6.4(a) and (b), open employment reports statistically significantly higher scores for both *empowerment/independence* and *quality of life* across all participants (Panel A, Table 6.5) (Z = -4.432, $p \leq .001$ and Z = -2.328, $p \leq .020$, respectively) and for participants in unskilled labouring positions (Panel B, Table 6.5) (Z = -4.020, $p \leq .001$ and Z = -2.479, $p \leq .013$, respectively). Also similar to Tables 6.4 (a) and (b), for the sub-samples matched based on living environment (Panel C, Table 6.5) and living and occupation type (Panel D, Table 6.5) only *empowerment/independence* is found to be statistically significantly different between participants in open employment and those in supported employment (Z = -3.676, $p \leq .001$ and Z =

-3.693, $p \leq .001$, respectively); with participants in open employment reporting higher scores. As in Tables 6.4(a) and (b), the matched-pairs sub-sample results (Panel E, Table 6.5) reveal that open employment participants have statistically significantly higher *quality of life* ($Z = -3.356$, $p \leq .001$) than supported employment participants.

Table 6.5(b):   Differences in means of original QOL.Q scores

	Satisfaction	Competence/ Productivity	Empowerment/ Independence	Social belonging/ Community integration	QOL
Panel A: All occupations (n=117)					
Open employment	24.17	25.16	25.28	22.58	97.19
(n=64)	70.86%[a]	75.78%	76.41%	62.89%	71.48%
Supported	24.51	25.64	22.51	21.13	93.79
employment (n=53)	72.55%	78.21%	62.55%	55.66%	67.24%
Z	-0.353	-0.637	-4.432**	-2.118*	-2.328*
Significance (p)	.724	.524	.000	.034	.020
Panel B: Unskilled labouring occupations (n=94)					
Open employment	24.44	25.11	25.35	22.67	97.58
(n=43)	72.21%	75.58%	76.74%	63.37%	71.98%
Supported	24.51	25.65	22.49	20.92	93.57
employment (n=51)	72.55%	78.24%	62.45%	54.61%	66.96%
Z	-0.149	-0.531	-4.020**	-2.302*	-2.479*
Significance (p)	.882	.595	.000	.021	.013
Panel C: Living with family (n=68)					
Open employment	23.79	25.21	24.70	22.44	96.14
(n=43)	68.95%	76.05%	73.49%	62.21%	70.17%
Supported	25.32	26.36	22.00	21.68	95.36
employment (n=25)	76.60%	81.80%	60.00%	58.40%	69.20%
Z	-1.905	-1.261	-3.676**	-0.927	-0.746
Significance (p)	.057	.207	.000	.354	.456
Panel D: Unskilled labouring occupations and living with family (n=54)					
Open employment	23.97	24.77	25.03	22.84	96.61
(n=31)	69.84%	73.87%	75.16%	64.19%	70.77%
Supported	25.39	26.43	21.91	21.26	95.00
employment (n=23)	76.96%	82.17%	59.57%	56.30%	68.75%
Z	-1.516	-1.689	-3.693**	-1.644	-1.061
Significance (p)	.129	.091	.000	.100	.288
Panel E: Matched-pairs sub-sample (n=34)					
Open employment	25.00	25.65	25.88	22.88	99.41
(n=17)	75.00%	78.24%	79.41%	64.41%	74.26%
Supported	24.35	24.65	23.12	20.41	92.53
employment (n=17)	71.76%	73.24%	65.59%	52.06%	65.66%
Z	-0.726	-0.940	-3.622**	-3.028**	-2.772**
Significance (p)	.468	.347	.000	.002	.006

a   All percentages reported in this table are percentage of scale maximum.
*   Significant at the 5 percent level.
**   Significant at the 1 percent level.

Of noticeable difference between the results for the refined QOL.Q (Tables 6.4(a) and (b)) and the original QOL.Q (Tables 6.5(a) and (b)) is that when using the original QOL.Q, the results for *social belonging/community integration* are statistically significantly higher on three occasions for participants in open employment; these being when the data are analysed for all participants (Panel A, Table 6.5) ($Z = -2.118$, $p \leq .034$), for participants in unskilled labouring positions (Panel B,

Table 6.5) (Z = -2.302, $p \leq .021$), and the matched-pairs sub-sample (Panel E, Table 6.5) (Z = -3.028, $p \leq .002$). The results for the matched-pairs sub-sample also has another notable difference to Tables 6.4(a) and (b) in that, in addition to there being a statistically significant difference in terms of *quality of life*, there is also a statistically significant difference in *empowerment/independence* (Z = -3.622, $p \leq .001$), with participants in open employment reporting the higher scores.

The differences between the *social belonging/community integration* factor of the refined QOL.Q and the original QOL.Q are most likely due to the low Cronbach alpha score of .589 for *social belonging/community integration* for the original QOL.Q, which was discussed in Section 4.5.2 (Reliability Analysis of the QOL.Q). Given that the scores for this factor cannot be assumed to be reliable, little weight can be placed on the statistically significant results obtained for the *social belonging/community integration* factor for the original QOL.Q.

On the face-of-it, the different result for the *empowerment/independence* factor for the matched-pairs sub-sample (Panel E of Tables 6.4 and 6.8), depending on which instrument is used (refined QOL.Q or original QOL.Q), would appear unusual. However, with the exception of the matched-pairs sub-sample, participants in open employment consistently report statistically significantly higher *empowerment/independence* scores when analysing the refined QOL.Q results (Table 6.4). As mentioned above, this non-significant result appears inconsistent with the other results for this factor, even more so given that when the original QOL.Q is used a significant result is found. As such, the above stated argument that the small sample size of the matched-pairs sub-sample is causing this one atypical result (when using the refined QOL.Q) appears justifiable. Moreover, as noted earlier, this factor does approach statistical significance ($p \leq .10$). Consequently, I believe it is possible to conclude that *empowerment/independence* is higher for participants in open employment.

6.3.1 Quality of Life Results for Participants with High Functional Work Ability
Tables 6.6(a) and (b) show the results for the refined QOL.Q for those participants classified as having high functional work ability (low refined FAI). Panel A of Table 6.6 reveals that across the entire sample of participants with high functional work ability (refined FAI ≤ 12) participants in open employment score statistically significantly higher scores than participants in supported employment for *empowerment/independence* (Z = -3.861, $p \leq .001$), *social belonging/community integration* (Z = -1.969, $p \leq .049$) and *quality of life* (Z = -2.978, $p \leq .003$). When occupation type is controlled for by analysing only unskilled labouring positions (Panel B, Table 6.6) *social belonging/community integration* is no longer found to be statistically significantly different. Though, participants in open employment again score statistically significantly higher scores than participants in supported employment for *empowerment/independence* (Z = -3.816, $p \leq .001$) and *quality of life* (Z = -2.854, $p \leq .004$). When the living environment is controlled for, by only analysing participants who live with their family (Panel C, Table 6.6), *quality of life* is no longer found to be statistically significantly different between open employment and supported employment. However, *empowerment/independence* (Z = -2.863, $p \leq .002$) is still found to be significantly different between open employment and supported employment; with participants in open employment again reporting statistically significantly higher scores than participants in supported employment.

The results in Table 6.6 for participants with high functional work ability (low refined FAI) are similar to those reported in Table 6.4 for the entire sample, in that across all occupations (Panel A, Table 6.6) and the unskilled labouring occupations (Panel B, Table 6.6), participants in open employment have statistically significantly higher scores for *empowerment/independence* and *quality of life*. The results for participants who live with their family (Panel C, Table 6.6) are also similar between Table 6.6 (participants with high functional work ability) and Table 6.4 (the entire sample), in that the only statistically significant difference between participants in open

Table 6.6(a): Differences in medians of refined QOL.Q scores for people with high functional work ability (refined FAI $\leq$ 12)

	Satisfaction	Competence/ Productivity	Empowerment/ Independence	Social belonging/ Community integration	QOL
Panel A: All occupations (n=46)					
Open employment	23.75	25.00	26.67	22.50	100.42
(n=34)	68.75%[a]	75.00%	83.33%	62.50%	75.52%
Supported	25.00	24.38	21.67	21.25	91.25
employment (n=12)	75.00%	71.88%	58.33%	56.25%	64.06%
Z	-0.101	-0.353	-3.861**	-1.969*	-2.978**
Significance (*p*)	.920	.724	.000	.049	.003
Panel B: Unskilled labouring occupations (n=36)					
Open employment	24.38	25.00	28.33	22.50	100.21
(n=24)	71.88%	75.00%	91.67%	62.50%	75.26%
Supported	25.00	24.38	21.67	21.25	91.25
employment (n=12)	75.00%	71.88%	58.33%	56.25%	64.06%
Z	-0.170	-0.321	-3.816**	-1.208	-2.854**
Significance (*p*)	.882	.753	.000	.237	.004
Panel C: Living with family (n=27)					
Open employment	23.75	25.00	26.67	22.50	98.75
(n=23)	68.75%	75.00%	83.33%	62.50%	73.44%
Supported	25.00	26.88	18.33	21.25	88.54
employment (n=4)	75.00%	84.38%	41.67%	56.25%	60.68%
Z	-0.724	-0.724	-2.863**	-1.220	-1.775
Significance (*p*)	.489	.489	.002	.243	.082

a   All percentages reported in this table are percentage of scale maximum.
*   Significant at the 5 percent level.
**   Significant at the 1 percent level.

Table 6.6(b): Differences in means of refined QOL.Q scores for people with high functional work ability (refined FAI $\leq$ 12)

	Satisfaction	Competence/ Productivity	Empowerment/ Independence	Social belonging/ Community integration	QOL
Panel A: All occupations (n=46)					
Open employment	23.81	24.82	26.81	24.15	99.59
(n=34)	69.03%[a]	74.08%	84.07%	70.77%	74.49%
Supported	24.27	24.38	21.67	21.25	91.25
employment (n=12)	71.35%	71.88%	58.33%	56.25%	64.06%
Z	-0.101	-0.353	-3.861**	-1.969*	-2.978**
Significance (*p*)	.920	.724	.000	.049	.003
Panel B: Unskilled labouring occupations (n=36)					
Open employment	24.19	24.79	27.01	22.97	98.97
(n=24)	70.96%	73.96%	85.07%	64.84%	73.71%
Supported	24.27	24.38	21.67	21.25	91.25
employment (n=12)	71.35%	71.88%	58.33%	56.25%	64.06%
Z	-0.170	-0.321	-3.816**	-1.208	-2.854**
Significance (*p*)	.882	.753	.000	.237	.004
Panel C: Living with family (n=27)					
Open employment	23.51	24.84	26.23	23.97	98.54
(n=23)	67.53%	74.18%	81.16%	69.84%	73.18%
Supported	25.00	26.25	18.33	20.63	90.21
employment (n=4)	75.00%	81.25%	41.67%	53.13%	62.76%
Z	-0.724	-0.724	-2.863**	-1.220	-1.775
Significance (*p*)	.489	.489	.002	.243	.082

a   All percentages reported in this table are percentage of scale maximum.
*   Significant at the 5 percent level.
**   Significant at the 1 percent level.

employment and supported employment is for *empowerment/independence*, with participants in open employment reporting the higher scores.

However, unlike the results for the entire sample (Table 6.4), the results for participants with high functional work ability (Table 6.6) show that when considering all occupations (Panel A, Table 6.6) participants in open employment report statistically significantly higher *social belonging/community integration* scores than participants in supported employment. This result is unusual, in that it is the only time that a statistically significant result is found for the *social belonging/community integration* factor using the refined QOL.Q. No emphasis is placed on investigating the potential causes of this result, given that once demographic differences are controlled (for example, by looking only at unskilled labouring positions: Panel B, Table 6.6) the result no longer holds. Also, it is noted that the result is only just statistically significant ($p \leq .049$).

The results reported in Tables 6.7(a) and (b) for the original QOL.Q are largely consistent with those reported in Table 6.5 for the refined QOL.Q. That is, participants in open employment report statistically significantly higher scores for *empowerment/independence* and *quality of life* when analysing all occupations (Panel A, $Z = -3.377$, $p \leq .001$ and $Z = -2.220$, $p \leq .026$, respectively) and only unskilled labouring occupations (Panel B, $Z = -3.313$, $p \leq .001$ and $Z = -2.407$, $p \leq .015$, respectively). Similar to the refined QOL.Q (Table 6.6), when investigating the sub-sample of participants living with their family, those in open employment only report statistically significantly higher scores than participants in supported employment for *empowerment/independence* ($Z = -2.565$, $p \leq .008$). The only difference between Table 6.7 and Table 6.6 is that on no occasion when using the original QOL.Q (Table 6.7) is *social belonging/community* integration found to be statistically significantly different between participants in open employment and supported employment. Although it is acknowledged that it does approach statistical significance ($p \leq .10$) when all occupations are considered (Panel A, Table 6.7)

The results for the original QOL.Q for participants with high functional work ability (low refined FAI), which are presented in Table 6.7, are largely consistent with the results for the original QOL.Q presented in Table 6.5 for the entire sample. Similar to the entire sample (Table 6.5), when analysing the results for only participants with a high functional work ability (Table 6.7) open employment is found to report statistically significantly higher results compared with supported employment for *empowerment/independence* and *quality of life* when investigating all occupations (Panel A, Table 6.7) and unskilled labouring positions (Panel B, Table 6.7). Also similar to the entire sample (Table 6.5), when investigating those participants who live with their family (Panel C, Table 6.7), the only statistically significant result is for *empowerment/independence*, with participants in open employment reporting higher scores than participants in supported employment. However different from the entire sample (Table 6.5), when analysing the sub-sample of participants with high functional work ability (Table 6.7), on no occasions is the *social belonging/community integration* factor found to be statistically significantly different between the two methods of employment. Recall that for the entire sample (Table 6.5) I find that participants in open employment score statistically significantly higher on this factor across all occupations (Panel A, Table 6.5) and unskilled labouring positions (Panel B, Table 6.5). However, recall as noted in Section 4.5.2 (Reliability Analysis of the QOL.Q) that the *social belonging/community integration* factor of the original QOL.Q reported unsatisfactory Cronbach alpha scores, bringing the reliability of the scores for this factor into question.

6.3.2 Quality of Life Results for Participants with Low Functional Work Ability

Tables 6.8(a) and (b) reveal the results for the refined QOL.Q for those participants classified as having low functional work ability (high refined FAI score). The results reveal that for participants with low functional work ability (refined FAI ≥ 17) there are no statistically significant differences in *quality of life* or any of its four factors based on method of employment (open employment versus supported employment). These results are found for participants across all occupations

Table 6.7(a): Differences in medians of original QOL.Q scores for people with high functional work ability (refined FAI ≤ 12)

	Satisfaction	Competence/ Productivity	Empowerment/ Independence	Social belonging/ Community integration	QOL
Panel A: All occupations (n=46)					
Open employment	24.50	25.00	27.00	21.00	99.50
(n=34)	72.50%[a]	75.00%	85.00%	55.00%	74.38%
Supported	23.00	24.00	22.00	20.00	92.00
employment (n=12)	65.00%	70.00%	60.00%	50.00%	65.00%
Z	-0.833	-0.176	-3.377**	-1.782	-2.220*
Significance (p)	.405	.860	.001	.075	.026
Panel B: Unskilled labouring occupations (n=36)					
Open employment	25.00	25.50	27.00	21.00	99.00
(n=24)	75.00%	77.50%	85.00%	55.00%	73.75%
Supported	23.00	24.00	22.00	20.00	92.00
employment (n=12)	65.00%	70.00%	60.00%	50.00%	65.00%
Z	-0.974	-0.101	-3.313**	-1.593	-2.407*
Significance (p)	.361	.934	.001	.120	.015
Panel C: Living with family (n=27)					
Open employment	24.00	25.00	27.00	21.00	98.00
(n=23)	70.00%	75.00%	85.00%	55.00%	72.50%
Supported	23.50	26.50	22.00	20.50	93.50
employment (n=4)	67.50%	82.50%	60.00%	52.50%	66.88%
Z	-0.137	-0.858	-2.565**	-0.689	-1.063
Significance (p)	.921	.409	.008	.531	.303

a   All percentages reported in this table are percentage of scale maximum.
*   Significant at the 5 percent level.
** Significant at the 1 percent level.

Table 6.7(b): Differences in means of original QOL.Q scores for people with high functional work ability (refined FAI ≤ 12)

	Satisfaction	Competence/ Productivity	Empowerment/ Independence	Social belonging/ Community integration	QOL
Panel A: All occupations (n=46)					
Open employment	23.74	24.41	26.35	22.29	96.79
(n=34)	68.68%[a]	72.06%	81.76%	61.47%	70.99%
Supported	23.58	24.75	22.67	20.50	91.50
employment (n=12)	67.92%	73.75%	63.33%	52.50%	64.38%
Z	-0.833	-0.176	-3.377**	-1.782	-2.220*
Significance (p)	.405	.860	.001	.075	.026
Panel B: Unskilled labouring occupations (n=36)					
Open employment	24.00	24.54	26.54	22.04	97.13
(n=24)	70.00%	72.71%	82.71%	60.21%	71.41%
Supported	23.58	24.75	22.67	20.50	91.50
employment (n=12)	67.92%	73.75%	63.33%	52.50%	64.38%
Z	-0.974	-0.101	-3.313**	-1.593	-2.407*
Significance (p)	.361	.934	.001	.120	.015
Panel C: Living with family (n=27)					
Open employment	23.39	24.61	26.13	22.13	96.26
(n=23)	66.96%	73.04%	80.65%	60.65%	70.33%
Supported	24.50	26.50	21.75	20.75	93.50
employment (n=4)	72.50%	82.50%	58.75%	53.75%	66.88%
Z	-0.137	-0.858	-2.565**	-0.689	-1.063
Significance (p)	.921	.409	.008	.531	.303

a   All percentages reported in this table are percentage of scale maximum.
*   Significant at the 5 percent level.
** Significant at the 1 percent level.

Table 6.8(a): Differences in medians of refined QOL.Q scores for people with low functional work ability (refined FAI ≥ 17)

	Satisfaction	Competence/ Productivity	Empowerment/ Independence	Social belonging/ Community integration	QOL
Panel A: All occupations (n=47)					
Open employment	26.25	26.88	23.33	27.50	101.25
(n=18)	*81.25%*[a]	*84.38%*	*66.67%*	*87.50%*	*76.56%*
Supported	26.25	26.25	21.67	27.50	97.92
employment (n=29)	*81.25%*	*81.25%*	*58.33%*	*87.50%*	*72.40%*
Z	-0.675	-0.986	-1.893	-0.494	-1.402
Significance (*p*)	.499	.324	.058	.621	.161
Panel B: Unskilled labouring occupations (n=37)					
Open employment	27.50	27.50	25.00	28.75	104.38
(n=10)	*87.50%*	*87.50%*	*75.00%*	*93.75%*	*80.47%*
Supported	26.25	26.25	21.67	25.00	97.92
employment (n=27)	*81.25%*	*81.25%*	*58.33%*	*75.00%*	*72.40%*
Z	-1.246	-1.004	-1.651	-1.672	-1.952
Significance (*p*)	.229	.335	.105	.105	.052
Panel C: Living with family (n=27)					
Open employment	25.63	26.25	20.00	27.50	98.75
(n=12)	*78.13%*	*81.25%*	*50.00%*	*87.50%*	*73.44%*
Supported	26.25	26.25	21.67	27.50	101.25
employment (n=15)	*81.25%*	*81.25%*	*58.33%*	*87.50%*	*76.56%*
Z	-0.644	-0.522	-0.616	-0.025	-0.391
Significance (*p*)	.548	.614	.548	.981	.719

a   All percentages reported in this table are percentage of scale maximum.

Table 6.8(b): Differences in means of refined QOL.Q scores for people with low functional work ability (refined FAI ≥ 17)

	Satisfaction	Competence/ Productivity	Empowerment/ Independence	Social belonging/ Community integration	QOL
Panel A: All occupations (n=51)					
Open employment	25.90	26.39	23.15	24.58	100.02
(n=20)	*79.51%*[a]	*81.94%*	*65.74%*	*72.92%*	*75.03%*
Supported	25.22	25.47	20.11	24.57	95.37
employment (n=31)	*76.08%*	*77.37%*	*50.57%*	*72.84%*	*69.22%*
Z	-0.675	-0.986	-1.893	-0.494	-1.402
Significance (*p*)	.499	.324	.058	.621	.161
Panel B: Unskilled labouring occupations (n=37)					
Open employment	26.63	26.50	23.33	27.00	103.46
(n=10)	*83.13%*	*82.50%*	*66.67%*	*85.00%*	*79.32%*
Supported	25.19	25.56	20.06	24.26	95.06
employment (n=27)	*75.93%*	*77.80%*	*50.31%*	*71.30%*	*68.83%*
Z	-1.246	-1.004	-1.651	-1.672	-1.952
Significance (*p*)	.229	.335	.105	.105	.052
Panel C: Living with family (n=27)					
Open employment	25.52	25.94	21.25	24.79	97.50
(n=12)	*77.60%*	*79.69%*	*56.25%*	*73.96%*	*71.88%*
Supported	26.08	26.33	20.00	26.67	99.08
employment (n=15)	*80.42%*	*81.67%*	*50.00%*	*83.33%*	*73.85%*
Z	-0.644	-0.522	-0.616	-0.025	-0.391
Significance (*p*)	.548	.614	.548	.981	.719

a   All percentages reported in this table are percentage of scale maximum.

(Panel A), only unskilled labouring occupations (Panel B), and for those participants living with their family (Panel C).

Tables 6.9(a) and (b) report the results for participants with low functional work ability based on the original QOL.Q. Similar to the results using the refined QOL.Q (Table 6.8), Panel A (all participants) and Panel C (living with family) of Table 6.9 reveal that there are no statistically significant differences in *quality of life* or any of its four factors for participants with a low functional work ability based on method of employment (supported employment versus open employment). However, the results in Panel B of Table 6.9 show that for participants' with low functional work ability in unskilled labouring occupations, those in open employment have statistically significantly higher *quality of life* (Z = -1.973, $p \leq$ .048) than those in supported employment. No explanation can be given as to why such a result occurs for the unskilled labouring sub-sample and not the entire population. However, it is worth noting that when the analysis was repeated using different cut-off scores of the refined FAI (both higher and lower) this result no longer held. As such this result is considered spurious and no explanation will be attempted about the possible reason for the result.

The above examination of results for the high functional work ability and low functional work ability participants reveals that the statistically significant differences in Table 6.4 (refined QOL.Q) and Table 6.5 (original QOL.Q) are driven by participants with high functional work ability. Given that the median (mean) refined FAI scores for participants in the matched-pairs sub-sample (Panel E) is slightly higher than of those of participants living with their family (Panel C) and those living with their family and working in unskilled labouring positions (Panel D), this may help to explain why in Table 6.4 and Table 6.5 the results of the matched-pairs sub-sample (Panel E) reintroduced significant differences that were not evident when the responses of only participants living with their family were analysed (Panels C and D).[119]

6.3.3 Discussion of Quality of Life Results
The results based on the refined QOL.Q presented in Panel A of Table 6.4 and the results using the original QOL presented in Panel A of Table 6.5 show that prior to controlling for demographic differences between the two populations, both *quality of life* and *feelings of empowerment/independence* are statistically significantly higher for participants in open employment. This result also held when differences in occupation types between open and supported employment were controlled for by analysing the scores for participants only in unskilled labouring positions (Panel B, Table 6.4; and Table 6.8). However, once the living environment was controlled for by investigating only those participants who live with their family (Panel C, Table 6.4; and Table 6.8) and those participants who live with their family and work in unskilled labouring positions (Panel D, Table 6.4; and Table 6.8), the only statistically significant difference between participants in open employment and supported employment is *empowerment/independence*, with participants in open employment reporting the higher scores. When the matched-pairs sub-sample was analysed, the results using the original QOL.Q (Panel E, Table 6.5) were consistent with those above, *empowerment/independence* was found to be statistically significantly higher for participants in open employment compared with supported employment. However, when using the psychometrically superior refined QOL.Q, the difference in *empowerment/independence* between open and supported employment is not found to be significant. As stated earlier, I believe this non-significant result to be due to the small sample size for the matched-pairs analysis, and given that the result approaches significance I believe it confirms the results in Panels A, B, C, and D of Table 6.4 and Table 6.8 that people with intellectual disabilities in open employment have greater feelings of *empowerment/independence* than those placed in supported employment.

---

[119] The effect that living with family might have on the above results is also acknowledged, and discussed in the next section.

Table 6.9(a): Differences in medians of original QOL.Q scores for people with low functional work ability (refined FAI ≥ 17)

	Satisfaction	Competence/ Productivity	Empowerment/ Independence	Social belonging/ Community integration	QOL
Panel A: All occupations (n=47)					
Open employment	25.50	26.50	23.50	23.50	98.50
(n=18)	77.50%[a]	82.50%	67.50%	67.50%	73.13%
Supported	25.00	26.00	22.00	23.00	96.00
employment (n=29)	75.00%	80.00%	60.00%	65.00%	70.00%
Z	-0.154	-0.697	-1.693	-0.661	-1.151
Significance (p)	.877	.486	.090	.508	.250
Panel B: Unskilled labouring occupations (n=37)					
Open employment	26.00	27.50	23.50	24.00	101.50
(n=10)	80.00%	87.50%	67.50%	70.00%	76.88%
Supported	25.00	26.00	22.00	22.00	96.00
employment (n=27)	75.00%	80.00%	60.00%	60.00%	70.00%
Z	-0.741	-0.917	-1.461	-1.486	-1.973*
Significance (p)	.468	.371	.148	.148	.048
Panel C: Living with family (n=27)					
Open employment	24.00	26.00	22.50	23.50	93.50
(n=12)	70.00%	80.00%	62.50%	67.50%	66.88%
Supported	26.00	27.00	22.00	24.00	98.00
employment (n=15)	80.00%	85.00%	60.00%	70.00%	72.50%
Z	-1.505	-0.545	-0.172	-0.321	-1.126
Significance (p)	.139	.614	.867	.755	.277

a   All percentages reported in this table are percentage of scale maximum.
*   Significant at the 5 percent level.

Table 6.9(b): Differences in means of original QOL.Q scores for people with low functional work ability (refined FAI ≥ 17)

	Satisfaction	Competence/ Productivity	Empowerment/ Independence	Social belonging/ Community integration	QOL
Panel A: All occupations (n=47)					
Open employment	24.83	26.28	23.44	22.33	96.89
(n=18)	74.17%[a]	81.39%	67.22%	61.67%	71.11%
Supported	24.59	25.69	21.62	21.83	93.72
employment (n=29)	72.93%	78.45%	58.10%	59.14%	67.16%
Z	-0.154	-0.697	-1.693	-0.661	-1.151
Significance (p)	.877	.486	.090	.508	.250
Panel B: Unskilled labouring occupations (n=37)					
Open employment	25.40	26.40	23.30	23.40	98.50
(n=10)	77.00%	82.00%	66.50%	67.00%	73.13%
Supported	24.59	25.70	21.52	21.48	93.30
employment (n=27)	72.96%	78.52%	57.59%	57.41%	66.62%
Z	-0.741	-0.917	-1.461	-1.486	-1.973*
Significance (p)	.468	.371	.148	.148	.048
Panel C: Living with family (n=27)					
Open employment	24.33	25.92	22.17	22.17	94.58
(n=12)	71.67%	79.58%	60.83%	60.83%	68.23%
Supported	25.87	26.40	21.93	23.07	97.27
employment (n=15)	79.33%	82.00%	59.67%	65.33%	71.58%
Z	-1.505	-0.545	-0.172	-0.321	-1.126
Significance (p)	.139	.614	.867	.755	.277

a   All percentages reported in this table are percentage of scale maximum.
*   Significant at the 5 percent level.

This finding of open employment participants, reporting higher *empowerment/independence* scores, is consistent with the findings of Eggleton *et al.* (1999). However, caution needs to be exercised when interpreting this result and that of Eggleton *et al.* (1999), as it is possible those people who naturally have higher feelings of *empowerment/independence* self-select into open employment. The only way to prove or disprove this would be to conduct a longitudinal study of the impact of open employment on people with intellectual disabilities. *Empowerment/independence* would have to be assessed prior to employment and then afterwards at regular intervals. A longitudinal study of the impact of supported employment would also be warranted, as it is acknowledged that supported employment might also impact on a persons feeling of *empowerment/independence*, but to a lesser extent than open employment.

The matched-pairs analysis (Panel E, Table 6.4 (refined QOL.Q); and Table 6.5 (original QOL.Q)) not only found *empowerment/independence* to be statistically significantly different between the two populations (open employment versus supported employment) but also *quality of life*, with participants in open employment reporting the higher scores. This result was initially considered unusual given that the matched-pairs sample controlled for differences between the two populations in relation to occupation type and living environment (as well as other demographic differences), but when only living environment is controlled by analysing the responses of participants who live with their family (Panel C, Table 6.4; and Table 6.5) *quality of life* is not found to be statistically significantly different between open employment and supported employment. It is important to note that the matched-pairs sub-sample controls for the demographic difference in terms of living environment between open and supported employment by directly matching based on living environment. As such, the matched-pairs sub-sample includes not only participants who live with their family, but also those who live independently and in group homes. Indeed, as noted in Section 5.11 (Demographics of Matched-pairs Sub-Sample), the matched-pairs sub-sample has proportionately greater representation of participants living independently than the entire sample. Consequently, the result of *quality of life* being statistically significantly higher for participants in open employment in the matched-pairs sub-sample suggests that while method of employment (open employment versus supported employment) does not affect the *quality of life* of people with intellectual disabilities who live at home, it does so for those who live away from home (either independently or in a group home). As such, it appears that living with family moderates the effect of method of employment on participants' quality of life. As to the specific affect that living with family has on this relationship is an area worthy of further research.

When the analysis was repeated for participants classified as having high functional work ability (Table 6.6; and Table 6.7), the above results were found to hold. That is, *quality of life* and *empowerment/independence* were consistently statistically significantly higher for participants in open employment compared with those in supported employment, except for participants living with their family when *quality of life* was not statistically significantly different. For participants with low functional work ability (Table 6.8; and Table 6.9) these results were not replicated. That is, people with intellectual disabilities who have high functional work ability experience a statistically significantly higher quality of life in open employment compared with those placed in supported employment, while the method of employment (open employment versus supported employment) does not appear to affect the quality of life of people with intellectual disabilities who have low functional work ability. As such, it appears that the results in Table 6.4 and Table 6.5 are driven by those participants with high functional work ability.

That participants with high functional work ability experience a statistically significant difference in their quality of life, based on the method of employment, and that those with low functional work ability do not, is not surprising. As previously stated, Moseley (1988) notes that expressing degree of satisfaction necessarily involves some form of comparison with other people. Lam and Chan (1988) note that for people with high functional work ability they likely compare themselves to people without disabilities. However, the frame of reference for people with low functional work ability is more likely to be other people with intellectual disabilities. Consequently, if participants with high functional work ability are comparing their situations with those of people without a disability, those participants in supported employment would be aware of the differences in their employment situation compared with people without a disability. Given the high level of importance people with intellectual disability place on employment (see, Schneider and Ferritor 1982), it is not unexpected that people with high functional work ability in open employment (who are experiencing a more normalised setting) would therefore report higher quality of life scores.

The general finding that people with intellectual disabilities report higher quality of life scores in open employment (Table 6.4) is consistent with the findings of prior research (Inge *et al.* 1988; Pedlar *et al.* 1990; Sinnott-Oswald *et al.* 1991, Eggleton *et al.* 1999). However, it is worth noting that none of these studies explicitly controls for differences in the level of functional work ability between open employment and supported employment samples. The discussion above on the differing results based on level of functional work ability highlights the importance of controlling for the differing levels of functional work ability likely between open employment and supported employment samples. It is possible that the results of previous studies are being driven by differing levels of functional work ability in their samples. The different results, based on level of functional work ability, also highlight the importance of not generalising findings based on a sample of participants that does not cover the full spectrum of level of functional work abilities.

As mentioned previously, in relation to the findings for *empowerment/independence*, caution needs to be exercised when interpreting the result that participants with high functional work ability report statistically significantly higher *quality of life* scores in open employment compared with supported employment. It is possible that those participants with high functional work ability, who have a higher *quality of life* self-select into open employment. This, again, highlights the need for a longitudinal study on the impact of both open employment and supported employment on participants' quality of life. Participants could have their quality of life assessed prior to employment and then at regular stages throughout employment. This would allow a deeper understanding of the effects of both open employment and supported employment, on people with intellectual disabilities.

Also worth mentioning are the percentage of scale maximum figures for quality of life as well as the four sub-domains reported in Table 6.4 through to Table 6.9. Cummins (2000, p. 136) notes that "the average level of life satisfaction [quality of life] can be described by 75 ± 2.5" percent scale maximum. Using two standard deviations around the mean to determine a normative range, Cummins (1995, 2000b) notes that population quality of life can be predicted to range between 70 and 80 percent of scale maximum. He argues that the value of 70 percent of scale maximum holds significance in that values below this level indicate that homeostasis[120] has been defeated. That is, the environment experienced by that population "has become so aversive that, on average, it exceeds the average person's adaptational capacity" (Cummins 2000b, p. 137).

Looking at Table 6.4(a), Table 6.5(a), Table 6.6(a), Table 6.7(a), Table 6.8(a), and Table 6.9(a),[121] it can be seen that in all instances for participants in supported employment the scores for *empowerment/independence* (under both the refined QOL.Q and the original QOL.Q) are below 70 percent of scale maximum. According to Cummins (2000), these results would indicate that the

---

[120] Cummins (2000b, p. 193-194) argues the existence of a "psychological, homeostatic mechanism that maintains an average level of life satisfaction at around 75" percent of scale maximum. This homeostatic mechanism "operates to control the human sense of well-being such that it generally remains positive" (Cummins 1995, p. 326) and ensures that "under relatively stable but diverse living conditions, most people feel satisfied with their lives" (Cummins 2000b, p. 194). For further details on homeostasis and homeostatic theory of subjective well-being see Cummins (1995; 1998; 2000b).

[121] As the scores for overall quality of life and its four factors are non-normally distributed reference is made to only the percentage of scale maximum figures based on medians.

homeostatic subjective well-being system of participants' has been defeated in regard to this domain of quality of life. This result suggests that disability employment agencies need to pay attention to the needs of their clients who are placed in supported employment in terms of their levels of *empowerment/independence*. It is apparent that supported employment is not delivering outcomes in these areas and specific programmes that target these specific domains may need to be developed. This conclusion applies, irrespective of whether those participants with naturally lower feelings of *empowerment/independence* are self-selecting into supported employment, or the lower percentage of scale maximum score for *empowerment/independence* is a result of the nature of supported employment. Either way, it is apparent that participants in supported employment have low feelings of *empowerment/independence* which need to be addressed.

Table 6.8(a) reveals that for participants with low functional work ability, irrespective of whether they are placed in open employment or supported employment, the mean score for *empowerment/independence* percent of scale maximum scores is below 70 percent (except for Panel B, for participants in unskilled labouring positions in open employment were the median percentage of scale maximum score for *empowerment/independence* is 75 percent).[122] This result indicates that people with low levels of functional work ability (high level of intellectual disability) do not feel as empowered or independent as those with milder levels of intellectual disability. To some extent this result may be due to the nature and level of their intellectual disability. However, it may be worth agencies revisiting their programmes designed to increase the independence of people with higher levels of intellectual disabilities, to see whether they can be redesigned to achieve, if possible, better outcomes.

When analysing the percentage of scale maximum scores for the *social belonging/community integration* factor there is a divergence in the pattern of scores between the refined QOL.Q and original QOL.Q. Using the original QOL.Q (Table 6.5(a); Table 6.7(a); and Table 6.9(a)) the *social belonging/community integration* scores for participants in both open and supported employment on all occasions are equal to or below 70 percent of scale maximum. However, when the percentage of scale maximum figures for the refined QOL.Q (Table 6.4(a); Table 6.6(a); and Table 6.8(a)) are examined, such a pattern is not apparent, with only the scores for participants with high functional work ability being consistently below 70 percent of scale maximum. Given that the *social belonging/community integration* factor for the refined QOL.Q reports higher reliability statistics (discussed in Section 4.5.2. (Reliability Analysis of the QOL.Q), emphasis will be placed on these results over those of the original QOL.Q.

Interestingly, when using the refined QOL.Q, the only instance that participants across all occupations report *social belonging/community integration* scores below 70 percent of scale maximum is for participants with high functional work ability (Table 6.6(a)). That is, it appears as though homeostasis has been defeated in relation to participants feeling the *social belonging/community integration* aspect of quality of life, irrespective of whether they are in open employment or supported employment. It is possible to explain the result in relation to participants in supported employment based on the insights of Moseley (1988) and Lam and Chan (1988). As stated previously, Moseley (1988) notes that assessing personal satisfaction requires implicitly a comparison with others, and Lam and Chan (1988) contend that for people with high functional work ability the frame of reference is likely to be people without a disability. Consequently, it is not

---

[122] This result for the median percentage of scale maximum score for the empowerment/independence score for participants with a low functional work ability in unskilled labouring positions in open employment (Panel B of Table 6.8(a)) is unusual in that in when participants in all occupations (Panel A of Table 6.8(a)) and when those living with their family (Panel C of Table 6.8(a)) are considered the percentage of scale maximum scores for participants in open employment is below 70 percent. It should be noted that with the omission of two people from the sample of participants in unskilled labouring positions (Panel B of Table 6.8(a)) the percentage of scale maximum score would drop below 70 percent. Given the above, the results of this panel are seen as broadly supportive of the results in Panels A and C of Table 6.8(a).

surprising that those participants in supported employment with high functional work ability report such low *social belonging/community integration* scores. These participants would be well aware of the fact that they are employed in a segregated setting and not interacting socially with people without a disability.

However, what was initially surprising was that those participants with high functional work ability in open employment, who are interacting with people without disabilities, likewise report percentage of scale maximum scores for *social belonging/community integration* below 70 percent. A possible explanation is that people without disabilities are not interacting, on a meaningful level, with workers with intellectual disabilities. This is supported by the findings of prior research, which finds people with intellectual disabilities in open employment are interacting at only a superficial level (Chadsey-Rusch *et al.* 1989; Knox and Parmenter 1993; Test *et al.* 1993; Petrovski and Gleeson 1997). If this is the case, participants with high functional work ability would be aware that their social interactions with co-workers are different compared with those among solely co-workers without a disability. Given that people with intellectual disabilities consider social interactions with others as one of the more important aspects of their lives (Knox and Parmenter 1993; Knox and Hickson 2001), this recognition of being treated differently on a social basis, may result in lower feelings of *social belonging/community integration*.

These results for the *social belonging/community integration* factor of the refined QOL indicate that in relation to open employment, there may be a need for disability employment agencies to train (or better educate) co-workers without a disability to involve people with intellectual disabilities in a meaningful way in their social interactions. This need is further highlighted by the results of Yazbeck *et al.* (2004) who find the general Australian population to report statistically significantly less positive attitudes towards people with intellectual disabilities than do disability service staff or students. As they note, it appears that community attitudes in Australia towards people with intellectual disabilities might be lagging behind those in European countries. The training or education of co-workers without a disability may assist people with intellectual disabilities to hopefully feel a sense of belonging to their work community, which as previously noted in Section 1.3 (The Choice of the Disability Employment Sector), forms a major part of an individual's life.

Results for the *social belonging/community integration* factor of the refined QOL in relation to supported employment appear to be indicating that people with high functional work ability in this form of employment are also not feeling apart of their community. To overcome this may require people with high functional work ability to have more interaction with people without a disability, to whom they are likely to be comparing themselves. However, as just noted above, it appears that when interaction with people without disabilities is increased, participants with high functional work ability still do not feel part of the community. As such, the task of increasing participants with high functional work ability's *social belonging/community integration* score appears to be problematic; it appears that they are not interacting on a meaningful level with either people without disabilities or with people with low levels of functional work ability, who form the majority of the work-force in supported employment.

Interestingly, results on the *social belonging/community integration* for the refined QOL.Q are different from those achieved for the *social* factor of the JSQ (Section 6.2 (Job Satisfaction)). However, as noted in Section 6.2.3 (Discussion of Job Satisfaction Results), the social factor of the JSQ is not stable (see Section 4.4.3 (Factor Stability of the Derived JSQ) and does not report a satisfactory Cronbach alpha score (see Section 4.4.2 (Internal Reliability of the Derived JSQ Scores)). Consequently, no weight is placed on the results of the *social* factor of the JSQ.

Table 6.6(a), also shows that for participants with high functional work ability, supported employment results in quality of life scores of below 70 percent of scale maximum. This indicates that supported employment is resulting in a defeat of homeostasis for those participants with high functional work ability (low levels of intellectual disability). Given that people with low levels of intellectual disability (high functional work ability) are likely to compare their situation with those of people without a disability (Lam and Chan 1988) it is not surprising that working in a segregated employment setting results in this effect.

6.3.4 Summary of Quality of Life Results

In totality, the results reported in Tables 6.4 and 6.5 support the notion that people with intellectual disabilities report higher *empowerment/independence* and *quality of life* scores when placed in open employment compared with supported employment. However, as noted, caution needs to be exercised when interpreting these results as those people who naturally have higher feelings of *empowerment/independence* and higher *quality of life* could self-select into open employment.

When the analysis is repeated for only participants classified as having high functional work ability (Table 6.6; and Table 6.7), the above results are found to hold. For participants with low functional work ability (Table 6.8; and Table 6.9) these results are not replicated. These differences in results for participants with high functional work ability compared with those of low functional work ability highlight that people with intellectual disabilities who have high functional work ability experience a statistically significantly higher quality of life in open employment compared with those placed in supported employment, while the type of employment does not appear to affect the quality of life of people with intellectual disabilities who have low functional work ability. As such, it appears that the results in Tables 6.4 and 6.5 are driven by those participants with high functional work ability.

It was also noted that living with family appears to influence the results on whether method of employment effected a participants' quality of life. When the responses of only participants who lived with their family were analysed (Panels C and D, Table 6.4; and Table 6.5), quality of life was not found to be statistically significantly different between open employment and supported employment. However, in the matched-pairs sub-sample (Panel E, Table 6.4; and Table 6.5), when the responses of participants living not only with their family, but also those living independently and in group homes were included in the analysis, quality of life was found to be statistically significantly higher for open employment compared with supported employment.

Percentage of scale maximums were then investigated to determine whether participants homeostasis has been defeated (score below 70 percent, as per Cummins (2000b)) in relation to *quality of life* or any of its four factors. Irrespective of participants' level of functional work ability, *empowerment/independence* scores were found to be consistently below 70 percent for participants in supported employment (Table 6.4(a); Table 6.6(a); and Table 6.8(a)). Further, all participants with low functional work ability (Table 6.8(a)) were found to have *empowerment/independence* scores below 70 percent of scale maximum. In both instances it appears that a need exists for disability employment agencies to develop programmes for their clients to overcome the defeat of homeostasis on this quality of life factor.

The examination of percentage of scale maximum scores further reveals that for participants with high functional work ability (Table 6.6) homeostasis has been defeated in relation to the *social belonging/community integration* factor of the refined QOL.Q. Such low scores are understandable for participants in supported employment, given that they are likely to compare their employment situation with that of people without a disability. For those participants in open employment these low percentage of maximum scores possibly reflect that they are not interacting on a socially meaningful level with their co-workers and, as such, do not feel part of their work community. If this is the case, disability employment agencies need to educate/train the co-workers without disabilities how to meaningfully interact and socially involve people with intellectual disabilities.

152

6.4 Conclusion

This chapter presented the results from research undertaken to determine whether the method of employment (open employment versus supported employment) affected the job satisfaction and quality of life of people with intellectual disabilities. The results indicate that after controlling for demographic differences between the two populations no difference was apparent in terms of job satisfaction or its factors. In relation to quality of life it appears that for participants with high functional work ability, open employment results in higher *empowerment/independence* and *quality of life*. While for people with low functional work ability, no difference in quality of life or its four factors was apparent.

Combining the above discussion on job satisfaction and quality of life supported employment does not appear to deliver outcomes for participants with high functional work ability, and open employment may deliver superior outcomes for these people. In relation to people with low functional work ability, method of employment (open employment versus supported employment) does not appear to affect the outcomes being achieved. As such, the results of this thesis would tend to support people with intellectual disabilities with a high level of functional work ability being placed in open employment. However, I wish to state explicitly that I do not wish to make any recommendation that would force people of a certain level of functional work ability to partake in one type of employment at the exclusion of the other. Such a policy would only serve to disempower people with intellectual disabilities by further reducing their power of choice with respect to the type of employment preferred. Rather, a preferable outcome would be to provide the results of this thesis to people with intellectual disabilities and their parents/guardians to aid them in deciding for themselves as to whether they would prefer to be placed in open or supported employment. I believe the results of this thesis will be valuable in the formulation of such decisions.

Though not central to this research, Appendix 2 (Correlates of Job Satisfaction and Quality of Life) discusses correlates of job satisfaction and quality of life in an attempt to understand which, if any, of the demographic variables may be related to job satisfaction and quality of life. The results of the correlation analyses are related back to the findings of this chapter.

The next chapter summarises the research conducted and major findings of this thesis. Limitations with the research and impacts these may have on the findings are acknowledged, and avenues for future research explored.

Chapter 7 – Conclusion

7.1 Background

As noted in Chapter 1, performance measurement in the not-for-profit sector is extremely important in terms of measuring the efficiency and effectiveness of organisations in achieving their goals. Performance indicators assist management in strategic decision making and fulfilling their accountability obligations for the best use of limited resources to funders, purchasers, consumers, and other stakeholder groups.

7.2 Aim and Importance

Measurement of performance in the not-for-profit sector is an area of research that has received increasing attention over recent years. It is extremely important in terms of measuring the efficiency and effectiveness of organizations in achieving their goals. Performance indicators assist management in strategic decision making and in fulfilling their accountability obligations to funders, purchasers, consumers, and other stakeholder groups for the best use of limited resources (Eggleton *et al.*, 2005). This thesis sought to further the research into performance measurement in the not-for-profit sector by evaluating the effectiveness of different methods of employment (open employment and supported employment) for people with intellectual disabilities.

During the past two decades, governments around the world have faced increased pressure to reform their public sectors. Most governments have either undergone reform or are undergoing reforms, such as privatization, reduction in size, commercialization, and deregulation (Martin, 1993; Nolan, 2001). These reforms have significantly increased the focus on performance measurement in the public sector (Guthrie, 1998; McCulloh and Ball,1992; Newberry, 2003, Modell, 2005).

Modell (2004) notes that the initial development of performance measures in the public sector during the 1980s and 1990s was characterized by growing concerns with accountability and fiscal probity, resulting in an emphasis on measuring performance in financial terms (Carter, 1991; Carter and Greer, 1993; Hood, 1995). This initial emphasis on purely financial measures of performance led to calls for a broadening of the measures of performance to better reflect the public sector's multiple stakeholders (Kloot, 1997; Ballentine *et al.*, 1998; Chow *et al.*, 1998; Jones, 1999a, 1999b; Kloot and Martin, 2000).

Schalock (1999) noted that during the past two decades there had been a significant change in how the public viewed social service programs. There was a change in focus from inputs to outputs, clients were redefined as either consumers or customers, and citizens became more empowered (Schalock 1999). The above mentioned public sector reforms together with the *quality revolution*, with its emphasis on total quality management, resulted in human service providers managing for quality (Schalock 1996). This greatly increased the focus on performance measurement and consequently agencies involved in the provision of public services (such as those involved in the provision of services to people with intellectual disabilities (PWID)) have been required to demonstrate to governments the effectiveness of their services in terms of improved outcomes (Eggleton *et al.* 1999).

The initial focus of research into the issue of the benefits of open versus supported employment investigated whether the financial benefits (e.g., increased tax revenues, decreased government pensions) of open employment exceed the associated costs (e.g., employment agency funding, subsidies paid to employers) (Hill & Wehman 1983; Hill *et al.* 1987; Conley *et al.* 1989; Tines *et al.* 1990; Noble *et al.* 1991; McCaughrin *et al.* 1993; Rusch *et al.* 1993,Tuckerman *et al.* 1999, Shearn *et al.* 2000). However, Inge *et al.* (1988) contended that although it has been shown that open employment results in positive financial outcomes, it is equally important to determine whether open employment had a positive effect on the lives of the individual. DeStefano (1990) specifically noted that an assessment of quality of life was an essential part of any comprehensive outcome evaluation. In addition to quality of life, the customer-referenced outcome measure of job satisfaction was also selected as it related directly to the consumers satisfaction with their current employment.

7.3 Method
To determine the effectiveness of the two different methods of employment for people with intellectual disabilities, 117 people with intellectual disabilities were interviewed. These people, who were employed in either open or supported employment, were drawn from the registers of six disability employment agencies that operated within the metropolitan area of one of Australia's capital cities.

7.3.1 Research Instruments
The Barlow and Kirby (1991) job satisfaction questionnaire and Schalock and Keith (1993) quality of life questionnaire were selected to ascertain levels of satisfaction with regards to job satisfaction and quality of life, respectively. Both instruments were tested to ensure that they were psychometrically valid and necessary refinements were made when appropriate to enhance the internal reliability of both instruments. Given the previous extensive use of the Schalock and Keith (1993) quality of life questionnaire, results were also presented for the original version of this questionnaire.

7.3.2 Statistical Analyses
Non-parametric tests were then conducted to examine if there were any differences in job satisfaction and quality of life experienced by participants in open employment compared with participants in supported employment. Statistical analyses were also conducted on sub-samples that were selected to control for underlying demographic differences between participants in open employment and participants in supported employment. These sub-samples controlled for differences between the two methods of employment in terms of: (1) the type of occupation performed (by analysing responses of only participants in unskilled labouring positions); (2) living environment (by analysing the responses of only participants living with their family); (3) both type of occupation and living environment (by analysing the responses of only participants in unskilled labouring positions who live with their family); and (4) type of occupation, living environment, functional work ability, work hours, and gender (by conducting a matched-pairs analysis). The effect of functional work ability on the results of the statistical analyses was controlled by splitting the entire sample into participants with high functional work ability and participants with low functional work ability and re-running the statistical analyses on each sub-sample.

7.4 Results
The results of this thesis indicate that after controlling for demographic differences between participants in open employment and those in supported employment, there is no difference in terms of job satisfaction based on method of employment (open employment versus supported employment). In relation to quality of life it appears that for participants with low functional work ability there is no difference in quality of life, or its four factors, based on method of employment. While for people with high functional work ability, open employment results in higher *empowerment/independence* and *quality of life*. However, caution needs to be exercised when interpreting these results as it is possible participants with higher *empowerment/independence* and *quality of life* scores are self-selecting into open employment.

It was also observed that living with family was affecting the results as to whether a statistically significant difference in the quality of life existed between participants in open employment and supported employment. When responses of only participants living with their family were analysed there were no statistically significant differences, in terms of quality of life, between methods of employment (open employment compared with supported employment). However, when responses of participants living not only with their family, but also those living independently and in group homes were analysed, quality of life was found to be statistically significantly higher for open employment compared with supported employment.

Percentage of scale maximums were then investigated to determine whether participants' homeostasis has been defeated. Homeostasis was found to have been defeated in relation to *empowerment/independence* for all participants in supported employment, and for participants with low functional work ability in open employment. In these instances, it appears a need exists for disability employment agencies to develop programmes for their customers to increase their feelings of *empowerment/independence*.

The examination of percentage of scale maximum scores also revealed that for participants with high functional work ability, homeostasis had been defeated for the *social belonging/community integration* factor of the refined QOL.Q. For participants with high functional work ability in supported employment it is likely that this reflects that they compare their employment situation to people without a disability. For those participants with high functional work ability in open employment, it is probable defeat of homeostatic on this factor reflects they are not interacting on a socially meaningful level with their co-workers, and as such do not feel part of their work community. If this is the case, disability employment agencies may need to educate/train the co-workers without disabilities as to how to interact meaningfully and socially involve people with intellectual disabilities.

7.5 Conclusion

Taken as a whole, the results of this research indicate that for people with low functional work ability, there is no difference in the effectiveness of open employment compared with supported employment. However, for participants with high functional work ability, open employment appears to have a higher degree of effectiveness than supported employment. As such the results of this thesis would tend to support people with intellectual disabilities with a high level of functional work ability being placed in open employment as opposed to supported employment. However, as stated previously, it is not appropriate to force people with intellectual disabilities of a particular functional work ability to participate in one method of employment, to the exclusion of the other. Such an action would only serve to disempower people with intellectual disabilities, by reducing their power of choice with respect to the type of employment preferred. Rather, it is hoped that the results of this research will be available to people with intellectual disabilities and their parents/guardians to guide them in deciding for themselves as to whether they would prefer to be placed in open or supported employment.

In addition to people with intellectual disabilities and their parents/guardians it is also hoped that results of this thesis will available to: (1) the staff of disability employment agencies, so that the results can be used to guide the implementation of improvements in the quality of the services provided; (2) employers of people with intellectual disabilities and organisations that are considering employing people with intellectual disabilities, so that they can hopefully take steps to redress the apparent lack of meaningful social interaction occurring between people with intellectual disabilities and co-workers without disabilities; (3) the Department of Employment and Workplace Relations (who fund open employment agencies) and the Department of Family and Community Services (who fund supported employment agencies), so that an understanding of the customer-reference outcomes achieved by the two methods of employment will inform any future policy formulation; (4) the community at large, so that they to can gain an understanding of the effects that different methods of employment (open employment versus supported employment) have upon people with intellectual disabilities; and (5) researchers, so that they can continue researching the effects of employment on people with intellectual disabilities, and begin investigating some of the areas of further research previously identified.

7.6 Limitations and Further Research

A limitation of the results presented in this thesis is that it was not possible to control for all the demographic differences between participants placed in open employment relative to those participants placed in supported employment (for example, differences in current job tenure and total years of employment). However, as Cummins and Lau (2004, p. 198) note "when comparing groups that differ from one another in ways that are fundamental to the control of the dependent variable", as is the case in this instance in regards to current job tenure and length of employment, sophisticated statistical procedures may "obfuscate rather than enlighten".

Having stated this, it is believed one particularly fruitful area for future research would be to investigate the effect of income levels on the quality of life of people with intellectual disabilities. Given the disparity in the wages paid to participants in open employment compared with those in supported employment it was not possible to control for the differences between the two methods of employment with regards to this demographic variable. As such, I cannot be entirely sure as to the cause of my results. That is, whether it is the type of employment *per se*, or possibly the differences in income levels between participants in open employment and supported employment that are driving my results. This is all the more pertinent given that the findings of Cummins (2000) suggest that people with low socio-economic status (as may be expected of people with intellectual disabilities) report higher quality of life with higher levels of wealth; as the additional income can be used to help buffer themselves from their external environment. As such it would be interesting to survey people with intellectual disabilities placed in supported employment who received considerably higher wages than those interviewed for this paper. This research opportunity is currently available given the move in Australia by supported employment agencies to pay their employees with intellectual disabilities a supported wage.[123] This would allow a determination of whether it is the method of employment or income levels that are driving my results.

Another limitation of this thesis worth mentioning is that participants were drawn from six employment agencies from the metropolitan area of one Australian capital city. Further research is required to determine if my findings can be generalised to people from other areas (that is, non-metropolitan areas and other cities) and other countries, especially non-Anglo-Saxon countries.

As noted in the Section 7.4 (Results) caution needs to be exercised when interpreting the result that for people with high functional work ability, open employment results in higher *empowerment/independence* and *quality of life*, as it is possible participants with higher *empowerment/independence* and *quality of life* scores are self-selecting into open employment. This highlights the need for a longitudinal study on the impact of both open employment and supported employment on participants' quality of life.

As, also, noted in the Section 7.4 (Results), living with family was affecting the results as to whether a statistically significant difference in the quality of life existed between participants in open employment and supported employment. This suggests the need for more research on what effect living with family has on the quality of life of people with intellectual disabilities, and how living with their family might moderate the effect method of employment has on quality of life.

In addition to the areas mentioned above, there are many other fruitful avenues for further research into the effect employment has on the quality of life experienced by people with intellectual disabilities. It would be interesting to conduct further research to investigate whether within a method of employment (open employment or supported employment) the nature of the occupation (that is, labouring positions versus non-labouring positions) has a bearing on quality of life. It

---

[123] Supported wages are based on an assessment of the person with an intellectual disability's productivity relative to a non-disabled person. The person with an intellectual disability is then paid in accordance to his/her productivity relative to the minimum wage or the wage that a non-disabled worker would receive for that job.

would also be interesting to know whether within supported employment, the extent of opportunities for interaction with people without disabilities has a bearing on participants' quality of life. For example, people employed in a mobile gardening crew have greater opportunities to interact with people without a disability, compared with those people employed in a business service (sheltered workshop). This degree of interaction may impact on their quality of life. Additionally, it would be worth investigating the effect the length of employment has on a participants' quality of life. Anecdotal evidence would suggest that people with intellectual disabilities placed in either open employment or supported employment tend to have limited opportunities for promotion and consequently remain in the same position for extended periods of time. It would be interesting to investigate the effect this has on the person's quality of life as a basis for formulating appropriate career plans for people with disabilities.

While consumer-referenced outcome measures such as quality of life and job satisfaction are important outcome measures, a complete stakeholder analysis of the different methods of employment would also be extremely valuable. The different methods of employment could be examined relative to the impact they have upon family members of the person with an intellectual disability, employers, co-workers, and funders.

In terms of the instruments used in this research, a fruitful avenue of research would be the further refinement of both the JSQ and QOL.Q. As revealed in Chapter 4, both instruments have one factor that is not stable. The development of a JSQ and QOL.Q where all factors were stable, would enhance each instrument's psychometric properties, thereby increasing the reliability of the scores attained for both instruments, and is therefore worthy of future research efforts.

Bibliography

Anderson, P. R. (2000). Open employment services for people with disabilities in Australia, 1995 to 1997. *Journal of Vocational Rehabilitation, 13*, 79-94.

Atkinson, A. A., Waterhouse, J. H., & Wells, R. B. (1997). A stakeholder approach to strategic performance measurement. *Sloan Management Review, Spring*, 25-37.

Australian Bureau of Statistics. (1997). *ASCO - Australian Standard Classification of Occupations* (Second ed.). Canberra: Australian Government Publishing Services.

Australian Commonwealth Government. (1986). *Disability Services Act*. Canberra: Commonwealth Government Printer.

Australian Government Department of Family and Community Services. (2004). *Australian government disability services census*. Canberra: Australian Commonwealth Government.

Awty, A. (2001). Singapore unlimited. *Australian CPA, 71*, 48-49.

Awty, A. (2002). Hong Kong moves on. *Australian CPA, 72*, 30.

Bac, A. D. (2002). Dutch private sector and local government accounting regulations: A comparison. *Journal of Public Budgeting, Accounting and Financial Management, 14*, 595-618.

Baker, F., & Intagliata, J. (1982). Quality of life in the evaluation of community support systems. *Evaluation and Program Planning, 5*, 69-79.

Ball, I. (1994). Reinventing government: lessons learned from the New Zealand treasury. *The Government Accountants Journal, 43*, 19-28.

Ballantine, J., Brignall, S., & Modell, S. (1998). Performance measurement and management in public health services: a comparison of U.K. and Swedish practice. *Management Accounting Research, 9*, 71-94.

Barlow, J., & Kirby, N. (1991). Residential satisfaction of persons with an intellectual disability living in an institution or in the community. *Australia and New Zealand Journal of Developmental Disabilities, 17*, 7-23.

Barton, A. (1999). Public and private sector accounting - the non-identical twins. *Australian Accounting Review, 9*, 22-31.

Bellamy, G. T., Rhodes, L. E., Bourbeau, P. E., & Mank, D. M. (1986). Mental retardation service in sheltered workshops and day activity programs: consumer benefits and policy alternatives. In F. R. Rusch (Ed.), *Competitive employment issues and strategies* (pp. 257-272). Baltimore: Brookes.

Bellini, J., Bolton, B., & Neath, J. (1998). Rehabilitation counselors' assessments of applicants' functional limitations as predictors of rehabilitation services provided. *Rehabilitation Counseling Bulletin, 41*, 242-259.

Biklen, S. K., & Moseley, C. R. (1988). "Are you retarded?" "No, I'm Catholic": Qualitative methods in the study of people with severe handicaps. *JASH, 13*, 155-162.

Bledsoe, J. C., & Brown, S. E. (1977). Factor structure of the Minnesota satisfaction questionnaire. *Perceptual and Motor Skills, 45*, 301-302.

Boston, J., Martin, M., Pallot, J., & Walsh, P. (1996). *Public management: the New Zealand model*. Auckland: Oxford University Press.

Bowarnwanatha, B. (1996). Thailand: the politics of reform of the secretariat of the Prime Minister.

Australian Journal of Public Administration, 55, 55-64.

Bowd, A. D. (1988). *Assessment of residents' satisfaction and family perceptions index*. Ontario: Lakehead University.

Bradburn, N. M. (1969). *The structure of psychological well-being*. Chicago: Aldine.

Brignall, S., & Modell, S. (2000). An institutional perspective on performance measurement and management in the "new public sector". *Management Accounting Research, 11*, 281-306.

Broadbent, J., & Guthrie, J. (1992). Changes in the public sector: a review of recent 'alternative' accounting research. *Accounting, Auditing and Accountability Journal, 5*, 3-31.

Brown, R. I., & Bayer, M. B. (1992). *Rehabilitation questionnaire and manual: A personal guide to the individual's quality of life*. Toronto: Captus University Publications.

Browne, M. W. (1968). A comparison of factor analytic techniques. *Psychometrika, 33*, 267.

Burnett, P. C. (1989). Assessing satisfaction in people with an intellectual disability: Living in community-based residential facilities. *Australian Disability Review, 1*, 14-19.

Caballo, C., Crespo, M., Jenaro, C., Verdugo, M. A., & Martinez, J. L. (2005). Factor structure of the Schalock and Keith quality of life questionnaire (QOL-Q): Validation on Mexican and Spanish samples. *Journal of Intellectual Disability Research, 49*, 773-776.

Campbell, A. (1976). Subjective measures of well-being. *American Psychologist*, 117-124.

Campbell, A. (1981). *A sense of well-being in America*. New York: McGraw-Hill.

Campbell, A., Converse, P. E., & Rodgers, W. L. (1976). *The quality of American life*. New York: Russell Sage Foundation.

Carlin, T. M. (2004). Output based management and the management of performance: Insights from the Victorian experience. *Management Accounting Research, 15*, 267-283.

Carlson, R. E., Davis, R. V., England, G. W., & Lofquist, L. H. (1962). *The measurement of employment satisfaction*. Minneapolis: University of Minnesota.

Carter, N. (1991). Learning to measure performance: the use of indicators in organizations. *Public Administration, 69*, 85-101.

Carter, N., & Greer, P. (1993). Evaluating agencies: next steps and performance indicators. *Public Administration, 71*, 407-416.

Cattell, R. B. (1952). *Factor analysis*. New York: Harper & Brothers.

Cattell, R. B. (1966). The Scree test for the number of factors. *Multivariate Behavioral Research, 1*, 245-276.

Cattell, R., & Jaspers, J. (1967). *A general plasmode (No. 30-10-5-2) for factor analytic excercises and research*.

Chadsey-Rusch, J., Gonzalez, P., Tines, J., & Johnson, J. R. (1989). Social ecology of the workplace: An examination of contextual variables affecting the social interactions of employees with and without mental retardation. *American Journal of Mental Retardation, 9*, 141-151.

Chow, C. W., Ganulin, D., Haddad, K., & Williamson, J. (1998). The balanced scorecard: A potent tool for energizing and focusing healthcard organization management. *Journal of Health Care Management, 43*, 263-280.

Cimete, G., Gencalp, N. S., & Keskin, G. (2003). Quality of life and job satisfaction of nurses.

Journal of Nursing Care, 18, 151-158.

Cliff, N. (1988). The eigenvalues-greater-than-one rule and the reliability of components. *Psychological Bulletin, 103*, 276-279.

Conley, R. W., Rusch, F. R., McCaughrin, W. B., & Tines, J. (1989). Benefits and costs of supported employment: An analysis of the Illinois supported employment project. *Journal of Applied Behavior Analysis, 22*, 441-447.

Conroy, J. W. (1996). The Small ICF/MR Program: Dimensions of quality and cost. *Mental Retardation, 34*, 13-26.

Cragg, R., & Harrison, J. (1984). *Living in a supervised home. A questionnaire of quality of life.* Manchester: West Midlands Campaign for People with Mental Handicap.
Crew, N. M., & Athelstan, G. T. (1984). *Functional Assessment Inventory Manual.* Menomonie, USA: Stout Vocational Rehabilitation Institute, University of Wisconsin-Stout.

Crewe, N.M. & Athelstan, G.T. (1984) *Functional assessment inventory manual.* Stout Vocational Rehabilitation Institute, University of Wisconsin-Stout, Menomonie.

Cronbach, L. J. (1951). Coefficient alpha and the internal structure of tests. *Psychometrika, 16*, 297-334.

Cummins, R. A. (1993). *Comprehensive quality of life scale - Intellectual disability* (Fourth ed.). Melbourne, Victoria, Australia: School of Psychology, Deakin University.

Cummins, R. A. (1995). On the trail of the gold standard for life satisfaction. *Social Indicators Research, 35*, 179-200.

Cummins, R. A. (1997a). Self-rated quality of life scales for people with an intellectual disability: A review. *Journal of Applied Research in Intellectual Disabilities, 10*, 199-216.

Cummins, R. A. (1997b). *Comprehensive quality of life scale - Intellectual/cognitive disability manual* (Fifth ed.). Melbourne: School of Psychology, Deakin University.

Cummins, R.A. (1998). The second approximation to an international standard for life satisfaction. *Social Indicators Research, 43*, 307-334.

Cummins, R. A. (2000a). *Self-rated quality of life scales for people who have cognitive disability.* Unpublished manuscript, Victoria, Australia.

Cummins, R. A. (2000b). Personal income and subjective well-being: A review. *Journal of Happiness Studies, 1*, 133-158.

Cummins, R. A., & Baxter, C. (1994). Choice of outcome measures in service evaluations for people with an intellectual disability. *Evaluation Journal of Australasia, 6*, 22-30.
Cummins, R. A., & Lau, A. L. D. (2004). Cluster housing and the freedom of choice: a response to Emerson (2004). *Journal of Intellectual and Developmental Disability, 29*, 198-201.

de Vaus, D. A. (1995). *Surveys in Social Research* (Fourth ed.): Allen and Unwin.

Department of Human Services and Health. (1994). *Report on the survey of service costs.* Canberra: Department of Human Services and Health.

DeStefano, L. (1990). Designing and implementing program evaluation, in F. Rusch (ed) *Supported Employment: Models, Methods, Issues,* Sycamore Publishing Company, Sycamore.

Diener, E., & Suh, E. (1997). Measuring quality of life: Economic, social, and subjective indicators. *Social Indicators Research, 40*, 189-216.

Donegan, C., & Potts, M. (1988). People with mental handicap living alone in the community. *The British Journal of Mental Subnormality, 34,* 10-22.

E-QUAL & Donovan Research (2000). *National Satisfaction Survey of Clients of Disability Services,* A report prepared for the Steering Committee for the Review of Commonwealth/State Service Provision and the National Disability Administrators, Ausinfo, Canberra

Efraty, D., Sirgy, M. J., & Siegel, P. (2000). The job/life satisfaction relationship among professional accountants: Psychological determinants and demographic differences. *Advances in Quality of Life Theory and Research, 4,* 129-157.

Eggleton, I. R. C. (1991). *Performance measurement for public sector organisations.* Unpublished manuscript.

Eggleton, I., Robertson, S., Ryan, J., & Kober, R. (1999). The impact of employment on the quality of life of people with an intellectual disability. *Journal of Vocational Rehabilitation, 13,* 95-107.

Elliot, J. (1996). Japan: the prospect for public sector change. *Australian Journal of Public Administration, 55,* 45-55.

Ellwood, S. (2002). The financial reporting revolution in the UK public sector. *Journal of Public Budgeting, Accounting and Financial Management,* 14, 565-594.

Enthoven, A. C. (1988). *Theory and practice of managed competition in health care finance.* Amsterdam: North Holland.

Everett, J. E., & Entrekin, L. V. (1980). Factor comparability and the advantages of multiple group factor analysis. *Multivariate Behavioral Research, 2,* 165-180.

Fabian, E. S. (1992). Supported employment and the quality of life: Does a job make a difference. *Rehabilitation Counselling Bulletin, 36,* 84-97.

Fitzgerald, L. (1988). Management performance measurement in service industries. *International Journal of Operation and Production Management,* 8, 109-116.

Flanagan, J. C. (1978). A research approach to improving our quality of life. *American Psychologist,* 138-147.

Gill, M. (2005). The myth of transition: contractualizing disability in the sheltered workshop. *Disability and Society, 20,* 613-623.

Gillet, B., & Schwab, D. P. (1975). Convergent and discriminant validities of corresponding job descriptive index and Minnesota satisfaction questionnaire scales. *Journal of Applied Psychology, 60,* 313-317.

Gorsuch, R. L. (1983). *Factor analysis* (Second ed.). Hillsdale: Lawrence Erlbaum Associates.

Government of Western Australia. (1992). *Disability Services Act 1992.* Perth: Governnment of Western Australia.

Gray, B. L., & Weiss, D. J. (1971). *Pilot study of the measurement of job satisfaction of mentally retarded adults.* Paper presented at the 79th Annual Convention, APA.

Gunzberg, H. C. (1977). *Progress assessment chart of social development.* London: (P-A-C). N.S.M.H.C.

Guthrie, J. (1998). Application of accrual accounting in the Australian public sector - rhetoric or reality? *Financial Accountability & Management, 14,* 1-9.

Guthrie, J., Parker, L., & English, L. M. (2003). A review of new public financial management chance in Australia. *Australian Accounting Review, 13*, 3-9.

Hair, J. F., Anderson, R. E., Tatham, R. L., & Black, W. C. (1995). *Multivariate data analysis* (Fourth ed.). Upper Saddle River: Prentice Hall.

Hair, J. F., Anderson, R. E., Tatham, R. L., & Black, W. C. (1998). *Multivariate data analysis* (Fifth ed.). Upper Saddle River: Prentice Hall.

Hancer, M., & George, T. R. (1994). Factor structure of the Minnesota satisfaction questionnaire short form for restaurant employees. *Psychological Reports, 94*, 357-362.

Harman, H. H. (1967). *Modern factor analysis* (Second ed.). Chicago: The University of Chicago Press.

Harner, C. J., & Heal, L. W. (1993). The multifaceted lifestyle satisfaction scale (MLSS): Psychometric properties of an interview schedule for assessing personal satisfaction of adults with limited intelligence. *Research in Developmental Disabilities, 14*, 221-236.

Heal, L. W., & Chadsey-Rusch, J. (1985). The lifestyle satisfaction scale (LSS): Assessing individuals' satisfaction with residence, community setting, and associated services. *Applied Research in Mental Retardation, 6*, 475-490.

Heinemann, A. W., Crown, D., & McMahon, R. (2000). Utility of the functional assessment inventory in a post-stoke sample. *Rehabilitation Counselling Bulletin, 43*, 165-177.
Hemming, H., Lavender, T., & Pill, R. (1981). Quality of life of mentally retarded adults transferred from large institutions to new small units. *American Journal of Mental Deficiency, 86*(2), 157-169.

Hill, M. L., Banks, P. D., Handrich, R. R., Wehman, P. H., Hill, J. W., & Shafer, M. S. (1987). Benefit-cost analysis of supported competitive employment for persons with mental retardation. *Research in Developmental Disabilities, 8*, 71-89.

Hill, M., & Wehman, P. (1983). Cost benefit analysis of placing moderately and severely handicapped individuals into competitive employment. *TASH Journal, 8*, 30-38.

Hood, C. (1991). A public management for all seasons? *Public Administration, 69*, 3-20.

Hood, C. (1995). The 'new public management' in the 1980s: Variations on a theme. *Accounting, Organizations and Society, 20*, 93-109.

Hoover, J. H., Wheeler, J. J., & Reetz, L. J. (1992). Development of a leisure satisfaction scale for use with adolescents and adults with mental retardation: Initial findings. *Education and Training in Mental Retardation, 27*, 153-160.

Hopwood, A. (1984). Accounting and the pursuit of efficiency. In A. Hopwood & C. Tomkins (Eds.), *Issues in Public Sector Accounting*: Phillip Allen.

Hoque, Z., & Moll, J. (2001). Public sector reform: implications for accounting, accountability and performance of state-owned entities - an Australian perspective. *The International Journal of Public Sector Management, 17*, 304-326.

Houser, R., & Chace, A. (1993). Job satisfaction of people with disabilities placed through a project with industry. *Journal of Rehabilitation* (January/February/March), 45-48.

Human Services Research Institute. (1998). *Core Indicators Project – Progress Report No. 2*, Center on Managed Long Term Supports for People with Disabilities, Cambridge, Mass.
Humphreys, L. G. (1964). Number of cases and number of factors: An example where N is very large. *Education and Psychological Measurement, 24*, 457.

Inge, K. J., Banks, P. D., Wehman, P., Hill, J. W., & Shafer, M. S. (1988). Quality of life for individuals who are labelled mentally retarded: Evaluating competitive employment versus sheltered workshop employment. *Education and Training in Mental Retardation*, 97-104.

Jensen, L. (1998). Interpreting new public management: the case of Denmark. *Australian Journal of Public Administration, 57*, 54-65.

Jiranek, D., & Kirby, N. (1990). The job satisfaction and/or psychological well being of young adults with an intellectual disability and nondisabled young adults in either sheltered employment, competitive employment or unemployment. *Australia and New Zealand Journal of Developmental Disabilities, 16*, 133-148.

Jones, C. S. (1999a). Developing financial accountability in British acute hospitals. *Financial Accountability & Management, 15*, 1-20.

Jones, C. S. (1999b). Hierarchies, networks and management accounting in NHS Hospitals. *Accounting, Auditing and Accountability Journal, 12*, 164-187.

Judge, T. A., & Bretz, R. D. (1993). Report on an alternative measure of affective disposition. *Educational and Psychological Measurement, 53*, 1095-1104.

Kaplan, R. S., & Norton, D. P. (1992). The balanced scorecard - measures that drive performance. *Harvard Business Review, January-February*, 71-79.

Kaplan, R. S., & Norton, D. P. (1993). Putting the balanced scorecard to work. *Harvard Business Review, September-October*, 134-147.

Kaplan, R. S., & Norton, D. P. (1996). Using the balanced scorecard as a strategic management system. *Harvard Business Review, January-February*, 75-85.

Kaplan, R. S., & Norton, D. P. (2001). Transforming the balanced scorecard from performance measurement to strategic management: Part 1. *Accounting Horizons, 15*, 87-106.

Kaul, M. (1997). The new public administration: management innovations in government. *Public Administration and Development, 17*, 13-26.

Kendall, L. M., Smith, P. C., Hulin, C. L., & Locke, E. A. (Eds.). (1964). *The relative validity of the job description index and other methods of measurement of job satisfaction* (Vol. IV).

Kim, M. S., & Cho, K. H. (2003). Quality of life among government employees. *Social Indicators Research, 62*, 387-409.

Kim, P. S. (1996). South Korea: searching for a new direction of administrative reform. *Australian Journal of Public Administration, 55*, 30-45.

Kinicki, A. J., Schriesheim, C. A., McKee-Ryan, F. M., & Carson, K. P. (2002). Assessing the construct validity of the job descriptive index: a review of meta-analysis. *Journal of Applied Psychology, 87*, 14-32.

Kloot, L. (1997). Organizational learning and management control systems: Responding to environmental change. *Management Accounting Research, 8*, 47-73.

Kloot, L., & Martin, J. (2000). Strategic performance management: A balanced approach to performance management issues in local government. *Management Accounting Research, 11*, 231-251.

Knox, M., & Hickson, F. (2001). The meanings of close friendships: The views of four people with intellectual disabilities. *Journal of Applied Research in Intellectual Disabilities, 14*, 276-291.

Knox, M., & Parmenter, T. R. (1993). Social networks and support mechanisms for people with mild intellectual disability in competitive employment. *International Journal of Rehabilitation Research, 16,* 1-12.

Kober, R., & Eggleton, I. R. C. (2002). Factor stability of the Schalock and Keith (1993) quality of life questionnaire. *Mental Retardation, 40,* 157-165.

Kunin, T. (1955). The construction of a new type of attitude measure. *Personnel Psychology, 8,* 65-77.

Lam, C. S., & Chan, F. (1988). Job satisfaction of sheltered workshop clients. *Journal of Rehabilitation* (July/August/September), 51-54.

Landesman, S. (1986). Quality of life and personal life satisfaction: Definition and measurement. *Mental Retardation, 24,* 141-143.

Lapsley, I. (1996). Reflections on performance measurement in the public sector. In I. Lapsley & F. Mitchell (Eds.), *Accounting and Performance Measurement: Issues in the Private and Public Sectors.* London: Paul Chapman Publishing.

Lehman, A. F. (1988). A quality of life interview for the chronically mentally ill. *Evaluation and Program Planning, 11,* 51-62.

Linn, R. L. (1968). A Monte Carlo approach to the number of factors problem. *Psychometrika, 33*(1), 37.

Liss, P. E. (1994). On need and quality of life. In L. Nordenfelt (Ed.), *Concepts and measurement of quality of life in health care.* Netherlands: Kluwer Academic.

Locke, E. A. (1976). The nature and causes of job satisfaction. In M. Dunette (Ed.), *Handbook of industrial and organizational psychology* (pp. 1297-1349). Chicago: Rand McNally.

Martin, B. (1993). *In the public interest? Privatisation and public sector reform.* London: Zed Books.

Mason, A., & Morgan, K. (1995). Purchaser-provider: The international dimension. *British Medical Journal (International edition), 310,* 231.

McAfee, J. K. (1986). The handicapped worker and job satisfaction. *Vocational Evaluation and Work Adjustment Bulletin* (Spring), 23-27.

McCaughrin, W. B., Ellis, W. K., Rusch, F. R., & Heal, L. W. (1993). Cost-effectiveness of supported employment. *Mental Retardation, 31,* 41-48.

McCulloh, B. W., & Ball, I. (1992). Accounting in the context of public sector management refore. *Financial Accountability & Management, 8,* 7-12.

McGregor, W. (1999). The pivotal role of accounting concepts in the development of public sector accounting standards. *Australian Accounting Review, 9,* 3-8.

McVilly, K. R., & Rawlinson, R. B. (1998). Quality of life issues in the development and evaluation of services for people with intellectual disability. *Journal of Intellectual and Developmental Disability, 23,* 199-218.

Midwinter, A. (1994). Developing performance indicators for local government: the Scottish experience. *Public Money and Management, 14,* 37-43.

Modell, S. (2004). Performance measurement myths in the public sector: A research note. *Financial Accountability & Management, 20,* 39-55.

Modell, S. (2005). Performance management in the public sector: past experiences, current practices and future challenges. *Australian Accounting Review, 37,* 56-66.

Mosely, C. R. (1988). Job satisfaction research: Implications for supported employment. *JASH, 13,* 211-219.

Mote, T. A. (1970). An artifact of the rotation of too few factors: Study orientation vs. trait anxiety. *Revista Interamericana de Psicologia, 4,* 171.

Murrell, S. A., & Norris, F. H. (1983). Quality of life as the criterion for need assessment and community psychology. *Journal of Community Psychology, 11,* 88-97.

Neath, J., Bellini, J., & Bolton, B. (1997). Dimensions of the functional assessment inventory for five disability groups. *Rehabilitation Psychology, 42,* 183-207.

Newberry, S. (2003). Sector neutrality and NPM incentives: their use in eroding the public sector. *Australian Accounting Review, 13,* 28-34.

Nihira, K., Foster, R., Shellhaas, M., & Leland, H. (1974). *AAMD adaptive behaviour scale.* Washington D.C.: American Association on Mental Deficiency.

Nirje, B. (1969). The normalisation principle and its human management implications. In R. Kugel & W. Wolfensberger (Eds.), *Changing patterns in residential services for the mentally retarded.* Washington, D.C.: President's Committee on Mental Retardation.

Nirje, B. (1976). *The normalization principle: Implications and comments.* Washington DC: President's Committee on Mental Retardation.

Nirje, B. (1985). The basis and logic of the normalization principle. *Australia and New Zealand Journal of Developmental Disabilities, 11,* 65-68.

Nisbet, J., & York, P. (1989). Indicies of job satisfaction of persons with moderate and severe disabilities. *Education and Training in Mental Retardation,* 274-280.

Noble, J. H., Conley, R. W., & Banerjee, S. (1991). Supported employment in New York state: A comparison of benefits and costs. *Journal of Disability Policy Studies, 2,* 39-71.

Nolan, B. C. (2001). *Public sector reform - An international perspective.* New York: Palgrave Publishers.

Nordenfelt, L. (1994). Towards a theory of happiness: a subjectivist notion of quality of life. In L. Nordenfelt (Ed.), *Concepts and measurement of quality of life in health care.* Netherlands: Kluwer Academic Publishers.

Nunnally, J. (1967). *Psychometric theory.* New York: McGraw Hill.

O'Bryne, J., & Tyne, A. (1981). *The principle of normalisation in human services.* London: CMH.

Ormsby, M. J. (1998). The povider/purchaser split: A report from New Zealand. *Governance: An International Journal of Policy and Administration, 11,* 357-387.

Ouellette-Kuntz, H. (1990). A pilot study in the use of the quality of life interview schedule. *Social Indicators Research, 23,* 283-298.

Pallant, J. (2001). *SPSS survival manual.* Crows Nest, Australia: Allen & Unwin.

Parmenter, T. R. (1990). Evaluation and service delivery research in the area of severe intellectual disability in *Australia. Australia and New Zealand Journal of Developmental Disabilities,* 16, 187-193.

Parmenter, T. R. (1993). International perspective of vocational options for people with mental

166

retardation: The promise and the reality. *Mental Retardation, 31*, 359-367.

Parmenter, T. R. (1999). Effecting a system change in the delivery of employment services for people with disabilities: A view from Australia. *Journal of Vocational Rehabilitation, 13*, 117-129.

Parmenter, T. R. (2001). The contribution of science in facilitating the inclusion of people with intellectual disability into the community. *Journal of Intellectual Disability Research, 45*, 183-193.

Parmenter, T., Riches, V., Atkinson, N., McGaw, A., & Yazbeck, M. (1996). *Evaluation of funding classification instruments of people with a disability*: Report Commissioned by the Disability Services Access and Quality Branch of the Commonwealth Department of Health and Family Services.

Pascoe, S., & Lee, M. (1980). Employer attitudes towards hiring physically handicapped people. *National Rehabilitation Digest, 4*, 29-36.

Pedlar, A., Lord, J., & Loon, M. V. (1990). Quality of life outcomes of supported employment. *Canadian Journal of Community Mental Health, 9*, 79-96.

Petrovski, P., & Gleeson, G. (1997). The relationship between job satisfaction and psychological health in people with an intellectual disability in competitive employment. *Journal of Intellectual & Developmental Disability, 22*, 199-211.

Pfeiffer, B. A., McClelland, T., & Lawson, J. (1989). Use of the functional assessment inventory to distinguish among the rural elderly in five service settings. *Journal of the American Geriatrics Society, 37*, 243-248.

Rapley, M., & Antaki, C. (1996). A conversation analysis of the 'acquiescence' of people with learning disabilities. *Journal of Community & Applied Social Psychology, 6*, 207-227.

Rapley, M., & Lobley, J. (1995). Factor analysis of the Schalock & Keith (1993) quality of life questionnaire: A replication. *Mental Handicap Research, 8*, 194-202.

Rayner, M. (1995). International trends in redefining the role of the public sector: Canada's experience. *Australian Journal of Public Administration, 54*, 299-305.

Reiter, S., Palnitzki, A., Levi, A., & Levi, A. M. (1981). Social and vocational integration of mentally retarded adults living in the community and in two institutions. *British Journal of Mental Subnormality, 27*, 3-7.

Rosen, M., Bussone, A., Dakunchak, P., & Cramp, J. (1993). Sheltered employment and the second generation workshop. *Journal of Rehabilitation*, 30-34.

Rosen, M., Halenda, R., Nowakiska, M., & Floor, L. (1970). Employment satisfaction of previously institutionalized mentally subnormal workers. *Mental Retardation*, 35-40.

Rosen, M., Simon, E. W., & McKinsey, L. (1995). Subjective measure of quality of life. *Mental Retardation, 33*, 31-34.

Roznowski, M. (1989). Examination of the measurement properties of the job descriptive index with experimental items. *Journal of Applied Psychology, 74*, 805-814.

Rummel, R. J. (1970). *Applied factor analysis*. Evanston, USA: Northwestern University Press.

Rusch, F. F., Chadsey-Rusch, J., & Lagomorcino, T. (1987). Preparing students for employment. In M. E. Snell (Ed.), *Systematic instructions of persons with severe handicaps* (3rd ed., pp. 471-491). Columbus, OH: Merrill.

Rusch, F. R., Conley, R. W., & McCaughrin, W. B. (1993). Benefit-cost analysis of supported employment in Illinois. *Journal of Rehabilitation, 59*, 31-36.

Schalock, R. L. (1996). Reconsidering the conceptualization and measurement of quality of life. In R. L. Schalock (Ed.), Quality of Life: Volume I (pp. 123-139). Washington, DC: American Association on Mental Retardation.

Schalock, R. L. (1999, 27 September). *Could Mother Teresa survive an outcomes-oriented world?* Paper presented at the Australian Society for the Study of Intellectual Disability, Sydney.

Schalock, R. L. (2004). The concept of quality of life: what we know and do not know. *Journal of Intellectual Disability Research, 48*, 203-216.

Schalock, R. L., & Bonham, G. S. (2003). Measuring outcomes and managing the results. *Evaluation and Program Planning, 26*, 229-235.

Schalock, R. L., & Genung, L. T. (1993). Placement from a community-based mental retardation program: a 15-year follow-up. *American Journal of Mental Retardation, 98*, 400-407.

Schalock, R. L., & Keith, K. D. (1986). Resource allocation approach for determining clients' need status. *Mental Retardation, 24*, 27-35.

Schalock, R. L., & Keith, K. D. (1993). *Quality of life manual.* IDS Publishing, Worthington, OH.

Schalock, R. L., Keith, K. D., Hoffman, K., & Karan, O. C. (1989). Quality of life: Its measurement and use. *Mental Retardation, 27*, 25-31.

Schalock, R. L., Lemanowicz, J. A., Conroy, J. W., & Feinstein, C. S. (1994). A multivariate investigative study of the correlates of quality of life. *Journal of Developmental Disabilities, 3*, 59-73.

Schalock, R. L., & Lilley, M. A. (1986). Placement from community-based mental retardation programs: How well do clients do after 8 to 10 years. *American Journal of Mental Deficiency, 90*, 669-676.

Schneider, M. (1975). The quality of life in large American Cities: Objective and subjective social indicators. *Social Indicators Research, 1*, 495-509.

Schneider, M. (1976). The 'quality of life' and social indicators research. *Public Administration Review*, 297-305.

Schneider, M. J., & Ferritor, D. E. (1982). The meaning of work. In B. Bolten (Ed.), *Vocational Adjustment of Disabled Persons*. Baltimore: University Park.

Schuster, J. W. (1990). Sheltered Workshops: financial and philosophical liabilities. *Mental Retardation, 28*, 233-239.

Seltzer, G. B. (1981). Community residential adjustment: The relationship among environment, performance, and satisfaction. *American Journal of Mental Deficiency, 85*, 624-630.

Seltzer, M. M. (1984). Patterns of job satisfaction among mentally retarded adults. *Applied Research in Mental Retardation, 5*, 147-159.

Seltzer, M. M., & Seltzer, G. (1978). *Context for competence.* Cambridge, Massachusetts, USA: Educational Projects Inc.

Shanly, A., & Rose, J. (1993). A consumer survey of adults with learning disabilities currently doing work experience: Their satisfaction with work and wishes for the future. *Mental Handicap Research, 6*, 250-262.

Shearn, J., Beyer, S., & Felce, D. (2000). The cost-effectiveness of supported employment for people with severe intellectual disabilities and high support needs: a pilot study. *Journal of Applied Research in Intellectual Disabilities, 13*, 29-37.

Sinnott-Oswald, M., Gliner, J. A., & Spencer, K. C. (1991). Supported and sheltered employment: Quality of life issues among workers with disabilities. *Education and Training in Mental Retardation*, 388-397.

Sirgy, M. J. (1986). A quality of life theory derived from Maslow's developmental perspective: 'Quality' is related to progressive satisfaction of a hierarchy of needs, lower order and higher. *The American Journal of Economics and Sociology, 45*, 215-228.

Smith, P. (1995). Performance indicators and outcome in the public sector. *Public Money and Management, 15*, 13-16.

Smith, P. C., Kendall, L. M., & Hulin, C. L. (1969). *The measurement of satisfaction in work and retirement: a strategy for the study of attitudes*. Chicago, Ill: Rand McNally.

Stancliffe, R. J., & Keane, S. (1999). *Outcomes and costs of community living: Semi-independent living and group homes*: Centre for Developmental Disability Studies.

Stewart, B., Hetherington, G., & Smith, M. (1984). *Survey item bank: Volume 1 Measures of satisfaction*. Bradford, England: MCB Press.

Tabachnick, B. G., & Fidell, L. S. (1989). *Using multivariate statistics* (Second ed.). New York: Harper Collins Publishers.

Tabachnick, B. G., & Fidell, L. S. (2001). *Using multivariate statistics* (Third ed.). New York: Harper Collins Publishers.

Talkington, L. W., & Overbeck, D. B. (1975). Job satisfaction and performance with retarded females. *Mental Retardation*, 18-19.

Tan, P. P., & Hawkins, W. E. (2000). The factor structure of Minnesota satisfaction questionnaire and participants of vocational rehabilitation. *Psychological Reports, 87*, 34-36.

Test, D. W., Hinson, K. B., Solow, J., & Keul, P. (1993). Job satisfaction of persons in supported employment. *Education and Training in Mental Retardation*, 38-46.

Thorndike, E. L. (1939). *Your city*. New York: Brace and Co.

Tines, J., Rusch, F. R., McCaughrin, W., & Conley, R. W. (1990). Benefit-cost analysis of supported employment in Illinois: A statewide evaluation. *American Journal on Mental Retardation, 95*, 44-54.

Tsao, K. K., & Worthley, J. A. (1996). China: Administrative corruption - experience in a comparative context. *Australian Journal of Public Administration, 55*, 22-30.

Tucker, L. R., Koopman, R. F., & Linn, R. L. (1969). Evaluation of factor analytic research procedures by means of simulated correlation matrices. *Psychometrika, 34*, 421.

Tuckerman, P., Smith, R., & Borland, J. (1999). The relative cost of employment for people with a significant intellectual disability: The Australian experience. *Journal of Vocational Rehabilitation, 13*, 109-116.

Warr, P., Cook, J., & Wall, T. (1979). Scales for the measurement of some work attitudes and aspects of psychological well-being. *Journal of Occupational Psychology, 52*, 129-148.

Wehman, P., Kregel, J., Banks, P. D., Hill, M. & Moon., M. S. (1987) Sheltered versus supported work programs: A second look. *Rehabilitation Counseling Bulletin 31*, 42-53.

Weiss, D. J., Dawis, R. V., England, G. W., & Lofquist, L. (1969). *Manual for the Minnesota satisfaction questionnaire*: Work Adjustment Project, Industrial Relations Center, University of Minnesota.

Wilkinson, M. (1975). Leisure: An alternative to the meaning of work. *Journal of Applied Rehabilitation Counselling, 6*, 73-77.

Wolfensberger, W. (1983). Social role valorization: A proposed new term for the principle of normalization. *Mental Retardation, 21*, 234-239.

Wolfsenberger, W. (1972). *The principles of normalisation in human services*. Toronto: National Institute on Mental Retardation.

Worthington, A. C., & Dollery, B. E. (2002). An analysis of recent trends in Australian local government. *The International Journal of Public Sector Management, 15*, 496-515.

Wu, J. K. F., & Watkins, D. (1994). A Hong Kong validity study of the job description index. *Psychologia, 37*, 89-94.

Yazbeck, M., McVilly, K., & Parmenter, T. R. (2004). Attitudes toward people with intellectual disabilities. An Australian perspective. *Journal of Disability Policy Studies, 15*, 97-111.

Zwick, W. R., & Velicer, W. F. (1986). Comparison of five rules for determining the number of components to retain. *Psychological Bulletin, 99*, 432-442.

Appendix 1 – Questionnaire

JOB SATISFACTION

Physical	YES	NO	NOT SURE
1.1 Do you like the place where you work?	[ ]	[ ]	[ ]
1.2 Is it a nice building to work in?	[ ]	[ ]	[ ]
1.3 Is it a nice place to work?	[ ]	[ ]	[ ]
1.4 Do you have to stand up/sit down too much while you work?	[ ]	[ ]	[ ]
1.5 Is it too hot/cold, noisy there?	[ ]	[ ]	[ ]
1.6 Do the days seem very long, like they will never end, when you are working?	[ ]	[ ]	[ ]
1.7 Would you rather be working in a different section?	[ ]	[ ]	[ ]
1.8 Is this the best job you have had?	[ ]	[ ]	[ ]

If no, what was the best job you have had? (*validation question*)

_____

Why was it the best job you have had? (*validation question*)

_____

Task	YES	NO	NOT SURE
2.1 Do you think your work is interesting?	[ ]	[ ]	[ ]
2.2 Do you think your work is too easy?	[ ]	[ ]	[ ]
2.3 Does your work make you feel that you are doing something important?	[ ]	[ ]	[ ]
2.4 Is your work boring?	[ ]	[ ]	[ ]
2.5 Do you have enough to do at work?	[ ]	[ ]	[ ]
2.6 Would you rather be doing a different type of work?	[ ]	[ ]	[ ]
2.7 Do you have to push yourself very hard?	[ ]	[ ]	[ ]

Pay	YES	NO	NOT SURE
3.1 Is your pay too little to let you make ends meet?	[ ]	[ ]	[ ]
3.2 Do you think you should be paid more for what you do?	[ ]	[ ]	[ ]
3.3 Do you think that you get paid less than you are worth?	[ ]	[ ]	[ ]
3.4 Do you ever worry that the amount of your pay will change from week to week?	[ ]	[ ]	[ ]
3.5 Does your pay let you buy special things when you want to?	[ ]	[ ]	[ ]
3.6 Do you think that you are paid very well?	[ ]	[ ]	[ ]

Social	YES	NO	NOT SURE
4.1 Do you like the people you work with?	[ ]	[ ]	[ ]
4.2 Is it hard to meet people at work?	[ ]	[ ]	[ ]
4.3 Do you sometimes have lunch with the people you work with?	[ ]	[ ]	[ ]
4.4 Do they talk to you very much?	[ ]	[ ]	[ ]
4.5 Do you see them (socially) after work?	[ ]	[ ]	[ ]
4.6 Would you rather be working with different people?	[ ]	[ ]	[ ]
4.7 Would the people at work help you if you had a problem?	[ ]	[ ]	[ ]
4.8 Do the people you work with respect (understand) you?	[ ]	[ ]	[ ]

Staff	YES	NO	NOT SURE
5.1 Does your supervisor tell you honestly what he/she thinks about your work?	[ ]	[ ]	[ ]
5.2 Does he/she let you work by yourself enough?	[ ]	[ ]	[ ]
5.3 Is he/she there when you need help with your work?	[ ]	[ ]	[ ]
5.4 Does he/she praise you when you do a good job?	[ ]	[ ]	[ ]
5.5 If you had a personal problem would he/she help you?	[ ]	[ ]	[ ]
5.6 Do you think that he/she respects (understands) you?	[ ]	[ ]	[ ]
5.7 Does your supervisor help you to learn new work skills?	[ ]	[ ]	[ ]

QUALITY OF LIFE

Satisfaction	3 Points	2 Points	1 Point	Score
1. Overall, would you say that life:	Brings out the best in you? (*very good*)	Treats you like everybody else? (*good/average*)	Doesn't give you a chance? (*not very good*)	
2. How much fun and enjoyment do you get out of life?	Lots	Some	Not much	
3. Compared with others, are you better off, about the same, or less well off?	Better	About the same	Worse	
4. Are most of the things that happen to you:	Rewarding	Acceptable	Disappointing	
5. How satisfied are you with your current home or living arrangement?	Very satisfied	Somewhat satisfied	Unsatisfied or very unsatisfied	
6. Do you have more or fewer problems than other people?	Fewer problems	The same number of problems as others	More problems than others	
7. Do you ever feel lonely? (Yes/No) (If they answer no score as 3 point) If yes, how many times per month do you feel lonely?	Seldom, never more than once or twice	Occasionally, 3 or 4 times a month	Frequently, 5 or more times per month	
8. Do you ever feel out of place in social situations?	Seldom or never	Sometimes	Usually or always	
9. How successful do you think you are, compared to others?	Probably more successful than the average person	About as successful as the average person	Less successful than the average person	
10. What about your family members? Do they make you feel:	An important part of the family	Sometimes a part of the family	Like an outsider	

173

Competence/Productivity	3 Points	2 Points	1 Point	Score
11. How well did your educational or training program prepare you for what you are doing now? *Do you think that the things you learnt at school/course have helped you with your job?*	Very well *A lot*	Somewhat	Not at all well *Not a lot*	
12. Do you feel your job or other daily activity is worthwhile and relevant to either yourself or others?	Yes, definitely	Probably	I'm not sure, or definitely not	
13. How good do you feel you are at your job?	Very good and others tell me I am good	I'm good but no one tells me	I'm having trouble on my job	
14. How do people treat you on your job?	The same as all other employees	Somewhat differently than other employees	Very differently	
15. How satisfied are you with the skills and experience you have gained or are gaining from your job?	Very satisfied	Somewhat satisfied	Not satisfied	
16. Are you learning skills that will help you get a different or better job? What are these skills?	Yes definitely (one or more skills mentioned)	am not sure, maybe (vague, general skills mentioned)	No, job provides no opportunity for learning new skills	
17. Do you feel you receive fair pay for you work?	Yes, definitely	Sometimes	No, I do not feel I am paid enough	
18. Does your job provide you with enough money to buy the things you want?	Yes I can generally buy those reasonable things I want	I have to wait to buy some items or not buy them at all	No, I definitely do not earn enough to buy what I need	
19. How satisfied are you with the benefits you receive at the workplace?	Very satisfied	Somewhat satisfied	Not satisfied	
20. How closely supervised are you on your job?	Supervisor is present only when I need him or her	Supervisor is frequently present whether or not I need him or her	Supervisor is constantly on the job and looking over my work	

	Empowerment/Independence	3 Points	2 Points	1 Point	Score
21.	How did you decide to do the job or other daily activities you do now?	I chose it because of pay, benefits, or interests	Only thing available or that I could find	Someone else decided for me	
22.	Who decides how to spend your money?	I do	I do, with assistance from others	Someone else decides	
23.	How do you use health care facilities (doctor, dentist, etc.)? *When you need to go to the doctor, dentist etc. do you usually make the appointment and go on your own?*	Almost always on my own	Usually accompanied by someone, or someone else has made the appointment	Never on my own	
24.	How much control do you have over things you do every day, like going to bed, eating, and what you do for fun?	Complete	Some	Little	
25.	When can friends visit your home?	As often as I like or fairly often	Any day, as long as someone else approves or is there	Only on certain days	
26.	Do you have a key to your home?	Yes, I have a key and use it as I wish	Yes, I have a key but it only unlocks certain areas	No	
27.	May you have a pet if you want?	Yes definitely	Probably yes, but would need to ask	No	
28.	Do you have a guardian? *Do you have someone who takes responsibility for you or are you responsible for yourself?*	No, I am responsible for myself	Yes, limited guardian	Yes, I have a full guardian	
29.	Are there people living with you who sometimes hurt you, pester you, scare you, or make you angry?	No	Yes, and those problems occur once a month or once a week	Yes, and those problems occur every day or more than once a day	
30.	Overall, would you say that your life is:	Free	Somewhat planned for you	Cannot usually do what you want	

175

Social belonging/Community integration	3 Points	2 Points	1 Point	Score
31. To how many clubs or organisations (including church or other religious activities) do you belong?	2 to 3	1 only	None	
32. How satisfied are you with the clubs or organisations (including church or other religious activities) to which you belong?	Very satisfied	Somewhat satisfied	Unsatisfied or very unsatisfied	
33. Do you worry about what people expect of you? *For example, do you worry that people expect too much of you?*	Sometimes, but not all the time	Seldom	Never or all the time	
34. How many times per week do you talk to (or associate with) your neighbours, either in the yard or in their home?	3 to 4 times per week	1 to 2 times per week	Never or all the time	
35. Do you have friends over to visit your home?	Fairly often	Sometimes	Rarely or never	
36. How often do you attend recreational activities (homes, parties, dances, concerts, plays) in your community?	3 to 4 per month	1 to 2 per month	Less than 1 per month	
37. Do you participate actively in those recreational activities? *That is, do you get involved with what is going on?*	Usually, most of the time	Frequently, about half the time	Seldom or never	
38. What about opportunities for dating or marriage?	I am married, or have the opportunity to date anyone I choose	I have limited opportunities to date or marry	I have no opportunity to date or marry	
39. How do your neighbours treat you?	Very good or good (invite you to activities, coffee, etc.)	Fair (say hello, visit, etc.)	Bad or very bad (avoid you, bother you, etc.)	
40. Overall, would you say that your life is:	Very worthwhile	Okay	Useless	

Appendix 2 - Correlates of Job Satisfaction and Quality of Life

A2.1 Introduction
In this appendix I first discuss the correlates of job satisfaction and its four factors (*work and staff*, *task*, *pay*, and *social*). Correlation analysis is initially conducted for the entire sample, then separately for participants with high functional work ability, participants with low functional work ability, participants in open employment and participants in supported employment. This is undertaken to establish whether the relationship between the collected demographic variables and job satisfaction and its four factors is consistent across both levels of functional work ability and method of employment.

The correlations between the collected demographic variables and quality of life and its four factors (satisfaction, competence/productivity, empowerment/independence, social belonging/community integration) are then analysed in a similar manner to that described above. That is, correlates are first investigated for the entire sample, then separately for participants with high functional work ability, participants with low functional work ability, participants in open employment and participants in supported employment.

A2.2 Correlates of Job Satisfaction
Having investigated the differences in job satisfaction between open employment and supported employment in Chapter 6 (Results: Outcome Evaluation), Spearman Rank Order Correlation Tests[124] are conducted to gain an understanding of with which of the collected demographic variables the job satisfaction of people with intellectual disabilities is correlated. Spearman rhos are calculated between the collected demographic variables and the four factors of the JSQ, the total JSQ score, as well as total score excluding the *social* factor.

As can be seen from Panel A of Table A2.1 when looking at the entire sample there is a statistically significant positive correlation between the *work and staff* factor of the JSQ and both the refined FAI score ($r_s = .217$, $p \leq .019$) and the original FAI score ($r_s = .216$, $p \leq .020$). This relationship suggests that participants with a higher functional work ability (resulting in lower refined and original FAI scores) are less satisfied with the work they perform and the staff at the workplace than are participants with lower functional work ability. This lower level of satisfaction could be due to an observation made by Lam and Chan (1998), who note that people with lower levels of disabilities may in fact be comparing their situation to people without a disability, as opposed to people with higher levels of intellectual disability, who may be comparing their situation to other people with intellectual disabilities. If this is the case, it is likely that participants with higher levels of functional work ability would be less satisfied with the differences in the manner in which they are treated by their co-workers and the work they perform compared to their co-workers without a disability, than would be participants with lower levels of functional work ability. This would explain my finding of a negative (positive) statistically significant relationship between *work and staff* and functional work ability (refined FAI score and original FAI score).

When the type of occupation is controlled for by only investigating participants in unskilled labouring positions (Panel B, Table A2.1) the above relationship of a positive correlation between *work and staff* and both the refined FAI score ($r_s = .225$, $p \leq .029$) and the original FAI score ($r_s = .228$, $p \leq .027$) is still found. However, a positive statistically significant correlation is also found between the *social* factor of the JSQ and both weekly wage ($r_s = .240$, $p \leq .020$) and hourly wage ($r_s = .291$, $p \leq .004$). This suggests that jobs that pay higher levels of wages are associated with greater levels of satisfaction in regard to their social aspects. It is likely that this relationship is a function of the findings in Table 6.1 (Panels A, B, and E) which show that participants in open employment

---

[124] Spearman rank order correlation coefficients were calculated as opposed to Pearson correlation coefficients given the non-normal distribution of the data.

report statistically significantly higher scores for the social factor of the JSQ than do participants in supported employment. Given that open employment pays considerably higher wages than does supported employment the fact that a positive correlation should exist between the *social* factor of the JSQ and both weekly wage levels and hourly wage levels is not surprising. What is surprising is

Table A2.1: Spearman rank order correlation coefficients between job satisfaction and demographic variables

	Weekly wage	Hourly wage	Refined FAI Score	Original FAI Score	Age	Current job tenure (years)	Total years of employment
Panel A: All occupations (n=117)							
Work and staff	-.126	-.067	.217*	.216*	.007	.017	-.030
	(.175)[a]	(.473)	(.019)	(.020)	(.944)	(.853)	(.745)
Task	-.054	.060	.160	.158	-.091	-.145	-.085
	(.566)	(.522)	(.084)	(.088)	(.331)	(.120)	(.361)
Pay	.100	.104	-.020	-.035	-.080	-.054	-.070
	(.285)	(.267)	(.828)	(.710)	(.390)	(.561)	(.451)
Social	.117	.145	.080	.058	-.117	-.009	-.010
	(.209)	(.119)	(.389)	(.531)	(.208)	(.924)	(.911)
Total job satisfaction	.016	.083	.153	.138	-.139	-.086	-.104
	(.861)	(.373)	(.099)	(.137)	(.135)	(.357)	(.262)
Total job satisfaction (exc. social)	.009	.068	.147	.134	-.131	-.093	-.111
	(.924)	(.468)	(.133)	(.149)	(.159)	(.318)	(.233)
Panel B: Unskilled labouring positions (n=94)							
Work and staff	-.115	-.037	.225*	.228*	.140	-.036	.012
	(.269)	(.725)	(.029)	(.027)	(.178)	(.733)	(.910)
Task	-.039	.113	.121	.132	-.038	-.188	-.056
	(.706)	(.277)	(.208)	(.205)	(.718)	(.069)	(.591)
Pay	.110	.117	.007	-.006	-.099	-.065	-.093
	(.292)	(.260)	(.947)	(.956)	(.344)	(.536)	(.374)
Social	.240*	.291**	.087	.059	-.141	-.068	-.021
	(.020)	(.004)	(.407)	(.570)	(.175)	(.516)	(.842)
Total job satisfaction	.055	.166	.138	.125	-.079	-.151	-.087
	(.600)	(.110)	(.185)	(.230)	(.450)	(.147)	(.402)
Total job satisfaction (exc. social)	.026	.120	.133	.122	-.064	-.141	-.083
	(.803)	(.249)	(.201)	(.241)	(.542)	(.174)	(.428)
Panel C: Living with family (n=68)							
Work and staff	-.172	-.125	.209	.212	-.017	.045	-.023
	(.160)	(.310)	(.087)	(.082)	(.893)	(.714)	(.855)
Task	-.136	-.065	.187	.191	-.069	-.007	-.042
	(.269)	(.600)	(.127)	(.119)	(.575)	(.953)	(.733)
Pay	-.026	-.020	-.066	-.067	.034	.248*	.128
	(.833)	(.872)	(.595)	(.586)	(.784)	(.042)	(.300)
Social	.002	.075	.015	-.015	-.101	.034	-.024
	(.986)	(.546)	(.904)	(.905)	(.414)	(.781)	(.847)
Total job satisfaction	-.109	-.045	.100	.094	-.063	.095	.010
	(.377)	(.717)	(.419)	(.448)	(.611)	(.441)	(.938)
Total job satisfaction (exc. social)	-.109	-.063	.109	.105	-.044	.119	.036
	(.377)	(.610)	(.378)	(.395)	(.721)	(.333)	(.770)
Panel D: Unskilled labouring positions and living with family (n=54)							
Work and staff	-.216	-.140	.220	.239	.093	.049	.050
	(.117)	(.311)	(.109)	(.082)	(.505)	(.724)	(.718)
Task	-.077	.024	.178	.185	-.020	-.048	-.006
	(.578)	(.864)	(.199)	(.180)	(.886)	(.730)	(.963)
Pay	-.042	-.021	-.095	-.084	.084	-.236	.175
	(.760)	(.883)	(.494)	(.546)	(.547)	(.086)	(.206)
Social	.148	.234	-.029	-.063	-.138	.046	.035
	(.285)	(.088)	(.834)	(.651)	(.321)	(.741)	(.804)
Total job satisfaction	-.080	.026	.078	.081	-.013	.083	.073
	(.563)	(.851)	(.577)	(.560)	(.925)	(.551)	(.600)
Total job satisfaction (exc. social)	-.096	-.017	.088	.096	.044	.120	.118
	(.491)	(.900)	(.528)	(.491)	(.754)	(.388)	(.394)

Table A2.1 Continued

	Weekly wage	Hourly wage	Refined FAI Score	Original FAI Score	Age	Current job tenure (years)	Total years of employment
Panel E: Matched pairs sub-sample (n=34)							
Work and staff	.050	.177	.322	.269	.014	-.215	-.216
	(.781)	(.317)	(.063)	(.125)	(.935)	(.221)	(.221)
Task	-.018	.179	.291	.260	-.259	-.304	-.303
	(.917)	(.310)	(.095)	(.137)	(.139)	(.081)	(.082)
Pay	.206	.163	.058	-.020	-.018	-.265	-.024
	(.241)	(.358)	(.745)	(.910)	(.918)	(.130)	(.850)
Social	.259	.305	.018	-.041	-.231	-.146	-.089
	(.139)	(.080)	(.920)	(.818)	(.189)	(.410)	(.615)
Total job satisfaction	.167	.264	.237	.175	-.146	-.321	-.179
	(.346)	(.131)	(.176)	(.324)	(.411)	(.064)	(.311)
Total job satisfaction (exc. social)	.149	.246	.237	.183	-.133	-.334	-.188
	(.400)	(.161)	(.178)	(.301)	(.453)	(.054)	(.287)

a Figures in parentheses represent significance levels.
* Significant at the 5 percent level.
** Significant at the 1 percent level.
Note: *Method of employment* and *living environment* were not included in the above correlation analysis as both are categorical variables.

that this relationship is not found for the entire sample. However, it should be noted that the results in Chapter 4 (Psychometric Properties of Research Instruments) revealed that the scores for the *social* factor of the JSQ lack reliability and as such no emphasis is placed on the findings for this factor.

The results when controlling for the living conditions of participants, by only investigating those participants that live with their family (Panel C, Table A2.1), no longer reveal any statistically significant relationship between level of functional work ability and *work and staff*. However, a statistically significant positive correlation is found between the *pay* factor of the JSQ and current job tenure (r_s = .248, $p \leq .042$). This indicates that the longer a participant is employed in their current job the greater their level of satisfaction with pay. Why this relationship should only apply to participants who live with their family is not readily apparent. It is felt that given there is no obvious cause for such a relationship and the fact that this statistically significant positive correlation between *pay* and job tenure is not found in any of the other panels, this result may be spurious.

As can be seen from Panel D of Table A2.1, once both the type of occupation and the living conditions of participants are controlled for by using responses only for participants who work in unskilled labouring positions and live with their families, no statistically significant correlations are found. Likewise with the matched pairs sample (Panel E, Table A2.1). It should be noted that the lack of statistically significant correlations for these two panels and Panel C, given that the correlation between pay and current job tenure is considered spurious, could be due to the smaller sample sizes (n = 68, 54, and 34 for Panels C, D, and E, respectively) compared to Panels A and B (n = 117 and 94, respectively).

A2.2.1 Correlates of Job Satisfaction for Participants with High Functional Work Ability
To see whether there are any differences in the correlates of job satisfaction for participants with different levels of functional work ability, Spearman Rank Order Correlation Tests are conducted separately for participants with high and low functional work abilities.

Table A2.2 reports the results for participants classified as having high functional work ability. The results reveal that when considering all participants with high functional work ability (Panel A, Table A2.2), there is a statistically significant negative correlation between the *work and staff* factor of the JSQ and refined FAI scores (r_s = -.307, $p \leq .038$). This result is interesting on two counts.

First, it only occurs for the refined FAI and not the original FAI. However, the refinement of the FAI described in Chapter 4 (Psychometric Properties of Research Instruments) resulted in the instrument being more appropriate for people with intellectual disabilities than the original FAI and the reason that this result occurs only for the refined FAI could be due to this fact. It is also acknowledged that this result could be spurious. However, given that the positive correlation for this variable is present for all panels in Table A2.1 and that in Panel C (discussed below) there is also a statistically significant result this possibility is discounted.

Table A2.2: Spearman rank order correlation coefficients between job satisfaction and demographic variables for participants with high functional work ability (refined FAI ≤ 12)

	Weekly wage	Hourly wage	Refined FAI Score	Original FAI Score	Age	Current job tenure (years)	Total years of employment
Panel A: All occupations (n=46)							
Work and staff	-.144	.052	-.307*	-.240	.045	-.074	.039
	(.341)[a]	(.731)	(.038)	(.108)	(.764)	(.626)	(.796)
Task	-.013	.119	-.172	-.168	-.057	-.069	.040
	(.930)	(.429)	(.254)	(.263)	(.707)	(.649)	(.778)
Pay	-.050	.027	-.327*	-.326*	-.059	-.035	.001
	(.741)	(.861)	(.026)	(.027)	(.699)	(.817)	(.994)
Social	.285	.253	-.075	-.125	-.294*	.033	.020
	(.055)	(.090)	(.619)	(.406)	(.047)	(.827)	(.893)
Total job satisfaction	.046	.140	-.278	-.266	-.169	-.025	.021
	(.763)	(.355)	(.061)	(.074)	(.261)	(.869)	(.891)
Total job satisfaction (exc. social)	-.033	.072	-.279	-.262	-.104	-.047	.002
	(.828)	(.637)	(.060)	(.078)	(.491)	(.756)	(.992)
Panel B: Unskilled labouring positions (n=36)							
Work and staff	-.245	.000	-.225	-.112	.271	-.140	.182
	(.149)	(.999)	(.188)	(.517)	(.110)	(.415)	(.289)
Task	.029	.138	-.173	-.145	-.050	-.238	.057
	(.867)	(.423)	(.312)	(.397)	(.773)	(.162)	(.740)
Pay	-.013	.016	-.304	-.295	-.166	-.033	-.042
	(.938)	(.927)	(.072)	(.081)	(.333)	(.847)	(.807)
Social	.414*	.393*	-.057	-.152	-.337*	-.108	.014
	(.012)	(.018)	(.743)	(.375)	(.044)	(.529)	(.934)
Total job satisfaction	.051	.164	-.266	-.238	-.133	-.183	.041
	(.766)	(.339)	(.118)	(.163)	(.438)	(.286)	(.814)
Total job satisfaction (exc. social)	-.041	.066	-.257	-.216	-.079	-.182	.032
	(.812)	(.700)	(.131)	(.206)	(.648)	(.288)	(.851)
Panel C: Living with family (n=27)							
Work and staff	-.147	-.064	-.470*	-.455*	.058	-.093	-.060
	(.466)	(.751)	(.013)	(.017)	(.773)	(.645)	(.766)
Task	.076	.072	-.264	-.336	-.028	.056	.156
	(.708)	(.721)	(.183)	(.086)	(.889)	(.781)	(.438)
Pay	-.313	-.159	-.309	-.268	-.004	.233	.207
	(.112)	(.428)	(.117)	(.177)	(.985)	(.241)	(.301)
Social	-.028	-.045	.151	-.031	-.148	.092	.135
	(.889)	(.823)	(.453)	(.876)	(.460)	(.649)	(.501)
Total job satisfaction	-.130	-.029	-.295	-.334	-.078	.112	.165
	(.520)	(.885)	(.135)	(.089)	(.701)	(.577)	(.410)
Total job satisfaction (exc. social)	-.155	-.061	-.352	-.370	-.052	.126	.157
	(.441)	(.761)	(.072)	(.058)	(.798)	(.530)	(.434)

a   Figures in parentheses represent significance levels.
*   Significant at the 5 percent level.
**   Significant at the 1 percent level.
Note: *Method of employment* and *living environment* were not included in the above correlation analysis as both are categorical variables.

Second, the result is also interesting because the direction of the relationship is opposite to that in Table A2.1; in Panel A of Table A2.1 (for the entire sample) there was a statistically significant positive correlation between these two variables. What this suggests is that for participants who have a high functional work ability (refined FAI ≤ 12) the higher (lower) their functional work ability (refined FAI) the higher their satisfaction with *work and staff*. A possible explanation for this could be that participants with higher levels of functional work ability are treated on a more equal basis with their co-workers without a disability than are the participants with lower levels of functional work ability. As such, these participants express higher levels of satisfaction with work and staff than do their counterparts in this sub-sample with lower levels of functional work ability.

At first the above explanation seems contrary to the explanation given in Section A2.2 (Correlates of Job Satisfaction) which explains the relationship between higher levels of functional work ability and lower levels of satisfaction with *work and staff* observed for the entire sample as being due to participants with higher levels of functional work ability comparing themselves to people without disabilities. These people with higher levels of functional work ability may resent the fact that they feel they are treated differently to people without a disability and therefore express this with lower work and staff scores. However, the two explanations are not necessarily entirely incongruent. Given that all the participants in the current sub-sample could be classified a having mild intellectual disability, they may well be comparing themselves with people without a disability. But those who notice that they are being treated differently by their co-workers, which are likely to be the ones with lower levels of functional work ability, report lower levels of satisfaction with work and staff. Combining the explanations given in Section A2.2 (Correlates of job satisfaction) for the entire sample and the above explanation would suggest a U-shaped curve with a worker with very high functional work ability having higher work and staff scores (due to the fact that they perceive that they are being treated similarly to co-workers without a disability) and these scores decreasing as level of functional work ability decreases (due to the likelihood that as level of work ability decreases people with intellectual disability may be treated differently to co-workers without a disability and this is recognised by the person with the intellectual disability). This negative relationship continues until some point where it reverses and persons with lower levels of functional work ability start reporting increasing *work and staff* scores. Presumably this point where *work and staff* scores begins increasing would be at the point where participants stopped comparing themselves with people without a disability and started comparing themselves to other people with intellectual disabilities, thus no longer being as dissatisfied with being treated differently to workers without a disability. Such a relationship seems possible given a visual inspection of the scatter plots of the two variables for all occupations (Figure A2.1) and for participants living with their family (Figure A2.2). Though it must be acknowledged the espoused relationship does not seems as strongly borne out in the scatter plot as would be expected given the contrary results found in Panels A of Tables A2.1 and A2.2.

The results in Panel A of Table A2.2 also reveal a statistically significant negative correlation between the *pay* factor of the JSQ and both participants' refined FAI score (r_s = -.327, p ≤ .026) and their original FAI score (r_s = -.326, p ≤ .027). This suggests that as the level of work ability decreases (FAI gets higher) the satisfaction with pay also decreases. This result is not surprising given that Table 5.18 reveals a statistically significant positive correlation between both weekly and hourly wages and level of functional work ability (as measured by both refined FAI scores and original FAI scores). This indicates that within the sub-sample of participants with high functional work ability, the lower the level of functional work ability the lower the level of pay. As noted previously Lam and Chan (1998) stated it was likely that people with lower levels of intellectual disability (higher levels of functional work ability) compare their life situations to those of people without a disability. In such circumstances it is not surprising that participants in this sub-sample, who would all be considered to have a mild intellectual disability, who are receiving less pay (due to their lower level of functional work ability) would be displeased with this situation and express this displeasure through lower satisfaction scores on the *pay* factor of the JSQ.

Panel A of Table A2.2 also reveals a statistically significant negative correlation between a participant's age and their satisfaction with the *social* factor of the JSQ (r_s = -.294, p ≤ .047),

Figure A2.1:   Correlation between *work and staff* score and refined FAI score (n=117)

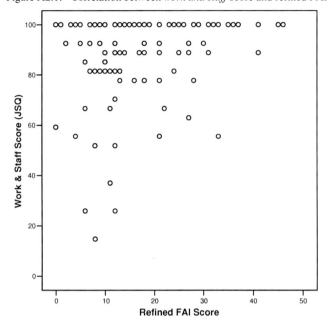

Figure A2.2:   Correlation between *work and staff* score and refined FAI score for participants living with their family (n=68)

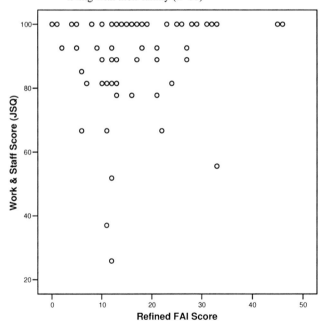

indicating that the older participants were less satisfied with the social aspect of employment than their younger counterparts. This result is not surprising since as revealed by Table 5.5 participants in supported employment are statistically significantly older than participants in open employment and Panel A of Table 6.2 reveals that participants with a high functional work ability in open employment score statistically significantly higher on the *social* factor of the JSQ than do participants in supported employment. However, as previously noted, the social factor of the JSQ was shown in Section 4.4.3 (Factor Stability of the Derived JSQ) not to provide reliable scores and as such no weight is placed on this result.

Panel B of Table A2.2, which only considers participants with a high functional work ability who work in unskilled labouring positions, reveals that there is a statistically significant positive correlation between a participant's *social* score on the JSQ and both their weekly wage ($r_s = .414$, $p \leq .012$) and hourly wage ($r_s = .393$, $p \leq .018$). Consistent with the explanation of the results in Table A2.1, this result is due the fact that participants report a statistically significantly higher social score in open employment than in supported employment and that open employment pays statistically significantly more than does supported employment. Consistent with the findings in Panel A of Table A2.2, Panel B also reveals a statistically significant negative correlation between age and the *social* factor of the JSQ ($r_s = -.337$, $p \leq .044$). As stated above no emphasis can be placed on the results of the social factor of the JSQ given the findings Section 4.4.3 (Factor Stability of the Derived JSQ), which found that the scores for this factor were not reliable.

Similar to the results of Panel A of Table A2.2, Panel C, which controls for a participants' with high functional work ability's living environment by only analysing the scores for participants who live with their family, finds a statistically significant negative correlation between work and staff and level of functional work ability; though in Panel C this relationship is found for both the refined FAI score ($r_s = -.470$, $p \leq .013$) and the original FAI score ($r_s = -.470$, $p \leq .017$). An intriguing aspect of this relationship is that it is found to be statistically significant in Panels A and C, but not in Panel B of Table A2.2. If the results were close to significant in Panel B it may be possible to claim that low sample size (n = 36) could be affecting the results. However the sample size of Panel C is even smaller (n =27), and the results are significant, and the significance levels in Panel B for both the refined FAI score and original FAI score are a considerable distance from the five percent significance level ($p = .188$ and $p = .517$, respectively). No plausible explanation can be offered as to why a statistically significant positive (negative) relationship should not exist between functional work ability (refined and original FAI scores) and *work and staff* for participants with a high functional work ability who are employed in unskilled labouring positions (Panel B, Table A2.2) when it does when considering participants across all occupations (Panel A, Table A2.2) and participants living with their family (Panel C, Table A2.2).

A2.2.2 Correlates of Job Satisfaction for Participants with Low Functional Work Ability
Table A2.3 reports the results of Spearman Rank Order Tests for participants classified as having low functional work ability. They reveal that when considering all participants with low functional work ability (Panel A, Table A2.3), there are statistically significant negative correlations between the *task* factor of the JSQ and both current job tenure ($r_s = -.417$, $p \leq .004$) and total years of employment ($r_s = -.313$, $p \leq .032$), as well as between job satisfaction and current job tenure ($r_s = -.297$, $p \leq .043$). The results in Panel B of Table A2.3, which considers only the responses of participants in unskilled labouring positions also reveals a statistically significant negative correlation between the *task* factor of the JSQ and current job tenure ($r_s = -.358$, $p \leq .030$). The results in relation to participants who live with their family (Panel C, Table A2.3) show no statistically significant correlations, which may in part be due to the low sample size of this sub-sample (n = 27).

The above results in relation to the statistically significant negative correlation between *task* and both current job tenure and total years of employment suggest that the longer a person works in the same job the less satisfied they are with the tasks they perform. In discussions with staff from several of the disability employment agencies involved in this research, it was mentioned that staff were concerned that people with intellectual disabilities once trained to perform a certain function, if they performed that function well, were then left in that position without any consideration of up-skilling or promoting the person. Given such a scenario a negative relationship between *task* and both current job tenure and total years of employment seems plausible. The above explanation is also likely to be the reason behind the statistically significant negative correlation between *job satisfaction* and current job tenure in Panel A of Table A2.3.

Table A2.3: Spearman rank order correlation coefficients between job satisfaction and demographic variables for participants with low functional work ability (refined FAI ≥17)

	Weekly wage	Hourly wage	Refined FAI Score	Original FAI Score	Age	Current job tenure (years)	Total years of employment
Panel A: All occupations (n=47)							
Work and staff	-.053	-.116	.242	.186	-.048	.000	-.158
	(.724)a	(.437)	(.101)	(.211)	(.747)	(.998)	(.289)
Task	-.057	.114	.054	-.003	-.125	-.417**	-.313*
	(.705)	(.446)	(.720)	(.986)	(.402)	(.004)	(.032)
Pay	.155	.226	-.051	-.067	-.067	-.155	-.152
	(.297)	(.127)	(.735)	(.656)	(.657)	(.298)	(.307)
Social	-.120	-.084	.192	-.106	-.019	-.014	-.063
	(.421)	(.574)	(.196)	(.477)	(.899)	(.924)	(.674)
Total job satisfaction	.006	.106	.096	.031	-.099	-.256	-.252
	(.969)	(.477)	(.523)	(.837)	(.510)	(.082)	(.088)
Total job satisfaction (exc. social)	.064	.167	.068	.020	-.114	-.297*	-.268
	(.667)	(.261)	(.651)	(.895)	(.444)	(.043)	(.068)
Panel B: Unskilled labouring positions (n=37)							
Work and staff	.000	-.109	.263	.176	.058	-.092	-.126
	(.998)	(.521)	(.116)	(.296)	(.733)	(.589)	(.459)
Task	-.144	.099	.096	.023	-.083	-.358*	-.240
	(.394)	(.561)	(.574)	(.892)	(.624)	(.030)	(.153)
Pay	.182	.313	-.015	-.022	-.046	-.242	-.126
	(.280)	(.059)	(.931)	(.898)	(.785)	(.149)	(.457)
Social	.153	.185	.028	-.056	.016	-.071	.021
	(.367)	(.274)	(.868)	(.744)	(.924)	(.678)	(.903)
Total job satisfaction	.033	.197	.076	.005	-.047	-.298	-.173
	(.848)	(.243)	(.654)	(.976)	(.783)	(.073)	(.306)
Total job satisfaction (exc. social)	.045	.171	.103	.041	-.023	-.271	-.149
	(.791)	(.313)	(.544)	(.808)	(.893)	(.104)	(.379)
Panel C: Living with family (n=27)							
Work and staff	-.047	-.123	.209	.148	.208	.132	.081
	(.712)	(.541)	(.296)	(.460)	(.298)	(.512)	(.686)
Task	-.321	-.160	.317	.288	-.114	-.239	-.271
	(.102)	(.426)	(.107)	(.146)	(.571)	(.230)	(.171)
Pay	.019	-.119	.014	-.044	.050	.165	.047
	(.925)	(.554)	(.946)	(.826)	(.806)	(.410)	(.817)
Social	-.312	-.110	.227	.088	-.264	-.160	-.380
	(.113)	(.586)	(.256)	(.661)	(.183)	(.425)	(.051)
Total job satisfaction	-.221	-.023	.181	.104	-.091	-.120	-.192
	(.267)	(.909)	(.365)	(.604)	(.653)	(.551)	(.338)
Total job satisfaction (exc. social)	-.211	-.045	.243	.189	-.001	-.061	-.105
	(.290)	(.823)	(.221)	(.344)	(.998)	(.763)	(.601)

a   Figures in parentheses represent significance levels.
*   Significant at the 5 percent level.
**   Significant at the 1 percent level.
Note: *Method of employment* and *living environment* were not included in the above correlation analysis as both are categorical variables.

It is interesting that these statistically significant negative correlations between *task* and both current job tenure and total years of employment and between *job satisfaction* and current job tenure were not revealed previously when the correlates of job satisfaction for the entire sample (Table A2.1) and for participants with high functional work ability (Table A2.2) were explored. As noted in Section 5.12 (Correlations among Demographic Variables) people in open employment have been in their current jobs fewer years than people in supported employment. Since open employment comprises of primarily participants with high functional work ability and supported employment comprises mainly of participants with low functional work ability, this employment pattern may partially explain this result. Another plausible explanation for this relationship is that participants with low functional work ability are more likely to be the ones who remain in a certain occupational position. It is possible that given the person's perceived low functional work ability, employers, and possibly disability employment agencies, may be contented with the fact that the person is satisfactorily performing a duty and therefore not consider training the person to perform new skills in a different job. Consequently, as time goes on the person, not surprisingly, receives less satisfaction from performing the same tasks.

A2.2.3 Discussion of Job Satisfaction Results
In relation to the correlates of job satisfaction several interesting results were revealed. First, when considering the entire sample it appeared that there was a significant negative (positive) correlation between functional work ability (refined FAI and original FAI) and the *work and staff* factor of the JSQ. This indicates that participants who have lower (higher) functional work ability (refined FAI and original FAI), score higher in regards to their satisfaction with work and staff. This result was explained by the fact that people with high functional work ability (low level of intellectual disability) tend to compare themselves to people without a disability as opposed to people with low functional work ability (higher levels of intellectual disability) who compare themselves with other people with intellectual disability (Lam and Chan 1988). Consequently participants with a high functional work ability realising that they are being treated differently from people without a disability and consequently are expressing less satisfaction with *work and staff* compared to participants with lower functional work ability.

However, when the responses from only participants with high functional work ability are considered the statistically significant correlation between functional work ability (refined and original FAI) and *work and staff* is in the opposite direction. This was explained by the fact that those participants in this sub sample of participants who would all be considered to have a mild intellectual disability, with higher levels of functional work ability, may be treated similarly to other people at work without a disability and as such they express satisfaction with the *work and staff* factor of the JSQ. However, those participants in this sub-sample who are not as highly functionally able may notice they are being treated differently to co-workers without a disability and thus express less satisfaction with the *work and staff* factor.

Combining the above two explanations would result in a U-shaped curve where starting with participants with a low refined FAI score, initially as the refined FAI increases, satisfaction with *work and staff* decreases until some point when this relationship reverses, then as refined FAI increases satisfaction with work and staff begins to rise. The point at which this change occurs could indicate the level of functional work ability were people with intellectual disability compare themselves less with people without disabilities and more to other people with intellectual disabilities.

The second interesting result in relation to the correlates of job satisfaction is the statistically significant negative correlation between the *task* factor of the JSQ and current job tenure[125] for

---

[125] It is acknowledged that there was also a statistically significant negative correlation between task and total years of employment in Panel A of Table A2.3. However, given that this relationship was not statistically significant in Panel B of Table A2.3 and that current job tenure and total years of employment

participants with low functional work ability. This negative relationship between a person's length of employment and their satisfaction with *task* is likely to be due to participants with low functional work ability performing the same work functions each day at work, without being up-skilled or promoted. Also it is more likely that people with low functional work ability are employed in a supported environment thus limiting opportunities for up-skilling or promotion. Therefore, it is not surprising that such continual repetition of tasks over an extended period of time results in lower levels of satisfaction with the *task* factor of the JSQ. This result confirms previous research which generally finds people with intellectual disabilities are placed into low-level positions with little opportunity for advancement (Parmenter 1993).

A2.3 Correlates of Quality of Life
Similar to the discussion above on job satisfaction, having determined the differences in outcomes achieved by participants in open employment compared to supported employment in terms of quality of life in Section 6.3 (Quality of Life), Spearman Rank Order Correlation tests are now conducted to determine the correlates of quality of life and its four factors. Spearman rhos are calculated for the correlations between the collected demographic variables and total quality of life as well as it four factors as measured by both the refined and original QOL.Q.

Panel A of Table A2.4 reveals that for the entire sample *empowerment/independence* is statistically significantly positively correlated with a participant's weekly wage ($r_s = .508$, $p \leq .001$) and hourly wage ($r_s = .497$, $p \leq .001$), and statistically significantly positively correlated with functional work ability, as measured by either the refined FAI ($r_s = -.447$, $p \leq .001$) or original FAI ($r_s = -.432$, $p \leq .001$). Panel A of Table A2.4 also reveals that *social belonging/community integration* is statistically significantly positively correlated with the refined FAI score ($r_s = .207$, $p \leq .025$)[126] and statistically significantly negatively correlated with both age ($r_s = -.260$, $p \leq .005$) and total years of employment ($r_s = -.249$, $p \leq .007$). *Quality of life* is found to be statistically significantly positively correlated with hourly wage ($r_s = .274$, $p \leq .003$).

When occupation type is controlled, by only analysing the responses of participants from unskilled labouring positions (Panel B, Table A2.4), the results are largely the same as those reported above. *Empowerment/independence*, as for the entire sample, is statistically significantly positively correlated with weekly wage ($r_s = .530$, $p \leq .001$) and hourly wage ($r_s = .503 \leq .001$) and statistically significantly negatively correlated with the refined FAI ($r_s = -.428$, $p \leq .001$) and the original FAI ($r_s = -.404$, $p \leq .001$). However, unlike the results for Panel A, in Panel B of Table A2.4 there is also a statistically significant negative correlation between *empowerment/independence* and current job tenure ($r_s = -.210$, $p \leq .042$). The results for the correlates of *social belonging/community integration* for Panel B of Table A2.4 are also similar to those of Panel A, in that there are statistically significant negative correlations with age ($r_s = -.271$, $p \leq .001$) and total years of employment ($r_s = -.246$, $p \leq .017$). In addition to the refined FAI being statistically significantly positively correlated with *social belonging/community integration* ($r_s = .334$, $p \leq .001$), as it was in Panel A, for Panel B of Table A2.4 the original FAI is also found to be statistically significantly correlated with *social belonging/community integration* ($r_s = .308$, $p \leq$

---

are highly correlated only the results in relation to current job years will be discussed in this section. The implications of the statistically significant correlation are similar for total years of employment and for current job tenure and it is felt not much would be gained in the discussion in this section by specifically referring to total years of employment.

Also, the statistically significant result between job satisfaction and current job tenure in Panel A of Table A2.3 is not mentioned as the significant relationship is not found in Panels B and C of Table A2.3. Additionally, the implications of this relationship are the same as discussed in the main body of this thesis.

[126] The Spearman rho between *social belonging/community integration* and original FAI for Panel A of Table A2.3 just fails to meet the five percent significance ($r_s = .181$, $p \leq .051$). Given that for Panels B, C, and D of Table 6.6 both the refined FAI and original FAI are statistically significantly positively correlated with *social belonging/community integration*, it is safe to conclude that functional work ability is negatively correlated with the *social belonging/community integration* factor of the QOL.Q.

.003). As per Panel A, the results in Panel B of Table A2.4 show that *quality of life* is statistically significantly positively correlated with hourly wages (r_s = .298, $p \leq$ .004).

The results in Panel C of Table A2.4, for participants who live with their family, are similar to those in Panel B of Table A2.4, in that *empowerment/independence* is found to have a statistically significant positive correlation with both weekly wage (r_s = .547, $p \leq$ .001) and hourly wage (r_s = .535, $p \leq$ .001) and a statistically significant negative correlation with the refined FAI score (r_s = -.531, $p \leq$ .001), the original FAI score (r_s = -.523, $p \leq$ .001), and current job tenure (r_s = -.240, $p \leq$ .049). The results for *social belonging/community integration* for Panel C of Table A2.4 are also similar to Panel B, with statistically significant positive correlations with the refined FAI score (r_s = .299, $p \leq$ .013) and the original FAI score (r_s = .299, $p \leq$ .013) and statistically significant negative

Table A2.4: Spearman rank order correlation coefficients between refined QOL.Q and demographic variables

	Weekly wage	Hourly wage	Refined FAI Score	Original FAI Score	Age	Current job tenure (years)	Total years of employment
Panel A: All occupations (n=117)							
Satisfaction	-.055	-.040	.151	.123	-.007	.025	-.060
	(.553)[a]	(.667)	(.103)	(.188)	(.938)	(.786)	(.519)
Competence/	.008	.005	.083	.099	.027	.019	-.116
Productivity	(.928)	(.961)	(.376)	(.288)	(.521)	(.836)	(.215)
Empowerment/	.508**	.497**	-.447**	-.432**	.086	-.165	.026
Independence	(.000)	(.000)	(.000)	(.000)	(.356)	(.075)	(.779)
Social belonging[b]	-.073	.099	.207*	.181	-.260**	-.098	-.249**
	(.433)	(.291)	(.025)	(.051)	(.005)	(.291)	(.007)
QOL	.166	.274**	-.028	-.037	-.108	-.111	-.175
	(.074)	(.003)	(.767)	(.691)	(.246)	(.233)	(.060)
Panel B: Unskilled labouring positions (n=94)							
Satisfaction	.008	.034	.146	.121	-.013	-.063	-.135
	(.938)	(.747)	(.159)	(.244)	(.899)	(.543)	(.194)
Competence/	.047	.030	.075	.080	.119	.030	-.049
Productivity	(.650)	(.775)	(.475)	(.441)	(.254)	(.777)	(.640)
Empowerment/	.530**	.503**	-.428**	-.404**	.032	-.210*	-.031
Independence	(.000)	(.000)	(.000)	(.000)	(.762)	(.042)	(.766)
Social belonging	-.172	.074	.334**	.308**	-.271**	-.091	-.246*
	(.097)	(.480)	(.001)	(.003)	(.000)	(.383)	(.017)
QOL	.148	.298**	.039	.031	-.121	-.150	-.192
	(.154)	(.004)	(.707)	(.768)	(.191)	(.148)	(.064)
Panel C: Living with family (n=68)							
Satisfaction	-.322**	-.274*	.297*	.276*	.052	.129	-.027
	(.007)	(.024)	(.014)	(.023)	(.676)	(.294)	(.828)
Competence/	-.138	-.192	.091	.119	.228	.185	.027
Productivity	(.261)	(.116)	(.461)	(.336)	(.061)	(.131)	(.829)
Empowerment/	.547**	.535**	-.531**	-.523**	-.085	-.240*	-.096
Independence	(.000)	(.000)	(.000)	(.000)	(.491)	(.049)	(.435)
Social belonging	-.269*	-.091	.299*	.299*	-.267*	-.104	-.317**
	(.026)	(.459)	(.013)	(.013)	(.027)	(.401)	(.008)
QOL	-.075	.041	.056	.062	-.129	-.109	-.271*
	(.545)	(.738)	(.652)	(.618)	(.293)	(.377)	(.025)
Panel D: Unskilled labouring positions and living with family (n=54)							
Satisfaction	-.301*	-.219	.370**	.354**	.054	.073	-.101
	(.027)	(.111)	(.006)	(.009)	(.700)	(.599)	(.486)
Competence/	-.138	-.221	.078	.109	.287*	.282*	.152
Productivity	(.320)	(.108)	(.576)	(.431)	(.036)	(.039)	(.272)
Empowerment/	.589**	.584**	-.533**	-.517**	-.131	-.307*	-.107
Independence	(.000)	(.000)	(.000)	(.000)	(.344)	(.024)	(.443)
Social belonging	-.400**	-.120	.478**	.464*	-.301*	-.090	-.294*
	(.003)	(.389)	(.000)	(.000)	(.027)	(.517)	(.031)
QOL	-.108	.084	.171	.173	-.177	-.131	-.247
	(.437)	(.548)	(.215)	(.212)	(.200)	(.344)	(.072)

Table A2.4 continued

	Weekly wage	Hourly wage	Refined FAI Score	Original FAI Score	Age	Current job tenure (years)	Total years of employment
Panel E: Matched pairs sub-sample (n=34)							
Satisfaction	.155	.374*	.306	.232	-.088	-.167	-.269
	(.380)	(.029)	(.078)	(.187)	(.622)	(.345)	(.125)
Competence/	.205	.249	.103	.032	.075	.019	.020
Productivity	(.245)	(.156)	(.561)	(.855)	(.675)	(.914)	(.912)
Empowerment/	.482**	.583**	-.030	.001	.281	-.008	.189
Independence	(.004)	(.000)	(.866)	(.997)	(.108)	(.966)	(.283)
Social belonging	-.204	.124	.251	.223	-.192	-.168	-.281
	(.248)	(.485)	(.151)	(.204)	(.276)	(.343)	(.107)
QOL	.181	.537**	.240	.189	-.020	-.155	-.135
	(.306)	(.001)	(.172)	(.285)	(.911)	(.382)	(.446)

a   Figures in parentheses represent significance levels.
b   Abbreviation for *social belonging/community integration*.
*   Significant at the 5 percent level.
**   Significant at the 1 percent level.
Note: *Method of employment* and *living environment* were not included in the above correlation analysis as both are categorical variables.

correlations with age (r_s = -.267, $p \leq .027$) and total years of employment (r_s = -.317, $p \leq .008$). However, unlike the results in Panel B, Panel C of Table A2.4 also shows a statistically significant negative correlation between *social belonging/community integration* and weekly wage (r_s = -.269, $p \leq .026$). Also, for the first time statistically significant correlations are found between *satisfaction* and weekly wage (r_s = -.322, $p \leq .007$), hourly wage (r_s = -.274, $p \leq .024$), refined FAI score (r_s = .297, $p \leq .014$), and original FAI score (r_s = .276, $p \leq .023$). Also for the first time a statistically significant negative correlation is found between *quality of life* and total years of employment (r_s = -.271, $p \leq .025$).

Panel D of Table A2.4, which controls for both the living and working environment by analysing the responses of only participants who work in unskilled labouring positions and live at home, also reveals similar results to the above Panels. Panel D of Table A2.4 shows the same demographic variables to be statistically significantly correlated with *empowerment/independence* and *social belonging/community integration* as does Panel C. That is, *empowerment/independence* is statistically significantly positively correlated to weekly wage (r_s = .589, $p \leq .001$) and hourly wage (r_s = -.584, $p \leq .001$), and statistically significantly correlated with the refined FAI score (r_s = -.533, $p \leq .001$), the original FAI score (r_s = -.517, $p \leq .001$), and current job tenure (r_s = -.307, $p \leq .024$). *Social belonging/community integration* is statistically significantly positively correlated with both the refined FAI score (r_s = .478, $p \leq .001$) and the original FAI score (r_s = .464, $p \leq .001$), and statistically significantly negatively correlated with weekly wage (r_s = -.400, $p \leq .003$), age (r_s = -.301, $p \leq .027$), and total years of employment (r_s = -.294, $p \leq .031$). Also similar to Panel C, the results in Panel D of Table A2.4 show satisfaction to be statistically significantly positively correlated with the refined FAI score (r_s = .370, $p \leq .006$) and the original FAI score (r_s = .354, $p \leq .009$), and statistically significantly negatively correlated with weekly wage (r_s = -.301, $p \leq .027$). However, unlike the results in Panel C, no statistically significant correlation is found between *satisfaction* and hourly wage for those participants working in unskilled labouring positions and living with their family (Panel D, Table A2.4). Different to the results in the prior three panels, the results in Panel D of Table A2.4 show no statistically significant correlations for total *quality of life*. Also different to the results of previous panels is the emergence of a positive statistically significant correlation between *competence/productivity* and the two demographic variables of age (r_s = .287, $p \leq .036$) and current job tenure (r_s = .282, $p \leq .039$).

Panel E of Table A2.4 displays the results of the Spearman correlations for the matched pairs sub-sample. The results for this sub-sample are noticeably different to the above sub-sample in the lack of statistically significant correlations between quality of life and its four factors and the demographic variables. This lack of correlation is probably in large part due to the small sample size (n = 34), which prohibits any extensive analysis. However, despite the small sample size several statistically significant relationships are still apparent. As per the results in Panels A to D, the results in Panel E of Table A2.4 still show *empowerment/independence* to be statistically significantly positively correlated to both weekly wage (r_s = .482, $p \leq$ .004) and hourly wage (r_s = .583, $p \leq$ .001). Similar to the results in Panel C, Panel E of Table A2.4 shows a positive statistically significant correlation between satisfaction and hourly wage (r_s = .374, $p \leq$ .029). The results in Panel E of Table A2.4 also show a significant positive correlation between *quality of life* and hourly wage (r_s = .482, p $\leq$ .004).

The above results are by-in-large as would be expected given the statistically significant differences in quality of life and its factors shown in Table 6.4 (for the entire sample) and the statistically significant differences in demographic variables between open employment and supported employment participants highlighted in Table 5.5 (for the entire sample), Table 5.11 (for participants in unskilled labouring positions), Table 5.13 (for participants living with their family), Table 5.15 (for participants working in unskilled labouring positions and living with their family), and Table 5.17 (for the matched pairs sub-sample). The results in Table 6.4 reveal that for Panels A to D, *empowerment/independence* is statistically significantly higher for participants in open employment. As such, given that Tables 5.5, 5.8, 5.10, and 5.12 reveal that for the entire sample and the relevant sub-samples participants in open employment compared to their counterparts in supported employment receive statistically significantly higher weekly and hourly wages, score statistically significantly lower refined and original FAI scores, are statistically significantly younger, and have been employed statistically significantly less years in their current job and in total, it is not surprising that *empowerment/independence* is found to be statistically significantly correlated with these demographic variables.

Likewise, given that *social belonging/community integration* is found to be significantly different between open employment and supported employment in Panels A and B of Table 6.4, it is not surprising that it is correlated with several demographic variables (refined FAI score, original FAI score,[127] age, total years of employment) in Panels A and B of Table A2.4. However, the correlations are also present for Panels C and D, which is interesting given that Panels C and D of Table 6.4 did not report any statistically significant differences between open employment and supported employment for *social belonging/community integration*. In fact an extra demographic variable (weekly wage) is found to be statistically significantly correlated with *social belonging/community integration* in Panels C and D of Table A2.4, compared to Panels A and B.

Given that participants in open employment are statistically significantly younger (Table 5.5) and have been employed statistically significantly less years (Table 5.5), the statistically significant negative correlations between *social belonging/community integration* and age, and total years of employment, are consistent with the results in Table 6.4, which reports participants in open employment to have statistically significantly higher *social belonging/community integration* scores than participants in supported employment. However, what is surprising is that *social belonging/community integration* is positively correlated with the refined and original FAI scores (across Panels A to D of Table A2.4), suggesting that the lower (higher) a person's functional work ability (refined and original FAI score) the higher their score on this factor of the QOL.Q. Given that participants in open employment are shown to have a higher (lower) functional work ability (refined and original FAI score) (Tables 5.5, 5.8, 5.10, and 5.12) this positive correlation appears contrary to the results of Panels A and B of Table 6.4, which reveal that participants in open

---

[127] It is acknowledged that the Spearman rho between social belonging/community integration and original FAI for Panel A of Table A2.4 just misses statistical significance (rs = .181, p $\leq$ .051). However, given the Spearman rhos between these two variables are statistically significant for Panels B to D of Table A2.4, the result in Panel A is still seen as supporting a correlation between the two variables.

employment score statistically significantly higher *social belonging/community integration* scores than participants in supported employment.

The fact that Panels A to D of Table A2.4 consistently report a positive correlation suggests that there is possibly a U-shaped relationship between *social belonging/community integration* and functional work ability, which could be attributed to differences in whom people with low level of disability compare themselves to relative to people with high levels of disability (see, Lam and Chan 1988; Moseley 1988). That is, participants with high (low) functional work ability (refined and original FAI scores) report high scores for *social belonging/community integration*, as they are more likely to be accepted into a community including people without disabilities, who are their reference point. This level of acceptance is likely to decreases as the person with an intellectual disability's level of functional work ability (refined and original FAI scores) decreases (increases), thus resulting in lower *social belonging/community integration* scores. However, once people with intellectual disabilities level of disability reaches a certain point their reference group begins to move towards other people with intellectual disabilities, a community to which they would be accepted, and as such their scores on the *social belonging/community integration* factor of the QOL.Q would then begin to increase. Such a scenario is weakly supported by a visual inspection of the scatter plot (Figure A2.3) and the sign of the correlations for *social belonging/community integration* presented below for participants with high functional work ability in Table A2.6 (negative correlation, though not statistically significant) and low functional work ability in Table A2.8 (positive correlation, though not statistically significant).

Figure A2.3:   Correlation between *social belonging/community integration* score and refined FAI score (n=117)

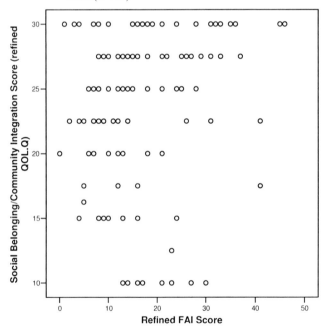

Initially, the statistically significant negative correlation between *social belonging/community integration* and weekly wage shown in Panels C and D of Table A2.4 appears surprising. However, this can be explained by the fact that both refined and original FAI scores are statistically significantly positively correlated with *social belonging/community integration* and that refined and original FAI scores are statistically significantly negatively correlated with weekly wages (Table 5.18).

The results for the *satisfaction* factor of the refined QOL.Q will not be discussed given that Section 4.5.2 (Reliability Analysis of the QOL.Q) reveals that reliability cannot be attributed to the scores of this factor.

Quality of life is found to be statistically significantly positively correlated with hourly wage in Panels A, B, and E of Table A2.4. This coincides exactly with the Panels in Table 6.4 where *quality of life* is found to be statistically significantly different between participants in open employment and supported employment. Given that *quality of life* is found to be statistically significantly higher for participants in open employment (Panels A, B, and E of Table 6.4) and hourly wages are statistically significantly higher in open employment compared to supported employment (Table 5.5), this positive correlation between *quality of life* and weekly wages is not unexpected.

Table A2.5 reports the Spearman rhos for the original QOL.Q. In many respects the results are very similar to those shown in Table A2.4 for the refined QOL.Q. Similar to Table A2.4, Table A2.5 show *empowerment/independence* to be statistically significantly positively correlated with weekly wages (Panel A, r_s = .527, $p \leq$ .001; Panel B, r_s = .536, $p \leq$ .001; Panel C, r_s = .533, $p \leq$ .001; Panel D, r_s = .557, $p \leq$ .001; Panel E, r_s = .507, $p \leq$ .002) and hourly wages (Panel A, r_s = .504, $p \leq$ .001; Panel B, r_s = .509, $p \leq$ .001; Panel C, r_s = .540, $p \leq$ .001; Panel D, r_s = .576, $p \leq$ .001; Panel E, r_s = .658, $p \leq$ .001) and statistically significantly correlated with refined FAI score (Panel A, r_s = -.468, $p \leq$ .001; Panel B, r_s = -.463, $p \leq$ .001; Panel C, r_s = -.521, $p \leq$ .001; Panel D, r_s = -.526, $p \leq$ .001), original FAI score (Panel A, r_s = -.460, $p \leq$ .001; Panel B, r_s = -.451, $p \leq$ .001; Panel C, r_s = -.517, $p \leq$ .001; Panel D, r_s = -.520, $p \leq$ .001), and current job tenure (Panel A, r_s = -.194, $p \leq$ .036; Panel B, r_s = -.228, $p \leq$ .027; Panel C, r_s = - .243, $p \leq$ .046; Panel D, r_s = -.297, $p \leq$ .029). The results in Table A2.5 for *social belonging/community integration* are also similar to the results shown in Table A2.4, in that for panels A to D of Table A2.5 *social belonging/community integration* is found to be statistically significantly negatively correlated with age (Panel A, r_s = - .307, $p \leq$ .001; Panel B, r_s = -.353, $p \leq$ .001; Panel C, r_s = -.271, $p \leq$ .025; Panel D, r_s = -.331, $p \leq$ .014) and total years of employment (Panel A, r_s = -.260, $p \leq$ .005; Panel B, r_s = -.295, $p \leq$ .004; Panel C, r_s = -.291, $p \leq$ .016; Panel D, r_s = -.276, $p \leq$ .044). However, different to the results shown in Table A2.4, there is never a statistically significant correlation between *social belonging/community integration* and refined FAI score (Panels B to D of Table A2.4), original FAI score (Panels A to D of Table A2.4), and weekly wage (Panels C and D of Table A2.4) in Table A2.5.

The results for *satisfaction* shown in Table A2.5 (original QOL.Q) are different to those revealed in Table A2.4 (refined QOL.Q). Like the results in Table A2.4, there are no statistically significant correlations in Panels A and B of Table A2.5. However, the results in Table A2.5 also reveal that there are no statistically significant correlations in Panels C and D. This is unlike Table A2.4, where Panels C and D reveal statistically significant correlations with weekly wage, hourly wage, refined FAI score, and original FAI score. Similar to Table A2.4, Panel E of Table A2.5 shows a positive statistically significant correlation between *satisfaction* and hourly wage (r_s = .374, $p \leq$ .029).

Similar to Table A2.4 (refined QOL.Q), the results for *competence/productivity* reveal no statistically significant correlations in Panels A, B and E of Table A2.5 (original QOL.Q). Also similar to the results in Panel D of Table A2.4, Panel D of Table A2.5 reveals a statistically significant positive correlation between *competence/productivity* and age. However, unlike Table A2.4, Panel D of Table A2.5 does not report a statistically significant correlation between *competence/productivity* and current job tenure. Though it must be acknowledged that the result in Panel D of Table A2.5 for the correlation between *competence/productivity* and current job tenure

191

only fails to reach significance by .001 percent ($r_s = .267$, $p \leq .051$), which given the limited sample size (n = 54) can probably be seen as supporting the results in Table A2.4. Another difference between the results in Table A2.4 and Table A2.5, is that unlike Panel C of Table A2.4, where no statistically significant correlations were present for *competence/productivity*, the results in Panel C of Table A2.5 show a statistically significant positive correlation with age ($r_s = .251$, $p \leq .039$).

The results for quality of life also vary between Table A2.4 (refined QOL.Q) and Table A2.5 (original QOL.Q). Similar to Table A2.4, the results in Panels A, B and E of Table A2.5 reveal a statistically significant positive correlation between quality of life and hourly wages (Panel A, $r_s = .252$, $p \leq .006$; Panel B, $r_s = .300$, $p \leq .003$; Panel E, $r_s = .519$, $p \leq .002$). However, unlike the results in Table A2.4, Panels A and B of Table A2.5 reveal not only a statistically significant correlation

Table A2.5: Spearman rank order correlation coefficients between original QOL.Q and demographic variables

	Weekly wage	Hourly wage	Refined FAI Score	Original FAI Score	Age	Current job tenure (years)	Total years of employment
Panel A: All occupations (n=117)							
Satisfaction	.035	.009	.090	.047	-.003	.081	-.056
	(.709)[a]	(.921)	(.332)	(.614)	(.970)	(.388)	(.549)
Competence/	-.026	-.060	.108	.115	.060	.040	-.087
Productivity	(.777)	(.521)	(.248)	(.216)	(.521)	(.666)	(.354)
Empowerment/	.527**	.504**	-.468**	-.460**	-.033	-.194*	-.060
Independence	(.000)	(.000)	(.000)	(.000)	(.726)	(.036)	(.522)
Social belonging[b]	.014	.157	.075	.049	-.307**	-.117	-.260**
	(.885)	(.091)	(.424)	(.600)	(.001)	(.207)	(.005)
QOL	.216*	.252**	-.080	-.097	-.130	-.085	-.183*
	(.020)	(.006)	(.388)	(.296)	(.164)	(.361)	(.048)
Panel B: Unskilled labouring positions (n=94)							
Satisfaction	.097	.078	.088	.043	-.036	-.016	-.127
	(.352)	(.454)	(.399)	(.683)	(.729)	(.878)	(.224)
Competence/	.025	-.010	.082	.080	.171	.054	-.001
Productivity	(.814)	(.923)	(.434)	(.446)	(.099)	(.604)	(.989)
Empowerment/	.536**	.509**	-.463**	-.451**	-.071	-.228*	-.082
Independence	(.000)	(.000)	(.000)	(.000)	(.496)	(.027)	(.432)
Social belonging	-.036	.159	.148	.114	-.353**	-.146	-.295**
	(.731)	(.127)	(.154)	(.274)	(.000)	(.159)	(.004)
QOL	.237*	.300**	-.061	-.083	-.136	-.145	-.202
	(.022)	(.003)	(.561)	(.428)	(.191)	(.164)	(.051)
Panel C: Living with family (n=68)							
Satisfaction	-.199	-.234	.168	.134	.113	.225	.052
	(.104)	(.054)	(.171)	(.275)	(.358)	(.065)	(.676)
Competence/	-.124	-.195	.100	.120	.251*	.179	.032
Productivity	(.313)	(.111)	(.418)	(.328)	(.039)	(.144)	(.797)
Empowerment/	.533**	.540**	-.521**	-.517**	-.165	-.243*	-.158
Independence	(.000)	(.000)	(.000)	(.000)	(.179)	(.046)	(.199)
Social belonging	-.188	-.034	.145	.139	-.271*	-.157	-.291*
	(.124)	(.780)	(.237)	(.258)	(.025)	(.201)	(.016)
QOL	.003	.042	-.045	-.048	-.057	-.048	-.174
	(.979)	(.731)	(.715)	(.700)	(.646)	(.699)	(.155)
Panel D: Unskilled labouring positions and living with family (n=54)							
Satisfaction	-.143	-.186	.215	.176	.094	.174	.003
	(.301)	(.179)	(.118)	(.204)	(.501)	(.207)	(.984)
Competence/	-.131	-.219	.086	.111	.323*	.267	.153
Productivity	(.345)	(.112)	(.538)	(.423)	(.017)	(.051)	(.270)
Empowerment/	.557**	.576**	-.526**	-.520**	-.216	-.297*	-.149
Independence	(.000)	(.000)	(.000)	(.000)	(.117)	(.029)	(.282)
Social belonging	.221	.015	.252	.229	-.331*	-.151	-.276*
	(.109)	(.916)	(.066)	(.096)	(.014)	(.276)	(.044)
QOL	.020	.089	.024	.015	-.077	-.049	-.121
	(.886)	(.524)	(.866)	(.912)	(.581)	(.724)	(.383)

Table A2.5 continued

	Weekly wage	Hourly wage	Refined FAI Score	Original FAI Score	Age	Current job tenure (years)	Total years of employment
Panel E: Matched pairs sub-sample (n=34)							
Satisfaction	.085	.303	.359*	.267	-.140	-.069	-.236
	(.634)	(.082)	(.037)	(.127)	(.430)	(.696)	(.180)
Competence/	.195	.213	.103	.008	.137	.001	.062
Productivity	(.269)	(.226)	(.562)	(.963)	(.439)	(.994)	(.728)
Empowerment/	.507**	.658**	.052	.022	.035	-.127	-.002
Independence	(.002)	(.000)	(.769)	(.903)	(.843)	(.475)	(.993)
Social belonging	-.046	.252	.096	.038	-.293	-.112	-.324
	(.798)	(.151)	(.588)	(.832)	(.093)	(.527)	(.061)
QOL	.200	.519**	.309	.194	-.160	-.192	-.250
	(.257)	(.002)	(.075)	(.272)	(.366)	(.277)	(.154)

a   Figures in parentheses represent significance levels.
b   Abbreviation for *social belonging/community integration*.
*   Significant at the 5 percent level.
**   Significant at the 1 percent level.
Note: *Method of employment* and *living environment* were not included in the above correlation analysis as both are categorical variables.

between quality of life and hourly wages, but also one with weekly wages (Panel A, r_s = .216, $p \leq$ .020; Panel B, r_s = .237, $p \leq$ .022). A negative statistically significant correlation is also shown in Panel A of Table A2.5 between quality of life and total years of employment (r_s = -.183, $p \leq$ .048), when no such result is found using the refined QOL.Q (Table A2.4). The other difference between Table A2.4 and Table A2.5 in terms of statistically significant results is that in Panel C of Table A2.5 no statistically significant correlation is found with total years of employment when such a relationship was shown in Table A2.4.

A2.3.1 Correlates of Quality of Life for Participants with High Functional Work Ability

Having established the correlates of quality of life for the entire population, comprising both participants with high and low functional work ability, Spearman Rank Order Correlation Tests were conducted separately for participants with high functional work ability and for participants with low functional work ability. Table A2.6 reports Spearman rhos for those participants who were classified as having high functional work ability (refined FAI ≤ 12).

As can be seen from Panel A of Table A2.6, when analysing the responses of participants with high functional work ability across all occupations, *satisfaction* has a negative statistically significant correlation with original FAI score (r_s = -.380, $p \leq$ .009). Panel A of Table A2.6 further reveals that *empowerment/independence* is statistically significantly positively correlated with both weekly wage (r_s = .431, $p \leq$ .003) and hourly wage (r_s = .552, $p \leq$ .001) and statistically significantly negatively correlated with refined FAI score (r_s = -.389, $p \leq$ .007), original FAI score (r_s = -.329, $p \leq$ .026), and current job tenure (r_s = -.291, $p \leq$ .050). *Quality of life* is found to be statistically significantly positively correlated with weekly wage (r_s = .336, $p \leq$ .022) and hourly wage (r_s = .413, $p \leq$ .004) and statistically significantly negatively correlated with both the refined and original FAI scores (r_s = -.332, $p \leq$ .024; r_s = -.351, $p \leq$ .017, respectively).

Panel B of Table A2.6, which controls for the type of occupation by reporting only the responses of participants in unskilled labouring positions, reveals similar results to Panel A, which did not control for occupation type. As with the results in Panel A of Table A2.6, Panel B shows *satisfaction* to have a negative statistically significantly correlation with the original FAI score (r_s = -.380, $p \leq$ .009). The results for *empowerment/independence* in Panel B of Table A2.6 are also similar to the results in Panel A, with statistically significant positive correlations with both weekly and hourly wages (r_s = .567, $p \leq$ .001; r_s = .624, $p \leq$ .001, respectively) and statistically significant negative correlations with both the refined and original FAI scores (r_s = -.337, $p \leq$ .045; r_s = -.290, p

≤ .086, respectively). However, unlike the results in Panel A, Panel B of Table A2.6 reveals no statistically significant correlation with current job tenure, but instead a negative statistically significant correlation with total years of employment ($r_s = -.339$, $p \leq .043$). The two statistically significant positive correlations for *quality of life* reported in Panel B of Table A2.6, with weekly wage ($r_s = .376$, $p \leq .024$) and hourly wage ($r_s = .424$, $p \leq .010$), were also reported in Panel A. However, these are the only two statistically significant correlations for *quality of life* for this panel of Table A2.6.

Table A2.6: Spearman rank order correlation coefficients between refined QOL.Q and demographic variables for participants with high functional work ability (refined FAI ≤ 12)

	Weekly wage	Hourly wage	Refined FAI Score	Original FAI Score	Age	Current job tenure (years)	Total years of employment
Panel A: All occupations (n=46)							
Satisfaction	.159	.044	-.267	-.380**	.094	.125	.119
	(.290)ᵃ	(.772)	(.073)	(.009)	(.533)	(.408)	(.431)
Competence/	-.004	.079	-.246	-.153	.008	.001	-.130
Productivity	(.980)	(.601)	(.099)	(.311)	(.956)	(.993)	(.391)
Empowerment/	.431**	.552**	-.389**	-.329*	-.188	-.291*	-.279
Independence	(.003)	(.000)	(.007)	(.026)	(.212)	(.050)	(.060)
Social belongingᵇ	.124	.209	-.014	-.116	-.083	.143	.020
	(.413)	(.163)	(.928)	(.444)	(.582)	(.344)	(.894)
QOL	.336*	.413**	-.332*	-.351*	-.104	-.021	-.115
	(.022)	(.004)	(.024)	(.017)	(.491)	(.892)	(.445)
Panel B: Unskilled labouring positions (n=36)							
Satisfaction	.180	.016	-.263	-.402*	.178	.064	.181
	(.292)	(.927)	(.121)	(.015)	(.299)	(.711)	(.292)
Competence/	-.009	.053	-.282	-.173	.104	-.069	-.085
Productivity	(.957)	(.757)	(.096)	(.314)	(.548)	(.690)	(.624)
Empowerment/	.567**	.624**	-.337*	-.290*	-.255	-.299	-.339*
Independence	(.000)	(.000)	(.045)	(.086)	(.133)	(.076)	(.043)
Social belonging	.037	.084	.200	.086	.038	.267	.136
	(.833)	(.627)	(.242)	(.619)	(.828)	(.116)	(.428)
QOL	.376*	.424**	-.222	-.253	-.009	-.037	-.029
	(.024)	(.010)	(.192)	(.136)	(.957)	(.828)	(.865)
Panel C: Living with family (n=27)							
Satisfaction	-.074	-.245	-.139	-.340	.354	.279	.266
	(.715)	(.217)	(.488)	(.083)	(.070)	(.159)	(.182)
Competence/	-.252	-.155	-.327	-.240	.279	.128	.009
Productivity	(.205)	(.440)	(.096)	(.227)	(.158)	(.525)	(.963)
Empowerment/	.313	.360	-.256	-.224	-.287	-.397*	-.295
Independence	(.112)	(.065)	(.198)	(.261)	(.147)	(.040)	(.135)
Social belonging	.061	.067	-.073	-.160	-.155	.236	-.013
	(.762)	(.741)	(.717)	(.424)	(.440)	(.235)	(.947)
QOL	.104	.138	-.331	-.416*	-.069	.000	-.095
	(.606)	(.491)	(.092)	(.031)	(.733)	(.999)	(.639)

a   Figures in parentheses represent significance levels.
b   Abbreviation for *social belonging/community integration*.
*   Significant at the 5 percent level.
**   Significant at the 1 percent level.
Note: *Method of employment* and *living environment* were not included in the above correlation analysis as both are categorical variables.

Panel C of Table A2.6, which controls for living environment, by only analysing the responses for participants living with their family, shows only two statistically significant correlations for the entire panel. *Empowerment/independence* is found to be statistically significantly negatively correlated with current job tenure ($r_s = -.397$, $p \leq .040$) and *quality of life* shows a negative statistically significant correlation with the original FAI score ($r_s = -.416$, $p \leq .031$). The lack of statistically significant results for this panel is not surprising, given that there are only 27 people in this sub-sample.

Not taking into consideration the results in Panel C, due to the small sample size, the results in Table A2.6 indicate that *empowerment/independence* is positively correlated to both weekly and hourly wages and negatively correlated to both the refined and the original FAI scores. The positive correlations between *empowerment/independence* and weekly and hourly wages is not surprising given that open employment pays statistically significantly higher weekly and hourly wages (Table 5.5), and that Table 6.6 reveals that participants with high functional work ability report statistically significant higher *empowerment/independence* scores in open employment compared to supported employment. Likewise a statistically significant negative correlation between *empowerment/independence* and refined and original FAI scores are not unexpected, given the statistically significantly higher functional work ability of participants in open employment. These results tend to support the results for *empowerment/independence* in Table A2.4 for the entire sample.

The results in Table A2.6 also indicate that *quality of life* for participants with high functional work ability is correlated with weekly and hourly wages. Again, given the statistically significant difference in weekly and hourly wages between the two forms of employment (Table 5.5), and given that Panels A and B of Table 6.6 reveal that participants in open employment report statistically significantly higher quality of life scores, this result is to be expected. These results for quality of life are slightly different to those reported in Table A2.4 for the entire sample. The results in Table A2.4, reveal *quality of life* to be positively related to hourly wage, though interestingly not weekly wage.

It is also interesting to note that for the entire sample (Table A2.4) *social belonging/community integration* is correlated to several demographic variables, but on no occasions for the high functional work ability sub-sample (Table A2.5) are there any statistically significant correlation between *social belonging/community integration* and any of the collected demographic variables.

Given the lack of reliability that can be attributed to the satisfaction scores of the refined QOL.Q, which were discussed in Section 4.5.2 (Reliability Analysis of the QOL.Q), the implications of the results for this factor will not be discussed.

Table A2.7 presents the Spearman rhos for participants with high functional work ability using the original QOL.Q. Reassuringly the results are very similar to those reported in Table A2.6 using the refined QOL.Q. There are only two differences in the results presented in Panel A of Table A2.7 compared to Panel A of Table A2.6, which relate to the fact that no statistically significant correlation is found between *quality of life* and hourly wages in Table A2.7, whereas one was reported in Table A2.6, and that a statistically significant negative correlation between *empowerment/independence* and total years of employment ($r_s = -.346$, $p \leq .019$) is reported in Table A2.7, when no such relationship was found in Table A2.6.

Similarly, in Panel B of Table A2.7, the results closely mirror those reported in Panel B of Table A2.6, with, again, only two differences between the two panels. The results in Panel B of Table A2.7 reveal a statistically significant negative correlation between *quality of life* and the original FAI score ($r_s = -.363$, $p \leq .030$), when such a correlation was not reported in Panel B of Table A2.6. Also, the results show no statistically significant correlation between quality of life and hourly wages in Panel B of Table A2.7, when a statistically significant positive correlation was reported in Panel B of Table A2.6.

Comparing the results in Panel C of Table A2.7 to those in Panel C of Table A2.6, only one difference is apparent, which relates to the fact that in Table A2.6 a statistically significant correlation is shown between *empowerment/independence*, when Panel C of Table A2.7 does not find this correlation to be statistically significant. Overall, the results of the original QOL.Q (Table A2.7) are seen as confirming the results, and the implications drawn from those results, presented earlier in relation to the refined QOL.Q (Table A2.6).

Table A2.7: Spearman rank order correlation coefficients between original QOL.Q and demographic variables for participants with high functional work ability (refined FAI ≤ 12)

	Weekly wage	Hourly wage	Refined FAI Score	Original FAI Score	Age	Current job tenure (years)	Total years of employment
Panel A: All occupations (n=46)							
Satisfaction	.215	.085	-.191	-.335*	-.042	.030	-.128
	(.150)[a]	(.574)	(.202)	(.023)	(.783)	(.841)	(.395)
Competence/	.052	.033	-.288	-.226	.043	-.009	-.075
Productivity	(.730)	(.825)	(.053)	(.132)	(.778)	(.950)	(.620)
Empowerment/	.386**	.441**	-.407**	-.381**	-.303	-.296*	-.346*
Independence	(.008)	(.002)	(.005)	(.009)	(.041)	(.046)	(.019)
Social belonging[b]	.058	.099	-.094	-.199	-.154	-.105	-.079
	(.700)	(.515)	(.536)	(.185)	(.307)	(.489)	(.601)
QOL	.306*	.251	-.373*	-.428**	-.157	-.077	-.198
	(.039)	(.093)	(.011)	(.003)	(.298)	(.610)	(.187)
Panel B: Unskilled labouring positions (n=36)							
Satisfaction	.245	.078	-.165	-.342*	-.022	-.056	-.126
	(.150)	(.649)	(.338)	(.041)	(.901)	(.748)	(.463)
Competence/	.017	.012	-.293	-.212	.186	-.052	.020
Productivity	(.919)	(.944)	(.082)	(.213)	(.278)	(.765)	(.906)
Empowerment/	.441**	.501**	-.365*	-.362*	-.294	-.277	-.368*
Independence	(.007)	(.002)	(.028)	(.030)	(.082)	(.102)	(.027)
Social belonging	.064	.067	.143	.005	-.105	.155	-.060
	(.711)	(.700)	(.407)	(.975)	(.544)	(.367)	(.730)
QOL	.341*	.280	-.287	-.363*	-.066	-.120	-.149
	(.042)	(.098)	(.089)	(.030)	(.703)	(.484)	(.385)
Panel C: Living with family (n=27)							
Satisfaction	-.084	-.195	-.122	-.323	.173	.097	-.045
	(.678)	(.330)	(.546)	(.100)	(.389)	(.630)	(.825)
Competence/	-.088	-.093	-.362	-.316	.374	.103	.067
Productivity	(.664)	(.645)	(.064)	(.109)	(.054)	(.610)	(.739)
Empowerment/	.216	.333	-.296	-.271	-.336	-.343	-.327
Independence	(.280)	(.090)	(.134)	(.171)	(.087)	(.080)	(.096)
Social belonging	-.207	-.204	-.144	-.257	-.171	-.131	-.087
	(.299)	(.307)	(.475)	(.195)	(.394)	(.515)	(.665)
QOL	.024	-.023	-.326	-.416*	.016	-.057	-.129
	(.906)	(.908)	(.097)	(.031)	(.938)	(.776)	(.523)

a   Figures in parentheses represent significance levels.
b   Abbreviation for *social belonging/community integration*.
*   Significant at the 5 percent level.
**   Significant at the 1 percent level.
Note: *Method of employment* and *living environment* were not included in the above correlation analysis as both are categorical variables.

A2.3.2 Correlates of Quality of Life for Participants with Low Functional Work Ability

Table A2.8 reports the results of Spearman Rank Order Correlation Tests for participants with low functional workability using the refined QOL.Q. Panel A of Table A2.8 shows that *empowerment/independence* is statistically significantly positively correlated with weekly wage (r_s = .324, $p \leq .026$) and hourly wage (r_s = .358, $p \leq .013$), and statistically significantly negatively correlated with the refined FAI score (r_s = -.320, $p \leq .029$) and the original FAI score (r_s = -.301, $p \leq .040$). Panel A of Table A2.8 also reveals statistically significant negative correlations between *social belonging/community integration* and both age (r_s = -.317, $p \leq .030$) and total years of employment (r_s = -.433, $p \leq .002$).

Panel B of Table A2.8 reveals the Spearman rhos for participants with low functional work ability in unskilled labouring positions. The results reveal that *empowerment/independence* is statistically significantly positively correlated with both weekly and hourly wage (r_s = .332, $p \le$ .044; r_s = .372, $p \le$ .023, respectively), and statistically significantly negatively correlated with the refined FAI score (r_s = -.333, $p \le$ .044). *Social belonging/community integration* is found to be statistically significantly positively correlated with both hourly wages (r_s = .374, $p \le$ .023) and current job tenure, and statistically significantly negatively correlated with age (r_s = -.431, $p \le$ .008) and total years of employment (r_s = -.478, $p \le$ .003). Panel B of Table A2.8 also highlights a statistically significant positive correlation between *quality of life* and hourly wage (r_s = .408, $p \le$ .012) and a statistically significant negative correlation between *quality of life* and current job tenure (r_s = -.328, $p \le$ .047).

Table A2.8: Spearman rank order correlation coefficients between refined QOL.Q and demographic variables for participants with low functional work ability (refined FAI ≥17)

	Weekly wage	Hourly wage	Refined FAI Score	Original FAI Score	Age	Current job tenure (years)	Total years of employment
Panel A: All occupations (n=47)							
Satisfaction	.056	.131	-.064	-.065	-.147	-.113	-.205
	(.710)[a]	(.380)	(.669)	(.527)	(.325)	(.450)	(.166)
Competence/	.120	.088	.072	.044	.005	-.063	-.104
Productivity	(.422)	(.555)	(.629)	(.768)	(.974)	(.675)	(.487)
Empowerment/	.324*	.358*	-.320*	-.301*	.066	-.132	-.010
Independence	(.026)	(.013)	(.029)	(.040)	(.659)	(.378)	(.948)
Social belonging[b]	-.096	.093	.221	-.192	-.317*	-.259	-.433**
	(.521)	(.533)	(.135)	(.196)	(.030)	(.079)	(.002)
QOL	.093	.237	-.062	-.065	-.116	-.211	-.272
	(.533)	(.108)	(.677)	(.663)	(.436)	(.154)	(.064)
Panel B: Unskilled labouring positions (n=37)							
Satisfaction	.214	.296	-.165	-.216	-.183	-.226	-.228
	(.202)	(.075)	(.329)	(.200)	(.278)	(.179)	(.175)
Competence/	.268	.201	.015	-.036	.059	-.068	-.030
Productivity	(.101)	(.234)	(.928)	(.833)	(.727)	(.691)	(.858)
Empowerment/	.332*	.372*	-.333*	-.304	.061	-.282	-.072
Independence	(.044)	(.023)	(.044)	(.067)	(.720)	(.091)	(.673)
Social belonging	.048	.338*	.187	.152	-.431**	.374*	-.478**
	(.776)	(.041)	(.267)	(.368)	(.008)	(.023)	(.003)
QOL	.224	.408*	-.168	-.179	-.159	-.328*	-.284
	(.182)	(.012)	(.320)	(.289)	(.347)	(.047)	(.089)
Panel C: Living with family (n=27)							
Satisfaction	-.168	-.118	.100	.075	.050	.017	-.018
	(.402)	(.559)	(.621)	(.711)	(.805)	(.933)	(.928)
Competence/	-.063	-.217	.247	.245	.205	.193	.066
Productivity	(.755)	(.277)	(.213)	(.218)	(.305)	(.334)	(.744)
Empowerment/	-.044	.143	-.182	-.235	-.148	-.145	-.197
Independence	(.826)	(.478)	(.365)	(.237)	(.461)	(.470)	(.325)
Social belonging	-.310	-.136	.427*	.416*	-.190	-.317	-.387*
	(.116)	(.498)	(.026)	(.031)	(.342)	(.108)	(.046)
QOL	-.321	-.165	.238	.241	-.081	-.237	-.321
	(.103)	(.411)	(.231)	(.227)	(.689)	(.233)	(.103)

a   Figures in parentheses represent significance levels.
b   Abbreviation for *social belonging/community integration*.
*   Significant at the 5 percent level.
**   Significant at the 1 percent level.
Note: *Method of employment* and *living environment* were not included in the above correlation analysis as both are categorical variables.

The only statistically significant correlations revealed in Panel C of Table A2.8, which controls for living environment by analysing only the responses of participants living with their family, relate to *social belonging/community integration*. This factor of the refined QOL.Q is found to be statistically significantly positively correlated with both the refined and original FAI scores (r_s = .427, $p \leq .026$; r_s = .416, $p \leq .031$, respectively) and statistically significantly negatively correlated with total years of employment (r_s = -.387, $p \leq .046$). As stated in the previous section, the lack of statistically significant results for this panel is not surprising given the small sub-sample size. Given this small sub-sample size, not much weight is placed on the results in Panel C of Table A2.8.

Taken together, the above results indicate that for people with low functional work ability *empowerment/independence* appears to be positively correlated with both weekly and hourly wages and negatively correlated with refined FAI score. These results are similar to those presented for the refined QOL.Q for the entire sample (Table A2.4) and for participants with high functional work ability (Table A2.6). As per the results for the entire sample and for participants with high functional work ability, these results for participants with low functional work ability are not unexpected given the demographic differences between open employment and supported employment highlighted in Table 5.5, and the fact that participants in open employment report statistically significantly higher *empowerment/independence* scores compared to participants in supported employment (Table 6.8).

The negative correlations between *social belonging/community integration* and both participants' age and total years of employment are consistent with the results for the entire sample, reported in Table A2.4. Interestingly though, this is substantially different to the results for participants with high functional work ability for whom *social belonging/community integration* is not found to be statistically significantly related to any demographic variables (Table A2.6). This result indicates that the older participants with a low functional work ability (high level of intellectual disability), who would by default have been in employment longer given their age, are not as satisfied with their feelings relating to integration with the community. The result in Panel B of Table A2.8 showing a positive statistical significant correlation between *social belonging/community integration* and current job tenure is interesting, in that the longer a participant is employed in their current job, the greater their total years of employment, yet the two correlations are in opposite directions. This indicates that for participants with low functional work ability job stability helps to increase their feelings of integration with a community. However, given that this correlation is not found to be statistically significant in Panel A and furthermore the sign of the correlation is in the opposite direction in both Panels A and C, no great emphasis can be placed on this result, which is unique to Panel B of Table A2.8.

Table A2.9, which reports the Spearman rhos for participants with a low functional work ability using the original QOL.Q, are similar to the above results using the refined QOL.Q in Table A2.8. In fact the statistically significant correlations reported in Panel A of Table A2.9 are the same as those reported in Panel A of Table A2.8. Comparing the results in Panel B of Table A2.9, which relates to participants in unskilled labouring positions, with those in Panel B of Table A2.8, two differences are apparent. These two differences relate to a statistically significant negative correlation between *empowerment/independence* and the original FAI score, which is shown in Panel B of Table A2.9 (r_s = -.330, $p \leq .046$), but not apparent in Panel B of Table A2.8, and the fact that no statistically significant relationship is shown between *social belonging/community integration* and hourly wage in Panel B of Table A2.9, when one is revealed in Panel B of Table A2.8. Panel C of Table A2.9 does not reveal any statistically significant correlation between *social belonging/community integration* using the original QOL.Q and any of the demographic variables. This is in contrast to the results in Panel C of Table A2.8, which using the refined QOL.Q, reveals social belonging community integration to be statistically significantly correlated with the refined FAI score, the original FAI score, and total years of employment. However, as noted before given the small sample size of this sub-sample it is not surprising that no statistically significant results are revealed. The high degree of similarity between the results reported in Table A2.9, using the original QOL.Q, with those reported in Table A2.8, using the refined QOL.Q, lend support to the results previously discussed in relation to the refined QOL.Q.

Table A2.9: Spearman rank order correlation coefficients between original QOL.Q and demographic variables for participants with low functional work ability (refined FAI ≥17)

	Weekly wage	Hourly wage	Refined FAI Score	Original FAI Score	Age	Current job tenure (years)	Total years of employment
Panel A: All occupations (n=47)							
Satisfaction	.110	.055	-.156	-.195	.007	.001	-.076
	(.462)[a]	(.711)	(.296)	(.189)	(.964)	(.995)	(.610)
Competence/	.110	.062	.037	.012	.020	-.039	-.082
Productivity	(.460)	(.679)	(.804)	(.934)	(.893)	(.794)	(.582)
Empowerment/	.324*	.371*	-.321*	-.302*	.011	-.151	-.075
Independence	(.026)	(.010)	(.028)	(.039)	(.944)	(.313)	(.619)
Social	-.046	.155	.115	-.113	-.288*	-.253	-.362*
belonging[b]	(.758)	(.299)	(.443)	(.451)	(.050)	(.086)	(.012)
QOL	.151	.235	-.117	-.112	-.074	-.178	-.230
	(.311)	(.112)	(.433)	(.452)	(.620)	(.231)	(.120)
Panel B: Unskilled labouring positions (n=37)							
Satisfaction	.295	.201	-.256	-.315	-.064	-.130	-.108
	(.077)	(.234)	(.126)	(.057)	(.705)	(.444)	(.525)
Competence/	.274	.188	-.038	-.092	.083	-.033	.014
Productivity	(.101)	(.266)	(.824)	(.587)	(.626)	(.845)	(.933)
Empowerment/	.346*	.386*	-.359*	-.330*	.016	-.314	-.137
Independence	(.036)	(.018)	(.029)	(.046)	(.923)	(.058)	(.417)
Social	-.027	.268	.113	.092	-.391*	.402*	-.458**
belonging	(.875)	(.108)	(.504)	(.589)	(.017)	(.014)	(.004)
QOL	.298	.400*	-.215	-.232	-.126	-.377*	-.296
	(.074)	(.014)	(.201)	(.167)	(.458)	(.021)	(.076)
Panel C: Living with family (n=27)							
Satisfaction	-.139	-.313	-.089	-.130	.329	.319	.269
	(.489)	(.112)	(.660)	(.518)	(.094)	(.105)	(.176)
Competence/	-.020	-.169	.155	.164	.218	.134	.031
Productivity	(.920)	(.389)	(.440)	(.415)	(.275)	(.506)	(.878)
Empowerment/	-.030	.118	-.120	-.177	-.130	-.068	-.160
Independence	(.881)	(.558)	(.552)	(.377)	(.519)	(.737)	(.427)
Social	-.363	-.111	.279	.306	-.105	-.284	-.213
belonging	(.063)	(.583)	(.159)	(.120)	(.602)	(.152)	(.286)
QOL	-.292	-.257	.124	.127	.153	-.011	-.057
	(.139)	(.195)	(.538)	(.529)	(.446)	(.956)	(.777)

a   Figures in parentheses represent significance levels.
b   Abbreviation for *social belonging/community integration*.
*   Significant at the 5 percent level.
**   Significant at the 1 percent level.
Note: *Method of employment* and *living environment* were not included in the above correlation analysis as both are categorical variables.

A2.3.3 Discussion of Quality of Life Results

The following discussion provides a summary of the above results relating to the correlates of quality of life and relates these results to the findings of prior research. Initially, when the entire sample (comprising participants with both high and low functional work ability) was investigated (Table A2.4 and Table A2.5), *empowerment/independence* was found to be statistically significantly positively correlated to weekly and hourly wages, and to be statistically significantly negatively correlated to refined FAI, original FAI, and current job tenure. From Tables A2.4 and A2.5 *social belonging/community integration* is found to be statistically significantly positively correlated with the refined FAI score and the original FAI score, and statistically significantly negatively correlated with age and total years of employment. *Quality of life* is also found to have a statistically significantly positive correlation with hourly wages for the all participants (Panel A), unskilled labouring positions (Panel B), and the matched-pairs sub-sample. The fact that only hourly wage and not both hourly and weekly wages is found to have a statistically significantly positive correlation with quality of life is interesting. Exactly why such a result is achieved cannot be readily explained, especially given that it contradicts the findings of Schalock *et al.* (1994) who find weekly wages to be positively correlated with quality of life.

With the exception of the positive correlation between *social belonging/community integration* and both the refined FAI and the original FAI scores, the above correlations were not unexpected given that statistically significant differences noted in Section 6.3 (Quality of Life).

With the exception of the lack of a statistically significant correlation between *social belonging/community integration* with both the refined FAI and the original FAI scores, the results for both participants with high functional work ability (Table A2.6 and Table A2.7) and low functional work ability (Table A2.8 and Table A2.9) confirm the findings for the entire sample (Table A2.4 and Table A2.5).

Interestingly *social belonging/community integration* in Tables A2.4 and A2.5 is positively correlated with both the refined FAI and the original FAI scores, indicating that the lower (higher) the functional work ability (refined and original FAI scores) the higher the *social belonging/community integration score*. This correlation contradicts the results in Table 6.4, which show that participants in open employment (who on average have higher functional work ability) report statistically significantly higher *social belonging/community integration* scores than their counterparts in supported employment (who on average have lower functional work ability). Combining these two results possibly suggests a U-shaped relationship between *social belonging/community integration* and functional work ability.

The possibility of a U-shaped relationship existing can be explained based on who people with intellectual disabilities compare themselves to in determining their level of satisfaction. It is likely that participants with very high functional work ability (very low refined and original FAI scores) will be more accepted into a work community of people without disabilities, who are their reference point (see, Lam and Chan 1988). As such they are likely to report high *social belonging/community integration* scores. However, for participants with slightly lower levels of functional work ability they may be less accepted into the community of workers without disabilities. Given that these participants reference point is still people without disabilities, this decrease in acceptance is likely to be reflected in a decline in their *social belonging/community integration* scores. This partially explains the negative correlations observed in Tables A2.4 and A2.5.

However, once the functional work ability of participants decreases to a certain point it is likely that their frame of reference changes to other people with an intellectual disability and not people without disabilities (see Lam and Chan 1988; Moseley 1988). Further, given that people with lower functional work ability are more likely to be employed in a supported setting, they are also more likely to be accepted by this community and as such their *social belonging community/integration* score may begin increasing.

The above explanation for the contrary findings relating to *social belonging/community integration* and functional work ability across Table A2.4, Table A2.6, and Table A2.8 is weakly supported by an inspection of the scatter plot (Figure A2.3), the negative correlation (though not statistically significant) shown in Table A2.6 for participants with high functional work ability, and the positive correlation (though not statistically significant) shown in Table A2.8 for participants with low functional work ability. Given this weak level of support, it is apparent more research is warranted into the relationship between *social belonging/community integration* and functional work ability.

A2.4 Conclusion
This chapter has investigated the correlations between the collected demographic variables, job satisfaction (and its four factors) and quality of life (and its four factors). In relation to the correlates of job satisfaction two interesting results were revealed. First, the results suggested the

possibility of a U-shaped relationship between functional work ability (as measured by either the refined FAI or original FAI) and the *work and staff* factor of the JSQ.

The second interesting result in relation to the correlates of job satisfaction is the statistically significant negative correlation between the *task* factor of the JSQ and current job tenure for participants with low functional work ability. This negative relationship between a person's length of employment and their satisfaction with *task* is likely to be due to participants with low functional work ability being consigned to performing the same work functions each day. This suggests that it is important that disability employment agencies pay attention to the tasks being performed by their clients and where possible up-skill clients or persuade employers to consider varying the tasks of the person with an intellectual disability.

In relation to the findings relating to the correlates of quality of life, the possibility of U-shaped curve between the participants' functional work ability and *social belonging/community integration* was posited. However, as was noted only existed weak support for such a relationship, with more research required.

0 1341 1379751 5

D/

CPSIA information can be obtained at www.ICGtesting.com
Printed in the USA
LVOW100230231111

256202LV00001B/121/P

9 783639 219081